TSCHIFFELY'S

RIDE

TSCHIFFELY'S RIDE

*Being the account of 10,000 miles
in the saddle through the Americas
from Argentina to Washington*

A. F. TSCHIFFELY

PALLAS ATHENE

CONTENTS

PREFACE
For the Three Friends
Tschiffely, Mancha, and Gato

I have always held that the distinction some people make between instinct and reason is false, and that all animals reason and that all men have instinct.

Therefore I have written what I have above, as I know that the senior partner in the friendship will understand my meaning. I am just as certain that the other two would understand, did I but know their form of speech. Even if they would not understand me, I know that they understand the man who shared so many perils, hardships, hunger, thirst and weariness with them, in the long pilgrimage through the Americas that has placed them with the immortals of the equine race.

In the green Trapalanda, I have always thought that Providence, however hardly its judgments may bear on man, must have prepared for all the horses that have suffered here on earth, from overwork, ill-usage and neglect, as well as those so innocent and shy who in their lifetime ranged the pampas, steppes and prairies, Cæsar's eight-footed horse, Pascasas, and Bucephalus will be there to welcome them. May the time be long, before that they exchange their greetings, whinnying low, holding their velvet nostrils gently forward, till they touch, with their ears quivering.

I like to imagine their infinite, celestial home—for our imagination can but conceive what we have known on earth, however sublimated—as a great prairie, with the wind sweeping over the perennial grasses, till they roll like waves. Pasture shall never wither there, nor lose its succulence. Water shall never fail. There shall be neither 'cangrejal' or treacherous 'guadal,' still less stretches of arid sand, as in the steppes, or poisonous 'mio-mio,' to slay them cowardly. All shall be fresh and green. No winter blasts shall set their coats astare, or burning sun pour down upon their undefended heads, making the little foals seek shelter in the shadow of their dams.

No 'tabanos' shall pester them at noonday, nor vampire-bats suck out their blood at night, leaving them slack and listless after their attacks. The rivers shall not harbour alligators, nor shall electric eels discharge their current on them as they swim, to make them sink like lead. In shallows there shall be no 'rayas' to wound their feet as they prepare to swim, nor in the woods shall any tigers lurk to pounce upon them unawares, and stun them with a stroke of their fell paw. All shall be sweet, harmless and innocent as they were, in their Calvary on earth. Justice, deaf, blind and futile as she has always been in this world, there shall recover sight and hearing, and the perception of the meaning of her name. All this I wish, rather than look for, and that in the equine Paradise I have endeavoured to describe, and that for all my doubts I feel exists, my hope is that the three friends will not be parted. In the shade of some celestial Ombu, leafy and wide~spreading, in the hours of siesta, may they doze all together, and now and then recount—for then the barrier of speech will have been broken down—the incidents of their long Hegira.

R. B. CUNNINGHAME GRAHAM

FOREWORD

L et me start this foreword with an apology. I am well aware that critics may, and probably will, find fault with the style of writing. For that I apologise, but it is unavoidable. I have no pretensions to being a writer, and have only done my best to give an accurate description of the countries through which I passed and the many and varied types of people whom I met.

I rode some 10,000 miles in two and a half years. From Argentina I came north, over cold, barren 16,000-foot ranges then down into steamy jungles, across the Isthmus of Panama, up through Central America and Mexico, and so to the United States.

I reached Washington with the same two horses with which I started—ponies that were 15 and 16 years old when my ride began.

Remote from cities and seaports—far from white men's haunts—ran much of my lonely trail. One night camp might be pitched far from any human habitation; again, I ate and slept with ancient Indian tribes in stone villages older than the Incas.

Of high adventures, hair-breadth escapes, and deeds of daring, there were few; yet in all the annals of exploration I doubt if any traveller, not excepting Marco Polo himself, had more leisure than I to see and understand the people, the animals and plant life of the countries traversed.

Naturally an expedition of this nature was bound to entail a certain amount of adventure and risk, but I have purposely endeavoured to avoid anything that might give an armchair voyager the idea that I was exaggerating for the sake of effect.

What is particularly gratifying to me is the knowledge that I have been able to prove that the Argentine Criollo (Creole) horse is worthy of the reputation he has always held among the few that really know him, namely, that of being second to none for continuous hard work under any conditions. My two pals, 'Mancha' and 'Gato,' have shown powers of resistance to heat, cold, hunger, and every hardship imaginable that have surprised even the most sanguine admirers of the breed, and Dr. Emilio Solanet, who presented them to me, must indeed feel proud of them.

I sincerely hope that nothing I have said will hurt the feelings of any reader, for although it may seem that in some cases I have been unduly harsh in my criticism of people, that is not so; rather otherwise. Where

I have apparently been severe in my remarks I have in reality been mild, since the whole truth would in many cases be absolutely incredible to anyone who had not seen it with his own eyes.

Let me say in conclusion that I cannot properly express the gratitude I feel to those countless friends whom I met on the journey, whose hospitality knew no bounds, and whose help and encouragement enabled me to carry through to a successful finish.

A. F. TSCHIFFELY

INTRODUCTION

'Impossible!' 'Absurd!' 'The man's mad!'

In this way many people stated their opinions, some publicly, some privately, when the news came out that somebody was going to attempt to ride from Buenos Aires to New York with two native Argentine horses. And it cannot be denied that they had good grounds for their opinion. Those who know the topography of the country between Buenos Aires and the States might well doubt the ability of man or beast to undertake such a trip with any hope of success. Overland travelling is hard enough at the best of times, but in an undertaking of this nature the difficulties are so numerous and varied. Will there always be a sufficiency of food and water for the rider and his animals? Can the horses be expected to cross the vast mountain ranges and sandy deserts, and endure the severe variations of heat and cold? What about unfriendly Indians, rainy seasons, insects, fevers? In short, how can any animal be expected to overcome the thousand and one difficulties that are bound to be met?

Yes, the critics had right on their side, but nevertheless I continued with my preparations. It was not a sudden impulse on my part, but the result of several years' contemplation, although I had not mentioned the idea to anyone until I had actually determined to make the attempt.

After completing my education, I had spent some time teaching in England and had then come out to the Argentine, where I spent nine years in the largest English-American school in the country. For a long time I had felt that a schoolmaster's life, pleasant though it is in many ways, does not afford much prospect and is apt to lead one into a groove. I wanted variety: I was young and fit; the idea of this journey had been in my head for years, and finally I determined to make the attempt.

As a result of various enquiries I went to the office of *La Nación*, the leading newspaper of the Argentine, and put forward my idea. When once they were convinced that I was not one of the many who come to them for funds to assist in some imaginary exploit, but that I wanted information and nothing more, they received me with the greatest courtesy and gave me every possible assistance, and at length I was put in touch with Dr. Emilio Solanet, a most enthusiastic breeder of the Creole horse and one of the greatest authorities on the subject, and to whom I shall always be under debt of gratitude. He eagerly took up the idea and undertook to supply the two horses for the trip.

A few words on the origin of the Creole horse may help the reader to understand the reasons for their powers of resistance. They are the descendants of a few horses brought to the Argentine in 1535 by Don Pedro Mendoza, the founder of the city of Buenos Aires. These animals were of the finest Spanish stock, at that time the best in Europe, with a large admixture of Arab and Barb blood in their veins. That these were the first horses in America is borne out by history, by tradition, and by the fact that no native American dialect contains a word for horse. Later, when Buenos Aires was sacked by the Indians and its inhabitants massacred, the descendants of the Spaniards' horses were abandoned to wander over the country. They lived and bred by the laws of nature, they were hunted by the Indians and wild animals, drought would compel them to travel enormous distances in search of water, the treacherous climate with its sudden changes of temperature killed off all but the strongest, and, in short, they were forced to obey the natural law of 'the survival of the fittest.' The fitness of the race has been amply proved. During the War of Emancipation and the various Indian wars, the Creole horses performed marches that would appear incredible were it not an established fact. Dr. Solanet, in an admirable speech delivered at a conference of the Agricultural and Veterinary Faculties, said: 'Their marches for months during the War of Emancipation are not reckoned by kilometres but by leagues: a hundred, two hundred and more was the distance frequently covered in these wonderful raids, which terminated at the ranks of the Spanish soldiers, valiant it cannot be denied, since they are of our own race. And the horses of the Patriots arrived with sufficient energy to drive home a victorious charge. Afterwards, the same night, they would rest, feeding on whatever they could 'rustle.' Without covering they endured frosts, and on the following day, instead of a massage and grooming, came the violent hot gale that scorched them and lashed them with burning sand.'

The two horses given to me by Dr. Solanet were 'Mancha,' who was at the time sixteen years old, and 'Gato,' who was fifteen. They had formerly been the property of a Patagonian Indian Chief named Liempichun ('I have feathers') and were the wildest of the wild. To break them in had been a task that taxed the powers of several of the best 'domadores' for some time, and even when I took them over they were far from tame. I may state that even now (at twenty-two years of age) after a journey of over ten thousand miles, Mancha will not allow anyone except myself to saddle him. These two animals had, a very short time previously, come up to the 'estancia' (estate) with a troop from Patagonia and had performed a road march of over a thousand miles, in the course of which they had lived on what they could find, which was not much. To a European horse-lover they would appear, to put it mildly, curious. Mancha is a red, with heavy irregular splashes of white: white face and stockings. In the U.S. and in England this colour is sometimes called 'pinto,' or 'piebald.' Gato is more or less of a coffee colour, a sort of a cross between a bay and a dun, or what the American cowboys used to call a 'buckskin.' Their sturdy legs, short thick necks and Roman noses are as far removed from the points of a first-class English hunter as the North Pole from South. 'Handsome is as handsome does,' however, and I am willing to state my opinion boldly that no other breed in the world has the capacity of the Creole for continuous hard work. The horses obtained, there still remained many other points to be considered, primarily the question of riding and of pack saddles. For riding I chose the type of saddle used in Uruguay and the northern parts of Argentina. This consists of a light framework, about two feet long, over which is stretched a covering of hide. This sits easily on the horse, and, being covered with loose sheep-skins, makes a comfortable bed at night, the saddle forming the pillow. I used the same saddle throughout the trip, but was obliged to change the pack saddle in the mountainous regions. To take a tent was, of course, an impossibility, owing to the weight, so I had to be content with a large 'poncho' (cloak) for covering when sleeping out. A big mosquito-net in the shape of a bell tent was taken, as it folded up into a very small space and weighed practically nothing.

I then had to spend several weeks getting into riding condition and accustoming myself to long expeditions. As a schoolmaster I had had perforce to be content with riding during vacations and consequently a considerable amount of practice was necessary.

When the preparations were nearly complete, the horses were sent up to Buenos Aires and lodged in the fine premises of the Argentine Rural Society. This was not easy. Let the reader imagine the feelings of two savage warriors from the interior of Africa suddenly dumped into Piccadilly or Broadway. The nearest approach to a town that either of them had seen was an Indian village composed of a few 'toldos'—tents made of posts and raw hide. To bring them across the city, which was done in the early hours of the morning and by the least frequented streets, and finally to persuade them to enter the stables was a labour worthy of Hercules himself. The very streets and houses scared them, while an automobile!! They turned up their noses at the most luscious alfalfa, barley, oats, etc., with which they were provided and devoured with relish the straw put down for bedding. In this respect, however, they soon changed, and began to realise what was good, and, as they gradually filled out on good fodder, so did their spirits, none too tame before, rise, and exercising them became a really interesting, not to say exciting job.

When all was ready the press heard about the undertaking, and then came comments of the nature of the opening words to this chapter. Some were encouraging, others frankly sarcastic. One paper even went as far as to accuse me of cruelty to animals, the gifted writer apparently not having sufficient grey matter to realise that a man who was going to entrust his life absolutely to two horses would make the comfort and welfare of those horses his first consideration. Many who fancied themselves experts on the subject tried to put me off, others, and in particular a few members of the Rural Society and some prominent sportsmen, backed me up solidly and gave me all the encouragement in their power.

I had originally intended to take as companion a Belgian Police dog which had been presented to me by a friend. This plan, however, was upset by the fact that on the first day of the journey the dog came nearer to one of the horses than the latter approved of and received such a severe kick on the hip that I was obliged to leave him behind. This was in reality a blessing in disguise for the dog because, as things turned out, he would not have survived the journey. Lack of water affects dogs more than horses, their feet will not stand the wear and tear of stony roads, and the fact that a dog carries his nose so near the ground would render the journey across sandy deserts a matter of great distress; besides all these points there is the question of feeding. A small dog that could, when necessary, be carried on the pack-horse might do the trip, but even that is doubtful.

By way of conclusion to this introductory chapter I should state that I do not pretend to be an infallible authority on the various countries through which I passed. Naturally I learnt a lot about their customs, history and traditions, but to know a country thoroughly requires years of residence. I shall only attempt to describe what I actually saw and what actually happened to me, without floral embellishment. It can easily be understood that I did not find hospitality, hygiene and comfort everywhere (!!), but I shall give credit where credit is due.

THIS BOOK IS DEDICATED

*To all lovers of the horse and the wide
open spaces;
And to many friends—of whatever race,
nationality or creed—
Who did their utmost to make rough
places smooth.*

The First Day

I propose to tell the story of the first day's trip at some length for various reasons: it naturally impressed itself on my mind as the start of a great adventure: it contained enough variety to satisfy anyone; and it may give the reader a slight idea of some of the conditions prevailing in Argentina.

Early in the morning of St. George's Day I left my hotel and drove off to the premises of the Rural Society, accompanied by my dog, who seemed to scent disaster and had to be tied to a lead before he would accompany me. Trouble began early; the horses strongly objected to being saddled, each part of the saddle seemed to annoy them more than the previous one, and for a long time we were just a whirling mass of kicking horses and cursing stable-boys. At last, however, everything was ready, and the horses, having expressed their opinions of the girths by a vigorous display of bucking, became more or less quiet, and I was ready to start.

By this time some press photographers, who had in some mysterious manner learnt that I was setting out, had arrived obviously regarding the whole thing as a huge joke:—'A lunatic proposing to travel overland to New York, que loco'—etc., etc. However, I can appreciate a good joke myself and consented to pose for them, which led to another merry five minutes before the horses could be got into position; the shutters clicked, and the gentlemen of the press bowed and retired, with ill-concealed chuckles at my idiocy. I felt strongly tempted to quote to them the saying, 'Let fools laugh; wise men dare and win,' but a doubt assailed me as to which of us really was the fool, so I refrained.

I rode Gato, he being the quieter of the two, leading Mancha, who did duty as pack-horse, and we were accompanied by a stable-boy to show the best way out of the town. This lad was mounted on a big thoroughbred which made my stocky little animals look more diminutive than ever. The dog followed, but very unwillingly. After about an hour we came to a newly-made dirt road with a wire fence on each side and my guide, having informed me that by following this I would get to the main road, returned home. His thoroughbred was steaming with perspiration while the two Creoles showed no signs of having travelled at all. Recent heavy rains had converted this road into a river of soft mud into which the horses sank deep at every step. Mancha had evidently decided that he would much prefer to go back to his stable, and I had to haul him along by main force. To make matters worse, a fine rain began to fall and, with one thing and another, I came to the conclusion that this was the worst bit of road in the world. As a matter of fact it was Fifth Avenue and Regent Street combined compared with some of the trails I encountered later.

Disaster came soon; I heard a dull thud followed by a squeal of pain, and saw the dog fly through the air and land in a pool of water, where he lay as though dead. He had approached nearer to Mancha than the latter approved of and had suffered accordingly. On examining him I found that he had received a severe blow on the hip and that his shoulder-blade was broken. Here was a situation worthy of a cartoonist's pencil. Far away from any habitation, stuck in the mud, the rain soaking into my skin, with two half-wild horses and a crippled dog: hardly an encouraging start. I did not want to shoot the dog, much less leave him where he was, and as there was about as much chance of meeting any vehicle on that road as there is of seeing Polar bears in the Sahara Desert I decided to carry him to the main road. It was no easy job to carry the heavy dog some two hundred yards, deposit him by the roadside, return to the horses and drag them along, and repeat this over and over again. At last we reached the road and I sat down to await a passing motorist. The first car to pass was an exceedingly antiquated 'Tin Lizzie.' I beckoned to the driver to stop and asked him if he would carry the dog to the nearest town and leave him for me. With an accent that clearly betrayed his Spanish origin he inquired how much I was prepared to pay for the service, explaining that times were not as they used to be, and so on and so forth. He became so flowery in his speech that I cut him short with a cordial request that he would betake himself to a warmer climate and he departed, his old bus rattling like an ironmonger's store in an earthquake. Presently another car came along and the two gentlemen who were in it readily consented to help me, and carted the dog off to Moron where I decided to put up for the night. My first act on reaching there was to telephone to a friend, asking him to look after the dog, and when I returned after over three years' absence I was delighted to find him in the best of condition.

The next job was to look for board and lodging for the horses. One would imagine this a simple matter so near to the capital, but it was no such thing. All available stabling was occupied, but at length I obtained permission to leave them at the Police Station for the night, and having, after a lengthy search, purchased a bale of hay, and carted it on my back to the corral, I was free to look after myself. Accordingly I had a fairly respectable dinner and retired to bed, fondly imagining that my troubles were over for the day. Alas for the frailty of human hopes! The hotel was of a pattern almost universal throughout the Camp towns, as country towns are called in the Argentine. The rooms are built round a square patio, or courtyard, and have large double doors but no window, consequently no through ventilation. Each room has two, three, or four beds, and happy is the man who gets a room to himself. I was not one of these, for I had hardly retired when another man was shown in, and shortly afterwards two more arrived. As is the custom of many of the lower class Argentines, my companions insisted on the doors being shut, thus cutting off all ventilation, while to make matters worse the two last comers started to smoke, dividing their time pretty evenly between puffing and spitting. Everything comes to an end sometime, and at last with many grunts and groans they composed themselves to sleep.

I was just about to do the same when I felt—something. At first I took no notice, but when that something began to multiply itself by hundreds I got up and struck a match.—!!! My bed was like some plain during army manœuvres—regiments, army corps, marching to and fro and scuttling to take cover from the light. I switched on the lamp and hurled the mattress on to the floor, awakening one of the sleepers in so doing. He was interested and even amused at my excitement, and assured me that the 'bichos' were quite harmless, and that I was very 'delicado' (fastidious) to make such a fuss. After a strict search into dug-outs and trenches in the frame I lay down on the wire and slept, disturbed only by a few individual attacks and by the snoring of my sleeping companions. I was very glad when morning came and I was able once more to breathe the fresh air.

Towards Rosario

From now on this stage of the trip was most uninteresting. Once the city bounds are passed the traveller finds himself in the wilds, the dividing line being very slender. This can very easily be understood when the relation of population to area is considered. The area of the Argentine Republic is roughly 1,200,000 square miles; the population is eleven and a half millions, of which two and a half millions are in the city of Buenos Aires, Rosario holding another half million.

Between these two towns (180 miles) and indeed right on to the Andes the country is dead flat. As far as the eye can reach there is nothing visible but large herds of cattle grazing in the 'potreros' (paddocks), or vast expanses of crops, chiefly wheat and corn. Wire fences and windmills are everywhere, trees being conspicuous by their absence, except round the estancia houses and in a few isolated patches of 'monte' (scrub). The roads are either very dusty or very muddy, being simply dirt-tracks bordered by wire fences and running dead straight from one right-angled turn to the next, a curve being practically unknown. In the neighbourhood of a village skinny horses and cows belonging to the poorer inhabitants pick up a scanty living from the grass on the roadside, and if an animal dies on the road it is left to be devoured by 'chimangos' (a kind of hawk) or stray dogs.

During the harvest season one frequently sees grain-carts, with enormous wheels up to ten feet in diameter, drawn by an unlimited number of horses. The official team of six or eight is arranged in a fan-shape formation, but when the roads are heavy as many extra horses as are available are attached to any part of the vehicle to which a rope may be tied, the other end of the rope being fastened to the cinch of the horse. It is heavy work for the animals, but they are for the most part willing labourers.

The further I went from Buenos Aires the worse became the roads. Constant rain had reduced them to soft mud, and progress was necessarily slow. The pack-saddle was constantly slipping; the only sounds to break the monotony of the splashing horses through the mud were the blasphemous screech of a prairie-owl sitting on a fence-post and the whistling and yammering of the wind through the telegraph wires. Occasionally, to my astonishment, an automobile would come plodding its way through the mud, and more than once I was asked to assist in pulling one out of a mud-hole, a request I was obliged to refuse as my horses were not accustomed to such work. Anyway, I grew to hate automobiles; the drivers showed very little consideration for me and seemed to delight in seeing the horses rear and plunge when they passed us. They were my pet aversion from the beginning of the trip to the end, and if all my wishes had been carried out, Hades would be well supplied with motors and motorists. Being only human, I must confess that, while driving about in a comfortable car I hold other views about them, but I am speaking here from the point of view of the horseman.

Miles away from the next village I was caught in a heavy storm and was very pleased to arrive at a small wayside ranch where guests were received. The horses were turned loose in a good field and with feelings of relief I went inside to shelter and warmth. This ranch, or hut, was a small two-roomed place and several men were inside drying themselves at a good fire. When I had introduced myself in the proper manner, i.e., by shaking hands with everyone, I was given a seat near the fire and presented with a 'mate.' This is a pear-shaped gourd with an opening at the narrow end, which is half-filled with 'yerba' (Paraguayan tea) and filled up with hot water. The resulting infusion is sucked up through a metal tube ('bombilla'). It is very refreshing and stimulating and is the national drink. No peon starts his day's work until he has had three or four mates, which, with a piece of 'galleta' (hard biscuit), keep him going until he has his breakfast, which is taken about midday. Only one mate is used for a party; the host usually takes the first brew which is supposed to be inferior to the others, and is sometimes just sucked up and spat out; it is then refilled with boiling water and handed to the first guest, and so on until it becomes too weak. It is surprising how long one charge of yerba will last. To a stranger the idea is a bit repugnant at first, but one gets used to it in time, and to refuse to participate would be considered an insult.

There was also an 'asado' to be eaten. This is a strip of meat, preferably the ribs, stretched on a wire or a kind of spit and roasted slowly over the ashes. When properly cooked—and the natives are nearly all experts at the job—it is most delicious. Forks are not considered necessary, the fashionable way to eat it being to take one end of the portion in the left hand, grasp the other with the teeth, and then cut a mouthful off with a knife.

The fireplace was extremely primitive and the room was full of acrid wood smoke which made my eyes smart and brought me to tears.

We all slept in the same room and as there were no beds, which perhaps was just as well, we made ourselves comfortable on the floor with the help of our saddles, the saddle-cloths and sheepskins making a comfortable couch and the saddle doing duty as a pillow.

The type of saddle used in the plains of Argentina is different from that used in the mountain districts, the saddle proper being formed of two pads connected by strips of hide, and so formed that when it is placed on the horse it presents a flat surface. First of all one or, more usually, two saddle-cloths are placed in position, then comes another of leather; on this is placed the saddle and the whole secured by a broad cinch of raw hide, sometimes as much as a foot in breadth; over these are placed sheepskins, and finally a covering of soft leather—the best are made from the skin of the 'carpincho' or water hog. These are fastened down with a narrow over-cinch. This gives the rider the appearance of a man sitting astride a dining-table, but yet the gaucho of the pampas seems very comfortable in this strange saddle.

I slept very soundly that night and next day proceeded on my journey. After this one day was like another; there was nothing to be seen but flat country, the only thing to break the monotony being a very occasional 'boliche' or wayside inn. Here, although often there is no other house in sight, are usually to be found a few people buying household necessities, chatting over a glass of wine, or 'bochas,' a game resembling bowls, except that the bowl is thrown instead of rolled. Every man wears a wide belt into which is stuck, at the back, a large sheath knife; the more silver there is about the belt the greater the owner's pride. These knives are not primarily for fighting, as some people imagine, but for practical use; killing and skinning cattle, repairing leather, cutting the meat at meals. It is an uncommon thing to-day to hear of a serious fight, and if knives are drawn it is usually out of bravado. Occasionally serious harm is done, and to prevent this there is a law that every man on entering an inn must hand over his arms to the proprietor. This law is more honoured in the breach than the observance and sometimes when the news arrives that a police-man is approaching there is a scramble to hand over weapons before his entrance. When a fight does occur the landlord is held responsible.

In the villages the two places where people assemble are the station and the 'almacen'. In the outlying districts, where a train passes perhaps once in two or three days, the whole population turns out to greet it. In the 'almacen'—the word really means a store—almost anything can be obtained, and it is the news centre of the district. As long as it is open there will be horses tied to the posts outside, patiently waiting for their masters who are inside making purchases or having a game of cards over a drink and, of course, gossiping. The acknowledged king of the place is the local 'comisario' (chief of police). A 'vigilante' has to be on the platform when the train is in and the rest of his time is usually spent round about the almacen. Although people spend a long time over their drinks they really do not drink very much, and there is very little drunkenness among the Argentines, except in the north where possibly a large strain of Indian blood may have something to do with it. Outbursts take place occasionally, especially when an unprincipled dealer has diluted a jar of wine with two or three jars of water and then fortified the mixture with a bottle of 'caila' (spirit made from the sugar-cane) in which tobacco has been steeped. This concoction has a punch more powerful than Dempsey's best and is the cause of a lot of trouble and even if the victims do not get into a fight, they are totally unfit for work the next day.

The weather continued abominable, but fortunately I was in no hurry, for I had calculated on reaching the Bolivian border in August which marks the commencement of the dry season. I slept under cover whenever possible and was usually fortunate. One evening I arrived at a monastery and as it was getting late decided to try my luck. Having knocked at the door and been duly inspected through a small window, I was admitted,

and found myself in an Irish community. Father Superior O'Connor made
me welcome, my horses were cared for, and the Brethren showed me the
greatest hospitality. We all sat down together at the supper-table but, to
my dismay, I found I was the only one eating. It was a fast day, but nevertheless the good monks made me an excellent dinner, after which I was
conducted to a comfortable guest-chamber, where I slept the sleep of the
just until 6 a.m., disturbed only by the chanting of the Brethren while celebrating Matins in the small hours. When I left after breakfast I was given
a cordial send-off by the entire community. I shall always have a soft spot
in my heart for these kindly brothers.

Whenever the day's journey ended in a village I would pass the night
in the local hotel (?) if such a thing existed, and if there was no other place
for the horses would put them in the corral of the 'comisaria' (police
station). On one occasion while I was looking after the animals at one of
these places two tramps were brought in. I have seen tramps and hobos
in many countries, but for real class commend me to the 'linghera' or
Argentine variety. The majority have long hair and beards, and their
torn and ragged 'bombachas' (baggy trousers), from frequent patching,
would resemble Joseph's coat were it not for the fact that all trace of colour
is usually concealed by age and dirt. These two gentlemen had been
brought to the comisaria, not because they had committed any crime, but
just in case of accidents, that they might be safe for the night. To use an
Irishism, they were not drunk but had drink taken, and never have I heard
protest expressed in such flowery language as that used by those elderly
wayfarers. 'Why should the finer feelings of poor but highly desirable citizens be trodden on by the tyrant police? It was gross injustice to strangers
and they would certainly put the matter in the hands of their solici-
tors....' The comisario and his assistant listened patiently for some time,
apparently with the greatest respect and admiration, but at length, growing tired of it, they conducted their guests to the calabozo and turned the
key on them. The torrent of righteous indignation continued for some
time, and then they drowned their sorrows in song until sleep finally over-
came them.

At last we arrived at Rosario. Heavy storms forced me to postpone our
departure for some days, and the newspapers began to hint delicately that
I was getting 'cold feet': as a matter of fact I had plenty of time and to
spare to reach Bolivia in the dry season, and there was no sense in
getting unnecessary wettings; there would be plenty of unavoidable
ones later.

The Rolling Pampas

After some time the weather cleared and we were able to resume our journey. From Rosario I took a north-westerly course towards the Bolivian border and for over two hundred miles travelled through fertile cattle and corn country. It was dull, to put it mildly. I can imagine nothing more uninteresting than continuous journeying along these straight roads, bordered by wire fences and telegraph poles, the tops of the latter usually decorated with the wonderfully constructed nests of the 'hornero' (oven-bird). The 'lechuza' (burrowing owl) peeping out of his burrow, or sitting on a fence-post, greets the traveller with a hideous screech, and, particularly in swampy ground, the 'tero-tero', the *bête noire* of shooters, alarms all the game in the vicinity with the squawk from which it gets its name. There is no stone to be found in these parts, which accounts for the state of the roads. All the stone used in the country has to be brought either from the mountainous districts in the West, or across the river from Uruguay. Incidentally, it might be of interest to add here that many of the granite paving-stones used in Buenos Aires are shipped across the seas from Scandinavia!

There was one ever-present danger in this district, namely, the 'romerillo' (or 'mio-mio'), a poisonous weed somewhat resembling Scotch heather, which is fatal to horses. Those reared in the neighbourhood do not touch it, but animals that are strangers are apt to do so with unfortunate results. Horses can be trained to avoid this in either of two ways: by rubbing their teeth with the bitter-tasting weed or by burning it and well smoking the animal's nostrils with the fumes. I used both of these precautions, but to make assurance doubly sure, took care not to turn them loose where there was romerillo about.

I was struck with the fact that the further I got from Buenos Aires the more hospitable were the people. Possibly this is due to the fact that the influx of foreigners to the neighbourhood of the capital has brought about mistrust of strangers and has caused a breakdown of the old traditions. In the outer districts one is more among the old type of settler who holds by the unwritten law of the open door to the stranger. Many is the night I have spent in a hospitable ranch where I was made welcome to the little they had to offer, but which was offered with a warm heart. Occasionally I stayed at one of the larger estancia houses, and at one of these had the luck to witness a real camp 'fiesta.' It was Saturday night when

I arrived and the 'patron' (boss) informed me that on the morrow they were going to hold a fiesta to celebrate a good sale of cattle. I was up and out early, and it was easy to see that there was something doing. As I strolled towards the men's quarters my nostrils were greeted with a most appetising odour of roasting meat. This emanated from a mighty 'asado' that was in course of preparation. The *pièce de résistance* was 'carne con cuero,' or meat roasted with the hide on, a most delicious dish, while to help it out were two or three lambs and a couple of sucking-pigs. This was suspended on grids or spits over a great bed of red-hot ashes of some special hardwood, and the 'chef' never took his attention off it during the several hours necessary for the proper cooking. The men were in their gala attire, wearing black caps with gaily-coloured tassels, or broad-brimmed black hats carefully pressed and ironed. Each man had a coloured silk scarf round his neck and, of course, carried his 'facón' (long knife) in a broad belt; the 'swells' having their belts studded with silver coins. 'Bombachas' (trousers) of enormous width, and top boots or embroidered shoes of soft leather helped to complete a picturesque costume. Some men wore spurs of silver or baser metal with huge rowels, as much as four inches in diameter, and the real exquisite had his reins and bridles studded with silver, and sometimes a semi-lunar plate of the same metal swung loosely under the horse's jaws.

Visitors began to arrive early; the men on horseback and the women-folk in sulkies. The latter were not one whit behind their men in the matter of personal adornment, and very pretty indeed were many of the girls in their gay dresses and neat stockings and shoes—it is rarely that one sees an Argentine girl badly shod and hosed, whatever her station in life may be—their deep black eyes and glossy hair, derived from a touch of Indian blood, added to a perfect natural complexion, making as pleasing a sight as one could wish to see. As the majority had been on the move since the small hours they were not slow in getting to work on the 'asado,' and by eleven o'clock the feast was in full swing, the meat being washed down with adequate supply of wine or beer. They were in no hurry; they had the whole day before them, and it must have been close on one o'clock before the last knife was cleaned and replaced in the owner's belt.

The majority composed themselves for siesta, while a few of the more active retired to a shady spot for a game of 'taba.' The taba is the astragalus (heel-bone) of a bullock, on to one side of which is screwed a metal plate. The object of the game is to toss the taba over a line some ten to fifteen yards away so that it will land with the metal uppermost. A childish enough game at first sight, but the players get desperately excited, and enough money has been lost and won over it to make it illegal in any public place.

When the fierce heat had somewhat abated and the carne cuero digested, the real business of the day commenced with horse races. These races are almost invariably matches between two horses, sprints of two to four hundred metres, and are very interesting to watch. The jockeys ride bareback and start themselves, although there is an official at the starting-post to see fair play. A lot of time is wasted by the riders 'kidding' each other to break away to a false start, this being one of the first arts of camp jockeyship. Eventually, however, they appear mutually agreed and down the course they come hell for leather. The 'juez de raya' (judge) does not publish the result but whispers it to an assistant who announces it to the anxious public.

A lot of money changes hands at these meetings, and I was greatly amused at the excitement of one gentleman before the first race. This was between an 'alazan' (chestnut) and a 'colorado' (red bay). He waved his hand, in which was a bundle of notes, and commenced roaring, 'Mil pesos al colorado' at the top of his voice. As a thousand pesos was more than most of them earned in a year it was small wonder that there were no takers. Accordingly he reduced his offer to 'quinientos pesos' (five hundred pesos) but still without success. Gradually the amount grew smaller and smaller until finally it came down to 'diez pesos' (ten pesos). At this stage another shouted, 'Che, te juego cinco pesos' (I bet you five pesos). 'Muy bien' shouted the plunger, and at once deposited his entire wad with the necessary third party: it was exactly five pesos.

I noticed that the betting on the last race was not nearly so brisk as on the earlier ones, and on enquiring the reason was informed that one of the horses engaged belonged to the local comisario (chief of police) and therefore was unlikely to lose.

The racing over, everyone who possessed or could borrow a horse took part in a contest of 'sortija.' For this a sort of gallows is erected and from the crossbar a ring, not much if any larger than an ordinary finger ring, is suspended by a hook. Each competitor is armed with a pencil or small stick and attempts to carry off the ring while galloping at full speed. This is very popular, and, with the galloping and the dust and the shouting, the horses seem to get as excited as their riders. Anyone who is successful—and these are not many—is a popular hero for at least two minutes, and the 'patron' usually puts up a prize of one or two pesos for each success.

At length night began to close in and an adjournment was made for dinner, but the fun was not by any means over yet. When dinner was finished the whole family came over to a large 'galpon' (shed) which had been cleared and cleaned, and was lit up with candles and lanterns. Along one side were seated all the ladies of the community, while the men occupied the other side: in one corner was the 'musica,' two guitars and an accordion. Everyone was deadly solemn as befitted the seriousness of the occasion.

The appearance of the 'patron' was the signal for the orchestra to strike up, and after a few awkward moments one of the men plucked up courage to cross the room and held out his right hand to the girl of his choice. She at once got up and the couple began to walk slowly round the room arm in arm. This broke the ice and soon there were seven or eight couples following one another in slow procession. At last they decided to start the dance, while the 'patron' made doubly sure by leading off with the washer-woman, a sprightly young damsel of about forty-five who looked seventy. The dance finished, each man solemnly led his partner back to her seat, dropped her like a red-hot coal, and returned to his place. To avoid soiling the pretty dresses of the girls every man carried a clean handkerchief in his right hand. The round dances, the waltz and polka, were slow and stately affairs, but the 'jota' and 'gato' were fast and furious. Foxtrots and tangos were other favourites, and a couple of men gave a clever display by dancing the 'Malambo,' which is an old gaucho dance that is danced with heavy spurs on, making them drum on the floor very much as in a tap-dance.

I had an amusing experience. The patron and his family had retired but I had stayed on to watch what was a novelty to me. I must have been looking lonely or forlorn, for suddenly one of the girls came over to me and held her hand, evidently taking pity on my rawness. Accordingly we danced, and when the music ceased my pretty partner led me back to my seat and left me. This absolute reversal of the general law, though it must have surprised many, did not cause even a smile; they were much too polite.

At another estancia I had the opportunity of witnessing a 'domada,' or horse-breaking. The 'domador' (breaker) was occupied in taming a troop of 'potros' (broncos), from three to four years old, some of them as wild as cats. He was a tall, slim young fellow, about twenty-four years of age, dark and handsome, and concerned himself solely with the riding. The catching and saddling were in the hands of two assistants. These entered the corral, lasso in hand, and with shouts and waving of the rope caused the horses to gallop wildly round and round until the object of their search was clear of the others, when the rope was dropped on his neck with unerring aim. It was almost uncanny the way in which the horse that was wanted divined their intentions. He would twist and turn about, always keeping two or three other horses between himself and the men, while the rest appeared to be helping him deliberately. However, in the long run he was caught and the lasso immediately whipped about a 'palenque' (post) in the middle of the corral. As he kicked and struggled his legs were roped and he came to earth with a crash. While he was down the 'bocado' was slipped into his mouth. This is used instead of a bit and is simply a strip of raw hide tied firmly round his lower jaw and to which the reins are attached. He was then allowed to rise, but his hind legs were roped together, one foreleg slung up and his head tied close to the palenque. Then one of the assistants saddled him while the other looked after the ropes. The cinches were tightened until the unfortunate animal looked like an early Victorian belle, and when all was ready he was dragged out cautiously on three legs, the foreleg still slung up, into the open field. Even with only three legs to walk on he could spare one to kick with, and the men were extremely careful.

Once in the potrero the domador mounted, the ropes were cast off and then the band began to play. Plunging, kicking, bucking, the maddened potro strove to rid himself of his rider, but each buck only resulted in a vicious whack from the broad raw-hide lash of the 'rebenque' (whip). Changing his tactics he tore off at full speed, and now found another horse on each side of him, whose riders frustrated any attempts he made to get to the fence where he might brush this burden from his back. Round and round the field they galloped, the domador occasionally forcing him to slow down by hauling with all his strength on the reins, at other times encouraging him to dash along with shouts and lashes. Finally he was brought to a standstill; the first lesson was over. The rider dismounted and calmly lit a cigarette without—as far as I could see—the slightest sign of a tremor in his hand, and waited for the next animal to be saddled.

The Desolation of Santiago del Estero

We were slowly nearing the desolate parts of Santiago del Estero and the land became more and more arid. Cactus plants of different varieties were to be seen everywhere, and in the low parts pampas grass grew in abundance, its silvery white flowers waving in the air like a sea of spearheads of an army of the middle ages. The only animals that seem to thrive in some sections of this semi-desert are goats, which roam about in large herds.

As a railroad crosses this region I had sent small bundles of hay to some of the stations, and was fortunate in obtaining good water, which is brought for the station-masters by train from the Andes. This water is kept in concrete wells which are always padlocked to prevent other people from helping themselves too freely.

The few huts I came across were very miserable, and the people of darkish hue, showing a fair strain of Indian blood. How they are able to exist on the few goats they raise is a mystery to me. Naked children can be seen playing outside in the sand, and living skeletons of dogs nose around in search of some bone among the rubbish that is thrown out of the huts.

A few more journeys and we were in the midst of the worst parts of the region where the horses raised thick clouds of fine dust, so dense at times that it was difficult to see the way, especially if a slight wind happened to be blowing from behind us. In some places the ground looked as if it were covered with snow, saltpetre giving it this strange effect. The very shrubbery and thick, coarse grass that grew here and there had a strong, salty taste, but the only plants that seem to thrive there are cacti, some of which grow to enormous heights.

We travelled whole days without passing a hut or meeting a living being excepting 'cuises' (a kind of guinea pig) or some snake that glided away, probably frightened by the heavy trampling of the horses' hoofs. Again I would see some brightly-coloured lizard who looked at us as if wondering what we were doing there. Strange to say, foxes abound in this neighbourhood and I am still wondering what they live on, unless they hunt lizards or little bright-green parrots which fly about screeching in flocks.

The few habitations one finds scattered far apart from each other are of the most primitive kind imaginable, and the same applies to the people who live in them. Near the hut there is usually a hollow, filled with dirty, yellow water that has a strong taste of salt. To prevent the animals from drinking more than their allowance to keep them alive, thorn branches are piled up around this only drinking-place, forming an impenetrable barrier, and the corrals are constructed in a similar manner. People obtain their water out of this same ditch, but sometimes the liquid is filtered through a dirty cloth. I was prepared for such situations, and mixed my water with bicarbonate of soda, doing the same for the horses, to prevent them from getting colic. I had brought a folding canvas bucket of the kind one uses to fill radiators of cars. For my own use I usually mixed a few drops of iodine in a bottle before drinking the contents, and although it did not exactly help to improve the already repulsive taste of the water it disinfected it.

He who is delicate in the food line does well to keep out of Santiago del Estero, for dried goats' meat is the order of the day, but only if one is lucky enough to find a hut where they are willing to let one have a little of their reduced supply. The making of this 'charqui,' as the dry meat is called, is not very appetising, to say the least, and when one sees the dirty hands that cut it up, and the clouds of flies that swarm about it whilst it is hanging in the sun, it is apt to spoil even the most ferocious appetite.

One day, as I was riding along, partly dazed by the heat and sleepy with boredom, I suddenly became aware that the sun was hidden behind a dark cloud. Shortly after, the light became dim and I expected a heavy thunderstorm to break, but presently I recognised this dark cloud to be a swarm of locusts, a swarm so large that it was at least an hour before they had passed. Obviously even locusts had no desire to settle in so desolate a region as the one through which I was riding. A few days later we came to a part where some of these pests had settled, and only he who has seen an invasion of locusts knows what this means. The ground was covered with a thick carpet of them, every cactus plant and shrub was overhung with a grey mass, and some clung together in clusters, hanging down like bunches of grapes. At first the horses shied a little and refused to move, and when one flying along hit their heads they gave a nervous jump. However, very soon they found out that there was no danger and walked along, leaving a patch of mashed bodies behind with every step, the crushed locusts being devoured at once by the others. Luckily we were out of the infested area within a few hours and I was looking forward to reaching better parts again.

Semi-deserts and even real deserts have their charms, and it is probably owing to this that people who are born and raised in such will always return; what particularly struck me in Santiago del Estero were the marvellous sunsets. After some of those scorching days, when even the cactus plants appear to suffer from the merciless sunrays that seem to penetrate to the very bones, and when even the little parrots keep quiet in some shady spot, then the sun often sets behind a dark curtain of red. The cactus plants stand out in black silhouettes, looking like fantastic beings stretching their octopus-like feelers towards the sky as if in agony, or again they look like human arms groping in all directions. The shrubbery, standing out black against the crimson horizon, reminded me of the classical Japanese silhouette pictures. As soon as the sun has disappeared below the sea of flame nature seems to breathe once more and the first shrill shrieks of some night birds can be heard or, maybe, the silence is broken by the ugly, cough-like bark of some prowling fox.

My faithful horses stuck to their work like heroes, and in spite of the fact that they had eaten next to nothing for several days, and the lack of water, they seemed as fit and willing to move as they had been in the fertile sections far behind us. I felt like spurring the horses to a fast gallop when we entered the first forest land, for now we were out of Santiago del Estero, and our first real victory was won. My face was scorched and burnt, and my lips cracked with the salty sand and dust, but I was happy and proud, for we had crossed the region experts had told me no horse could cross from end to end, unless it be an animal raised and trained in this part.

Tucuman, 'The Argentine Eden'

The country now became hilly, and the forest with its gigantic trees had the appearance of a beautiful park, but, best of all, there was cool, clear water running in the irrigation canals.

The first sign of human life I encountered was a group of women riding on small mules and burros, one of the animals carrying two hefty females without seeming to mind the weight. Some of the women were smoking pipes which they handled with the dexterity of old mariners.

Very soon the first farmhouses appeared in a forest clearing where alfalfa grew in abundance. (When such a clearing is made the felled trees are cut into logs which are burnt to make charcoal, an important industry in this part.) Feeling we had done enough I stopped at the first hut, where I was immediately given hospitality. The horses once more were able to fill themselves with good grass and water, and after I had washed off the sand and dust that had accumulated during the past few days I was ready for a good meal. In the evening we all sat and chatted, and, as usual, strange tales of the region were told. When the conversation drifted to foxes I heard remarkable stories about Mr. Reynard and his cunning. Some might be true, others were undoubtedly the works of imagination, but nevertheless they were entertaining.

'Yes,' said one of the men, 'if there are no dogs without fleas, there certainly are no foxes without them,' and then he related the following story which I have heard in other parts before and since and which I have no reason to disbelieve.

Shortly before sunset Mr. Fox usually comes out of his burrow to see how things go outside, and to find out if the weather is suitable for a good night's hunting. If there is an 'arroyo' (stream) near, he then goes down to wet his dry throat. Presently he slowly dips the lower part of his belly in the water and, by degrees, gently and very slowly, goes in deeper, until finally his back is covered. The hairs along his spine are bristled as if he were facing an enemy, and as the fleas have been forced higher and higher by the rising water they will finally take refuge on the bristles that are still out of the water. When the time comes the fox suddenly goes completely below the surface, and then immediately swims away, leaving most of the fleas to float on the water, where minnows and other small fish snatch them.

I felt much relieved when I sighted the first village and, to my surprise, there existed a very nice inn where the horses were fed on green alfalfa and where I had a decent meal and a comfortable bed to sleep in. I had an excellent night's rest, which was at one time disturbed by a drunken rascal who walked up and down the only street threatening some imaginary enemy and firing shots into the air. Here nearly all the houses are built of a hard wood called 'quebracho,' the gaps between the logs being filled in with mud. The roofs are made of straw, which keeps the interior very cool during the hot summers. As quebracho wood does not rot, these huts can almost be said to be everlasting.

The next journey brought us to the outskirts of La Banda, a town of considerable importance near Santiago, the capital of the province. When we arrived at a nice 'finca' (farm) I entered to ask if we might spend the night there. The owner, an elderly gentleman, received me with warm words of welcome and assured me that he would never allow me to proceed before I had spent a whole week with him. Nothing was left undone to make me comfortable, and the horses, having been bathed, were turned loose in a beautiful alfalfa field. After they had rolled and shaken themselves they settled down to make up for what they had missed during the previous ten days or so, and soon they were munching the juicy mouthfuls of grass, the noise of mastication sounding like sweet music to me.

I stayed a whole week with my kind host, and besides other entertainments I was taken to a travelling circus one night. The circus show was much the same as anywhere else: a couple of acrobats, a horribly painted, high-kicking señorita of at least forty winters, a few trained dogs and horses went through a lot of useless figures whilst H.M. the manager, dressed in greasy tailcoats with a rubber shirtfront and collar, cracked the whip and twitched his plastered 'Kaiser Bill' moustache.

Once the circus part was over, a stage was arranged and all the artistes (?) dressed to present the eagerly-waiting public with a drama. All such circus dramas in the Argentine are supposed to take one back to the old gaucho times, but I doubt if ever so much blood ran in all the dramas of real life as is supposed to run in one of these plays alone. One great and very interesting difference exists between one of these Argentine circus dramas and what is called a 'drama' in the moving pictures. The movie hero invariably comes out top dog and fades away from the sighing public of sentimental ladies with one of those long-drawn kisses that make the young ladies shiver. Now the final scene of an Argentine circus drama is utterly different, for here the hero must be killed on a stage strewn with dead or dying friends and enemies, some having been stabbed, others shot, clubbed or strangled in a regular hurricane free-for-all fight; in other words, these circus dramas have ultra-dramatic final scenes, so dramatic in fact that they are first-class comedies.

Like all good things, my stay here had to come to an end, and it was with regret that I parted from my kind host and his family. He accompanied me for some distance, riding on one of the small but hardy ponies of the region, and as he turned after the final farewell I noticed that his eyes were wet. This gentleman belonged to the old Argentine type; people whose religion was hospitality and whose friendship was a guarantee at any time.

After two long journeys we arrived in Tucuman, a pretty town at the foot of the first range of the Andes. The country round this town is beautiful and exceedingly fertile, and the sugar industry is the chief source of wealth. Tucuman is often called the 'Eden' of the Argentine, and here federal state was declared in the year 1816. The small, old-fashioned house in which the document was signed still stands and is now protected by a glass building enclosing it. I was invited to stay at the military barracks, where both the horses and myself were shown every consideration. Military service in the Argentine is compulsory, one year in the army or two in the navy. The barracks are of modern construction and kept spotlessly clean, and I found the officers and men thoroughly enjoying themselves.

Leaving Tucuman I took a northerly direction towards the Bolivian frontier. I was happy to have reached the Andes, but I was much more pleased when I waved my last farewell to them, nearly one year later, in the extreme north of the continent. For a few days we travelled through green sugar-cane fields where Bolivian Indians and 'mestizos' (half-castes) were busy cutting the cane with large 'machetes' (long, broad knives, some two feet in length). The apparently simple operation of cutting sugar-cane requires great skill before the necessary speed and endurance are acquired, and I was fascinated watching these men do their work. The settlements and villages in this sector are about as primitive as I have ever seen, and the huts are usually swarming with insects of all kinds. The majority of the men are heavy drinkers, and here, unlike all other parts of the Argentine I know, drunkenness is not only common but general. Strange to say, I found similar conditions all the way up the Andes as far as the extreme north of the continent and later in Central America and Mexico; as the U.S. are theoretically 'dry' my observations in this line have to stop at the very wet Rio Grande.

In the town of Tucuman I could not help noticing the many exceedingly pretty and well-dressed girls, but once out in the open, on my way towards the Bolivian border, I found the type to be much darker and showing a very strong strain of Indian blood. Girls of eleven and twelve years are fully developed, and mothers of that age are not uncommon.

Entering the Mighty Andes

From Tucuman north the country is very picturesque and the mountain trails lead through fine forests and through deep 'quebradas' (gulleys) or again along vast and rocky river-beds, and often we were threading our way along giddy paths on mountain sides with deep precipices in straight drops down to the valleys below. Luckily I had been well advised and arrived at a time of year when the rivers were low, and it could easily be seen what these must be like when they come romping down in full flood on their way down to the distant Atlantic.

Occasionally a rider crossed us, probably on his way to the next settlement or on some errand to the distant town. The shaggy and sturdy mountain ponies were usually saddled and rigged out in their best and the rider wore some gaily coloured poncho and carried his few belongings in saddle-bags behind on the animals' haunches. It is no use asking these people the way, for they have only one' answer and will invariably reply, 'siga derecho no mas' (just go straight ahead), although the trail may wind and twist through a regular labyrinth of deep canyons and valleys. If one enquires as to the distance to the next place the monotonous and aggravating reply is always 'aqui la vuelta no mas' (here, just round the corner), or 'cerquita,' which means 'quite close,' although there may be scores of bends and side valleys and a whole day's riding to be done before one reaches the place—if one is lucky enough not to lose oneself completely. However, in spite of these useless answers, I made a point of asking every passer-by, even if it was only to break the monotony of lonely hours without hearing a human voice. Like most mortals, these people are very inquisitive and curious, and they usually asked me where I came from and where I was going. My stock answer to these questions was that I came from the south, and that I was on my way north, which always seemed to satisfy their curiosity, and wishing me 'que le vaya bien' (good luck to you) in a peculiar singing bass voice they would spur on their mounts.

It was no easy matter to follow the right trail, and more than once we had to retrace our steps a long way when I realised that we had gone wrong. Such incidents did not improve my temper, and as we were returning I usually went through a special vocabulary from alpha to omega, and I am certain that if the horses had realised what it was all about they would have nodded approval with every step.

Several rivers had enough water to make fording a ticklish proposition, and on one occasion the horse I was riding lost his footing and the strong current carried both of us down into a pool below the shallow rapids where we had attempted to cross. Luckily the two of us came out of it with only a thorough soaking and a good fright, and after all, this was only one of the many lessons we had to learn, lessons that can only be learnt by experience. The pack-horse was luckier than we had been and had enough sense to go on until he reached the other side safely, where we once more joined company.

By this time the horses and myself were the best of friends, or 'amadrinado' as the gauchos call it. The bell-mare of a 'tropilla' (troop) is called 'madrina' in the Argentine, from which noun this pretty adjective 'amadrinado' is derived. In order to appreciate fully the friendship of a horse, a man has to live out in the open with him for some time, and as soon as the animal comes to a region that is strange to him he will never go away from his master but will look for his company and in case of danger seek his protection. By this time both my horses were so fond of me that I never had to tie them again, and even if I slept in some lonely hut I simply turned them loose at night, well knowing that they would never go more than a few yards away and that they would be waiting for me at the door in the early morning, when they always greeted me with a friendly nicker.

Ostriches are very common in these parts, but as they are often hunted they are extremely shy. These birds belong to the South American variety (*Rhea Darwini*) and are smaller than the African kind. The females lay the huge eggs in a common nest that has been roughly scratched out in some hidden-away place, and there as many as thirty eggs may be deposited. Once the laying season is over one of the males takes charge of the hatching and later of the raising of the young. The females and other males take not the slightest notice of the eggs or the young, and once the laying is done all but the one male go back to their normal life. Should anybody disturb the nest during the temporary absence of the male which hatches them, he will immediately find it out on his return. Should there be one egg missing, and even if this has been taken from the bottom and with great care, he will at once find it out, and then he often smashes all the others by trampling on them and kicking them in every direction. I do not believe nor suggest that the birds are able to count, but I am convinced that they possess some instinct which enables them to know when eggs are missing. I have known an ostrich to break all the eggs in his nest after I had observed him for a while from a considerable distance.

The large grey lizards or iguanas which are very common in the northern provinces of the Argentine are great egg eaters. However, the eggs of ostriches are too big for their mouths, and their tails too weak to break the thick shells by striking them. Although a good-sized iguana measures two feet or more from head to the tip of the tail, and in spite of his formidable teeth, he will not venture near an ostrich nest whilst the male is anywhere near. If he happens to be away eating, the lizard will then go to the nest and push out an egg a foot or so and then roll it rapidly against the others so as to crack the hard shell. Once this has been done the rest is easy. I have often eaten ostrich eggs and found them to taste much like ordinary hens' eggs, and I am inclined to think that the average man would not know the difference.

Although ostriches abounded in the pampas until recent years they are rapidly disappearing now. On some estates they are allowed to live, but on most estancias where fat stock is raised the owners object to their presence owing to their bad habit of running about flapping their wings when they are in a playful mood. When the cattle see this they become curious and begin to follow them, and finally they will stampede. If the weather happens to be hot this ruins the cattle, and often many animals die. Only a young ostrich can be overtaken by a man on horseback, and this only after a considerable amount of chasing. A full-grown bird is much too fast for a man and horse, but by hunting in groups one can often take them by surprise. The sporting way of catching them is with the bolas*, but there are not many men who know how to use them properly these days.

Pumas, as the South American lions are called, give a great deal of trouble to the sheep and goat-raisers, but they are not dangerous to men, excepting when they have cubs and one should happen to pass near their caves. Wild cats also are often seen in these forests, but unless they are disturbed they will not attack a human being. Occasionally some tiger which has strayed to these parts from the Chaco regions to the north-east has been killed, but such a thing is rare.

Cattle roam about in the forests or among the thorny shrubbery, and

*Bolas, or sometimes called boleadoras or 'Las Tres Marias'. A weapon of Indian origin, consisting of three balls, fastened together with leather thongs.

it was in this district that I saw some of the cleverest horsemen. It is amazing to see them chasing an animal through the thick bush, the fleet ponies twisting through the shrubbery like eels, galloping at full speed whilst the riders are dodging thorny branches and twigs by bending from side to side, all the while swinging their raw-hide lassos and waiting for the opportunity to make a successful throw if the chased animal happens to pass through an open gap in the bush. Lassoing in the open is child's play when compared with this, and, to add to the obstacles the country presents, one has to consider that the cattle are small, very agile and wild, and therefore able to dodge like wild goats. In these forest regions in the north of Argentina both rider and horse are protected by huge flaps made of leather which are called 'guarda montes' (shrub guards), without which both man and mount would be torn to pieces by the terrible thorns. For further protection the men often wear leather skull caps and jackets made of the same material, and an extra leather protector is strapped across the horses' chests.

The next place of importance we reached was Jujuy, a pretty town in a big, fertile valley. Here, as in Tucuman, sugar is grown and fine orange groves adorn the steep slopes. Nearly all the plantation workers are pure Indians who come down from Bolivia for the harvest. There is a saying that so long as sugar and coffee are consumed there will be slavery in the world, and I had opportunity to observe that there is a great deal of truth in this. The ignorant and poor Indians earn relatively fair salaries, but at the end of the harvest all the money paid to them is back in the safes of the companies. Some of these concerns prohibit merchants to sell their goods within their vast stretches of land, and run their own stores where things are sold at criminal prices to the ignorant Indians, who sleep in huts made of sugar-cane, and the least said about the conditions they live in the better. Pay-day is one of the worst sights in drunken orgies that can be imagined, and, of course, all the drinks must be purchased at the company's stores. Chemical wine and cheap sugar-cane alcohol are sold at champagne prices, and when I expressed my disgust to one of the superintendents of a certain company he told me that I was ridiculously sentimental and that this was—commerce! I should not be at all surprised if these same people are ardent supporters of some mission to Indians, and I can picture them, with uplifted eyes, generously putting a bank note into the plate when the collection is handed around the church whilst people behind whisper to each other what charming and liberal people Mr. and Mrs. So-and-So are. After pay-days there is no work done for two or three days, most of the Indians not being in a condition to move or not having quite spent all their earnings.

The fame of these pay-day scenes had reached me long before, whilst I was in Buenos Aires, but now I had the opportunity to see for myself that the accounts I had heard were only too true. Early in the morning, after having received their pay 'without scruple knowing they were justly entitled to it,' the mestizos and Indians came flocking to the store. Coca leaves (from which cocaine is extracted, and which the Indians chew as some do tobacco), machetes, knives, clothing, tobacco, etc., were bought at high prices, and spirits and wine were consumed in unbelievable quantities. At first there was hardly any conversation, but as time went on, and the alcohol began to take effect, the place sounded like a stock exchange during a sensational day. The store was filled with villainous-looking fellows, all drinking, smoking, chewing coca and arguing in loud voices, some in bad Spanish and others in Quichua, the language of these Indians. Some bought their supplies and took them outside where they drank squatting on the ground or leaning against the wall, whilst others took the wine away in buckets and went staggering towards their filthy quarters; a few were already sleeping where they happened to have fallen. The store stood on a little hill and steps led up to its entrance, and I could not help feeling amused when several men stumbled, rolled and bounced down into the ditch against the fence below, where they remained fast asleep until next day. Behind the store some had started cockfights. These are strictly illegal in the Argentine, but where there are Indians there are fighting-cocks. The betting was as fast as the drinking, and the winners every now and again slouched away to the store to fetch a fresh supply of alcohol. A little further away stood a small wooden box, placed lying on its side and without a lid. When night came several candles were put inside to illuminate the ground near there whilst the men played a game of taba. (The game with the heel-bone of a bullock I have described in a former chapter.) Some ten paces from either side of the box, almost in complete darkness, stood the throwers, and around the box stood or squatted all the others who took side bets, for there, in front of them, where the candles illuminated the ground the bone had to be thrown and so they were in the best position to see the result. The expressions on the men's faces were a rare study, and the strong shadows the candlelight threw on them made the scene almost grotesque when the eager winners clutched the money with greedy hands whilst the losers' eyes flashed with disappointment.

Fights of a serious nature are the order of the day, and that night was no exception, for two started slashing each other with their machetes until one had his head split open, the blood squirting all over the place. Nobody seemed to take more than a casual interest in the duel, and once the wounded man was dragged away by his friends and the victor had escaped, everybody who had money left again settled down to drinking and gambling, and thus they continued until finally the last cent was back with the company. Next morning I went to see how the wounded man was getting on, and I arrived just as they were curing him. His friends had put handfuls of red pepper on the deep skull wound to stop the bleeding, and this mixed with blood and with the coarse black hair had formed a regular knob, about the size of two fists. These people are so tough that almost nothing short of cutting their heads clean off will kill them, and although this man had his skull split open and had lost much blood, he walked away immediately after he had been roughly fixed up, and two days later was at work again as if nothing had happened, and was only waiting for the next pay-day to come. The police are supposed to interfere when fights take place, but then it suits the company to keep the men at work, and a little 'propina' (tip) for the 'comisario' (sheriff) does wonders, as in most other places in the world.

Preparing the Rough Mountain Travel

Before leaving I had carefully to consider the changing of my equipment. The packs that I had used so far had given fairly good results in the plains, but for mountain travelling a more suitable type of pack-saddle had to be acquired. Throughout the Argentine up to this point there was no need to carry firearms, although I had taken a .45 Smith & Wesson with me. I did not use the automatic type but the old-fashioned six-shooter which is not so likely to jam when travelling through sandy country, and does not need to be kept so clean as the automatic. I also carried a 12-gauge repeating shot gun and a Winchester .44. The firearms, excepting of course the revolver, were strapped on top of the pack-saddle; ammunition being rather difficult to obtain in many countries I added a .45 long (six-shooter) to my collection. Besides firearms, I had to think about other important details; thus I added a cooking-pot, a kettle, rice, beans, coffee, tea, sugar, salt, biscuits, etc., to my little store, for they might come in handy in places where it would be impossible to obtain food. At the same time I had to try to keep the weight of the pack to a minimum. The horse I rode always carried the money, which is a considerable weight in parts where Indians will only accept silver coins. This animal also carried my documents (letter of credit, passport, maps, etc.), compass, barometer, and a couple of books to pass away dull moments. Although the sheepskins of the saddle made quite a comfortable bed, and knowing that we should encounter some very cold places in the mountains, I added a big woollen blanket to my equipment. I also took a light rubber poncho, which is simply a square sheet with a slit in the middle through which one puts one's head, making quite a good overcoat in case of rain. I took good care that the saddle blankets that had to go next to the skin of the horses were of the best quality and large enough so that I should be able to use them as extra blankets during exceptionally cold nights. Of course I could not carry a tent, nor a sleeping-bag, the weight and bulk of such being too much for the horses on so long a journey. However, I had with me the large mosquito-net I have already described and to protect my face I had a net made to fit over the broad-rimmed hat and wide enough to fall over the shoulders. This had a larger mesh and was made of black material to give better visibility and at the same time to protect the eyes against the glaring sun. Naturally I had very little use for these things in the highland of Bolivia, although I was worried by gnats and sandflies in several places where I had never expected to find such.

Later, as I reached the low swamp regions in the tropics, these mosquito-nets must have saved my life. To protect my face and eyes against wind and sand I acquired a woollen mask and green goggles, and these were most useful later. The horses shod, and many other details attended to, I packed up and saddled, and confidently started out to tackle what I then thought would be the toughest part of the whole journey, the part over the Andes down to the Pacific Ocean. Had I guessed what obstacles and difficulties were in store for me after that, I really believe I would never have started out, but then, 'fools rush in where angels fear to tread.'

Through Mighty Quebradas and Over Windswept Mountains Towards the Bolivian Border

From July on we travelled in a vast and deep valley leading practically due north. Every now and again Indians with troops of llamas, packed with rock salt and woven goods, passed us on their way down to the towns, where they exchange these articles for corn, sugar, coca leaves and other necessaries that cannot be obtained in the regions where these people live. They usually make one trip a year, and this during the dry season, because it is utterly impossible to travel when the rivers are high.

Not only do these Indians use llamas; many put their loads on small, shaggy burros. It is rare to see the natives ride, they seem to prefer to trot behind the animals and drive them along. The loads the llamas carry are not heavy, for should one of them be overloaded it is likely to lie down and not get up until the extra weight is taken off it. Llamas never eat during the daytime but only after the sun has gone down, and they are able to subsist on fodder which would not even keep a burro or mule alive. Up in the Bolivian highland there are practically no trees and therefore fuel is scarce and accordingly expensive. The droppings of the llamas might well be called 'Bolivian coal,' for they serve as fuel everywhere, even in La Paz, the capital, where I have frequently seen Indians unload their precious burdens at private houses and hotels where this excellent fuel is used for cooking, etc.

We were slowly advancing towards the Argentine-Bolivia border, and the imposingly broken and rough valley we were using as a road was walled in by high mountains which had wonderful tints. Some appeared reddish, some green and others violet. Travelling was very bad and exceedingly hard on the animals, for the stony river-beds were strewn with huge boulders and rocks. As we passed during the dry season most of the rivers were absolutely dry, but a few had water and made things unpleasant at times, the current being very strong and often dangerous. The horses stumbled and tripped and we had to cross and re-cross the valleys from one side to the other. One evening I had arrived at a little village in a narrow, deep side-valley. All the houses there are made of 'adobe' (mud) and are covered with peculiar round-tiled roofs. Behind every house there is a huge square corral made of high, thick mud walls. Not a soul was to be seen. I rode through two narrow streets without seeing the slightest sign of life until I came to a place where a mule was tied to a post, to all appearances fast asleep. After a while a door opened and a curious darkish face looked at me. After no little trouble I found the house of the 'comisario.' The gentleman was asleep on the floor of his office. After I had shaken him several times he opened his eyes and turned over on his back. It did not take me long to realise that he was very drunk; however, I managed to revive him sufficiently to make him understand what I wanted. When he was able to move again he provided me with the best he had, which, by the way, was very little.

The office consisted of a room that had not been swept nor dusted since it was built, and in it were a couple of rickety chairs, a bench and a worm-eaten table. On the latter I made my bed, and the horses were put into the backyard where they were given a feed of straw, which is considered a luxury for animals in these parts. Next day we continued up the main valley which is known as the Quebrada de Humahuaca. This name is due to an old fable that is still told to this day by people of the region and which an old half-caste Indian, in a hardly audible, soft and singing voice, told me whilst sitting beside the fire in his poor little hut.

'In the time of our old ancestors a powerful and prosperous tribe of Indians lived on one side of the valley, and on the opposite mountain slopes an equally strong and well-organised tribe had settled. At first these two tribes were the best of neighbours and traded honestly and freely, but, as time went on, ambition and jealousy had converted them into bitter enemies, and many fierce battles were fought between the two. The "cacique" (chief) of one tribe had a son, and his enemy on the other side had a beautiful daughter, and one day the two happened to meet and immediately fell in love with each other. The cacique's son often disappeared quietly during the night, and after following perilous trails he would meet his beloved. However, soon they aroused suspicion, and the father of the girl sent a messenger to the young man's father, threatening to execute his enemy's son should he ever catch him. Even this threat was not enough to frighten the young lover, who continued his visits during dark nights. On one occasion he was waylaid, taken prisoner, and brought before his father's enemy, who ordered the young man to be beheaded at once. Once the head had been severed from the body it was taken to the girl who hysterically caressed it, and according to the fable the eyes of the still warm head opened wide and tears began to flow out of them, and ever since this valley has been called Humahuaca, which means "Weeping Head".'

Not only are the inhabitants of these regions full of mystery and superstition; the very mountains and atmosphere seem to be filled with it.

I stopped for two days at some prehistoric ruins called Tilcara. They are situated on the very peak of a high hill from where one has a marvellous view of the vast valley below. There is no history attached to these ruins, but archæologists have taken a keen interest in them.

It was no easy matter to find a man to accompany me to make a few excavations, people here being very superstitious about the ruins and especially so about graves. Finally I found a man who was willing to come with me, and it was obvious that he had been there before. He was an expert at locating graves, which he did by stamping on the ground, and every now and again boring down with a thin iron rod. I could not notice the difference in sound, but here and there the man would stop to bore with the rod, and if he struck a hollow below the surface he then used a spade to clear away the soft, sandy soil. In this manner we found several graves, all having been built in the shape of old-fashioned beehives, but lined and covered with stones. The dead had obviously been buried in a sitting position, much the same way as is still customary to this day among certain South American Indian tribes. In some graves we found pottery and stone implements and in all were well-preserved skeletons. What particularly struck me about these was the strange shape of the skulls which appeared as if the foreheads had been pushed back. The main thing I was searching for was one of the golden masks, which were usually placed over the faces of dead chieftains, several having been found by expeditions which had previously made excavations in these ruins. In one grave, among pottery and other things, we found the bones of a llama, probably the remains of a sacred animal; the ancient Indians having adored white llamas.

Putting my hand into one grave we had just opened, a small thorn entered one of my fingers, and within a few hours a very nasty infection set in and after a few days the consequent blood poisoning looked as if it might cost me my life. At first I took but very little notice of the swelling, but when the infection broke out in the other hand, in my face and in the right leg, I began to feel alarmed. There was no doctor anywhere near and so I was obliged to travel some days before I reached a village where there was a more or less qualified medical man who could not even as much as guess what kind of poisoning it was, and in spite of his treatment my condition did not improve in the slightest. He advised me to return to Buenos Aires, telling me that even if I were cured I was not in a condition to undertake so arduous and dangerous a journey as the crossing of the mountains to La Paz, the capital of Bolivia.

However, I had not come all this distance only to return home again and be laughed at by fools who get pleasure out of making others look ridiculous, even if they themselves are not capable of doing anything better, and so I sadly packed up, willing to risk it and to see if fate would be kind to me. We were in high altitudes where mountain-sickness affects strangers, and that morning, when I was pulling at the girth whilst putting on the pack-saddle, my nose began to bleed profusely; I had 'puna,' as this affliction is called in this region. It was a sick and sad man who slowly and painfully wound his way up the rocky river-beds, even the horses seeming to sense that something was wrong with their master.

In a lonely hut of a mountaineer I was told about an Indian herb doctor who had great fame in the neighbourhood, and when I agreed to it somebody went to call him. After four days the messenger arrived with him. He was an elderly and obviously poor Indian, and not of the type who might inspire the average patient with confidence, but when he asked me a series of highly intelligent questions, which were interpreted to me by a person who could speak both Quichua and Spanish, I began to realise that he knew far more than I had given him credit for. He declared that the case was not a serious one and immediately set to work boiling some dry herbs which he carried in a poncho on his back. When they were ready for use, the steaming herbs, which looked very much like spinach, were laid on the open sores. He stayed with me for two days, and prior to leaving he recommended that I should drink no alcohol, eat no meat nor eggs, and drink tea made from herbs he gave me. His fees for his 'professional services,' including the long journeys, amounted to one boliviano, or roughly 6d., and when I gave him five times that amount his appreciation could be read on his rugged face. Within five days I was able to proceed, but, of course, the wounds were not closed and I could not wear a boot on my right leg, so I made myself a sandal and wore some thick woollen stockings over the bandages. These stockings are made of llama wool and are skilfully knitted by the industrious Indians.

We were still in a vast and desolate valley, where nothing grows excepting a few cactus plants and where terrific winds come down from the cold regions above, making travelling unpleasant in the extreme. Fine sand and even little pebbles were continually being blown into my face which was badly chapped. My lips were so badly cracked that they had swelled considerably, causing a great deal of discomfort.

One day I met some Indian 'arrieros' (troop drivers) who were driving a troop of loaded burros back to their distant mountain home. Having nobody to talk to, I entered into conversation with them and was very glad when I found out that they spoke Spanish quite well. I told them that I was on my way towards the border and they offered to show me a short cut that would take us over a better trail in the mountains. At first my new acquaintances were very shy, but a few coca leaves and a 'traguito' (swig) of alcohol soon made them more talkative. We had some very interesting conversations as we were threading our way between boulders, or bordering precipitous mountainsides and these men taught me quite a number of things that were useful to me at later periods. Among other things they warned me against some poisonous herbs that grow in these and other mountain regions, herbs that will kill mules and horses should they eat them.

Towards evening we arrived at a lonely hut, high up in the mountains. This was very small and built entirely of big stones that were merely piled on each other. We called, but as nobody answered we crawled through the door—a small opening in one of the walls. At first I could see nothing, but once my eyes became accustomed to the dusk, I discovered an old man lying on some dry goat-skins in one corner. In the middle of the room there was a hollow in the ground, the ashes in it suggesting that a fire had been made there lately. When I approached the old man he became aware that somebody was near and enquired who it was. The poor old man was practically blind and almost deaf, and when I asked him if there was anything to eat, both for men and beasts, he replied that he had absolutely nothing and that he was waiting for his son who brought him food every other day and who looked after the few goats he possessed. The smell inside the hut was so repulsive that I had to go outside for fresh air every now and again. After a considerable time an old man, dressed in rough mountaineer's clothes and wearing heavy sandals, appeared. He introduced himself as the son of the old man in the hut, and judging by his appearance he must have been some eighty years of age. (He later told me he was ninety.) I offered him a drink and some coca leaves and promised to pay him well if he brought grass for my starving horses. In these regions there is no vegetation excepting in some of the hollows which a stranger is not likely to find. Fortunately the man agreed to bring some much-needed fodder and immediately left, taking a large net with him, and soon he disappeared, leaping over rocks and from boulder to boulder with the sure-footedness and agility of a chamois. After about two hours, when it was already getting dark, he returned with a big bundle of grass on his back.

Having attended to the horses I began to think about having something to eat myself, but it was difficult to make the man admit that he had some dry goat's meat and oats hidden away somewhere outside, but after a little more alcohol and a few more coca leaves he brought in what we wanted, and lit the fire to boil water in an earthenware pot. Although the wooden plates and spoons we were using had never been washed, I thought I had never tasted anything so good in all my life, for the mixture of dry goat's meat and oats made an excellent soup. It was late when we finished the meal, and then we squatted around the fire to warm ourselves, for outside the temperature had already fallen below freezing point. As usual, the conversation became livelier once the stomachs were full, and when I produced more coca leaves and even a few cigarettes, the men's eyes fairly sparkled with joy. Many were the tales of mystery I heard that night whilst sitting near the fire in that lonely hut high up in the cold and windswept mountain near the Bolivian border.

When the time came to make our beds it was no easy matter to make everybody fit in the small space available, but soon we were all rolled up in our blankets on the floor, and as the glow of the embers became less and less, the cold became more intense, and outside I could hear the animals munching their fodder, every now and again giving one of those peculiar snorts horses are accustomed to give when the cold penetrates their nostrils.

For two days I had the pleasant company of these arrieros, with their small, shaggy burros, and although the trail was bad and dangerous in parts, I am certain that I saved a considerable number of miles and probably avoided worse travelling along the route I had originally intended to follow. I was sorry when my companions had to take a different direction from mine, and I saw them disappear behind some cliffs in a side valley, leaving me once more alone with my two faithful horses.

Further north we passed through several small villages and settlements, where I noticed a very different type of people, most of them being half-castes or pure Indians. The women carry the babies in a cloth on their backs and wear long skirts of different colours, sandals, and high white hats that look like over-sized 'bowlers.' Some of the people make their sandals out of old motor-car tyres, and before I knew this I was puzzled on several occasions when I saw what I took to be tracks of cars, and this in places where no automobile could possibly move. We passed Indians, men and women, who were travelling along our trail, probably on their way to some distant market. Whilst they were trotting along they were continually spinning woollen thread. This is done by twirling a piece of wood, not unlike a wooden toy-top but through which another piece is driven, about as thick as a pencil. The top-like wooden piece acts as flywheel, whilst the thread is wound around the stick that is stuck into it.

In the north of the Argentine I spent two days with a settler on his small farm. He possessed several burros, and as we discussed the relative sense of the different domestic animals, my host, who was an ardent supporter of the donkeys, told me that no puma could kill a burro born in that region. In that particular neighbourhood there were many pumas and in order to entertain me, and at the same time to prove his statement, the man led a donkey away to a hollow, where he tied him to a solitary bush with a rope. This done we went away some 10 yards and lay down to wait to see what would happen. It was just growing dark, and after a wait of some two hours I began to think there were no pumas in the district.

It was a bright night, and with the help of my field-glasses I could see the burro quite well. Presently he doubled his legs and rolled over on his side, and then my host touched my arm and pointed towards the animal, and, sure enough, there I could see the puma, like a, shadow, slowly creeping towards the poor burro, who then rolled right over on his back and started to kick wildly with all fours, at the same time making noises that were terrible to hear. The puma made a large circle around him and then slowly slunk away and disappeared. The man then told me that the burros there seem to know that a puma will only attack by jumping on the neck of his prey, and I had to admit that I had never suspected burros to have as much sense and cold blood under such trying circumstances as his shaggy little animal had just proved himself to possess. Good for donkey sense!

After some extremely rough journeys and some most uncomfortable nights we reached the border village—La Quiaca—having successfully crossed the highest pass at a point called Tres Cruces (Three Crosses) which is over 11,000 feet above sea level. Mountain sickness had worried me considerably at times and my nose had bled profusely, but the horses did not seem to be affected by the rarefied air and never behaved in an abnormal manner, even when we crossed high ridges, and I was delighted to see them reach the border in better condition than they had been when we left Buenos Aires. (It must be remembered that when they arrived in the capital they had then just completed the overland journey up from the southernmost regions of the continent.) We had covered roughly 1,300 miles (from Buenos Aires), and, although the animals arrived at the Bolivian border in such good condition, I still had my doubts as to whether they would be able to cross the main Andean ranges of Bolivia and Peru which we had necessarily to negotiate in order to reach the Pacific Ocean.

We took a well-earned rest at La Quiaca, although the place is most unattractive, to say the least, cold and windswept. No trace of vegetation is to be seen in the whole neighbourhood, and strong winds blew day and night, carrying with them clouds of sand that were almost blinding at times. I had some hay sent to this place by train, for I knew that the neighbourhood produced no fodder and the horses had to be fed up well to be fit for the next trying stage, the trip from here to La Paz. There being no stables or corrals, I put them behind the station where there was a fenced-off square, but unfortunately there they were exposed to the winds and to the intense cold day and night, and, sorry as I felt for them, I had no remedy. My health had improved considerably, but it still left much to be desired. A good bed, regular meals, and reasonable amount of sleep soon worked wonders with me, and in between times I attended to the horses, again modified my equipment and rectified little defects I had noticed here and there.

Into the Land of the Quichuas

After a good rest, and with everything arranged to my satisfaction, we crossed a small, shallow river near the international railway bridge, and soon I was jogging over desolate, sandy country and big, rolling and barren 'lomas' (hills). For two days we continued thus, and on the second day, reaching the top of one of these hills, I beheld a sight that will for ever live in my memory.

Deep down before us a beautiful valley came in view and for the first time in nearly three weeks I saw a big stretch of beautiful green grass, and, better still, I saw some trees again. Even the horses seemed to quicken their steps as we were winding our way down the mountain side, and never in my life had the song of birds filled me with as much joy as it did here, for many days had passed without having seen even as much as a trace of birds. We came to a little village where I actually found what they called an 'hotel.' The traveller must not be delicate in these parts, for such hotels are merely mud huts, and the rooms have no other ventilation but the door, for windows do not exist. The bed, if he considers himself lucky enough to have found one and is foolish enough to use it, is simply a framework on four legs with boards laid across.

Early in the morning I was awakened by the beating of drums and the shrill notes of whistles and Indian reed flutes. I got up to see what this signified and saw a large crowd of Indians walking up and down the street, making this unearthly noise, or music as they call it. The proprietor of the hotel informed me that this was the day of Saint Roque, and when I admitted my ignorance, telling him that I had never heard the gentleman's name before, my visibly surprised host immediately explained that San Roque was the patron saint of dogs and that this day was dedicated to him, being observed once a year. Looking about me, I noticed that most dogs were decorated with ribbons and pieces of coloured wool. I wandered to the church, following behind the band, and later entered to see what was going on inside. The roof had fallen in in several places, so the light inside was good, although there were no windows.

The Indians brought their dogs and had them blessed whilst the band kept on playing outside. On this day all dogs are let loose, even those which are normally tied up day and night. When I had seen enough, in and around the church, I returned to the hotel, where I sat outside my room, watching more dog fights than I had seen in all my life before, and then suddenly a regular whirlpool of canine warriors of all colours and sizes came fighting up the street. During the heat of battle one big growler knocked me off my chair, and whilst this was happening other retreating fighters took refuge in my room where a regular battle royal ensued. One mongrel had obviously mistaken one of my saddle sheepskins for one of his enemies and dragged it outside, all the time shaking it and snarling viciously as if he were holding one of his foes by the throat, and had I not thrown my chair at him he would probably have torn my precious sheepskin to pieces.

A long day's ride through deep ravines and canyons brought me to Tupiza, where I was again awakened by music next morning, for another feast was being celebrated. It did not take me long to become accustomed to all these Bolivian 'fiestas,' and after a few days I hardly noticed them.

The most practical suggestion I can bring forward for Bolivia is to abolish calling every other day after some saint; I think it would be a lesser strain on people's memories if the days were simply called St. Sunday, St. Monday, and so on, and should there not be sufficient, it would be easy to shunt in an extra fiesta every now and again. After all, there is no need to have an astronomical calendar for the average Bolivian, sowing and harvest time is sufficient to see him through happily, and as to the hours, any fool knows whether it is day- or night-time. Be it well understood that I am only considering the Indian and mestizo population of the country, but then this amounts to about eighty or ninety per cent of the total.

Whenever time permitted, I never failed to visit the market places, where the essence of local life can be seen. The market is about the only place where anybody ever seems to move, excepting, of course, during fiestas. At the 'mercado' coca leaves, spices, dyes, alcohol, grain, woven goods, pottery, medical herbs, meat, etc., are sold at stalls or are merely spread out on the ground on a dirty poncho. Bolivian markets always reminded me of eastern bazaars, and I could watch for hours how the people bartered and argued without getting tired of it.

From Tupiza a railroad runs to La Paz, but I could not follow it because I knew that I should find absolutely no fodder for the animals if I went that way, so I decided on another route, picking our way through valleys and over mountains where I would at least find sufficient food to see the horses through alive.

All Indians near Tupiza speak Quichua and I was obliged to make myself a small dictionary to be able to ask for the most necessary things, for only very few Indians understand Spanish. They are very interesting people, but exceedingly primitive, especially so in the almost inaccessible districts hidden among the network of mountains.

Many still live in tribes, a 'cacique' (chief) ruling them. These caciques are appointed by tribal election and rarely leave their huts without carrying a staff which is adorned with silver rings, these staves being the insignia or badge of office. Caciques have a great deal of power in certain tribes, and the Indians submit to them and accept their word as final. Not unlike their Inca forefathers, many tribes live on communistic principles; thus, when the land of a member has to be worked, all men of the tribe assemble there, and with their wooden spades, resembling oars, they dig the ground, chanting weird songs. Having tilled the land of one fellow-tribesman, the men then proceed to the property of another, and thus they continue until every man's land has been worked.

During the time of the Spanish conquest and subsequent occupation, a gold trail that started in Potosi led through these parts and down towards Tucuman in the Argentine. Whilst making their hasty retreat, during the War of Emancipation, the Spaniards buried much treasure along this trail. In many places I could see where treasure-hunters had dug in search of a 'tapado,' as such hidden treasures are called among the Spanish-speaking people in this region. The native treasure-hunters claim that where 'luces,' or strange lights, appear during the night, wealth is sure to be lying buried. I myself have seen such lights which I put down to escaping gases. Some wriggled along the ground like luminous snakes, others stood upright like columns of Grecian temples, and some looked like high coco palms, the light being of a greenish phosphorus-like colour. If ever a native sees one of these lights and is able to locate the exact spot where it appeared, he drives a stake into the ground, or leaves some other mark in order to be able to find the place next day, for he usually is far too superstitious to work there by night, and there are many who would never dare to touch an ancient grave or treasure, even if they knew that they would encounter great wealth.

The Roman Catholic church predominates throughout Bolivia, and although most Indian tribes have their patron saints I am afraid they know next to nothing about the religion itself. They are very fond of building little chapels on the very tops of hills or mountains that happen to overlook their villages and settlements, and the trails that lead up to these shrines are invariably absolutely straight and very steep, so steep in fact that a white man would find it difficult to reach the top.

Bolivian Indians are very superstitious and mystical, and they can often be seen on their way to a fiesta in some distant village, carrying a hideously painted wooden saint with them, the whole tribe marching to the music of flutes and whistles and to the beating of huge drums. Every now and again they stop to take a rest and to drink to the health of their idol, alcoholic drinks being carried in earthenware pots, in calabashes, or in bottles.

In one little village I saw a particularly lively Indian fiesta for which people from far and near had assembled, some having come long distances over the mountains and through desolate valleys. Standing or kneeling before the image of some saint there was a large number of girls who were going through all manner of movements, all the time wailing and murmuring in their language, which I could not understand. Luckily the local government official who accompanied me spoke both Quichua and Spanish and inter-preted some of the things they were telling to their saint. All these girls were imploring the wooden figure to assist them in finding husbands, and whilst they were doing this the men were looking on without showing the slightest trace of emotion, which is a characteristic among most Indians, who show neither pleasure nor sorrow by facial expression.

A short distance from the place where these girls were begging the saint to have compassion on them, there was another saint in front of which a group of rather older women were lamenting and whining and waving their arms like Dutch windmills. These women were asking their partic-ular saint to punish their bad husbands or to strike them with sudden death for all the ill-treatment they were receiving at their hands.

In spite of all these side-shows, the main attraction of any Indian feast is the alcohol that is consumed in unbelievable quantities and only those who have balance enough dance to the music of all manner of strangely-shaped reed instruments.

Indian Superstitions

Wherever I looked I saw proofs of the extraordinary superstitions these people believed in. At the top of the mountains, near the high-est point of a trail, there is always one, or several heaps of stones, and I noticed the same near every village alongside the trail that leads into it. All these mounds have a meaning attached to them, for if an Indian has been on a long journey and approaches his village on his way home, he picks up a large stone and carries it for a mile or two, and when he comes to one of the heaps near the village he deposits it there. The same is done when he approaches the top of a long and steep incline, and thus, in the course of time many large heaps have accumulated. The natives believe that by performing this simple ceremony they leave the pains, fatigue and sorrows of the journey behind.

When they travel with a troop of llamas and turn them loose after having made camp for the night they often make a circle with pebbles, which is supposed to represent a corral. For every animal they have, they put one llama dropping into this circle, firmly believing that this brings good luck, and that, although the animals roam about loose, they will all be safe and sound in the morning, just as if they had been in their corrals at home. Again, I had often noticed miniature houses built of a few small, flat stones, and this always in places where Indians had camped whilst on a journey. It was explained to me that when a poor man goes travelling he makes one of these houses every evening, for his belief is that he will be the lucky owner of a real house when he returns home, and that he will possess fields and animals if he has made such stone houses every night before retiring to rest.

On every Indian hut there is a small wooden cross, and usually a bunch of barley, an earthenware pot filled with 'chicha' (the native beer), a bottle of alcohol, a pot filled with corn and with coca leaves, etc. All this is supposed to bring luck and to influence the gods to provide them with these necessaries of life throughout the year, and once in every twelve months these tokens of good fortune are renewed.

Should an Indian be wishing for a baby, he seeks a hollow spoon-shaped stone and into this he places a small pebble; the pebble represents the baby, the larger and hollow stone, the cradle.

A Long-Forgotten Spanish Gold Trail

We had to ford several dangerous rivers, and at times we were climbing up some giddy mountain sides, but my sure-footed horses soon developed into good and cautious mountaineers and never showed signs of nervousness, even if we were bordering deep precipices. This caused me great satisfaction and gave me confidence, for I had long been wondering how they would behave in rough and dangerous mountain country.

One day, as we were nearing the summit of a high pass I happened to meet an Indian who, unlike his kin, was not afraid of me, and although we could not understand each other we carried on a lively conversation chiefly by means of signs and much to our mutual amusement. The good Indian was continuously pointing towards the horizon where I noticed a strange, small, yellow cloud. It was obvious that my new acquaintance was trying to make me understand something, and when he beckoned to me to follow him behind a fair-sized rock I began to realise that something abnormal was about to happen with the weather. Within a few minutes a formidable wind began to sweep the mountain top, having arrived with the suddenness and strength of an avalanche. Presently hail-stones, some of which were the size of small eggs, were blown horizontally past us, and I am certain that we would have met with disaster if we had been caught out in the open. Both horses stood behind us with their heads down and, although the noise around us was deafening and the very ground was quivering, they never tried to move, for obviously even they knew that the safest place was behind the rock where we huddled together. The hurricane only lasted a few minutes, and then the sky cleared with the same suddenness as it had darkened, and before I could give the Indian some coca leaves I always carried for this purpose he had disappeared down the steep slope.

In spite of my face-mask and goggles my lips were badly cracked and bleeding; I only used these protections when it was absolutely necessary, for after a few hours wearing them I began to feel uncomfortable. More than once, when Indians saw me with this hideous protection, they ran away shouting and screeching with fright, for they must have taken me for some evil spirit.

In former times there were official government resting-places along the main trails in Bolivia, and these were called 'postas,' but to-day only very few of them exist. In days gone by the postas were, roughly, twenty miles distant from each other and there the needy traveller could hire Indians to act as guides and to carry some of the pack, and at the same time fodder could be obtained at reasonable prices. Many of these places had mules which were hired to carry people and pack, and thus a person was able to go from one posta to the other without having to buy his own beasts. A few of these places were still working when I travelled through Bolivia, but owing to the recently-constructed railroad they were no longer working as much as they had done previously.

High up, in a cold and barren region, I stopped at the first posta, consisting of a large, one-roomed stone building and corrals with stone walls. When I entered the house I saw two sturdy Indians who were wearing loosely-fitting trousers that had once been white, heavy ponchos and knitted skull-caps. In the middle of the room there was a large table, made entirely out of stone, and along the walls I noticed some long, square stone blocks, which I later found out were the beds on which the weary traveller has to make himself as comfortable as possible with his blankets and packs. I was in sore difficulties, for I could not make myself understood, but finally the horses were given straw to eat and I feasted on barley soup and a kind of coarse, black biscuit which is called 'tanta,' this being the Indian word for bread. Shortly before sunset several other Indians arrived, and it was obvious that they had been working their little plots of land high up on the mountain-sides. As usual, I gave them coca leaves and a cigarette each, after which they were the best of friends, and then I showed them a few simple conjuring tricks I happened to remember, and I should not be surprised if they are still talking about that wonderful entertainment to-day. In the morning I let them look through my field-glasses, a mysterious marvel that seemed to fascinate them in the extreme and, judging by their signs, they must have thought field-glasses were intended to make the mountains appear to be dancing.

Chicha, the native beer, can be found almost everywhere. Even along some of the trails one sometimes meets an Indian woman who is sitting near a bush with a pot filled with this beverage, patiently spinning wool whilst waiting for some thirsty traveller to stop to buy a bowlful from her. When drinking chicha it is distinctly 'bad form' and shows lack of manners if one drinks the bowl empty, for the general custom is to spill a certain amount of the liquid on the ground, this being supposed to bring good luck to the person who is offering it. Should Indians happen to be ploughing a field and a traveller pass near there, they often come running towards him to offer a bowl of chicha, and even if he does not feel inclined to drink, the correct thing is to spill the liquid on the ground. In so doing the traveller is supposed to be blessing the soil, and for this reason the passer-by is offered the drink—not so much out of hospitality and generosity as for purely selfish motives.

Although the account is not very appetising it may interest the reader to know how Bolivian chicha is prepared.

I had been drinking it in preference to water, which is often bad and never safe, and one morning when I woke up in an Indian hut I saw a group of men and women squatting in a circle and speaking in muffled voices which made me wonder what was wrong with them. Upon watching them I found out that this was due to the fact that they were trying to speak with their mouths full. They were chewing corn, and when they had masticated it into a paste they spat it into a wooden bowl that was placed in the middle of the circle. I made enquiries as to what might be the object of this strange proceeding, whereupon one of the men, who spoke some Spanish, informed me that they were preparing the 'moco.' More puzzled than before I asked what so original a preparation might be used for, and the Indian seemed quite surprised at my question and explained that this was the first step towards the preparation of chicha. At later periods I had several opportunities to see Bolivia's national beverage being prepared, and this is roughly how it is done.

Corn is first of all soaked in water for a day, after which it is spread out on the ground and covered with a damp cloth. Thus covered, the corn begins to ferment, and next day it is put into large earthenware pots and boiled for some thirty-six hours. When it has been taken off the fire and has cooled down, the chewed corn, or the 'moco' is added to it, and this acts in a similar manner as yeast does with flour-paste to make bread. What actually happens is that the chewed corn becomes impregnated with saliva, which contains an enzyme, diastase. When added to a mass of hot boiled corn, the diastase acts upon the starch of the corn, converting it into malt sugar, and a sweet wort is obtained. Thanks to the climate, and with plenty of accidental infection this mash becomes infected with yeasts, or perhaps intentionally by adding some of a previous 'brew.'

In any case, fermentation sets in and alcohol is derived from the malt sugar. Within twelve hours the huge pots are fairly fizzing and humming with the fermentation and the brew begins to froth; the miracle has been performed; chicha has been made! According to the age it becomes stronger and stronger, but usually it is consumed before it is three days old, and even then it is already very strong and has a great deal of 'authority.' I must remark that in spite of my acquaintance with the finer points of the art of chicha making, I continued to drink it. Possibly some of my American friends will be eternally grateful to me for disclosing this recipe, and it might help them to prepare an especially original and tasty kind of 'home-brew' wherewith to entertain their thirsty friends.

Bolivian Indians cook everything in earthenware pots, and the food is served in wooden bowls that are rarely washed, but the traveller who arrives at a hut where he is lucky enough to find anything at all to eat does not notice such trifles.

If the natives' way of interpreting distance in the north of the Argentine was aggravating, the Indians' vague and laconic information was far more annoying, for if one enquires how far it is from one point to another, and if the Indian happens to understand and speak a little Spanish, he points in some direction as if he could see the place one asks about and says, 'cerquita' (quite near) or 'aquicito' (just here), though the distance may be anything between ten and a hundred miles.

Indians are industrious people and unlike the mestizos, who are untrustworthy and extremely lazy. Wherever there is a patch of ground, even high up on the mountain-sides, Indians cultivate it, and between harvests they spend all their time making thread and weaving. The latter is done on a primitive framework on the ground, but the quality of the material turned out is remarkably good and often of very artistic design. They are skilful in preparing natural dyes, but modern aniline dyes are often used today and are sold at all markets.

Many of Bolivia's mountains contain rich mineral deposits, some of which were exploited long before the Spaniards invaded these regions. To this day some of the old Spanish smelting-ovens can be seen, and here and there large heaps, some the size of small hills, are found. These heaps are the refuse of the ore the invaders had smelted, and to-day some of these mounds are of great value, and several companies are re-smelting the wasted ore, for the Spaniards could only extract some forty per cent of the metal by the old smelting process.

Along some of the mountain slopes there are terraces or 'andenes' that were built by the ancient Indians. On these andenes they had their cultivations which were irrigated by wonderfully constructed 'acequias.' Even to-day the Indians show great skill in making such irrigation canals, and it is amazing how they are able to judge decline entirely by eye and without the help of instruments.

The highland of Bolivia is said to have the most extraordinary climate in the world. During the daytime it can be very hot, but immediately after sundown the glass falls considerably below freezing point. This phenomenon is due to the fact that the mesa of Bolivia is situated on a tropical latitude and at great elevation above sea level. I spent many unpleasant nights in small stone huts where many of us, men and women, slept on the mud floor like dogs, and it was no easy matter to find sufficient barley straw to keep the horses going. I was very glad when I sighted the mountain of Potosi, but although it appeared to be near, I had to ride for two long days before I saw the town, shortly after crossing a high pass near the snow line. The mountain of Potosi is proverbial for its mineral wealth, and its slopes are of all colours, where refuse of the mines has been thrown out.

Potosi, the Old Mecca of Greedy Spanish Conquistadores

The town of Potosi was built at the foot of this mountain by the Spanish invaders, for they had not been long among the unfortunate Incas before they heard about the rich mines this mountain contains, and to this day old and new shafts are being exploited by different companies. Whilst conversing with a mining expert I asked him if the mineral wealth of this mountain was not going to be exhausted soon, and to this he replied that one could safely say that its exploitation, in relation to the wealth it contained, had not even properly started!

The history of Potosi, with the horrors of the early Spanish colonial days, is best left unwritten, for the Indians' sufferings there were probably never equalled in history. One of the old Spanish mines, called Socabon, is still to be seen and the Spanish coat of arms which was carved in the rocks over the entrance is still well preserved. Under it, it is estimated that some 20,000 Indians were driven into the darkness of this mine, and none who entered there ever saw daylight again.

The town is very much the same as it must have been during the Spanish days. Most of the houses have quaint balconies and small windows with iron gratings, and the very streets with their rough cobble-stone pavements make one feel as if one were still living in the old colonial days. One of the most remarkable buildings in South America is the old Spanish mint of Potosi. In place of the modern steel girders enormous hardwood beams were brought up from the forests of what is now the north of the Argentine, while others were painfully dragged up by the Indian slaves from to-day practically unknown forest regions of Western Brazil. This happened some three hundred years ago and one can guess how many lives must have been lost, and how much suffering the transportation of these colossal beams must have caused.

Thanks to the almost everlasting quality of the wood used, the old minting machines have remained in a perfect state of preservation. These ingenious machines were made entirely of different hardwoods, and the various parts were cleverly joined together, or tied with strips of raw hide. Mules supplied the driving power, treading a circle while pulling on a pole that turned an upright shaft by means of which the machine was set into motion. Unfortunately most of the relics and treasures of art disappeared out of the old mint during revolutionary times some years ago, but in spite of that I consider the old 'casa de monedas' of Potosi to be one of the most interesting things I saw on the whole ride.

Among the Aymara Indians

We experienced some very cold weather, and the day we started out again the mountains and the town were clad in a mantle of white. In spite of all the advice to the contrary I had decided to follow the shortest trail over the mountains towards Lake Popo. Formerly this had been one of the principal Spanish gold trails, but to-day it has been almost forgotten and is only used by Indians who occasionally come to town, but the majority of them who live on the hills or in some of the small valleys among this labyrinth of mountains never venture as far as Potosi, and are content to live and die where they were born.

The parts we were coming to are inhabited by Aymara Indians, who speak a language of their own; I think the Aymara language must rank among the least musical of tongues and seems to be spoken down in the throat and stomach.

I found the Aymaras to be very sulky and sullen, and bloody uprisings against their white oppressors often take place, and on such occasions their bloodthirstiness and cruelty know no bounds. Fights between the different neighbouring tribes are common, the origin of most of them being a dispute over the ownership of land, and some of these tribal feuds I am told have lasted for generations.

These Indians will rarely give or sell food to a white, and whenever I asked them for anything the one and only answer I received was 'jañua,' which is pronounced 'janeooah,' the 'j' being very guttural, not unlike the Scotch way of pronouncing the 'ch' in the word 'loch.' Before leaving Potosi I had again made myself a small dictionary, and with the help of this very useful 'book of words' I was able to make myself understood, but whenever an Indian happened to reply to me he might just as well have done it in Chinese or in the language of Hottentots for the only word I ever learnt to understand was the eternal 'jañua' which means 'there is nothing.'

People who knew how to deal with these natives had told me to take no notice whenever they said this, and simply to enter their huts and see if there was any food and to help myself to anything I happened to find. The very idea of doing such a thing shocked me and I determined to try politer methods, but once I was among these Aymaras I soon found out that kindness and consideration were out of place, and on more than one occasion I obtained the food for which I was craving on the principle that might is right. Much to my surprise the people never objected to this procedure and were quite pleased when I offered to pay for what I had taken, which was probably more than the average native whites (?) and mestizos do.

Today the only visible remains of the old Spanish gold trail is a wonderfully-built stone bridge which spans a deep canyon far below in a narrow gulley between high mountains. The bridge is called 'Puente del Diablo' (Devil's Bridge) and has an old legend attached to it.

An Old Indian Legend

Once upon a time a young Indian was on his way to visit his sweetheart, who lived on the other side of the river, and when he arrived there he found that the waters were so high and wild that it was impossible to cross. Bitterly disappointed, the young man sat down and lamented his misfortune in a loud voice. Suddenly the devil appeared before him and offered to build a bridge, but under the condition that the young man would sell him his soul in payment for his services. The youth agreed to this, but with the understanding that the bridge be completed before sunrise, whereupon the devil immediately set to work, but when the first rays of the sun came over the mountain tops there was still one stone missing to complete the bridge, and the devil, finding himself thus defeated, jumped down the precipice into the foaming waters below.

I later heard a similar legend about a bridge in Guatemala, as will be seen later, which makes me think that it must be a story of Spanish origin, and the fact that the devil is mentioned suggests that it is a white man's legend, for the Indians had never heard about that gentleman until the Spaniards told them about him and tried to convince them that they would all make his acquaintance in after-life.

Towards Lake Popo

In many places the trail was so bad that I feared for the horses. Seemingly eternal zig-zags took us slowly and painfully up terrific inclines and down again on the other side, and often did I breathe with relief when we had finished bordering some yawning precipice.

I had a most unpleasant and yet amusing incident in one miserable Indian settlement where I arrived very late, when it was already dark. Not a soul could be seen, and so I went from hut to hut until finally I found a solitary hag. I had no end of trouble to make her understand that I wanted to see the 'cacique' (chief), and when she made signs to me to listen I could plainly hear the beating of drums in the distance. Being no longer a novice among Indians I surmised that some feast was being celebrated, or possibly a wedding had taken place that day. It was so dark that I did not venture along the winding and uneven path, for the chances were that I would never have arrived at the place where the noise came from, so I pushed the old woman in that direction saying, 'cacique!' Without protesting she waddled away and soon disappeared in the dark, and I had to wait a long time until she appeared again with three men, one of whom was the cacique. The trio were so intoxicated that they could hardly stand, and when I asked the chief for food he seemed very annoyed and, judging by his voice and gestures, he was insulting me. Being tired and as hungry as a wolf I did not feel inclined to argue, and when I realised that I would not get far with kindness I changed my tactics, and grabbing the drunken rascal by the neck gave him a sound shaking. This frightened the other two men and the woman so much that they ran away in the direction they had come from. When I let the cacique go he also made off as fast as his balance permitted.

When I was alone once more I began to consider my situation, and it struck me that something very unpleasant might happen if these people went to tell their friends what had just happened to their chief. To resume travelling in the pitch dark was out of the question and, anticipating trouble, I prepared for a hostile encounter. Near the hut I saw one of the beehive-shaped ovens in which the Indians bake the 'tanta' (bread), and there I decided to make my fortification. I unstrapped the rifle and shot-gun from the packhorse, and taking all the ammunition I had with me I crawled under the oven, ready to make a possible attack as expensive as possible. The horses were standing near by and so I waited for things to develop. Time went on without anything happening, and by degrees I found it difficult to keep awake, and once or twice I caught myself dozing off, but finally I must have given way to nature, for when I woke up the first daylight had appeared and I heard the voice of the cacique, who had arrived with boiled eggs, soup and tanta. I had been asleep on old ashes, and when I crawled out from under the oven I saw that the horses, which were still saddled, were eating straw somebody had given them, and when I looked at myself in the small steel mirror I always carried I could not help smiling, for I was as black as the ace of spades. The cacique felt very sheepish and sorry for himself, not so much on account of the shaking I had given him as for the 'kick' the alcohol must have had. One of the men, who could speak a few words of very broken Spanish, told me that one of their tribe had died, and that they had been holding the wake, which among most Indians means a dance and a drunken orgy.

When I had finished my much-needed meal I watered the horses and prepared to continue the march, but as I had no idea which way to go in order to reach a certain lagoon I knew I had to pass, I ordered the cacique to come along with me and act as guide. When my interpreter told him this he doubled up as if he were in great pain and pretended to be lame and pointed at his 'alcalde,' as the next man of importance after the chief is called, but he also had something wrong with his legs. He at once hobbled towards his hut and returned with what appeared to be his wife, who was to come along and show me the way. When I realised that no man was willing to come with me, and to prevent making trouble, I started out alone.

I did not know whether I was following the right trail—or not, as the case might be—until, towards evening, a lagoon came in sight. It was situated on a mesa high up among the mountains and I was certain that this must be the point for which I was looking. All along the edge of the water were a number of flamingoes and, better still, I noticed many ducks.

Although I had no notion where to get fuel, the prospects of a good meal filled me with joy, so when I was near enough I fired a cartridge of duckshot into the middle, where the birds were thickest. This may sound very unsporting to many, but then it must be remembered that I was not out for a day's shooting for pleasure, furthermore I had to be careful with my ammunition, for if I wasted any I might be left without a single shot, and this perhaps at enormous distance from where I might be able to get a new supply.

A few moments after I had fired some Indians came running towards me over a hill, and I half suspected there was going to be trouble, but as they came nearer I heard them shouting and laughing, and presently one greeted me with a hearty 'buenas tardes' (Spanish for 'good evening'). The same fellow, who spoke good Spanish, then asked me to do them the favour to shoot some flamingoes for them, and told me they wanted their feathers to make themselves headgear which some Indians use for dancing on certain festive occasions. I agreed to kill as many as they wished, but under condition that they cooked my ducks for me, fed the horses, and gave me hospitality for the night.

The mutual bargain was immediately agreed upon, and not long after I was greedily devouring some excellently roasted ducks whilst the Indians were sorting out their treasured feathers and the horses were making the best of barley straw behind the hut. As usual, I handed out some coca leaves and a few cigarettes and, after I had stuffed down as much duck as I could hold, we started a merry conversation, my Spanish-speaking friend translating to those who could not understand me. I told them the story about what had happened to me the night before, and when they heard that I had tried to make the cacique come with me the listeners jumped up, shouted and waved their arms. I thought they were angry with me for having shown so little respect for a neighbouring chief, but my interpreter explained that they were merely disappointed because I had not brought him along with me.

It appears these two tribes are old enemies, and then it dawned on me why none of the men down in the valley were willing to accompany me, and they had offered to send along a woman because they knew only too well that not even one of their enemies would harm her.

Whenever Indians in the interior of Bolivia wish to speak to a white (or more or less white) man they usually take off the large hats they wear over their woollen skull-caps and come crawling up on their knees and often kiss his feet. This degrading custom dates back to the Spanish times when the natives were treated like dogs, although not much worse than they are being treated to-day.

Most government 'autoridades,' who usually are repulsive mestizos, have a whip hanging behind the doors of their offices, if such the miserable and filthy places can be called, and with these whips, which are made of a certain part of a bull's anatomy, they frequently beat the unfortunate Indians, whose wives and daughters they do not respect any more than they do their property. My comments may sound rather hard and bitter, but it must be remembered that I did not visit only the cities, but that I crossed the country from south to north and had better opportunity to see and observe things than the educated natives who spend most of their time abroad, or perhaps every few years come to La Paz, which is incidentally the only city in Bolivia worthy of the name.

When the first streaks of violet and purple announced the dawn of another day, the horses were saddled and, having taken leave of my Indian friends near the lagoon, I mounted, and soon we were merrily jogging along a fairly good trail; our stomachs were full and so our hearts were happy.

Here and there I saw herds of alpacas grazing and some lifted their heads to watch us with curiosity. Alpacas are very much like llamas, excepting that they have much longer wool, and some have such heavy and fluffy coats that they appear like huge woolly balls. During this journey I saw a herd of vicuñas in the distance. These small and elegant animals belong to the same family as the llama and the alpaca, they have the same type of long and upright neck as their cousins, but they are much smaller and look more like gazelles On account of their valuable skins vicuñas have been so much persecuted that they are threatened with extinction and, although the law to-day protects them, they are still being hunted by whites and Indians alike. With their wool, expensive and excellent rugs and blankets are made, and the South American who possesses a vicuña poncho feels very proud of it. These ponchos are waterproof and protect against the heat and cold alike. Up in these mountains the rare and almost priceless 'chinchilla real' is sometimes found, another inoffensive little animal which has practically disappeared owing to its highly valuable fur.

I rarely ate at midday, but if I found a spot where there was a little grass I unsaddled and let the horses roll and graze for an hour or so whilst I made my notes, took the altitude and the temperature. If I had anything to smoke with me, I puffed away, and before saddling up again I revised the animals' backs and hoofs and then changed horses, that is to say that the one which had carried the pack in the morning had to carry me in the afternoon. Very often the same animal carried me all day and sometimes two or three, the changing over entirely depending on the type of country we were travelling through, or again on the conditions of their backs. There is one thing I am very proud of to-day, which any horseman will appreciate, and that is to be able to say that my horses never had sore backs, excepting, of course, little minor troubles that are inevitable.

The journey from the lagoon on was pleasant, partly because the trail was fair and easy to follow, and partly because we had eaten well, and possibly the idea that there was another cold duck in my saddle-bag helped to make things appear rosy. In the evening we arrived at a posta, where I immediately prepared to spend the night. This was the busiest posta I struck on my way through Bolivia, the movement being due to the proximity of a mine, and to the fact that some valleys further in among the mountains are inhabited by Indians who pass this place on their way to and from Challapata, a small town down on the main plateau, where they go to sell their goods and products, and whence they return loaded with salt and other supplies which their region does not provide.

Owing to the rarefied atmosphere in these high parts the Indians, by constant deep breathing, have developed enormous chests, and the capacity of their lungs, as well as their extraordinary physique, enables them to perform amazing feats of endurance, and this in altitudes and over rough and steep mountain trails where a white man could hardly move and where strangers frequently suffer from fainting fits, caused by 'puna' or mountain sickness. I have seen Indians come from the distant interior carrying heavy loads on their backs, and after a long journey, which they do practically entirely at a slow trot, they would halt at some posta or hut, and when they had taken their loads off I actually saw some who had sore backs on which they sprinkled cold cinders to dry the sores. Several times I saw runners on arriving at a place lie on their backs near a wall and put their feet up against it, and when I asked why they were drying this, I was told that this was the most restful position after a long run and that it made the blood run back into the body. I often wondered what a Bolivian Indian would think of our Olympic Marathon runners, who would look like mere babies alongside these tough and rugged sons of the mountains.

Soon after sunset it became intensely cold, so after I had made the horses as comfortable as possible, and had given them as much of the straw as the 'postero' was willing to sell, I entered the big stone hut again and spread my blankets out on my stone-block bed and prepared to pass the night as well as was possible under circumstances. The straw is brought up from the valleys by Indians, who carry it on their backs. Instead of doing military service they are expected to work in the postas for a certain length of time, or to help in the construction of roads and trails.

I had been asleep for a short time when I was awakened by the trampling of hoofs and people talking in loud voices. This meant that I had
to get up to see that the newly-arrived animals were not put with mine,
lest they eat the fodder I had bought or fight with my horses. An Indian
was outside with two heavily-packed mules, and he told me that he was
carrying mail to some mine in the interior. As soon as I had seen the animals
accommodated I returned to my hard and cold bed, where I was soon
dreaming of better places! A tired body is the softest mattress.

The stars were still glittering when everybody began to stir, and as my
stomach was out of order I made myself some tea with coca leaves,
which I found to be a good remedy. I remembered my ducks and an old
South American verse that goes as follows:

'El que comió, tomó y montó,
No preguntes de que murió.'

(He who had eaten, drunk, and mounted,
do not ask what he died of.)

When the postman's mules were ready for the day's march he came back
into the house, where he went through an extraordinary ceremony. In
the middle of the large stone table that stood in the spacious room he
placed a bottle filled with alcohol, and in each corner he deposited some
coca leaves and some grains of corn on which he later put pieces of smoul-
dering embers. Once the coca leaves began to smoke he blew the rising
fumes towards the alcohol bottle in the middle, and moving from corner
to corner repeated the performance, all the time going through a series
of most complicated manoeuvres. I watched him with the interest of a
child following the mysterious movements of a conjurer, and when he
had finished I asked him what the meaning of all this was. In good
Spanish he told me that this was to protect himself against bad weather
and accidents on the journey, and that he never undertook a trip without first going through this ceremony, which he said was commonly
observed among his people.

Saddling up was no easy matter, for my fingers were stiff and painful with
the cold, and as usual in such cases, I could only tighten the girth by pulling
with my teeth, which is the customary way of doing this among the
gauchos of the pampas. All day long we wound our way through high
quebradas, where not a living being was to be seen, and had it not been
for the shifting clouds above I might have believed myself to be travelling
through a vast tomb, for the stillness of these places is most impressive.

Towards evening we reached the top of a long incline, and from there I beheld a panorama that would defy the brush of the cleverest master. Straight to the west, in front of us, the main mesa of Bolivia spread in all its vastness at our feet, and the evening sun made Lake Popo glitter like a huge golden mirror on which the gorgeously-coloured clouds were reflected like rolling masses of molten ore. Far beyond the lake I could see the dark and shaggy outline of the next mountain range, and to the north and south the vast, flat and barren mesa or altiplano, lost itself in glimmering horizons. It seemed impossible that this lake is over 11,000 feet above sea level, and only then did I fully realise how high up we had been for the last two or three weeks.

I could have remained there until dark, watching these heavenly fireworks, but knowing that our trail down would be long and steep, and possibly even dangerous in parts, I lost no time, and when I had resaddled the horses we started off along the rocky trail. I was glad to think that we would soon hit the railroad that passes towards La Paz, and that we would make better time on the plain below. Night overtook us long before we had reached the plain, but fortunately the moon was bright, and so we could see sufficiently to continue without running serious risks.

Over the Vast and Barren Bolivian Altiplano towards La Paz

Tired and weary we entered a little village where most of the people were already asleep. After no little trouble I found the house of the local 'autoridad,' where I was given shelter for the night. The horses fed and watered and having eaten a few bites myself, I was shown a room where I could sleep. I found the place packed with Indians, who were curled up in their blankets on the floor, and after making some of them shift I had enough room to squeeze in my saddles and myself. Next day there was to be a fiesta, and for this reason these men had arrived in good time to start merrymaking early in the morning.

Although the atmosphere in the stuffy room was not what health apostles might recommend, and in spite of a regular mass attack of crawlers and jumpers, I was soon dreaming about more pleasant things, and never stirred until one of the early risers stumbled over me in the dark. I had made up my mind to rest for a day before proceeding onward in the direction of La Paz, and as there was an abundance of fodder here I decided to stay, although my quarters were anything but attractive; after all, I had been in many more uncomfortable, and further along my luck might be even worse.

Indians came flocking into the village in groups, men, women and children, all at a slow trot. Many of the women carried babies in ponchos on their backs and I noticed that for once nobody was spinning wool.

The fiesta, like most of its kind, merely amounted to drinking and dancing, if such the hopping and bobbing about can be called. Drums and flutes provided the monotonous music that consisted of a few notes in minor keys, repeated time after time, and without interval for hours on end. By degrees the alcohol began to take effect and intoxicated men were lying here and there, nobody seeming to take the slightest notice of them. The dance continued all day, and after dark, when it was getting cold, crowds flocked to different huts, where they continued making merry.

Curious to see what was going on I approached a small, one-roomed adobe hut from which came the sound of music. The only opening through which I could see into the interior was a small, square hole, about two feet from the ground, which was door and window all in one. In one corner a few pieces of grease with wicks in them provided a dim and flickering light that enabled me to see a crowd of Indians packed together like sardines. The band was in a corner, and as there were too many people to dance they merely bobbed up and down to the rhythm of the drums. The rank smell of dirty and perspiring human bodies, mixed with the fumes of strong alcohol, was too much for me and I was glad when I breathed the cold and dry night air once more.

I was outside my quarters when a regular stampede came up the road, some chasing, others fleeing. A fight had started and missiles were flying in all directions. Some were throwing stones with the slings that Indian men and women use to keep their flocks together, and after a while the fighting mob disappeared in the darkness of the night. Such fights frequently occur at the fiestas when two or more tribes assemble, but as a rule next to no harm is done and when the losers have been chased far towards their distant homes the victors return, and both parties wait for the next opportunity to have another go at one another.

I had heard about an old thermal bath somewhere near the village and did not miss the chance to go there and to get clean once more, and to have a much-needed shave. That night I had to sleep among drunken people in the same house where I had spent the previous night, but I was getting so used to it that it hardly worried me.

Progress was easy, for we were now on the flat and sandy 'altiplano' (tableland or plateau), where I was at last able to make the horses trot again, a thing that had been impossible up in the mountains where I often considered myself lucky to have been able to proceed at all. Very little is to be seen in this flat desert, and often we were short of water. The atmosphere is so dry and clear that one can see enormous distances, which is the case throughout the Bolivian highland. I did not follow the railway line, leaving it to our west, for along the route I had just chosen I knew that we would pass several villages where I was likely to find fodder for the animals.

In one of those small places I ran into another of the many fiestas I saw in that happy land, and this time the Indians were dancing a kind of devil dance. The musicians were standing in a circle playing on huge drums or on strangely-shaped flutes. They were wearing enormous headgear of brightly-coloured feathers, mounted on light bamboo frames, and I could not help thinking of my friends up near the lagoon. Other men were dressed up as devils and some as what, to me, appeared intended to represent ugly Spanish conquerors with hideous white masks and beards. Some of the devils were wearing heavy black alpaca skins and masks with double noses; in short, these disguises were the most grotesque I had ever seen. None of the women were disguised, but forming a long snake line, led by a devil, they threaded their way in and out among the musicians, and the disguised men jumped around within the circle, shrieking and yelling whilst crowds of other Indians looked on with great solemnity.

After some extremely dull journeys we arrived in Oruro, a relatively busy town that owes its movement to important mines near there. Not far from this town we passed some prehistoric graves which are in the shape of high, square structures made of adobe, but, as far as I could find out, there is no history attached to them. Mirages are very common on the altiplano, and I often thought I could see water ahead, and even the mountains had the appearance of floating islands. Often I turned back to have a look at the country we had just left behind us, and lo! even those stretches appeared to be vast lagoons.

I had hoped to find good fodder for the horses in Oruro, but here also there was nothing but barley straw. At first my animals had trouble with the bristles of the barley ears, for many of them stuck in their gums, which became very sore and seemed to cause considerable discomfort. To cure them I had to pull these bristles out, after which I rubbed common salt on the sores, which I did with a stick around one end of which I had wrapped a piece of cloth, using it much in the same way as a tooth-brush.

I took quarters in quite a fair hotel facing the main plaza, but when the owner first saw me he obviously had his doubts about admitting so rough a specimen of humanity as I looked in my leather suit, with my fire-arms and horribly chapped and burnt face. In the dining-room I was placed into the farthest corner, and the sheepish looks some of the diners gave me were a real study. Somehow a newspaper reporter had guessed at the identity of this Robinson Crusoe who had arrived, and came to interview me in the evening; next day the change of attitude in the dining-room was very marked.

Oruro is by no means an attractive town, for most of its houses are old-fashioned, and many of them as dirty as are its rough cobble-stone-paved streets. The horses were lodged in a 'tambo,' as public corrals are called there, and when I went to feed them I found two young Beau Brummells in the corral, one of them chasing the horses around the small enclosure by hitting them with his walking-stick. I introduced myself to these 'caballeros' in language that suited the occasion, whereupon one told me that he merely wished to see if the animals had a good gallop. I recommended both of them to go to a certain place, or at least to do me the favour of leaving the corral I had hired. One of them protested, and added that he considered these horses to be public property, and that he could do as he liked in his town, and then he turned and hit one of the frightened horses once more. I fully realise that every dog is entitled to bark in his own kennel, but it is out of place for a puppy to try to bark like a dog, and had that caballero carried this in mind, he would have saved himself a sound beating and being rolled in the filth of the corral. Before disappearing he swore that he would have me prosecuted for so vile and brutal an offence against the dignity of a Bolivian gentleman, but that was the last I heard and saw of him.

After leaving Oruro we once more went towards the mountain range, leaving the railroad to the west. We passed through several miserable villages, in some of which fiestas were being celebrated. In one place I was invited to join the dance, and when I started to hop and charge about like a Jersey heifer the onlookers were delighted, and asked me if this was the way we were accustomed to dance.

We were still among Aymara Indians, and I was able to see a great deal of their ways an habits, and to observe what kind of treatment they receive at the hands of the 'corregidores,' as the government officials are called, most of whom are mestizos. No office is without its bull-whip, which is used more often than the occasion might possibly demand, and considering all in all, I am surprised that uprisings do not take place with more frequency.

Once I saw an Indian murderer brought into the office where I was given shelter for the night. Unfortunately I could not understand the conversation which was held in Aymara, but it was easy to guess what it was all about. The accused man stood against one of the walls with the corregidor, a dark-skinned specimen with bloodshot eyes and a thin, drooping Chinese moustache. Being strictly on business, he had his whip in his hand, and every now and again struck the accused man with it, on the head, in the face, or wherever he wished. The accusers were kneeling on the floor in a semi-circle, the men in front and the women behind. At times all started to chatter at once, and then the corregidor stepped in among them and lashed his terrible whip in all directions in order to restore quiet. The poor Indians merely doubled up, covering themselves with their arms and ponchos, and neither women nor children escaped the blind fury of this human monster, but no more than a suppressed or muffled exclamation of pain ever escaped these stoics. My fingers fairly itched to pull my guns out of their holsters and to riddle that corregidor with bullets, but then I had to remember that I was in a foreign land, and that I had another mission to fulfil.

Trouble was evidently brewing, for not far from there Indians had assaulted a white man's place, and two villages I passed through seemed to be completely deserted. However, I knew that this was not the case, and that the Indians were in their houses, for I noticed one or two doors gently open and close, just enough to see who might be moving about outside with horses. This was like the calm before a storm, for I had only been out of these villages a day or two when trouble began, and later I saw crowds of prisoners being herded into La Paz by strong, armed escorts. This uprising was the cause of our not eating a bite for nearly forty-eight hours, and I was forced to spend one night in a deserted hut, into which, to be on the safe side, I even took both the horses.

We struck the railway line again when we came to Viacha, a town on the altiplano, some eighteen miles from the capital. The military authorities were very kind to me and made me comfortable in their quarters, and next day I followed an excellent sandy road that leads as straight as an arrow towards La Paz, which, being situated in a deep hollow or pan, cannot be seen from the plain.

Many Indians were moving along this road, driving llamas and burros, which were loaded with things they were taking to the market. Some men trotted along with heavy loads on their backs, reminding me of the South American worker ants. The men wear long trousers which are split open behind as high up as their knees, and use tight-fitting woollen caps with flaps hanging over their ears. I am told that the object of the split trouser-legs is to be able to double them up over the knees when wading through mud or water.

On and on we trotted along this straight road, and being impatient I thought we were never going to reach the end that had seemed so near owing to the clearness of the atmosphere. My long waiting was fully recompensed when we came to the edge of the deep bowl at the bottom of which the town is situated; I felt like shouting with joy and triumph, for we had battled hard and won, and there was La Paz, the place many had said we could never reach. The horses arched their necks and looked down with ears pricked, and nostrils wide open, for they had seen the patches of green, things they had not beheld for days. From above, the town looked like a miniature toy with its quaint churches, steeples, houses and small gardens. On the far side mountains towered high, and to the south the snow-covered Andean monarch Illimani glittered in the radiant sun and seemed to be so near that one might believe a shot would reach it. I dismounted and watched for a while, and then followed behind some Indians who were taking a short cut down a narrow, rocky trail.

La Paz: 'The Hidden City'

The horses' hoofs were clattering and drumming on the cobble-stones in the outskirts of the town, and shortly afterwards we were mixed up among the little traffic that exists in the centre. A few guessed who we were and joyfully greeted us, and when I asked a policeman the way to the Argentine Embassy he kindly guided me towards it. The ambassador and his staff received me with joy and hearty congratulations, for they had never expected us to arrive there, and within a few minutes the horses were unsaddled, groomed and fed, and munched away happily in the stables of the embassy. They looked as if they had only been out for a morning's trot and nobody would ever have believed that these were the hardy ponies which had come from Patagonia to this place.

My stay in this city was very pleasant, and everybody with whom I came in contact treated me excellently, and I was struck by the exquisite manners and education of many who belonged to what is usually called the upper class. Many of these persons had obviously been educated or had travelled abroad, and taking all in all, I dare say that French influence predominated. However, the masses one sees in the streets are mestizos or Indians, and many of the latter speak no Spanish. The town is very hilly and some streets are so steep that only powerful cars are of any use.

Daily, masses of Indians come flocking to the markets, which are very colourful and lively, and there they sell and barter the most extraordinary things. Woven goods can be purchased at very low prices provided the buyer knows how to 'beat the Indians down,' an art that requires far more skill and practice than one might at first think. No market is without its stand where medicinal herbs and even amulets are sold, and among the many strange remedies I often noticed was dried star-fish, skinned and dried squirrels, and other queer articles that I thought must be more charms than anything else.

The city has a very fine museum of archæology, where I spent several most interesting and instructive hours. Like many other towns in Latin America, La Paz is a bad mixture of neglected colonial architecture and modern construction. In many European cities the old style has been preserved and has been worked into modem buildings, and thus a charming and uniform style of architecture prevails throughout, but this has not been done in Latin America, excepting in one or two cities like Buenos Aires, where splendid efforts are being made in this line, not so much to preserve the old as to give the streets an elegant appearance through graceful uniformity.

People in Bolivia are very fond of eating what they call a 'picante' about four o'clock in the afternoon. This very appetising dish is prepared with turkey, chicken or different meats, and one day I could not resist the temptation to try one. When I had taken the first mouthful I had to run outside to rinse my mouth with water, for the 'picante' was so 'hot' with the most wicked and devilish spices that I felt as if I had taken a mouthful of glowing charcoal. We had a good rest in this city, and when the horses and myself had fully recuperated I took leave of my many friends and acquaintances, and soon we were winding our way up the steep slopes. When we came to the place whence I had first seen La Paz I once more stopped to have a final look at the city where I had spent some delightful days.

Titicaca, the Sacred Lake

We were again on the plains above La Paz and trotting along the straight road towards Viacha. Our stay in the capital now seemed like a pleasant dream that had come to a sudden end, but this was part of the game, and so I fought against the softer sentiments within me. I remembered that self-pity is useless and foolish, and when I observed how happily the horses jogged along I tried to follow their example and take things as they came, and soon my mind was fixed on one object, to conquer the two next main ranges of the Andes and to reach the Pacific Ocean! I felt annoyed for having been 'soft,' and urged the horses on faster, but Mancha, instead of obeying my heels, turned his head round and looked at me with one eye and seemed to be telling me, 'Now then, old boy, what's all that about? Give us a chance,' and he continued in his regular and rhythmical jog-trot, his head slightly moving up and down with every stride, as if he were saying to himself, 'Yes, we'll do it,' and the loose bridles were swinging from side to side like the pendulum of a clock, and alongside us faithful old Gato loped along with the pack. He, too, was game to follow wherever I happened to go.

Without stopping at Viacha we continued in the direction of Lake Titicaca, and in the evening we halted at an 'hacienda' (farm) that belonged to a friend of mine in La Paz. The man in charge happened to be absent, and as none of the Indians who were there could understand Spanish, I had no end of difficulty in making myself understood by gesticulating and jabbering. However, I was finally admitted and given a cow-hide on which to spread my bed on the dirt floor in a room where several Indians slept.

Nearing the famous mountain lake we passed the pre-historic ruins of Tiahuanaco (or Tiahuanacu), a relic of the past I had been looking forward to seeing.

To-day there is not much left of what was once a colossal temple, excepting enormous stone pillars which stand in rows, and one of the big, grotesque monoliths (stone idols) which were adored by the ancients. The 'puerta del sol' (gate of the sun), with its remarkable carvings, stands in a perfect state of preservation, and at the western extremity there is an enormous one-piece block in which steps were hewn; probably the main entrance of the temple. In the close vicinity there are other remains of what probably was a temple or palace, and these are locally called 'el palacio del Inca.' One of the carved stone-blocks in the latter ruins measures some 25 by 18 feet, and has a thickness of roughly 4½ feet.

The manner in which all these colossal stones were transported to the place is veiled in mystery, for they had obviously been brought from the distant northern shores of Lake Titicaca, where ancient quarries have been discovered that give the kind of rock which was used in the building of Tiahuanaco. Personally I believe that they were transported across the lake in huge rafts and that the water-level was higher in those days, and that consequently the shores were somewhere near the place where the ruins are located. Later, when I rode over the plain in the direction of the lake, I saw a few hewn rocks, identical to those of the ruins, and I came to the conclusion that they must have fallen off the rafts, and as no means of salvaging them were known in those days, these blocks had to be left and were replaced by others. No matter what theory experts or mere guessers like myself might bring forward, the transportation of these hewn giants is likely to remain among the unknown and unexplained engineering marvels of the primitive world.

About two miles from the ruins stands the village Tiahuanaco, where I stayed in a small and dirty hotel. Unfortunately the Spanish invaders did not appreciate the priceless value of the old temples and wilfully destroyed them, and even until recent years stones were carried away to pave streets, and carved blocks were used to make entrances for houses, etc. The church is entirely built with material taken from the ruins, and two big stone idols were placed at its entrance, where they stand with their owl-like eyes, as indignant witnesses of ignorance and destruction. In the back yard of the 'hotel' I saw several beautifully carved troughs that had once belonged to the temple. These were being used to feed pigs, and to do the washing in, when this rare ceremony is performed.

From Tiahuanaco we went north over the sandy plain until we came to a hill, from the top of which I had the first sight of Lake Titicaca. Its deep blue reflected the mountains in the distance, and the dazzling white peaks to the east made a glorious background against the delicate blue sky.

We halted in a village called Guaqui, where the steamers arrive from Puno, the Peruvian port at the far extreme of the lake. He who casually glances at a map might think Lake Titicaca to be very small, but suffice it to say that modern steamers take twelve hours to make the trip from one end to the other. These steamers were built in England, and after having sailed all the way to the Pacific port, Mollendo, they were dismantled and transported by rail up to Puno. Here they were re-assembled for service on the lake, which is the highest navigable water in the world, being some 11,400 feet above sea level.

A Bolivian regiment was stationed in Guaqui, and I spent a happy day as their guest. The officers did everything to make my stay a pleasant one, and my horses were well looked after, and in the evening a dance was arranged to which the few white girls of the village were invited.

Late in the evening a globe-trotter, who had arrived on a lake steamer, appeared at my door. He wore a kind of boy scout uniform and on his left arm he had pinned an American flag. Having saluted me in an exaggerated military style, he handed me a card on which his photograph was printed. Without saying a word he made me a sign to read the text that was printed under the picture, and this is what I saw in Spanish:

'JHONNY WELINTON, the deaf and dumb American explorer and foot-walker, who on a wager has undertaken to walk around the world twice in ten years, visiting every capital and city, using no other means of loco-motion but his feet. This card is given away free of charge, but any donation you are willing to make will be thankfully received.'

Having read this highly interesting text, I had a good look at this, to me, unknown celebrity, who, besides the clue of the badly-spelt name, gave me anything but the impression of being an American, and somehow I thought he did not 'look' deaf and dumb. When I spoke to him he made signs that I should put my words on paper, which I then did in Spanish in order to put him to a test. Having read my question, he answered it in faultless Spanish, and his handwriting was of the type that is taught throughout the schools in Latin America. I then produced one of my maps and asked him to show me the route he had followed from the States down, but it was evident that he had not the slightest idea about the geography of the countries, and I was convinced that he was travelling just like all the other globe-trotters I had run into—namely, by using ships and rail-ways from place to place where money can be picked up, and carefully avoiding uninhabited and poor regions.

After a while I was able to get rid of this fellow by giving him a small present, but in the evening he again appeared at the officers' quarters where the dance was being held. At first some were inclined to feel sorry for this poor deaf and dumb 'Americano,' as they called him, but when I told them about my suspicions, we hit on a plan to find out the truth. We invited him into the refreshment-room, where we started by giving him as much food and liquor as he was willing to take, and in order to show how 'Amer-ican' he was he naturally gave preference to the whisky bottle, but unfortunately his desire to act his part to perfection was more than his capacity to stand the effects of the alcohol, and after the second stiff drink he began to sway to the music of the piano, and presently he even danced, and when our hero of the dark and unknown forests and scorching deserts had quietly 'passed out,' we tied a bunch of fire-crackers to the tail of his coat, and these performed the great miracle, for no sooner had they started to fizz and explode with loud bangs than our deaf and dumb friend shot into the air like a rocket, and the kind of exdamations he shrieked at the top of his voice were strictly Spanish, although they do not figure in the average dictionary.

Next morning the poor deaf and dumb 'Americano' was seen taking the train that left for La Paz, and even if he still muttered classical curses to himself, I hope he had time enough to cool down sufficiently to be deaf and dumb again before he reached his destination.

Leaving Guaqui we followed a fair trail along the western shores of the lake. The scenery was as delightful as the dry, clear and cool atmosphere, and whilst we were slowly moving along I had ample time to observe things around me, and for hours I thought about the fascinating history and mythology of the ancients. Here the Aymaras used to live, and their supreme being was Pachacamac. They adored objects of nature which they believed to be manifestations of their god, but they particularly adored a rock called Inti Karka, which is situated on the largest island of the lake, this island being known to-day as the Island of the Sun. The Aymaras, an ancient race of warriors, have made little or no progress for centuries, and they seem entirely unaffected by civilization, neither has the influence of religion proved beneficial to them. They have preserved many of their ancient customs and ways, and show distrust towards all who are strangers to them. On the other hand, the Quichuas (or Quechuas) are entirely different, for they are peaceful and industrious, and there is but little criminality among them.

According to the old legend, the first Inca, Manco Capaj, and his wife, Mama Ocllo, first appeared among the Aymaras. Some say that they rose out of the lake and that they founded Cuzco, the capital of the Quichuas. This legend, to a certain extent, shows that neither Manco Capaj nor Mama Ocllo found acceptance among the rebellious Aymaras, who were only conquered and subdued by the fifth Inca king. At a later period the Inca Tapaj-Yupanqui visited Inti Karka, the Aymara sanctuary on the largest island, and ordered the temple of the sun to be built, and minor temples to the lightning and thunder. Another island was consecrated to the moon, and was called Coya (the female, or wife of the sun).

The ruins of the Temple of the Sun and the house of the Inca show the magnitude of Incaic buildings and the skill of the builders. There are many people who confuse the Inca ruins with the idols and colossal remains of the temples of Tiahuanaco which I have already described, and which are probably thousands of years older, and show a much more advanced degree of culture than can be found in ruins of Incaic origin.

To-day the Aymaras extend as far as Puno, on the northern end of the lake, and from there on we were more among the Quichuas, who speak a slightly different language from those of the south. The name Titicaca is derived from the old Aymara word Inti Karka.*

When the Spaniards, under the leadership of Pizarro, conquered the Inca empire they found incredible quantities of gold. This metal had no commercial value among the Incas, and as it was considered sacred, the gold

*Titi-caca according to Garcilaso de La Vega, the old Spanish-Inca historian means 'Lead-Mountain.'

was almost exclusively kept in places of worship. Soon the Incas became aware that the Spaniards' chief ambitions were to obtain gold, and after the Inca Atahuallpa had been put to death, in spite of the fabulous ransom paid to the brutal invaders for his release, the Indians stripped all the temples of gold and hid it away. This gold is said to be the largest hidden treasure known, and is commonly known as 'Atahuallpa's treasure.'

Many people and even expeditions have spent their time and money searching for this and other historical hidden treasures, for at a later period the Jesuits buried great quantities of their valuables, and so did the Spaniards, on their hasty retreats during the War of Independence. Many are the tales I have heard about such hidden treasures, and countless people have, off and on, explored desolate valleys, hoping to become wealthy from one day to the other. I spoke to one American who had spent close on twenty years searching without success, but in spite of all he was still as optimistic as he must have been the first day he started— 'Seek and ye shall find.' (?)

Off and on we travelled on the very shores of the lake, and many a cool drink did the horses have. Often I counted the gulps they swallowed, watching them go down their necks with the regularity of the pulse. When they had taken their fill they would open their nostrils wide and give a long snort, rather like a German when he has drained the last drop of beer out of his massive pewter; and then they often pawed the water in play, as if annoyed at not being able to drink more.

It was interesting to watch the Indians make their balsas, as the strange canoes on Lake Titicaca are called. They are made of bullrushes cleverly tied together in the shape of two long and pointed sausages, the ends being turned up. The sails are also made from the same plants, but the long stems are split in two and tied together to make a large, square sheet, something like a Japanese blind. The balsa is guided by means of a long pole, and if there happens to be no wind, the same pole is used to propel it. Rough weather seems to make little difference to them, and on one occasion while I was there, a heavy storm raged on the lake, but in spite of the choppy waves the Indian fishermen were out in their balsas, and I was amazed to see how they could keep their balance whilst their boats plunged and reared like bucking horses.

If the Indians happen to be ploughing a piece of land for the first time, they celebrate the occasion by sticking many small flags into the ground, and the oxen which pull the primitive wooden ploughs are also gaily decorated with pieces of coloured cloth and ribbons. Only once or twice have I seen natives use modern steel ploughs, for they believe the steel poisons the soil, and so they stick to the old system. Needless to say, chicha flows freely whereever a new plot of land is being ploughed, women and children turning out in a body to witness so important an event. As a rule, the Indians are very kind to their animals, and I have never seen the beasts being ill-treated. What a humanitarian lesson the average white citizen of these countries could learn from them!

One day, when I was hungry—a frequent occurrence—an Indian woman passed me, and my mouth watered when I saw that the basket she was carrying on her head was full of eggs. I immediately took out my dictionary and looked up what was the Aymara for eggs, and having rehearsed my 'sesame' I trotted after her, and showing a silver Boliviano (one shilling and sixpence), I said 'gauna' (egg). Having examined my coin she emptied the whole basket on the ground, and I think there must have been some fifty eggs there. I sucked as many as I could and put a few into my pockets, and when I beckoned to the woman to take the rest away, she looked at me in great surprise, and, muttering something I could not understand, was off again with her load.

On Peruvian Soil

We came to the outlet of the lake called the 'desaguadero,' and crossing over a narrow bridge entered the Republic of Peru. On both sides of the stream are small settlements, one on the Bolivian side, and the other on Peruvian soil. In the middle of the bridge there is a steel trapdoor that is let down at night, more for show's sake than for practical purposes, for if anybody wishes to cross from one side to the other without being seen, there are many easy ways of doing it. Not a soul was to be seen when we crossed over the bridge, and the few low houses on the other side seemed to be deserted. Between the rough cobble-stones grass was growing, and the tiled roofs were covered with bright green mosses. After a while a fellow who was dressed in a uniform and cap that gave him the appearance of a French gendarme, came slouching out of a house, and when he saw me he lazily shuffled in our direction. He introduced himself as the border official, and asked me a few stupid questions, and when I showed him a recommendation I had with me, his attitude immediately changed, and he no longer called me 'señor,' but tried to flatter me by addressing me as 'general' and 'doctor,' titles which I later found out every Peruvian who wears a collar seems to possess.

My first day in Peru was an unpleasant one, for to begin with I could get no fodder in the settlement near the desaguadero, and in spite of the late hour of the day, we had to continue in the direction of the next village, where I hoped luck would be kinder to us. We had not gone far when a heavy storm broke out, and an icy rain soon soaked me to the skin. When night fell I was still chasing around the village, and I considered myself fortunate when somebody finally sold me a small ration of straw. With all my belongings wet through, and with the penetrating cold of the night, I was glad when the time came to start again.

We passed through several interesting and picturesque villages which are situated along the western shores of the lake. One of them was built by the Jesuits, and some of the old churches still remain, but, as they were not looked after, most of them are mere ruins to-day. Like many Jesuit ruins, they show great architectural skill and artistic taste, and some of the splendidly carved entrances to these churches are regular gems. Quite a number of the buildings in this particular village date back to the same period, and the massive police quarters where I stayed were also of Jesuit origin, as could easily be seen by the arched entrance gate, the massive walls, and what must have been dungeons in the old times. The 'gobernador' is the local government authority and mayor of the village all in one, and a stranger does well to make it his first duty to get acquainted with these local tin gods in Peru, for without their assistance it would be next to impossible to find a roof to sleep under where there are no inns.

When I expressed my desire to visit some of the ruins near the village the gobernador immediately offered to accompany me. It seems that nobody ever takes the trouble to look at these old churches, some because they are not interested, and others because they are too superstitious. As we entered one of these churches by the big heavy, wooden entrance door that had probably not been opened for years, it began to creak and crack and suddenly fell down with a loud crash, but luckily both of us were able to jump out of harm's way in time.

As the roofs of these churches have long ago fallen in, their interiors are overgrown with grass and even shrubbery. Statues of saints were lying about, and it was obvious that some of the old graves had been disturbed by treasure-seekers. A few old paintings remained hanging high up on walls where they happened to be sheltered from the weather, but the majority have been taken out by villagers, and I saw some hanging in their houses, and as far as my judgment goes in this matter, some of them may be of artistic value.

My pleasant and interesting day was spoilt in the evening by an occurrence which I was powerless to prevent: it would have been as much as my life was worth to interfere. I saw one of the 'autoridades' outrage an

Indian girl of some twelve years, which he did by imprisoning her father and mother, and when the girl came to bring her parents some food he forced her to follow him into one of the rooms which surrounded the yard where I kept my horses. When he returned with the sobbing creature, he released her parents and chased the three away as if they were dogs. I could quote several similar and even worse examples of how the Indians are sometimes treated; as I accidentally happened to witness the whole of this vile deed whilst I was with the horses in the dark courtyard I will not dwell further on so distasteful and revolting a subject, but I might add that when I later told the man concerned that I had caught him in the act, he thought it was an excellent joke and bragged about his cunning idea of arresting the parents, and when I protested as far as circumstances and wisdom permitted, he told me I was ridiculously sentimental and childish, for who cared a damn about an Indian wench?

Had it not been for the constant worry about fodder, I would have considered the trip along Lake Titicaca a joyride, but unfortunately there are no roses without thorns. In one little place a wedding was being celebrated, and so things were lively. In the centre of the plaza Indians were squatting on the ground, spinning thread and chewing coca leaves whilst they were watching the wedding-party dance to the music of flutes and drums. The musicians started at one corner of the plaza where they shuffled around in a small circle whilst the dancers hopped, pirouetted and charged about in all directions near them, all the time waving handkerchiefs in the air. After the dancing had continued for a while in one corner the musicians moved to another whilst all the dancers behind them, hopping like courting sparrows, or spinning around like puppies with wasps on their tails. After having gone round the plaza several times they danced their way to the best man's house, where alcohol and food were served, but soon they were back on the plaza again, where they once more started from corner to corner.

The bride was dressed in white woman's clothes, and to imitate further her fair-skinned cousins, and to add to her charms, her face was thickly powdered. She wore a pair of white football-boots that were several sizes too large for her—in fact, her tout ensemble might have made one believe she was dressed up for a fancy-dress ball or a students' rag. The bridegroom had also made efforts to look 'IT', and stiffly hopped about in what had once been a business suit that was much too tight for him, and every time he bent slightly I fairly held my breath, expecting the seemingly inevitable disaster to happen. The other women each wore several long woollen skirts, one over the other, and the bulk might have made one believe they were wearing crinolines. Every time they spun around during the dance they made these skirts fly to show their different colours, which gave them the appearance of big toy tops.

After a few visits to the best man's house the alcohol began to take effect. Then the men's charging around began to resemble the actions of infuriated bulls, some of the women's feet seemed to be getting too heavy to perform the fancy spins they had been so fond of before, and one or two looked as if they had become entangled in their own feet. Within an hour or so one might have believed that some of the dancers were walking on a carpet of chewing-gum whilst others moved as if they were on ice, and every now and again one lost his balance and fell, but whether they were men or women, nobody helped them to rise. The squatting and spinning onlookers watched without showing the slightest trace of emotion, nor even a smile when a woman who had tried a fancy pirouette turned head over heel like a shot hare. There is no limit to these feasts, and they simply last as long as there are alcohol and food and if there is sufficient of these the dance lasts for three or four days or even longer, and when the best man's stock is exhausted they often begin afresh at the newly-married couple's house-warming. White men would find it difficult to dance in such altitudes, for the air is so rarefied that even the slightest physical effort fatigues one.

In the mountains to the west of Lake Titicaca live the Tunquipa Indians, who are great fighters and have a bad reputation in the neighbourhood. The Tunquipas are skilful with the lasso and use modern fire-arms. They wear clothes made entirely of leather and ride on small but remarkably hardy ponies. From time to time they make raids on villages, but the white authorities leave them carefully alone because it would be very difficult and dangerous to reach their strongholds up in the mountains.

Whilst I was in Peru the feeling against the Chilians was very bitter, and owing to this I had a very unpleasant experience in a village near Lake Titicaca. As I was riding towards the plaza to find the 'gobernador' several men and boys shouted 'Perro chileno' (Chilian dog) after me, but I continued without taking any notice of these mestizo ruffians. When I arrived at the 'town hall,' a tumbledown adobe house that had been whitewashed when it was built, I asked for the gobernador, but a dark, pock-marked fellow with Mongolian eyes laconically informed me that the 'señor' was out. I produced my letter of recommendation, and on the strength of it (although he could not read) I was given permission to put the horses into the back yard. I then threw my packs and saddles into a bare room and went out fodder-hunting. When my efforts had met with partial success, but at high cost, I went from house to house until I found an old woman who was willing to cook something for me.

During the evening, as I sat on the doorstep of my room and puffed away at a rank-smelling cigarette, I noticed several groups of men come slouching past me, casting foxy glances in my direction and whispering to each other. I began to feel somewhat uneasy, and although I did not show it, I kept a weather eye on these fellows, and before curling up in my blankets and extinguishing the candle, a supply of which I always carried in my saddle-bags, I made the necessary preparations to receive visitors. However, I spent a good night, and all went well until I had saddled up in the morning. When I was just about to leave the gobernador arrived on the scene and came dashing up to me on a mule which seemed to be as excited and heated as the rider, who fairly barked and snorted 'perro chileno' and other not very complimentary names at me. A group of men had assembled, some being armed with clubs and one or two with pitchforks, ready to storm the bastille. They were, still a good distance away from me, and did not seem any too keen to advance more than a few short steps at a time. In order to impress me the gobernador whipped and spurred his excited and panting mule, and whenever the animal moved he pulled it back with a violent jerk on the bit which made it dance around in a circle. Of course I knew that nobody was any too keen on showing fight, for the two guns that were in my holsters looked too dangerous, and the average mestizo, although plucky with knives, is terrified of fire-arms, quite the reverse of Anglo-Saxons, who fairly freeze when they see the flashing of a knife, but who will usually face bullets without losing their heads.

I tried hard to get a word in, but it was impossible to penetrate the verbal barrage of the raving gobernador, who every time I tried to speak, barked: 'Shut your mouth, perro chileno!' The men did not seem inclined to come any closer, and remained at a safe distance, and so I stood there with my document in my hand, waiting until the gobernador's batteries of insults should run down sufficiently to allow him to listen to reason. Although my situation was not a very pleasant one, I could not help seeing the humorous side of it; I compared myself to a dog who had ventured into a strange village, and there before me was the big growler, snarling and showing his teeth whilst all the other mongrels were waiting in the distance for the fight to begin. Once the gobernador's admirable vocabulary was exhausted he grabbed the document I had been holding towards him and began to read it. It took him a long time to decipher its contents, and I noticed that the seal was the thing that most interested him, and in order to read it he turned the paper round in a circle several times, and then he suddenly shouted: 'Viva la Republica Argentina!' and turning towards the men he again shouted the same, and this time his call was answered by a chorus of 'Viva!' although I suppose the majority of the men had about as much idea where the Argentine is as wives have of their husbands' real whereabouts when they are 'away on business.' I was immediately invited to stay in the village as long as I might wish; and as I had already lost half the morning, I accepted the invitation to eat something, and took advantage to ask for a good feed for the horses, who could well do with it.

A kind of woolly seaweed that grows in the lake makes excellent feed for the small cattle the Indians raise. Men and boys wade out as far as they can where the water is shallow, and forming a line slowly move towards the shore, thus catching the seaweed with their legs. I have often watched cows, ponies and goats in shallow pools and have been surprised to see them submerge their heads to pull out some of these weeds, and it was remarkable how long they could keep their heads under water.

With the small grain of a certain plant the natives prepare a kind of flour that is of great nutritive value. In Spanish this flour is called 'pito de cañagua,' but among the Aymaras it is known as 'acu.' It is only made in very small quantities, but being keen on trying it I hunted everywhere until I finally obtained a supply. It is simply mixed with water and stirred until there are no lumps left and then this tasteless mixture is ready for consumption.

In these regions it is not advisable to be out in the open after sunset, for the Indians are apt to attack white men; considering the way they are being treated this is not to be wondered at and it is only astonishing that acts of revenge are not more frequent.

We were slowly nearing the northern end of the lake, and although I had enjoyed the scenery and had seen new and interesting things every day, I was glad when I unsaddled in Puno, where I had promised ourselves a day's rest.

Early next morning I was down at the wharf to see the natives arrive from far and near in their balsas. They were coming to the market and brought grain, goats, pottery, woven goods, etc. Others travelled overland, driving their patient, heavily-laden burros before them. On the top of several loads I saw fighting cocks, but those who took better care of their pet birds carried them under their arms to prevent them from being jolted about and thus handicapped for the coming fights. Cockfighting is a passion among these Indians, but according to the region the style of fighting varies, and the birds are especially trained for the manner in which they have to face their enemies.

Outside nearly every hut one can see one or several cocks tied by short pieces of string to small stakes, and there the birds spend the day crowing and scratching, excepting when the proud owner unties them for the daily training. This is done by taking a cock in both hands and swooping him past and around another bird. This so infuriates the latter that he jumps, pecks, hacks and turns, all according to the way in which the man moves the bird he is holding. When the owner considers a pupil in fit condition, he takes him to the nearest village or town, where he hopes to win easy money by betting on him.

In some places, such as Lima, a long, pointed half-moon-shaped knife is tied to one of the cock's legs, and all the birds are trained to use this formidable keen-edged weapon and never their beaks. In other places I have seen the animals taught to fight with both their spurs sharpened to fine points, and at the same time they are trained to make effective use of their beaks.

Personally I could get no amusement or excitement out of cockfights, but this was possibly due to the fact that my eyesight was not trained to see the amazingly rapid movements of the fighting birds, and thus I missed what might perhaps be called the finer points of the art.

Towards the Ancient Capital of the Mighty Incas

When the low houses of Puno had faded away in the distance we came to a range of hills, and after descending the other side we found ourselves on a plain where short, coarse grass grew. Much to my surprise the ground became boggy, but wishing to save time and distance I continued straight towards a cut in the mountains far ahead of us. I knew that this was the way we had to go towards Cuzco, for the Puno-Cuzco railway line went that way, though making a big, sweeping detour. The horses had already waded through soft puddles that gurgled in a very unpleasant way with our weight, and when we came to a broad strip of water which appeared to be traversing the plain from side to side, Gato, whom I was riding, refused to move further. The water was only some four inches deep, but the horse propped with the stubbornness of a bad-tempered mule, and when I hit him with the lead line he reared up and snorted like a bronco. I tried every means of persuasion to make the horses enter the water, but all my efforts were of no avail. Presently I saw an Indian in the distance who seemed to be shouting and waving his arms whilst he came running in my direction. When he was near enough I heard

him calling to me in broken Spanish to stop. Once he had sufficiently
recovered his breath to speak he told me that this was a very dangerous
place and that we would meet with disaster if we entered the treacherous
pool. He then guided us to a spot far away and put us on a safe trail. Gato
had taught me a good lesson, and I never interfered with him again when
he refused to step on a doubtful piece of ground. The good old boy had
not forgotten the lessons he had learnt in his youth whilst roaming over
the plains of Patagonia, and the instincts of the wild horse had warned him
that danger was lurking below the innocent-looking water.

It is surprising that neither of the horses was ever badly bogged on the
whole trip—more so when it is considered that we went through regions
where deadly quicksands and horrible, slimy pools wait to swallow the
unfortunate traveller who happens to step into them.

Putting it roughly, the three main ranges of the Andes extend from the
extreme north to the south of the South American continent, but in
several sectors cross ranges exist, and these run from east to west. These
cross ranges have formed a regular network of high, broken mountains,
between which there are deep canyons and vast, winding valleys, and these
intricate sectors are known as 'nudos' (knots). We had struck the first of
these in the Potosi sector, and now we were entering the second, but the
worst of them all was the formidable nudo we had to cross after leaving
the town of Cuzco, and later on we struck another bad place in southern Ecuador. In the high parts of Peru these criss-cross valleys produce
extraordinary atmospheric conditions; thus it often happened that we were
in glorious sunshine whilst only a few miles away a terrific storm was
raging, and the thunder sounded as if we were in the midst of this heavenly bombardment, which made the ground quiver and tremble.

We passed Indian shepherds who were grazing their small flocks of
sheep. To keep their animals together they do not use dogs, but instead
they cleverly handle slings, and if a sheep strays too far from the others
they pick up a stone, and with unerring aim throw it somewhere near the
wandering animal, which, thus frightened, returns back to the flock.
Women and children are as expert in the use of this primitive and useful
weapon as are the men.

The Indian women around here wear heavy, large and flat felt hats, and
whenever they greet a passing traveller they take them off, using both
hands, and although it is not the custom for men to return their greeting
in the same manner, I found it difficult at first to pass them without
doing the same.

We were caught in several storms, but luckily these never lasted long,
and the warm sunshine soon dried my dripping clothes.

At Chuquibambilla, on a high plain, north of Lake Titicaca, we came to a Peruvian Government experimental farm that was being run by Colonel Stordy, an ex-officer of the British Army. Both he and his charming wife gave me a warm welcome, and as both of them were great horse-lovers, my animals reaped the benefit. Formerly the colonel had kept a number of horses which he had imported from England, but owing to the altitude all had died and his stables were empty.

It was a treat to be with real white and educated people once more, and I felt like a new man after a glorious hot bath, and what a treat it was to sleep in a soft and clean bed, into which the colonel's kind and thoughtful wife had even put two hot-water bottles. Although I would have loved to enjoy a long stay with these hospitable people, we pushed on in a northerly direction, and entered the valley of Cuzco, the gateway to the ancient capital of the old Inca empire.

The day before we sighted this Mecca of archæologists I had to stay in a filthy inn where a group of drunkards made sleep impossible. Again I must have been taken for a Chilian, for throughout the night I heard some men exercising their powerful mountaineers' lungs by shouting, 'al mar con los chilenos!' (Into the sea with the Chilians!) Between these exclamations they roared like lions, as if they were competing to see who had the loudest and most terrifying voice.

Glorious Old Cuzco

In a valley, situated at the foot of a high, steep hill, Cuzco came in sight; we had penetrated through the mountains to what had once been the heart of a mighty empire: the city of the Incas.

A military detachment happened to be stationed in the town, and the commander was kind enough to take my horses into one of the corrals they had installed in a spacious backyard.

Neither man nor horse must be particular about quarters in Peru, and he who looks for a stable, or perhaps even for a lavatory, in villages and small towns might just as well seek Atlantis. My education in this line started in the north of the Argentine, near the Bolivian border, when I asked my host, the comisario (sheriff), the way to the lavatory. With a merry twinkle in his eyes he reminded me that I was no longer in Buenos Aires, and taking me by the arm he led me outside his house, and with a waving gesture of his outstretched arm told me, 'My friend, here you have the whole universe at your disposal, and I am sure it is large enough.' One soon gets used to these primitive and unsanitary conditions, and after a while one does no more than casually notice people committing what we call indecency, a thing one sees daily even in busy streets in towns, women being as unconcerned about the matter as are men and children.

I took a room in one of the hotels in Cuzco, and although I was used to far worse quarters or even none at all, I objected to the high charges. Conversing with acquaintances I had made there I found out that I was being charged twice as much as a Peruvian gentleman; an Englishman paid double my fees, and an American tourist was 'bounced' out of enough to leave no doubt that they had not mistaken him for a Scotchman.

To-day Cuzco has some 80,000 inhabitants, but it is estimated that its population amounted to 130,000 in the time of the Incas. Like most towns that were founded or rebuilt by the early Spanish settlers, it has an almost incredible number of churches and chapels. The twenty principal churches were built on the bases of ancient Inca constructions, and several have subterranean chapels that date back to the time of the Jesuits. Some of the old churches are noteworthy for their architecture, magnificent wood-carving and gorgeous altars. The pulpit in the cathedral is a masterpiece, being of the finest wood, beautifully carved, and the main altar is made of solid, beaten silver.

On the hill, to the north-east of the town, is the old Inca fortress, Sacsaihuaman, and in the vicinity there are several other important ruins. Enormous boulders form the walls of the fortress. But few of these huge blocks were cut square, and yet all were made to fit into each other. Walls were constructed in a similar way, the stones used being of all shapes and sizes and with intricate curves and angles, yet all shaped to fit into each other so perfectly that it would be impossible to introduce the blade of a knife between them. Near the fortress there are other ruins, a peculiar relic among them being the 'rodadero,' which somewhat resembles a 'shoot' cut out of the rocky slope, similar to those sometimes seen in amusement parks; whether the Incas (or pre-Incas) used it for the purpose of sliding down is uncertain. On another hill, not far from the 'rodadero' is what is said to have been the Inca's throne, and in other places seats were hewn in the rocks, and so arranged as to lead one to believe that they are places where the ancients held council.

Another relic is known as 'The bath of the Inca,' but I am afraid all the theories and suppositions about these remains will never be proved, and the early history of the Incas and pre-Incas will for ever remain a mystery. Thus we have to be content with all the beautiful legends and tales that have been handed down by word of mouth from one generation to another.

There are other important ruins in the close vicinity of Cuzco, the most interesting being those of Ollantaytambo and Pisacc (or Pisac), but these were much more difficult to reach, especially the latter, which are on a high and precipitous mountain peak in a side valley, a few hours from the town. Pisacc is believed to have been an observatory, and from there one has a marvellous view of the valley below. I went with a group of tourists, but none of my companions were able to climb more than half-way up the steep trail that winds towards the peak, the rarefied air making further progress impossible, so they sat down until I returned, loaded like a burro with their cameras, which I had carried with me to take some pictures for them. Indian children, dressed in their picturesque costumes, were herding goats among the ruins, and soon I was so friendly with these hardy children of the mountains that they allowed me to photograph them.

The remains of a sun-dial can still be seen, this primitive instrument having been hewn out of rock. Things that have always puzzled archæologists and scientists are the small water canals that exist in some Incaic ruins, even up on high mountains, as is the case in Pisacc. How water was brought up in sufficient quantity to justify the building of these small canals has never yet been satisfactorily explained.

On All Saints' Day I made a short trip by train to see some of Cuzco's surroundings. Everywhere I noticed people selling and eating sucking pigs. Even at the different stations many left the train to buy pieces of this meat from vendors who were hustling among the crowd. Even the poor people who travelled in trucks or on the roofs of the railway wagons climbed down to buy themselves chunks of sucking-pig. In the evening I arrived back in town, and there also I saw the same meat being sold and wondering what the meaning of it all was I made enquiries and was told that it is an old custom for everybody to eat this delicacy on All Saints' Day.

One evening, as I was wandering around the town before turning in I saw a moving picture show being announced, and thought it might be interesting to see what it was like.

The 'teatro' as they pompously called the place was a dirty and stuffy wooden shanty. The 'alta sociedad' (high society) sat below, where rows of wooden benches formed the stalls. Proud mothers were squatting like clucking hens beside their—in some cases—pretty daughters, whilst father, grandmother, uncle, and a few aunts formed the regulation escort of chaperons, without which no respectable girl must be seen out at any time. Such escorts accompany girls 'de buena familia' (of good family) wherever they go, be it to church, to a dance or to any other social function, and even when a 'caballero' visits a girl in her home with the heavily-barred windows, the whole family assembles in the 'sala' or in the 'patio,' where they all sit like marble statues in old European cathedrals. A battered pianola with many missing notes supplied the tinny music, a barefooted guttersnipe doing the 'pumping' and straightening of the torn music rolls whenever they slipped.

The young caballeros, who had carefully plastered down their oily black hair, were wearing their very best clothes for the occasion and preferred to stand along the walls, from where they had a better view of the señoritas, who nervously and self-consciously fingered their dresses. If a young lady had the audacity to cast a quick glance around and happened to see the longing and lingering eyes of a gentleman acquaintance of hers who looked at her as a forsaken lover looks at the moon, she would greet him with a slight nod and a quick, nervous smile would flash over her face, and then all the chaperons would stiffly turn their heads like prairie-owls and look at the daring young fellow, who would finger his best necktie and loosen his collar as if he were choking. This is South American courting. The poor people, chiefly men and boys, were perched up on a wooden gallery, and from there their bare feet were dangling down like dummy legs in the window of a manufacturer of artificial limbs.

After a great deal of whistling and stamping by the excited crowd the show was ready to begin, well over an hour after the advertised time. As soon as the lights went out there was a general rustle as everybody shifted into a more comfortable position. The film they showed must have been many years old and flickered so much that my eyes were aching. I could not keep count of how often it tore or slipped, but the crowd was delighted, and whenever an exciting part came on, the howls and shrieks of the public made me think I was at a bull fight.

Long before the show was finished I was fast asleep in the hotel, but my slumbers were disturbed by visions of beautiful and smiling señoritas, surrounded by vulture-necked and pock-marked chaperons, who, when they discovered me sneaking towards the queen of my heart, overpowered me, and as they were rolling me on the floor I felt the pain of many pins being stuck into me. I woke up bathed in perspiration and entangled in the torn sheets of my bed; my body was hot with irritation and itching, and when I struck a match I saw legions of bed bugs running helter-skelter like a defeated army after battle.

I had made the acquaintance of an English lady who was visiting Cuzco, and as I was crossing the main plaza one morning, she came running towards me in a terrible state of excitement. 'Oh,' she cried, 'do come ovah theah and tell that impudent Indian woman what I think of har! how dar' she insult me, an English lady!' Upon enquiring what on earth all this excitement was about the indignant lady told me she had 'hahdly' entered the cathedral when an Indian woman had come up to her and pushed her out into the street. Not only this, but she had actually assaulted her and by force pulled her hat off. I at once realised what had caused all this trouble, and proceeded to explain to the excited lady, who threatened to do everything but organise a war between England and Peru, that no Indian woman ever wears a hat when entering a church, that even the white women are accustomed to wear only the traditional Spanish mantillas or veils, and that undoubtedly the ignorant Indian woman had thought it sacrilege to wear a hat in church. However, in spite of all my efforts to smooth out the matter, the almost hysterical lady now even started to go for me for taking sides with the Indian woman and she shouted that English customs and traditions were the best; when I meekly suggested that it was always best to do in Rome as the Romans do, I really thought my eyes and freckled complexion were in danger.

Strange circumstances caused me to meet Mr. W., an Englishman who had lived in the Argentine for many years. He had retired from business and was visiting the Inca ruins in upper Peru. In the course of our conversation we found out that we had many mutual friends, and that I had even helped to educate some of his relatives, and although he knew me by name we had never met before.

Now Mr. W. was one of these men who read many of the fascinating books that are written about Upper Peru, and having a splash of the adventurer in his blood, he longed to see the places he had read about. When he heard that I was going to continue my ride towards the Pacific Ocean by a certain route, he became more enthusiastic than ever, for all along the trail I proposed to follow were historical relics and ruins. Botanists and natural historians had described some of the valleys in vivid colours, and even Pizarro, the conqueror, had penetrated the mountains towards Cuzco by following almost the same trail.

During one of our conversations Mr. W. suddenly turned to me and said he would join me and that he was determined to cross the second range of the Andes with me. I tried to make him realise the discomforts and even the possible dangers he would have to face, mildly hinting that he was no longer a spring chicken and that he was not trained to stand the many climatic extremes we would encounter up in the cold mountains and below in the hot valleys. When I saw that all my warnings were in vain, we immediately started to make preparations for the expedition.

Mules had to be hired, and many essentials had to be purchased, and when the English lady of the cathedral incident heard about Mr. W.'s adventurous plans she insisted on joining the party as well. I told her that such a thing was out of the question and gave my reasons; she privately assured me that she was 'any day as "tough" as Mr. W.,' but I flatly refused to be responsible. She said that money was no object to her, and that she would hire men and animals, buy tents, provisions, a camp kitchen, etc., but I assured her that if she insisted on making the trip she would have to do so alone. Luckily she finally gave up the idea, and on the morning when my horses and Mr. W.'s mules were packed and ready for the start, the good lady was there sadly to bid us 'bon voyage.'

Mr. W. had not yet arrived, and so I chatted with a group of officers and friends who had come to see me off. After a while Mr. W. came hurrying towards me, but to my surprise he was dressed in his usual grey business suit and wore his customary neat, grey felt hat, and this led me to surmise that he had changed his mind about coming with me at the last moment. After a hasty 'good morning' to everybody he said he was ready to start whenever I was, but without wasting time I went to my pack-horse and took a set of riding togs and a cap out of the saddle bags and told him to go and change into this more suitable outfit, but I had to argue with him for quite a while before he trotted off to do as I had told him. Whilst he was away I had visions of what was going to happen, and I realised that he thought he was merely going out for a joy ride in a park. After a while he returned, and soon we were going along the road at a merry gait.

Into the Heart of the Andes

At first the road led over a flat stretch, but later we came to a hill. Mr. W. was going ahead at a lively trot, obviously not heeding my warning to be careful and to take his time. I had advised him to bear in mind that we were in high altitudes where animals must not be hurried lest they get mountain-sickness, but with the novelty of sitting on a mule he merrily trotted up the hill as if he were in a hurry to reach the mountains and valleys of his dreams. Presently his mule began to stagger and sway from side to side, and suddenly collapsed as if it had been pole-axed; what I had foreseen had happened; the animal was down with sorroche, as mountain-sickness is called in Peru.

Sorroche claims many victims among beasts of burden, and frequently even men die of it. There are several ways of giving relief to animals, and I always carried the necessary things with me in case of accidents. One cure is to take a sharp penknife and cut a gash in the roof of the mouth of the afflicted animal, the loss of blood relieving the pressure on the brain. Another, more pleasant first-aid is to crush garlic between two stones, mix it with pure alcohol in the hollow of the hand, and blow this strong-smelling concoction into the animal's nostrils. As a general rule this soon makes the invalid re-act.

Luckily Mr. W.'s mule soon showed signs of improvement and there was no need to give it more than a few minutes' rest before we resumed the journey. The lesson had been a good one, and Mr. W. remembered it, for I never saw him hurry his animals again when we had to climb a hill.

Still following the good road we traversed a long and monotonous plain, and towards evening reached a high loma, on the highest point of which are the ruins of an old Inca observatory called Kcasa Cancha (Tired Fox). The road now changed into a rough and winding trail, and when we came to the top of the loma an almost breathtaking view opened before our eyes. Far to the west, ranges and ranges of high peaks rose out of the tropical mists below, and the golden evening sun gave the high clouds the appearance of rolling masses of fire, smoke and vapour, whilst patches of sky were purple, violet and light green. Mr. W., who had never before beheld anything so wonderful and inspiring, stood there gazing at the in-describable vastness and wild beauty of the panorama, and seemed to have forgotten that we had a long way to go yet before the day's travelling was done. I almost had to pull my gazing friend away, for night would soon come, and it would be dangerous to be overtaken by darkness on the steep trail we had to follow down into the valley that lay hidden below the mists on which the mountains seemed to be floating. With the approach of late evening it was already getting chilly where we were, and without losing time I went ahead and commenced the descent.

The trail was very steep and rocky, and experience had taught me that I made quicker progress on foot than mounted, so I went in front to pick the best way, and the horses followed behind me like two dogs. When an animal has to zig-zag up or down a 45 degree slope, and this over a trail with loose rocks and steps that are one or two feet high, it is much safer and easier to dismount, for with less weight to carry, a horse or mule will have more confidence. When a rider has to go on a long trip he must consider the animals' backs, for should they get sore, he will be left on foot, and the best saddle is bound to injure the animal if the rider is not careful in such places. Apart from this, what would one do if a horse twisted or broke a leg far away from the nearest human habitation?

It is much more tiring to go mounted up or down such steep and rough inclines, and the danger of a nasty fall is ever present. Whenever I came to precipitous trails, and there were many, I divided the pack between the horses; if we had to go downhill I went ahead, but when climbing I put Mancha in front and caught hold of his tail, and in this way he pulled me along without much effort. I always put him in front because he obeyed my commands, and I could guide him in any direction by pulling his tail one way or the other. Gato was much too eager to go ahead, and even if I tried to make him stop he went on until he was out of breath; the trick of guiding by the tail did not work with him, and so he had often chosen the worst foot trail, for he obviously thought the straightest trail was the shortest. When the Indians go afoot they never follow zig-zags down hill, but make the descent in straight line, hopping and jumping over rocks like goats and sliding and running over loose stones and pebbles. It can therefore easily be imagined how awkward and even dangerous it is if a horse chooses to follow such foot trails. At first Mr. W. insisted on going mounted, but soon his bones were aching with the bumps and jolts he received, or possibly the beginning of saddle soreness made him change his mind, and so he dismounted and followed my example.

The further down we went the warmer it became, and after a while we were among semi-tropical vegetation, where numerous little green parrots screeched at our approach, as if protesting against our intrusion. Down and down we stumbled and slid, and presently mosquitoes and sand flies began to worry us. The rushing of wild waters could be heard, the atmosphere became damp and sticky, and I knew that we were near the bottom. It was already dark when we arrived at a little place called Limatambo, and we were fortunate in finding a fairly decent inn, where we were given shelter and food.

Vampire bats had often attacked my horses, and I suspected that there were likely to be some of these pests in this hot, narrow valley. I made enquiries, and when I was told that my fears were well founded I went into the backyard to sprinkle my horses' backs with a strong kind of Indian pepper that keeps the bats away. I had already finished with Mancha, and was approaching what I took to be Gato in the dark, but before I had time to jump away the animal had turned and given me a vicious kick with both hind legs, sending me sprawling against the adobe wall. Both my thighs were numbed by the violent impact of the hoofs, and as I sat there I wondered what could have caused so tame and gentle a horse as Gato to kick me. I soon found out that owing to the darkness I had mistaken one of Mr. W.'s mules for my horse, and I had paid the penalty. Luckily there were no bones broken, but I suffered severe pains for quite a number of days, and after that I took good care to avoid making a similar mistake again.

The name Limatambo is a corruption of the old Quichua name

Rimac Tampu (Speaking Fort) and there are some very interesting ruins in the place.

Not far from this little settlement are the practically unknown ruins of Huatta, but unfortunately time did not permit me to make an expedition to visit them. These ruins, together with those of Machupichu are said to be the finest in Peru.

I have often been asked if descendants of Incas still exist, and this is a question that is easily answered. Incas were what we would call kings or emperors, and the people under them were often called by the same name by the Spaniards. It is obvious that the majority of pure Bolivian and Peruvian Indians are direct descendants of the old subjects of the Incas, for it is inconceivable that the blood could have changed entirely in less than four centuries. The Indian languages that are spoken today are practically the same as when the first Spaniards under Pizarro set foot on what is now Peruvian soil. The excellent character of the old Quichua Indians is clearly shown in the way they greeted each other, for when they met the greeting was: 'Ama Ilulla, ama sua, ama gguella.' (Be not untruthful, be not a thief, be not idle.) The answer to this was: 'Ccampas nocca, jinollatacc.' (Be this the same for you as for myself.)

We had heard about an old Inca thermal bath that exists some two miles from the settlement, and as neither Mr. W. nor myself had had a bath in Cuzco, where such luxuries did not exist in the hotels, we thought it would not be a bad idea to spend the next day in getting clean, and seeing the ruins in and around the little village. By following a rough footpath we found the old thermal bath that had been hewn out of the rock on the mountainside. It lay hidden away in a pretty creek and was surrounded by shady trees. The water was delightfully warm, and it was amusing to think that we were soaping and scrubbing ourselves where formerly perhaps some mighty Inca had bathed whilst being accompanied by an escort of a chosen few.

After Limatambo our way lay through beautiful wooded valleys with marvellous and exuberant vegetation; veritable paradises for naturalists. The trail passed under enormous trees or again through regular forests of bamboo, and the rocks along the rushing and foaming streams were overhung with many varieties of delicate ferns. On some rocks there were big trees with peculiar roots hanging down like huge snakes, and on these roots grew big brown knobs that resembled enormous potatoes. Here the ride would have been like a beautiful dream, had it not been for swarms of mosquitoes and gnats that were tantalising us. The horses kicked and fidgeted and were frantically swishing their tails in vain attempts to free themselves from the masses of insects which had settled on them. The heat was considerable, and when I looked for the candles at night I found that they had melted into a soft, pasty mass, and so we had to use a plateful of grease with a wick stuck in it, which is the usual way of illuminating the huts among the primitive people in many parts of South and Central America.

Sometimes we were winding our way through narrow and deep valleys, with walls of rock that seemed to reach the clouds on either side, and then again we had to zig-zag up a rough trail, stumbling, scrambling and slipping. Men and beasts were dripping with perspiration, and every now and again we had to halt to recover our breath, and so we slowly climbed higher and higher. We no longer admired the gorgeous panorama, all we saw was the trail, and after some time of this I began to feel as if the whole thing were a never-ending nightmare. Often the track was cut out of a perpendicular mountain wall, with a giddy fall down to the river, which from above looked like a winding streak of silver. In some places these trails are so narrow that the pack animals have to walk near the edge to avoid bumping against the rocky wall, and it would be impossible to cross animals coming in the opposite direction. I have been told of incidents in the Andes when two riders happened to have met in such narrow places, and when the man who shot first was the one who saved himself, for neither turning back nor crossing each other would have been possible in these traps. Once I had a few anxious moments when a mule train caught us unawares in a narrow place, but generally the Indians and mule drivers halt when they come to such a passage, and one of them goes ahead on foot to see if the trail is dear and to give possible arrivals on the other side the necessary warning.

The few pack trains that passed us mostly carried spirits to the interior. The strong alcohol is carried in goat skins, one on each side of the pack animal, and sometimes a third on top. Natives say that these skins are useless and will crack unless the unfortunate goats are skinned alive!

My travelling companion was very much worried by the mosquitoes, and although I warned him not to do so, he constantly scratched where the bites were irritating. I offered him the use of my gloves and the black mosquito net that fitted over the hat like a veil, but he refused to use them on the grounds that they made him feel too hot. Within a few days nasty infections had set in in both his hands and face, and as time went on his condition became worse and worse. Luckily I had a supply of bandages and disinfectants with me; without them there is no knowing what might have happened.

We always went along in single file, and one day, whilst we were slowly moving along one of those giddy trails, Gato stepped too near the edge, and some loose rocks gave way under his hind leg. He lost his footing and shot over the side and went sliding towards the edge of a deep precipice. For a moment I watched in horror, and then the miracle happened. A solitary sturdy tree stopped his slide towards certain death, and once the horse had bumped against the tree he had enough sense not to attempt to move. I took off my spurs and climbed down towards him, and as soon as I had reached the trembling animal I began to unsaddle him with the utmost care, for should he move and fall, I would at least save my few precious belongings. Poor Gato had scented danger, and was pitifully neighing to his companion, who was above in safety. It was not his usual neigh—it had in it a note of desperation and fear.

Once unsaddled I made sure that he could not move from the spot until preparations were made to assist him from above. When all was ready the horse was hauled back to safety, but had it not been for the fact that Gato spread out his forelegs like a frog, he would have over-balanced backwards, and the chances were that he would have swept me with him, for I was guiding the salvage operations from below. My heart was palpitating so violently that I thought it would burst, but once both of us were safely back on the trail that now looked like a paradise to me, I looked through the saddle bags to see if there was a drop left to celebrate the miraculous escape; however, we were out of luck in that line and had to wait until we came to a spring, where we washed down the fright.

After crossing the Apurimac River we came to the roughest and most broken country imaginable. Little bridges spanned deep canyons and ravines, and the trail led over high passes and through deep gorges and winding valleys. The condition of my friend was getting worse every day, and he was no longer able to use his hands. The infections on his face had made shaving impossible, and so his beard had grown considerably. The matter that oozed out of his running sores had dried and mixed with his now stubby beard, making his appearance anything but attractive, to say the least.

Most horsemen, horsebreakers, and open-air men have a special vocabulary of their own, and as I did not believe in punishing my horses excepting on rare occasions, I had learnt to ease my feelings by going through a special vocabulary whenever something went wrong, and somehow this seemed to happen all day long, and often even during the nights. Now a horse did something wrong, again the pack slipped, the trail was rough, or a thousand similar things and happenings demanded suitable remarks at short intervals. I remember soon after we set out together Mr. W. giving me a moral lecture about my strong language, assuring me that if I thus continued I should become so used to this horrible, useless and degrading habit, that I should never be able again to mix with decent people. My habit of eating raw onions was another source of annoyance and even indignation to him, and although I am not particularly fond of the after-taste of this vegetable, and never eat them under ordinary circumstances, I took some every day because I was told that they helped to prevent mountain-sickness, and apart from their high nutritive value, they are very easy to carry in the saddlebags and keep good for a long time. Now it so happened that my good friend had not been long with me before he was very efficient in the use of my private vocabulary, and, thanks to his knowledge of the language, I was able to add a few very original and expressive words to my repertoire. And this was not all, for soon I had to keep a strict eye on our onion supply, for which he had suddenly developed a rare liking.

Vampire bats had given us a great deal of trouble, and many a morning I found my horses clotted with blood that had oozed out of the small, circular holes the bats had bitten into their backs and necks. I was puzzled how a horse or a mule could let so big an animal bite him, when a mosquito or a fly will make him defend himself. At a later period I had the chance to observe how these bats attack, and I feel inclined to believe in the theory of some mountain people.

Bats have a peculiar way of flying around the horse in circles until he becomes drowsy and half dazed. These blood-suckers usually exist in deep quebradas, as the rugged valleys are called, and owing to the hot and damp atmosphere the horses perspire even during the nights. Gradually the bats circle closer and closer around the now sleepy horse, and presently they hover near the spot where they intend to bite, all the time fanning air against the victim. Once the horse gets used to the pleasant sensation of feeling cool the vampire gently settles down and bites through the hide with his sharp little teeth, all the while keeping up the fanning with his wings. I have seen bats so full of blood that they were unable to fly after their feed, and when I stepped on them, amazing quantities of blood squirted out. These pests not only attack horses and cattle, but also do damage among poultry, and as the latter have but little blood they invariably die, one bat sucking enough blood to kill a hen. Natives say that vampires always return to the same wound for their next feed, and for this reason they smear a mixture of vaseline and strychnine over the spot where the animal has been bitten, and if the bat returns again he has to eat this mixture first, thus poisoning himself.

There are several ways of keeping vampires off horses, the most simple being to cover them with rugs, but as the bat-infested regions are always hot, the horses do everything to rid themselves of the uncomfortable

A. F. TSCHIFFELY
From an oil painting
by A. J. Drucker.
London, 1932

'MANCHA' AND 'GATO'
From an oil painting
by L. Cordiviola

'LIEMPICHUN' (I HAVE FEATHERS)
The Patagonian Tehuelche Indian Chief who was
the first owner of the horses 'Mancha' and 'Gato'

BRANDING COLTS IN THE ARGENTINE PAMPAS
Every 'estancia' (estate) has its own mark which
must be officially registered

GAUCHOS PREPARING AN 'ASADO' (ROAST MEAT)
Note the stools which are made of the hip-bones of the horses or cows.
The man who is standing up is sipping 'mate' (tea made with
the leaf of the Paraguayan ilex)

BREAKING IN A COLT
One gaucho covers the animal's eye whilst his assistant gently slips a rope
through the halter-ring. Note the customary belt of the pampas, also the
knife from the handle of which hangs the 'rebenque' (whip)

A Village in the North-West of the Argentine

Humahuaca (Weeping Head)

An Old, Old Man of the Mountains
(See page 48)

Excavating Graves among the ruins of Tilcara in
North-Western Argentina

A Mountaineer Rides Trail in North-Western Argentina
Usually the sturdy ponies in these desolate regions, are ridden
without a bit, and their hard hoofs are never shod

Towards the Bolivian Border
Cactus plants and tough 'puna-grass.' The only 'roads' in
these desolate regions are vast, wind-swept 'quebradas'

THE LLAMA IS THE PACK AMINAL OF THE ANDES
Once a year, during the dry season, the Bolivian and the Peruvian mountain
Indian drives his herd down to the distant villages and towns, where he
trades his pottery and beautifully-woven goods for necessities of life,
which are unobtainable in his inhospitable native regions

THE POTTER'S CLAY
A Quichua Indian woman practising the art of her ancestors

WEAVING A 'VICUNA' BLANKET

TOWARDS THE INTERIOR
Of the imposing net-work of mountains in
southern Bolivia. 'Mancha' and 'Gato' take
a short rest in a dry river-bed

An Indian 'Chicha' Vendor

The Author, Wearing a Sand-Storm
Mask in Bolivia

Long-haired Bolivian
Indian Runners

Primitive Aymara Indian Hut

A Street in Potosi (Bolivia)
The old mining town. Many of the buildings date
back to the early Spanish colonial times

The Ancient Royal Spanish Mint
At Potosí, Bolivia. This machine—made of hardwood, held together by raw-
hide and wooden pins—is as solid as when it was built, nearly 400 years ago

A Bolivian Aymara Indian
Though a very old tribe, the modern Aymara
has yielded, but little to the encroaching
civilization of to-day

Bolivian Devil Dancers
Note the huge headgear, made of a light bamboo
frame and brightly coloured feathers

CYCLOPEAN RUINS OF AN ANCIENT RACE
At Tiahuanacú, near Lake Titicaca. Majestic, mysterious, their origin lost in
the dim, forgotten centuries, these giant stone pillars challenge the
imagination of modern man, who speculates in vain as to who
put them up, or when, or how

EQUINE STUDY OF A MONOLITH
At Tiahuanacú. The horses stand on the foot of a pre-historic temple

INDIANS WEAVE THESE BOATS OF RUSHES
Known as 'balsas,' these skiffs are much used on Lake Titicaca.
Indian fishermen landing with their day's catch

PERUVIAN INDIANS EATING CORN AND DRINKING 'CHICHA'
By an odd local custom, these Indian women lift their hats when
greeting friends or strangers along the trails

A HIGH PASS IN THE 'CORDILLERAS'
Blizzards and thick, shifting fogs are great dangers in many of these high regions, where breathing is made difficult owing to the rarefied atmosphere

'ONE GOOD TURN DESERVES ANOTHER'
Quichua Indian women hunting unwelcome visitors

Made of tough fibre and roots, this Indian bridge is
anchored by weighting its ends with heavy rocks

THIS FAMOUS 12-ANGLE STONE
Appears in an ancient wall art Cuzco, Peru. Though fitting so closely that a
knife cannot be inserted between the stones, no mortar was used. To this day
scientists are puzzled how the ancient masons fitted these enormous stones

covers. Any strong smelling disinfectant would give good results, but these are apt to burn the horses' skins. I found that well-crushed garlic was the best preventative, and I usually gave my animals a thorough friction with this simple and cheap preparation, and sometimes sprinkled Indian pepper over them.

Experience teaches cattle to defend themselves against these blood-suckers, which weaken the strongest of them. My horses were bitten several times just in the place where the saddles made most pressure, and it was no easy matter to saddle them after without producing sore backs, but constant observation and care prevented pressure on the affected spots.

I have heard of cases when bats even attacked human beings, and it is said that their favourite spot for sucking blood is on a person's big toe, and that they only attack when the victim is soundly asleep. Personally I never had any trouble with them, although they fluttered in and out of my habitation all night.

Along our trail we saw some places where treasure hunters had been busy excavating, for we were again following one of the most important of the old Spanish gold trails, and in this vicinity several valuable and historic treasures are suspected to have been buried.

Some of the inclines we had to climb were almost heartbreaking, and we had to be very cautious not to overstrain our animals. Had the old Greeks known some of these Andean 'cuestas,' as the steep inclines are called, they surely would have added the climbing of an endless one to the trials of Tantalus. All along these cuestas were the bleached bones of burros and mules which had not been able to reach the top, and the skeletons served as a continuous warning to me not to overstrain my horses unnecessarily.

In a beautiful and fertile mountain valley we rested in a picturesque village, and there my companion was obliged to change his mules. The cunning people asked exorbitant prices, for they knew that he would either have to pay what they demanded or else go on foot. After having tried to cure his infections and having chased around for mules for five days we were finally ready to push on. In the interior of Peru the Indians will not accept paper money, so the traveller must carry the heavy silver 'soles', and when we left my friend's load was considerably lighter, for the mules had cost him the price of a motor-car. In mountain sectors I reduced my pack to a minimum, and when I had to carry silver coins enough to reach the next town where there was a bank, the coins, fire-arms and ammunition made up the main weight of my load. I have seen merchants who had to carry fair sums of money, and as the total amount was in silver, the weight and bulk were so much that they required a special mule to carry it.

Whilst we stayed in this village rumours were circulating that bandits were making a high pass unsafe, and this did not help to encourage my companion, whose only desire now was to reach civilisation again. His thirst for adventure had been more than satisfied, and by this time he had lost all the interest he had formerly taken in the surroundings; the beauty of nature and the scenery no longer appealed to him, and all day long he cursed the Spanish conquistadores for having chosen the highest and roughest trails. I had heard so many bandit stories before that I took next to no notice of this one, for after all there was nothing else to do but to go ahead and chance it, and should the worst come to the worst, I had an idea that I would be able to make things pretty hot if I were given half a chance. Indians sometimes attack government officials and others who make life a misery for them, not so much to rob them as out of purely revengeful motives. As I had no personal enemies to fear, nor much property worth taking, I knew that we were relatively safe.

Whilst climbing towards the very pass we had been warned about, a heavy rain began to fall, and the ground became so slippery that further progress was made difficult, and spotting a solitary hut, I proposed to spend the night there, hoping better weather would prevail on the morrow. The small hut was inhabited by a man and his two sons, and as there was not room enough inside for all of us, we were offered a place outside in the shelter of the far overlapping roof. We tied the animals to some bushes near us, and once I had cut sufficient grass to last them for the night we had a few bites to eat, and then I spread our saddles and blankets on the ground and made ready to retire. It was up to me to do all this work, for my companion's hands were rendered useless by the infections.

I could see that he was worried and uneasy about something, and after a while he reminded me about the bandits who were supposed to be lurking in this region. He insisted that I should prepare all the fire-arms and knives, and lay them alongside us. In spite of his bandaged hands he chose my repeating shotgun and practised the use of it, and when he was satisfied with his rehearsals he laid the weapon alongside him. The last words of advice I heard before sleep overtook me were not to aim at the head but at the body. He woke me up several times during the night to ask me if I had heard this or that noise, and once he swore that somebody must have taken the shotgun from him, but upon investigating we found that it was so near his body that he had reached and fumbled much too far away in his hurried efforts to find it in the dark. This amused me so much that I had to make great efforts to suppress a hearty laugh.

Next day, as we were nearing the heights near the top of the pass, a man on horseback appeared over a ridge and began to descend over a grassy slope, making a great semi-circle around us. Mr. W., who had been on the look-out for trouble all the time, was the first to spot this lone rider, and he followed him with his eyes, and every now and again had a quick look at the ridges ahead of us to see if all was clear there; for all the world he looked like a prairie owl gazing from side to side on a fence post. However, nothing happened, and our weary procession moved over high mountains where the climate was raw and cold, and again we came to valleys exuberant with tropical vegetation, where brightly-coloured humming birds darted from flower to flower, and where parrots frolicked and screeched on the tree tops. Up in the desolate regions we saw some condors majestically circling in the clear, blue sky. Probably these Andean kings were on the look-out for the carcass of some unfortunate beast of burden.

My friend's condition was getting worse and worse, and with it his temper. I took good care not to let him notice that I was beginning to feel alarmed about him, and thus he more or less kept up his spirits.

About eighty miles before we reached the town of Ayacucho we struck an hacienda (farm) where we were invited to unsaddle. After dinner we started chatting, during the course of conversation we discussed the marvellous resistance of the Indians. Our hosts told us that a serious accident had happened to one of their men not long before, and as a doctor happened to be staying on the place at the time, he sent an elderly Indian to the distant town to fetch some chloroform he needed to enable him to operate on the victim. The distance from that place to Ayacucho and back is roughly one hundred and fifty miles, and the rough trail leads over several mountains. According to several witnesses the Indian was back in seventeen hours, and after he had eaten something he carried on with his usual work until evening. True, natives on foot make short cuts, and thus save many miles, but on the other hand these foot-trails lead over places where white men would hardly make any progress.

Civilisation Again

In Ayacucho a doctor immediately attended to my friend, and high time it was, for the flesh of his hands had positively begun to rot. From here, Mr. W. could reach the railway terminus by automobile, and the train would take him over the last range down to Lima. The best hotel in the town was dirty and lacking in many respects, but we were happy to be

in it, and once the animals had been accommodated and fed we sat down
to a hearty meal, and shortly after we were making up for some of our
lost sleep.

The second main range of the Andes was behind us now, and the
horses were in such excellent condition that I had no doubt that only an
accident could prevent us from reaching Lima and the Pacific Ocean.
After a few days Mr. W. was well enough to travel without running a
risk, and accordingly he arranged to leave on a lorry that was about to make
the trip to the railway terminus.

Like most tourists, he was a keen souvenir-hunter and admirer of
antiques, and as he hoped to find some bargains on his way to Lima, he
changed all his remaining banknotes for silver coins. When the lorry
arrived he was ready to depart. His hands were wrapped up in bandages
and his face was still in a terrible mess. He had obviously forgotten that
one of the handbags was filled with coins, for, in spite of his infected hands,
he tried to lift it as if it only contained a few articles of clothing. When
he felt the weight of it he let go a stream of language that left no doubt
that he could hold his own with any horse-tamer or mule-driver. Yes, Mr.
W. had been a good and easy learner, and if ever he had to give a moral
lecture after his spell in the mountains, I have no doubt that he was able
to deliver it in most expressive and convincing language.

He had hardly left when heavy rains began to pour down, and when I
met him again some three years later, he told me that his adventures had
by no means come to an end, for the lorry was held up owing to landslides,
and further along some bridges had been washed away and he had to cross
over two rivers in baskets hung on cables. Finally he arrived in Lima, and
after two months his wounds had healed completely, leaving only a few
scars to remind him of his joy-ride across one of the Andean ranges.

The history and legends of Ayacucho are most fascinating. It was close
to this place that a small army of Independents defeated the Spaniards, a
little over a hundred years ago.

According to an old legend, an Inca was holding council with his
consort when a falcon rose in the distance, and pointing towards the bird
the Inca exclaimed, 'hua manca!' (there goes a falcon). This having been
considered a lucky omen, a village was founded there and named
Huamanca. When the Spaniards invaded Peru, this village at one time
marked the dividing line between conquered and unconquered territory
of the Incas, and the invaders changed the name of Huamanca to San Juan
de la Frontera. There the Spaniards built the first church in South America, and this is still standing.

The original village, Ayacucho, stood some twelve miles from where the town stands to-day. Ayacucho means 'corner of the dead,' and another legend tells us that two Incas once fought a battle on the plains near there. In the evening the victorious Inca stood on a hill, and as he looked over the battlefield, which was strewn with dead, he pointed to a corner where the fallen lay thickest and said, 'aya cucho' (corner of the dead) and there the village was founded. After the War of Independence, to commemorate the battle of Ayacucho, San Juan de la Frontera (formerly Huamanca) was re-named Ayacucho. Although the town is small and poor it has thirty-seven churches, and I fail to understand how the legions of ecclesiastics one sees in the streets are able to exist; yet I never saw one who looked anything but well fed.

The old-fashioned and tumble-down town is full of Indians and half-castes, and the pride of every citizen is a more showy than artistic monument in the main plaza. My chief delight was to wander around the market-square, where rows of Indian women squatted, suckling their dark-skinned and blob-eyed babies whilst waiting for customers to come and finger the goods that were spread out on the ground before them. Others cooked food in earthenware pots, and to give a little shade to their stalls they stuck big, flat parasols into the ground, tilting them according to the angle at which the sun shone. Everything the region produces, both agricultural and industrial, is sold in this market, and bye-products, such as mangy mongrels and clouds of flies were also much in evidence, and that other insects breed well can easily be guessed by the way the Indian hags scratch and de-louse each other, an art that is often practised in public in Peru.

A tall, white beggar with refined features and a long, flowing beard had often attracted my attention in the streets. He appeared to be deaf, dumb and blind, and whenever he had walked a few steps he suddenly stopped and went through a series of most peculiar nervous contortions. I was very friendly with the mayor of the town, and one day whilst we were dining together I asked him if he knew this man, and this is the extraordinary story he told me about him.

This beggar was the son of a good family and had enjoyed an excellent education. When his parents died he inherited a considerable fortune and became the owner of several prosperous 'haciendas' (farms). Being young and foolish he began to envy a friend of his who was married to a beautiful girl, and in the course of time he succeeded in winning her affection. One day the two eloped and went to hide in one of the young man's haciendas in the mountains. The injured husband soon heard where the couple were hiding, and consulted with some Indian friends of his to see if they were willing to help him to avenge the wrong his false friend had done him. The average Indian is by nature a gentleman, and moral crimes, such as the one they now heard about, are beyond the range of their understanding, so they agreed to punish the criminal. They followed the couple to their place in the mountains and mixed one of their mysterious poisons in the man's food, and soon after he returned to town deaf, dumb and blind, and shaking with nervous convulsions. He called various doctors from far and near. When they failed to cure him he travelled to Europe, where he consulted the best specialists, but all their efforts, too, were futile. By degrees he spent his fortune, and later returned to his native town, where he had ever since been living on the charity of passers-by.

Bats had bitten the horses where the saddles pressed on them, and one or two of these spots had become sore and infected. It would have been unwise to resume travelling before these sores were better, and this obliged me to spend several more days in Ayacucho than I had originally intended. In the meantime a thing I had been fearing all the time had happened; the rainy season had set in, but in spite of reports about landslides and turbulent rivers that reached me, I saddled up as soon as the horses' backs were well, and within an hour or two Ayacucho became only a memory.

Landslides, a Detour and a Mountain Storm

Landslides and swollen rivers made it impossible to follow the road and compelled me to make a large detour over the mountains to the west. Natives who knew these regions advised me to take a guide, for alone I should have difficulty in finding the direction among the numerous little Indian footpaths.

With the mayor's assistance I found an Indian in a village who agreed to come with me, but unfortunately the man could neither speak nor understand Spanish. I bought some provisions, and without losing time started out, the guide, like most Indians, preferring to go on foot, and even when the horses went at a trot he kept up with us with ease. After some time he led us into very rough country, and often he made a sign to me to go ahead, and then he took a short cut, and later I found him sitting somewhere far ahead, chewing coca whilst waiting for us.

We had crossed some giddy and wobbly hanging bridges before, but here we came to the worst I had ever seen or ever wish to see again. Even without horses the crossing of such bridges is apt to make anybody feel cold ripples running down the back, and, in fact, many people have to be blindfolded and strapped on stretchers to be carried across. Spanning a wild river the bridge looked like a long, thin hammock swung high up from one rock to another. Bits of rope, wire and fibre held the rickety structure together, and the floor was made of sticks laid crosswise and covered with some coarse fibre matting to give a foothold and to prevent slipping that would inevitably prove fatal.

The width of this extraordinary piece of engineering was no more than four feet, and its length must have been roughly one hundred and fifty yards. In the middle the thing sagged down like a slack rope.

I went to examine it closely, and the very sight of it made me feel giddy, and the thought of what might easily happen produced a feeling in my stomach as if I had swallowed a block of ice. For a while I hesitated, and then I decided to chance it, for there was no other alternative but to return to Ayacucho and there wait for the dry season. I unsaddled the horses, and giving the Indian the lead-line I made signs to him to go ahead with Mancha first. Knowing the horse well, I caught him by the tail and walked behind talking to him to keep him quiet. When we stepped on the bridge he hesitated for a moment, then he sniffed the matting with suspicion, and after examining the strange surroundings he listened to me and cautiously advanced. As we approached the deep sag in the middle, the bridge began to sway horribly, and for a moment I was afraid the horse would try to turn back, which would have been the end of him; but no, he had merely stopped to wait until the swinging motion was less, and then he moved on again. I was nearly choking with excitement, but kept on talking to him and patting his haunches, an attention of which he was very fond. Once we started upwards after having crossed the middle, even the horse seemed to realise that we had passed the worst part, for now he began to hurry towards safety. His weight shook the bridge so much that I had to catch hold of the wires on the sides to keep my balance. Gato, when his turn came, seeing his companion on the other side, gave less trouble and crossed over as steadily as if he were walking along a trail. Once the horses were safely on the other side we carried over the packs and saddles, and when we came to an Indian hut where 'chicha' and other native beverages were sold we had an extra long drink to celebrate our successful crossing, whilst the horses quietly grazed as if they had accomplished nothing out of the way.

Torrential rains began to pour down, and the mountain trails were soon converted into rushing streams that carried earth and loose stones with them, and often we had to wait until the downpour ceased before we could proceed.

The guide pointed towards a mountain-side that towered up into the sky like a wall, and it seemed to me that he tried to make me understand that we would have to climb up there, but as this looked like an impossibility to me I thought I must be misunderstanding him. Much to my surprise our path led straight towards this formidable mountain-side, and presently we started up a neck-breaking path which had been partly hewn and partly worn out of the rocky wall. It was so steep and slippery that at first I considered it a physical impossibility for horses to climb up there, and when we finally came to the top I saw that another similar obstacle was ahead of us. A traveller soon gets used to such disappointments in the Andes, for often, after having reached what one thought would be the end of a long and weary climb, one sees another ahead, and frequently one has by no means finished with the eternal zig-zags even when the second has been surmounted.

The Indians in these parts may appear to be sullen, but yet I found them kind and hospitable. I shall always remember how well a solitary woman treated us when we arrived at her hut. Her husband was away, and so she was left alone with the children. She prepared food for us, and in return I gave her and the children some chocolate, for the good woman refused to accept money. We spread our blankets under a low shelter where we slept alongside some pigs, but when one is tired and the nights cold one is satisfied with any kind of protection. When daylight permitted we were glad to be off again, for it was bitterly cold, and my fingers were stiff and aching.

Below us the valleys and hollows were still wrapped in inky darkness whilst the first rays of the sun gave the highest peaks the appearance of glowing heaps of charcoal. By degrees, as the sun rose higher, the light crept further and further down the slopes, until it shone on the heavy mists below. Soon our shivering bodies began to feel the agreeable warmth, and the puffs of vapour that came out of the horses' nostrils with every breath became fainter and fainter as the atmosphere warmed up.

After some time the sea of mist began to heave and roll, and here and there we could see the valley through an opening, but soon a drifting cloud again covered the gap. Every now and again a heavy mass of white would gather and rise above the rest, assuming grotesque shapes of gigantic human heads or strange monsters that looked as if they were rising out of an angry and foaming sea. Slowly the mists rose until they reached us; then for a while the sun looked like a grey disc until it completely disappeared behind a thick curtain, and then a damp chill began to penetrate through our clothes. I was hoping that the clouds and fogs would lift towards noon, but this did not happen, and as time went on it became darker and darker. Towards evening thunder began to rumble in the distance, and suddenly a furious storm began to rage around us. The Indian, who was carrying our small food supply on his back, hurried ahead, and when we found an overhanging rock we took shelter under it. The rain poured down in such torrents that I was thankful not to be on a slope or in one of those trails in a hollow.

When the storm had passed the Indian left me, and, thinking he had merely gone to see what the weather was likely to do, I sat down to wait for him. After about a quarter of an hour I began to wonder what was keeping the man away for so long, and went to look for him, but although I searched in every direction and called, there was no sign of him. It was already dusk and still he did not appear, so I unsaddled and prepared to spend the night under the rock where we had taken refuge during the storm. Obviously the cunning Indian had returned towards home, taking with him all my food supplies, and as I had paid him in advance he must have thought it foolish to face further hardships, especially during an abnormally severe rainy season.

This was by no means the first time I had been in similar situations, and so I settled down to make the best of it until dawn would permit us to continue. There was no grass, so the horses stood alongside me whilst I sat on the sheepskins of the saddle and puffed away at some cigarettes, whilst imagining myself to be picking my choice from a long menu in some luxurious Parisian restaurant, and possibly my animals were dreaming of green alfalfa fields and feed-boxes full of crisp, golden oats. To my great joy, I discovered a treasure wrapped up in a paper in the saddle-bags—a piece of unrefined sugar. In the morning I cut this into three pieces, and whilst I made ready to start, the three of us chewed away, and when we had finished our mouthfuls we tried to remember the pleasant taste by licking our slobbery lips.

For mountain travelling a compass is of no use, for it is impossible to leave the narrow trails, and when one happens to come to a place where a path branches off in another direction one has to guess which one to take, and leave the rest to chance. I was lucky that day, for in the evening I sighted a small settlement on a slope, and when I arrived there the 'alcalde' (alderman) told me I was in Paucara, and in spite of not being any the wiser for this piece of information, I was glad to be there, for at least there were hopes of getting something to eat. The Indian alcalde gave me quarters in an empty hut next to his, and after a while brought me a steaming plate of barley soup and a bundle of straw for the horses. I could have taken many times the amount of soup I was given, but even the small quantity I had made me feel like a new man. When I went to look at the horses I found that they had already finished their feed, and so I walked from hut to hut, trying my best to get them some more, and although I was willing to pay any price for it, only one man reluctantly parted with a very little of his limited supply.

At sunrise the alcalde put me on a trail, informing me that by following it I would hit the 'Mejorada,' which is the terminus of the Central Peruvian Railroad. More than once I thought I must have gone the wrong way, for evening was approaching, and still I could see no railway line. Rounding a bend my fears were dispelled, for far below us, in a green valley, I saw a thin line, like a black thread that wound and twisted along the foot of the mountain. We were safe, for this must be a railroad, a thing I had not seen for a long, long time.

At the top of a steep zig-zag I halted to re-saddle before starting the descent. Whilst I was doing this a man arrived on a mule, and introduced himself as Herr X., a German mining engineer. He almost cried whilst he related that he had been lost all night and that he felt as empty as a drum, and judging by his looks the experience had made a great impression on him. Together we slowly descended towards the houses which looked like mere specks from above. At the railway terminus there was a small restaurant and store in a newly-erected wooden house. The hungry German rushed into it without even wasting time in, first, unsaddling his sorry-looking mule, and presently he appeared again with a string of sausages and a big chunk of bread, into which he put his teeth with the ferocity of a starving tiger.

A Famous Indian Market–'The Roof of the World'–Down to the Pacific Ocean

From the railway terminus, going was easy to Huancayo, the first passably decent place we had struck for a long time.

This little town is noted for its Indian market, which is held every Sunday, and which is probably the most important and busy of its kind in the whole of South America. On Saturday afternoon, and early on Sunday morning, Indians come flocking into town from far and near. Pottery, leather goods, hand-woven blankets, dies, grain, cleverly carved and painted calabashes, herbs, etc., are sold at low prices, provided the buyer knows how to barter with the thrifty vendors. Up to thirty thousand people gather weekly in this town, and nowhere else have I seen such a busy and colourful Indian market.

Whilst here I had the pleasure of meeting Messrs. Campe and Goddard, who invited me to visit the Carnegie observation station of which they are in charge. There terrestrial magnetism and electric currents are being observed, and I spent a most pleasant and instructive day. As Mr. Goddard had formerly been a member of MacMillan's polar expedition we had plenty to chat about.

Most of the soldiers in Peru are recruited, or rather 'rounded up' among the Indians, the few whites one sees in uniform being officers, and whilst I was in Huancayo I saw a contingent of future warriors arrive. A cordon of armed soldiers marched ahead, followed by two long lines of frightened and depressed-looking Indians, who carried small bundles of personal belongings on their backs. At the rear another armed guard shut in this sad procession, and lines of soldiers with rifles marched on either side of the files of Indians, making any attempt to escape difficult and dangerous. Thinking that these dejected-looking Indians were criminals or rebels who were on their way to an internment camp, I made enquiries as to what had happened, whereupon a Peruvian friend of mine informed me that these were the volunteers from Ayacucho and that they were on their way to the military barracks where they would be stuck into uniforms and then told that they were soldiers. In front of the procession one man carried a small red and white Peruvian flag, and the people who had come out of their houses to look on, every now and again shouted, 'Vivan los voluntarios de Ayacucho,' and the poor Indians, most of whom could not even understand Spanish, then looked more frightened than ever and huddled together like sheep when a dog worries them. I came to the conclusion that either the word 'voluntario' (volunteer) must have a different meaning in Peru from what it has elsewhere, or else that some of the people there have a very strange sense of humour.

Very justly, the average Indian intensely hates the whites, and none of them have the faintest notion what Peru is—yet, after having been rounded up, and by force brought down from their mountain homes, these peaceful and industrious men are expected to defend their 'patria,' a thing the better class and rich white 'patriotas,' excepting those who are officers, would scorn to do. It is a well-known fact, and I have it from good authority, that these sturdy mountaineers do not resist the hot climate of the lowland, and malaria, tuberculosis and other dread diseases claim many victims among them.

I am certain that the horses enjoyed their stay in Huancayo as much as I did, and I was sorry when I had to take them out of their alfalfa field. It would not take us long now to cross the last mountain range.

Recent landslides again forced me to make a large detour, but luckily a fair trail led towards Tarma, a charming little town in a beautiful fertile valley where the climate is one of eternal spring. A very good road connects Tarma with Oroya where the Cerro de Pasco Mining Corporation has its smelting plant. I followed this winding road for a few miles, and then took a short cut over a mountain to save time and distance.

The mining corporation has a very good hotel in Oroya, and the officials did everything to make me comfortable. Near the smelter the Americans have even made a golf links, and the 'Inca Club' has an up-to-date clubhouse where every comfort exists, including an excellent dance floor, library, music-rooms, and the inevitable American bowling alleys. Not far from Oroya are the Cerro de Pasco mines, where some of the employees have founded a Masonic lodge, and as the place is some 17,000 feet above sea level they have very appropriately named this lodge 'The Roof of the World.'

I visited the smelters, and next day continued over the mountains to another American-operated mine, where I was again treated with great kindness. The following day we crossed over the Ticlio, the highest point we reached in the third Andean range, some 16,500 feet above the sea. The highest railroad in the world passes near to this peak. I was happy and proud when we came to the top of the last climb, for from there on travelling would all be on a steep down grade until we reached Lima, the capital of Peru. Owing to the atmospheric pressure we had to march very cautiously, for the slightest effort in such altitudes exhausts one, although if one happens to go downhill it is unnoticeable.

Between two gigantic walls of rock, towering on both sides of us, we stumbled down a steep and rocky trail towards Lima. Up these formidable canyons and over giddy chasms puff the trains and the more I looked at this stretch of the Central Peruvian Railway, the more did I admire this wonderful and daring piece of engineering, an outstanding example of what human brain, energy, and initiative can accomplish.

A most peculiar and yet mysterious disease exists in some parts of the Peruvian mountains. This horrible malady, which is commonly known as 'verruga,' is usually fatal, and manifests itself in great swellings or boils, and opinions as to how it is contracted are divided. Some maintain that certain waters are the cause, others say it is in the air, and some blame insects. I had been told to be particularly careful not to drink water in a certain part of the gulleys on the downward grade towards Lima, but only remembered the warning when both the horses and myself had taken a hearty drink out of a crystal clear pool in the very place I had been warned about however, no harm resulted to any of us.

In two days we were down in the hot plains near the Pacific coast. The sudden change of atmospheric pressure affected my hearing, for my ears were humming and buzzing, and I constantly heard noises like the ringing of bells.

Lima, the Stately Old City of Kings

Having no other change with me, I was still wearing my heavy leather clothes which made me feel the heat doubly. My face was so badly chapped with the cold winds of the high regions that I had not been able to shave for some days, and my appearance was such that even the street urchins on the outskirts of Lima shouted 'bandolero' after me. The three of us were covered with dust, and perspiration fairly dripped off us, so I could hardly blame the guttersnipes.

In the morning I had telephonically advised the Argentine minister that I would arrive in the capital at four p.m., but as I had timed it badly I was in the centre of the town over one hour before time. I dismounted in front of an hotel in the centre of the town, where we had arranged to meet. Soon a small crowd collected around us, and presently a policeman elbowed his way through the bystanders to see what was happening, and when he saw me he stared as if he were looking at the Wild Man of Borneo. When I explained who I was he gave me a broad smile, and kindly offered to look after the horses whilst I went into the hotel to see if anybody had arrived. When I walked into the lobby, the employees' looks were real studies, for they had probably never seen such a rough-looking specimen of humanity before.

I suddenly remembered that I still had my guns on me, and when I saw that nobody was there to greet me I thought it would be entertaining to have a little joke to pass away time. It was obvious that nobody suspected who I was, and so I walked to the room-clerk's desk and asked him for a room with a bath, but instead of answering he rushed away to consult with the manager, and I was not at all surprised when he returned and very apologetically informed me that all the rooms were occupied but that there was a quite good hotel not far from there.

Instead of leaving I returned to the lobby where I sat down and ordered a bottle of beer, and as they could not very well tell me that they had finished their stock, the waiter reluctantly placed a bottle and glass before me and quickly retired to the place where he had stood before, acting something like a performing dog running back to his stool after having gone through his repertoire of tricks.

After some time the Argentine minister, accompanied by a few prominent men and friends, arrived, and when the hotel people saw that they
had come to greet me, they looked as embarrassed as if they had suddenly
lost their trousers. An Argentine sportsman who owned several racehorses
immediately offered me his stables, and soon after Mancha and Gato were
trying to make up for what they had missed in the mountains.

I bought myself some suitable clothes for city wear, and next morning,
after having bathed and shaved, and generally 'dolled up,' I sat down at
my table to have breakfast. My appearance was now so different that the
waiter asked me kindly to move to another table, telling me that the one
I was sitting at was reserved for 'the Argentine rider.'

The Limeños, as the citizens of Lima are called, may rightly be proud
of their historic buildings and old churches which, to me, were the chief
attractions there. Many of them have been rather neglected, which is probably due to the lack of funds, a very common complaint in Latin America.

The cathedral, although not very striking from outside, contains gems
of Spanish colonial art, and ranks among the finest in South America. In
one of the wings, on a special altar, are the remains of Pizarro, the
conqueror of Peru. They are in a glass coffin and in a remarkable state
of preservation, even the wounds inflicted by his assassins being plainly
visible.

Alongside the cathedral stands the bishop's palace, which is of recent
construction, but the style of architecture is based strictly on the colonial type, as also are the wonderfully carved balconies and other
decorations.

One afternoon, as I was walking near the main plaza, an elderly man,
in a spotless white naval uniform, came up to ask me for some information. His appearance was very striking, and with his grey hair and
general bearing, I could not help thinking what a fine Hollywood admiral he would have made. He was the chief steward on an American ship
that was lying at anchor in Callao, and as we approached the big government house the officer on duty called out the guard. As we passed a double
file of 'soldados' stood to attention and saluted what they thought must
be some important foreign guest. The 'admiral' acknowledged the
honour by giving one of those casual salutes that are common with
men who have to do this all day, and when we were past the soldiers he
gave me a meaning wink, and his face wrinkled with the effort to suppress
a hearty laugh.

Lima has its charms, but on the whole I found it to be a 'dead' town, for after nine p.m. there is nothing to do but to loaf or sit in unattractive cafes. Between six and seven o'clock every evening it is fashionable among the better class to dress in their best and then to parade stiffly up and down one of the main streets, but after that there is nothing to do unless one happens to be fond of moving pictures or cockfights. Theatres worth calling such do not exist, and opera houses may have been read about in novels and newspapers. The great attraction of the year is the official bullfight season, and even the poor find money to attend these gory but colourful spectacles, and the rich, or their imitators, buy expensive season tickets for the reserved balconies, just as wealthy people have their private boxes in opera houses in other countries.

I happened to be in Lima when the bullfight season opened, and as I had never seen one of these exhibitions before I did not miss the opportunity to go to some. The first time I went I felt positively ill when I saw the unfortunate horses being gored and ripped open, and when I saw some of them return into the arena after having been stitched up, I felt like blowing up the whole place. I have actually seen horses trip over their own intestines as they were being dragged out to be stitched up, which was done after banana leaves and wet straw had been stuffed into the trembling brutes. After the blood had been washed off them with a few buckets of water they were dragged and clubbed back into the ring, where the bull once more charged into them. One horse was used three times before loss of blood and partial paralysis made it impossible for him to stand, and only then he was given the *coup de grâce*, which was done by stabbing him at the back of the head with a sharp instrument.

Undoubtedly bullfighting is a great art, and a 'matador' requires extraordinary agility, grace, and 'sang froid' to make a name for himself, and if his judgment and knowledge of 'bull psychology' ever fail him, the chances are that he will wake up in hospital, or possibly that he will be the star turn at a funeral.

Betting on cockfights is another favourite 'sport' among men in Lima, where several important cockpits flourish and are crowded every night. Here the birds are trained to fight with a very sharp, half-moon-shaped blade which is fixed to their left legs, the blades being held in place by means of tape wound around the cocks' legs. Betting is very lively and keen, and the dividends are paid on a totalising system.

An indoor tennis court also attracted many. There four Cuban girls played every night whilst the spectators made their bets by means of a clever system of placing their money on games or sets.

The race track is another favourite place for Lima's crowd of gamblers, and every Sunday thousands of voices are strained as the swift thoroughbreds dash towards the winning-post. When the meeting is over one can see the losers returning sadly to town on foot, whilst the smiling winners laugh and make merry in taxis.

Lima is situated at some distance from the coast, but about half an hour's run by car takes one to Callao, Peru's principal seaport. Both these towns have a considerable Chinese population and, as in most coastal places in the country, Chinese merchants make it difficult for others to compete against their extraordinary thriftiness. I happened to make the acquaintance of an American gentleman who had spent some years in China, and as he spoke the language fluently he took me through the Chinese quarters, where he had many friends. We visited a Chinese theatre, but as their show only consisted of two gloriously dressed men who squatted on the stage, making noises like babies who have swallowed tin-tacks, I was not keen on staying long. Obviously their conception of art is beyond the range of my understanding. It must take a foreigner as long to appreciate their art as it does to learn their difficult language, and after all life is short. We visited a restaurant, and I must say that Chinese food was a revelation to me, for not only were their kitchens exceptionally clean, but the dishes were as good as any I had ever tasted.

Chinamen, Japanese, gringos, and other foreigners are allowed to enter the strictly illegal, but officially sanctioned, opium dens, and as I was keen on seeing what these places were like my American friend took me to one. We walked along a busy street, and when we came to a door that was wide open my friend halted. A screen was placed behind the door and thus one could not see the interior of the place from the outside. My friend entered into the semi-dark room and I followed him. Along the walls some two feet above the floor, were boards, like broad shelves, but with a slight slope upward towards the walls. These shelf-like boards served as couches and were covered with carpets, while cushions were placed here and there so that the customers could rest their heads on them. A few Chinamen were lying there, mostly in couples, smoking and chatting in low tones, whilst an attendant at their feet rolled the opium pills for them.

My friend was obviously known in the place, for an oily-looking Chinaman, probably the boss, came shuffling up and greeted us with a foxy smile and rubbing his hands, whilst he bowed as if we were Eastern potentates. We lay down on the boards, and an attendant came with the various instruments necessary for smoking opium. On a small silver tray he had a lamp, covered with a thing that looked like a big drinking-glass upside down and with a hole at the bottom. In a saucer resembling a diminutive ash-tray there was something like very dark molasses, and to my surprise I was told that this was the opium. On the tray I also noticed an instrument like a crochet needle without a hook. The pipe was about two feet in length and elaborately carved and inlaid with gold, silver and ivory, but when I looked for the opening where I had thought powdered opium would be stuffed in, like tobacco into an ordinary pipe, I found that there was only a very small hole, about the size of a pin's head. Being puzzled, but not wishing to show that I was a novice, I waited for things to develop, in order to learn by experience rather than by asking foolish and, to these people, childish questions. Once the attendant had settled down at our feet he heated the point of the needle over the lamp, and when it was hot enough he dipped it into the semi-liquid opium in the little saucer. A certain amount stuck to the needle, and then he held it over the flame again until it boiled and bubbled like sealing-wax. Again and again he dipped the needle into the liquid and held it over the flame until sufficient opium had collected at the point to roll a small pill. When this was done the servant placed it on the small opening on the pipe and pushed the needle through to make a small hole through the pill, and then the pipe was ready for smoking. My friend, who was an expert, held it over the flame, and when the pill began to melt and smoke he inhaled the musty-smelling fumes, and without stopping he smoked until all the opium was burnt. Once more the attendant rolled a pill, and then it was my turn, but as I was a novice I did not know how to smoke evenly, and in consequence the opening of the pipe clotted up several times and the attendant had to help with the needle. The taste was so repulsive to me that I only took a few puffs, and then left my friend and the attendant to finish all the opium we had bought, and whilst the couple smoked and chatted away in Chinese I had a good look around the place. Strange Chinese lottery tickets were being sold, and as I was curious to see what they were like I bought one. Instead of the usual numbers there are series of words printed on them and the buyer has to choose some, which are marked with Chinese ink by the seller. The price of these tickets varies according to the number of words one picks, and in the same way the prizes are paid to the gamblers who have picked most words and have them all correct according to the drawing.

When my friend was ready we returned home. I awoke next morning feeling none too well, and could still taste the opium. My stomach was badly out of order, and it took me two days to recover. I was sorry I had not been able to smoke more, for I wanted to know what effect opium intoxication would have on me, and I wondered if all the stories about those marvellous dreams were true. My acquaintance assured me that all the opium dreams we read about are inventions of novelists, and that he had never known an opium smoker who had been affected that way.

Determined to find out for myself, even if I made myself sick again, I asked my friend to take me to another opium den in the Chinese quarters. This was a much more refined place than the other, and as we passed some curtained-off departments or niches, I caught glimpses of several white men and women who were smoking inside. The few private compartments all being occupied, we went into the main room where several groups of Chinamen were smoking and chatting in low tones, which is a peculiarity of all who are under the influence of the drug. I had smoked for a long time, but still I felt no effects whatsoever. I began to doubt that I was smoking real opium and, wishing to light a cigarette for a change, I rose to go across to the other side of the room where my jacket was hanging, but when I tried to walk I at once realised that I was badly intoxicated. My head was as clear as it had been before I entered the place, and my brain was very active, but yet I found it difficult to keep my balance. Somehow my body seemed to belong to another being that came staggering behind me; the sensation was disconcerting and yet almost comical. Feeling very dry and thirsty, I asked for a cup of tea, and when I had finished it I made ready to leave for the hotel, but the owner of the place was quite alarmed and tried his best to make me sleep there, for he said that I had smoked so much that I would never be able to get home. In spite of his advice I was determined to go. My walk back to the hotel was extraordinary, for my head seemed to be going in front whilst the numbed and intoxicated body came floating behind, bumping against walls and corners. I was expecting to have some of those marvellous dreams, but instead I slept heavily, and when I woke up the musty and repulsive taste of opium was still in my mouth, and the smell of my clothes was so obnoxious that I had to change them. Although I had several opportunities to smoke opium since that day, nothing could induce me to try again; my curiosity has been satisfied.

Wandering around the city I had often passed a strange monument standing in one of the city parks, and in spite of racking my brain to find out what might be the symbolic meaning of an empty chair on a square granite block, I remained puzzled and mystified until an acquaintance told me that the effigy of a former Peruvian president had once occupied this chair, but, as the man had many enemies, some students one day placed a cartridge of dynamite between the image of the most excellent gentleman and the chair, and the immediate result was that the bronze statesman was blown heavenwards, which was to serve future presidential candidates as a fair warning that they may be blown the other way before their turn comes to be perpetuated in solid bronze.

Besides seeing the sights in and around Lima I was busy gathering as much information about the next stage of the trip as possible, no easy matter when but very few natives know their own country and maps do not exist. To this day the best charts of Peru are still the ones made by Raimondi, an Italian scientist who lived two generations ago. Even among people who hold high official positions one finds this sad lack of geographical knowledge.

I had let the horses' manes grow long, to protect their necks and heads against the fierce sun, and their tails also, to fight off the different pests that tantalise horses in the tropics. When my animals were more or less acdimatised to the heat, and I had changed my equipment to suit conditions along the coast, I made final preparations to leave Lima, after having enjoyed a most pleasant stay.

The Sandy Deserts of the Peruvian Coast

The first day's ride was to take me to Ancon, some twenty-odd miles. Knowing that I would find no fodder there I had sent a bale of hay ahead by train, for a railway connects this little bathing resort with the capital. About half way I was stopped by a soldier of the 'guardia civil' who demanded to see my licence for firearms, a document I did not possess. He very politely asked me to accompany him to the local headquarters where I explained to the 'capitan' who I was, and this gentleman issued me a permit in order to prevent my being held up again.

This little incident proved to be a blessing in disguise, for the officer informed me that a river I had to cross a little further ahead was high and therefore dangerous, and the capitan kindly sent a soldier with me to show the best place to cross. I never minded swimming rivers, but when I had to do this right alongside railway bridges that are impossible to cross with horses, I was none too pleased. If it was possible to swim the horses near the bridge I usually unsaddled the animals and carried everything over on foot, walking on the sleepers, and thus saving myself the trouble of having to wrap everything up in a waterproof sheet.

A few miles before we reached Ancon we entered the first sandy desert. Near here the last battle between Chili and Peru was fought, and the dead were buried in this stretch of desert where they fell. In time the winds shifted the sand, exposing a mass of skulls and bones. What a resting place for those who gave their lives for their country!

It was a good thing that I had sent some hay ahead, for otherwise the horses would have had to pass another night on empty stomachs. Water is very scarce in many places along the Peruvian coast, and even in this fashionable bathing resort it is sold at 10 centavos a tin.

From Ancon north, practically to the border of Ecuador, I had planned to follow the coast. Rains are almost unknown in these regions, in fact, there are parts where people have never seen rain fall. A few towns and villages stand on the rivers that run down from the Andes and cross the dry coast to the sea, and when these rivers are high they are very wild and dangerous. Some of the valleys are watered by small irrigation canals, and where such irrigation exists, fine crops of sugar-cane, cotton, and rice are grown. Between the distant rivers are the vast, sandy deserts where nothing grows and where the sand dunes rise one after another, like huge ocean billows. In such places the heat is terrific and there is absolutely no water. The ancient Mochica Indians, later the Chimus, and then the Incas, had irrigated many of the regions which are now empty deserts, and I saw the ruins of their towns, forts, canals, and burial grounds, which tell the sad story of the white man's invasion.

Contrary to the practice of most travellers in dry regions, I carried no water. For my own use I had a flask of brandy, and another filled with lemon juice mixed with a little salt. This concoction was very stimulating but tasted so bad that I was never tempted to drink much at a time. The juice of canned fresh tomatoes is probably the best thirst quencher, but then this article is rarely found when it is needed. As for the horses, I calculated that the energy wasted by them in carrying water would be greater than the actual benefit derived from drinking it, so they only drank when we came to a river or some village. I believe my theory was sound; with a light load we gained in speed, and avoided the horses getting sore, for water is the most uncomfortable and clumsy load a pack animal can carry. Only on rare occasions did the animals seem to suffer from excessive thirst.

After leaving Ancon we travelled over high sand dunes, and at eventide, in a fertile plain, we arrived at a big 'hacienda' belonging to a Chinaman, whose hospitality I shall never forget. The next day's trip being a long one we started long before daybreak. When I saddled up I thought my saddle-bags were rather heavier than usual, and later I found out that my kind host had filled them with all sorts of good things during the night.

The first rays of dawn found us among sand dunes where the horses sank deep into the soft sand that had been blown about by the wind until it appeared like ripples on a lake. The imposing silence was broken only by the rolling of the waves that sounded like the snoring of some sleeping giant. The wind almost immediately covered our tracks, and soon the terrible heat rose in waves, making breathing uncomfortable. In some places I could follow the coast, riding along the wet sand, where I made the horses go at a fast trot or even at a slow gallop, for I knew that this would be impossible once the sun rose higher; and time was precious. Sometimes a wave, bigger than the average, would wash higher up the beach, and the moving foam would frighten the horses. The vastness of the ocean, and the regular roaring of the waves on the seemingly endless and glittering beach, and the rolling sand dunes, gave the impression of eternity. Thousands of sea birds hovered silently over our heads, and crabs of all sizes went running with amazing swiftness towards their holes in the sand as we approached. Their manner of walking sideways was almost comical, and often, whilst I gave the horses a few minutes to breathe, I amused myself trying to catch some of them. Once or twice I threw a dead one as far as I could, then watched the others come to devour it; the fights that ensued were fierce and terrible, and I could not help comparing these fighting crabs with human beings. The wet sand was white with sea-gulls waiting for the waves to wash up something to eat. The birds would only rise when we had almost reached them, flying a small circle around us, invariably towards sea, where the wind came from, and again settle behind us. Thousands of guanos (a kind of sea bird) were flying in regular clouds, dashing and splashing into the water after fish, for all the world resembling aeroplanes in the moment of crashing; and every now and again a curious seal would come to the surface and look at us as if wondering what we were doing there. The hot and very bright sunlight reflected off the wet sand and the waves, and the snow-white gulls circling silently around us made my eyes smart, obliging me to wear the green goggles I had used in the mountains. Journeys through such deserts are trying in the extreme. At first the body suffers, then everything physical becomes abstract. Later on the brain becomes dull and the thoughts mixed; one becomes indifferent about things, and then everything seems like a moving picture or a strange dream, and only the will to arrive and to keep awake is left. All thinking ceases, and when one finally arrives and falls to sleep, even the will temporarily leaves the body.

Dante's Inferno is a creation of stupendous imagination, but the Peruvian deserts are real; very real.

In most of the coastal villages I slept in the police stations, when there were any, and the horses spent the nights in the prison yards, which are surrounded by high adobe walls. Hardly any of these settlements have hotels or inns, and if there happened to be a hut masquerading under the name, it usually lacked a safe place where I could keep the horses. If I was lucky enough to find the prison empty, the 'jefe de policia' gave me the keys to the place. Thus I could lock up my things and then go to see if there was any fodder to be found, and whilst I took the animals to water, often at some distance from the place, my belongings were relatively safe. Once the animals had been attended to, frequently a difficult and heartbreaking job, I was free to go searching for food for myself. Restaurants have not even been heard of in many of these villages, so I had to enquire for any house or hut where they are accustomed to sell food to strangers, and when I finally found the place the food was invariably the same; the standard menu of the Peruvian coast being boiled rice, beans, fried bananas, fried eggs, and black coffee. Often I considered myself lucky when I found even that.

In one of the small coastal towns a Spaniard introduced himself to me. He looked a pleasant sort of fellow, and told me he had lived quite a number of years in the Argentine. In the evening we chatted for some time, and during the course of conversation he said that no man's education was complete unless he had seen one of the low 'dance-halls' that exist in some of the small towns along the Peruvian coast, and when I expressed my willingness to see and learn he offered to act as guide. Soon we were on our way towards the place that was situated about a mile out of the little town. The 'dance-hall' was merely a large adobe hut, and the interior was lit by two oil lamps. Along the walls were rough benches on which some dirty, ragged and bare-footed men sat, whilst others were standing in front of a counter made of old packing-cases where alcohol was being despatched. The boss of the place was a fat and greasy mestizo woman with strands of black hair hanging over her face, hair that was coarse and wiry like a horse's mane. Several equally repulsive females were acting as 'dancing-partners' to any man who wished to pay ten cents for the pleasure of having one of them. I have seen some villainous faces in some of the 'western hair-raisers,' but since I have been in that dance hall it is obvious to me that the producers of these films have not been 'educated,' as my Spanish guide would say. The type of villain we usually see in the 'movies' are mere cherubims compared to the men I saw that night. The majority were mestizos, or what I would like to call 'criss-cross breeds' between Indian, Spanish, Chinese and negro blood. One specimen was black, pock-marked, had Chinese slit eyes, and curly hair with a red tint!

Somehow our presence did not seem to please, and particularly one fellow kept casting nasty glances towards us, glances that said more than words could have done. When my companion became aware of it he took offence, and soon the inevitable happened; both jumping at each other like tigers. Some intervened and the two were separated, and then somebody suggested going outside to fight it out. The Spaniard took off his coat and handed it to me, and when we were outside the two started at each other.

Owing to the darkness it was impossible to see what was happening, but after some quick shuffling, wrestling, fierce growling and many terrible oaths there was a piercing shriek, and then all was silence, a silence that was only broken by the heavy breathing of the two exhausted fighters. Presently I heard moans, and then somebody struck a match. The Spaniard was standing over his opponent who was on the ground, and upon striking another match we noticed that the man who lay writhing on the ground had been stabbed in two places.

Only now did I begin to realise the seriousness of my situation, for here was I all alone with the Spaniard, who after all was only a chance acquaintance, and the others were many, and for all I knew they might try to avenge their badly-wounded friend, who was now moaning and rolling over on the ground. Whenever I was in a town or in a more or less decent village I never carried my firearms, for they were heavy, and the sight of them might offend people. On this occasion I had come out unarmed, and fearing the worst I thought I would try to get out of this ticklish situation by bluffing. I jumped on a low adobe wall that fenced off a field and shouted that if anybody moved I would shoot. Obviously somebody had long ago advised the police that there was trouble, for soon several terribly excited 'vigilantes' arrived on the scene, waving their arms, rifles and swords like actors in a stage version of the storming of the Bastille. One who had come with a lantern led the procession back towards the town, a few helping to carry the wounded man, who was evidently in a serious condition. Once at the police station the 'jefe' (chief) and a doctor were called, and everybody, excepting the Spaniard and myself were thrown into the filthy 'calabozo.' The jefe's language was most apologetic for what had happened to me, and the Spaniard, being a good friend of his, was told to embark on a sailing vessel that was to leave the little port next morning, for in case the wounded man should die it would be just as well if the guilty party could officially be announced as having escaped. When I saw the last of that little town, I promised myself never again to visit a 'dance-hall' in Peru, and I did not find it difficult to keep that promise!

Still following the hot, sandy coast, we came to a large sugar plantation, not far from which stands a fortress that was built by the ancient Chimu Indians. It is a colossal piece of work, entirely made of adobe and built in high terraces that appear like a square hill from the distance. Near the main fortress are high walls, and the way everything was built leaves no doubt that these ancients had a certain scientific knowledge of warfare. Some of the paint with which the walls were coloured still remains, neither weather nor centuries having been able to make it fade or to destroy it. The colours that exist are red, black and yellow, the same as are found on pottery that dates back to the Chimu period.

The fortress of Paramonga consists of two main strongholds. One of these is situated on a hill, the waves of the Pacific Ocean beating against its inaccessible cliffs which face west. The eastern side of that hill has a steep and sandy slope where numerous mummies, wrapped in coloured cloths, were buried and have now become uncovered by the shifting and sliding sands. The main fortress is roughly half a mile east from there, and the two were probably separated by a swamp in former times, but to-day the low flat stretch of land between the two is dry, and sugar-cane is successfully cultivated by a Japanese settler who entertained me splendidly when I happened to call at his place during my rambles among the ruins. Although subterranean passages and burial places exist here, the natives are afraid to explore them, for many strange tales and superstitions have been handed down from one generation to another. As I had not time enough, I could not do more than have a general look over these interesting relics of the past.

From Paramonga north there is a vast desert, close on a hundred miles from one river to the next, and as there is no water to be found there I was obliged to make the crossing in one journey. For this reason I had to wait for the full moon before I could, with a certain degree of safety, attempt this long ride.

There was an outbreak of bubonic plague whilst I was there, and quite a number of plantation workers died, whilst many more were ill. The authorities raided their filthy quarters, and it was a pathetic yet amusing sight to see their owners howling and wailing as they walked behind their filthy belongings which were being carted out to be burnt, together with some ancient mummies that had been discovered near there in an old burial ground. I took every precaution against the horrible disease and was particularly careful never to lie down to rest unless I had previously sprinkled my bed with insect powder, for fleas and similar pests transmit the germs of bubonic plague. It was uncomfortable to have to remain in this place with the danger of catching the plague, but I was between the devil and the deep blue sea; for before attempting to cross the desert ahead of us I had to be careful to make my plans, and as I intended to start in the evening it was necessary to wait until the moon was at its brightest. I had heard many terrible stories about this sandy wilderness, its very name, 'Matacaballo' (Horse-killer), gave me food for reflection.

After four days' waiting I was ready to start, and as I did not intend to carry water for the horses, I was careful not to give them anything to drink the day before we left, for I wanted them to be thirsty and therefore not likely to refuse a good drink immediately before starting out. For myself I packed two bottles of lemon juice in the saddle-bags, and the only food I took with me were a few pieces of chocolate that had been in my pack for some days. Towards evening we were ready, and when the sun was setting we crossed the river, on the other side of which the rolling desert starts. I waited until the horses had finished their drink, and after they had pawed and played with the cool water I mounted, and soon we were on the soft and still hot sands that made a peculiar hissing sound under the hoofs of the animals. The indescribable colours of a tropical sunset were reflected on the glittering waves of the ocean, and the old Indian fortress assumed a tint of gold. Even the inhospitable sandy wastes had changed their dread and desolate appearance, for now the sand dunes and undulations were one mass of colour, from golden brown to dark purple, according to light and shadows. A few belated sea-birds were hurriedly flying towards their distant roosting-places on some rocky island; everything seemed to be different now, except the regular, eternal rolling of the breakers on the shore. No sooner had the last clouds ceased to glow like fading beacon fires than darkness set in, and after a while the moon rose over the mountain ranges in the far east, slowly, majestically; and more than welcome to me.

The sensation of riding on soft sand is a peculiar one at first, until the body becomes used to the peculiar springless motion of the horse. Knowing that such conditions mean a great strain on the animal I could not help moving in the saddle, uselessly endeavouring to assist my mount. We were twisting and winding our way through among high sand dunes and, whenever it was possible, I guided the animals down to the wet sand on the beach where I would urge them into a slow gallop. Often we came to rocky places or to land-points which stretched far out, and thus I was forced to make a detour inland again, frequently for considerable distances. For the first few hours I observed everything around me and admired the brilliance of the moon that made the ocean glitter like silver, and gave the often strange sand formations a ghostly appearance. Soon even all this became monotonous to me, and every time I stopped to rest the horses for a while or to adjust the saddles, I lit a cigarette to help pass the time away. Shortly before dawn I had to halt for quite a long time, for the moon had gone down behind some clouds and we were left in darkness; it would not have been wise to continue lest I should take the wrong direction or lead the horses into places where the sand is so soft that they would sink in up to their bellies.

My instinct for finding the direction had developed to a notable degree by this time, probably because I had not very much to think about besides keeping the horses' noses facing the right way, but even when I knew exactly which way to go, fogs or darkness on several occasions made me think it wiser to wait until I could see. The first rays of the morning sun were hot, and I rightly anticipated that the day was going to be a 'scorcher.' The horses plodded along as if they realised that they were in the midst of a serious test, and when it was about one hour after noon I noticed that they lifted their heads and sniffed the air. Immediately after they hurried their steps, and I believe they would have broken into a gallop if I had permitted them to do so. I was wondering why the horses were so keen to hurry along, and within an hour I knew the reason, for we arrived at the river, and I am certain that the animals had scented water long before I could see it; obviously Mancha and Gato still possessed the instincts of the wild horse.

Great were my feelings of relief when we left the Matacaballo desert behind us and, in spite of my already high opinion of the horses' resistance, I admired the splendid behaviour they had shown during so long and trying a journey—a journey that would have killed most horses unaccustomed to such conditions. After I had unsaddled them they had a good drink, and then I gave them a much-needed bath. When this had been done I turned them loose in a small field with good grass, and after both had rolled, stretched and shaken themselves they started to eat, and anybody might have believed they had only just returned from a short canter. I only realised how tired and played out I was when I sat down on my saddles whilst a woman in a hut prepared some food for me, and I thought I had only dozed off to sleep for a few moments when I awoke in the evening. The good woman, knowing that I needed sleep more than food, had kept my meal warm for me, and once I had the first taste of it I did not stop until the last grain of rice and the last bean had disappeared. It had taken us exactly twenty hours to cross the desert, and I have no desire ever to make another such ride.

All the coastal villages are much alike, equally depressing, hot and miserable. A few houses and huts, a couple of uneven and sandy roads, sometimes a tumbledown adobe church, hens and pigs roaming about in search of refuse that is simply thrown out of the houses into the street, and on the roofs a few mournful-looking 'gallinazos' (buzzards) waiting to pick up bits of filth at which other animals refuse even to look. At the doors of some houses, and particularly in front of the 'palacio municipal' (?), a primitive construction that is no better than the rest of the dilapidated houses, men can be seen loitering all day and, although they never seem to work, they always appear to have money enough to buy alcohol, and once they are stimulated by its temporarily elevating effects they talk in such sums of money that even the most powerful Wall Street magnates would prick up their ears. Rich mines, large estates, social reform, etc., are discussed and debated, and once the bottle is empty and the men full, they again fall into silence or shuffle home, happy and satisfied after a good day's work.

Malaria is very common in some of the regions along the rivers, and Indians who come from the mountains to work in the cotton and sugar plantations invariably fall victims to this tropical fever. Once the effects of malaria have rendered them unfit for work, the landowners simply dismiss them, the existing law that is supposed to protect the unfortunate semi-slaves against this crime hardly ever being observed.

Whilst I was riding along in company of a native who was on his way to another village, we had a most unpleasant experience with a snake. On a sandy plain we had dismounted to have a short rest, when suddenly the man shouted to me in a very excited manner. A small snake had crawled under his mule, probably in order to take advantage of the only shady spot within miles. The frightened man said that this was a particularly venomous reptile, and that its bite would without doubt kill his mule. We tried to tease the snake away by throwing pebbles at it, and fortunately the mule was very tame and did not move. However, instead of coming away from under the beast, the snake tried to climb up one of its legs, and I held my breath, expecting the mule to move or stamp, but somehow it did not seem to feel anything. We were lucky to be able to attract the snake away at last, and I immediately killed it with a leather strap I had ready for that purpose.

I had sometimes hired guides to take me through bad and tricky parts, but most of these men were so useless, lazy and impertinent that I much preferred to travel alone, and leave the rest to chance.

We had crossed another long and weary stretch of sandy desolation in which walls and other remains of the old Indians could be seen, and when we arrived at the river it was already dark. I knew that a village was not far from the opposite banks of the river, and as I had eaten nothing all day I was keen on crossing in spite of the prevailing darkness. I rode along the bank until I thought I had found a suitable place to cross, and there I made the horses wade out. I had not expected to find such a strong current and began to wonder if it would not be wiser to turn back, and just then the horse I was riding was swept off his feet. Very foolishly I still had the pack-animal tied to the wide girth of my mount, the usual manner in which lead-horses are taken along in the pampas. Before I had time to think, the three of us were swept downstream, and it was due more to luck than to ability that we landed safely back on the shore from which we had started. Besides having had a longer drink than I had bargained for, I rightly suspected in what a mess I would find the contents of my saddle-bags next day. I had no desire to make a second attempt to cross the river that night, so I resigned myself to fate and prepared to wait for daylight. I let the horses look after themselves among the coarse grass near the river, whilst I went to spread my soaked blankets at the foot of a sandy hill close by, for there it would not be damp, and the sand was still comfortably warm after the day's terrific heat. In spite of my raving appetite and my wringing wet clothes I was soon fast asleep, but during the night I was several times awakened by a strange noise that sounded like the beating of drums, or as if a motor launch were travelling on the river. As I could see nothing I continued to sleep, and only awoke when the sunrays were beginning to be hot. When I looked about, I found that I had slept near a 'gentilar' as the ancient Indian burial-grounds are called. There are many of these along the Peruvian coast and, after seeing a few, one takes hardly any more notice of all the skulls and bones that lie about on the sand, which has shifted with the passing of centuries. The horses must have had a good feed, for they were waiting for me, and when all was ready we crossed the river without much difficulty, and when we arrived in the village I fully made up for arrears in the food line.

While conversing with some people I told them about my nasty experience in the river the night before, and when they heard where I had slept all wanted to know if I had heard the 'manchang.' This word sounding rather like Chinese to me I asked them what it meant, whereupon they all started to explain in chorus that the sand-hill where I had slept was haunted, and that the dead Indians of the 'gentilar' danced every night to the beating of drums. So many terrible superstitious stories did they tell me about the 'manchang' that I began to think I was lucky to be still alive. Later I had occasion to speak to an educated gentleman who had come to visit me, and he said that both Baron von Humboldt and Raimondi had once upon a time investigated the strange phenomenon of that hill, and that they had expressed the opinion that the peculiar sounds that are frequently heard during the night due to underground waters which moved as the temperature changed. Another theory that has been brought forward is that when the sea breezes blow from a certain direction and the air hits the sandy ripples on the slopes of the hill, it will produce this strange sound. Somehow both explanations appealed to me as being sensible, but I feel inclined to think that the former is more likely to be correct.

After all these trying journeys I rested for two days, for there was plenty of grass for the horses, and I, for a change was able to even enjoy a few decent meals again.

One evening I thought I would pass a couple of hours away by going to see some moving pictures which were announced for that night. The 'teatro' was merely a large shed with a tin roof, and the films shown were old and worn out, but yet the audience seemed delighted with the show. All of a sudden everybody made a rush for the door; there were a few shrieks from women, and the whole place shook. Before I had even time to think what was happening the place was empty, only myself and two women who had fainted remaining there. Even then I could not make out what had happened, but when I went outside I was told there had been an earthquake. I had been under the impression that the trampling and rushing crowd had shaken up the place. Luckily nobody was hurt in that stampede for the open, but a few had sustained minor bruises and knocks and the rest had come out of it with only a good fright. No one seeming keen on going back, the management announced the show as having terminated; much to my surprise nobody protested or asked for 'money back.'

Earthquakes are very common occurrences along the Peruvian coast, but as the houses and huts are so lightly built, and the roofs being merely light covers to protect against the fierce sun, it is rarely that much harm is done. As I have mentioned before, rains are practically unknown in these regions, and so the houses are simply covered with bamboo canes, mud and straw.

Fording some of the wide and usually slow-flowing rivers was not without its dangers, treacherous quicksands lurking where one least expects to find them. If anybody happened to live near a river I had to ford, I always offered a good reward if he were willing to show me the best place where to cross, but often I had to try my luck alone.

One evening, after a long day's riding, I came to a solitary hut near the mouth of a river where a fisherman and his family lived. I was very hungry and thirsty, and looked forward to a change of diet, for I had lived on sardines and biscuits for some days. Two children were playing in the sand outside the hut, and as it was always my policy to make friends with the youngsters in order more easily to approach the parents, I thought I would do the same here, and so gave them my last biscuits and the remaining tin of sardines. I thought this was a good investment and a safe gamble to get something more agreeable to my taste from the grateful parents later on, but to my bitter disappointment I was told that they had run out of supplies and that there would be nothing to eat until next morning when the man was going out fishing. I was given some hot water with which I brewed myself some tea, and even this I had to drink without sugar, my supply having come to grief whilst crossing a river. The next journey being a long one I had to start early, and so I had to do another day's hard riding on an empty stomach, and it can easily be imagined how I blessed those children and how pleased I was with myself for having given them that tin of sardines and the biscuits.

After a few hours we came to a river that had a very bad reputation for quicksands, and so I rode up-stream until I came to a hut where another fisherman lived. He was willing to help me across. He had a pony which, he told me, served to drag his net through the shallow water along the beach. Mounted on this animal he came to show me the way, but he only did this after having received five *soles* (Peruvian standard currency) in advance for his services. We had nearly reached the other side of the shallow but wide river when suddenly his pony's hind-legs sank into the sand. Knowing what this meant, I hurried my horses along, made a semi-circle around my guide, and was fortunate enough to reach the dry shore. Without losing a moment I untied the lasso I always had handy, and then cautiously waded back to where the man was still sitting on his animal, which was sinking deeper and deeper. As soon as I had thrown him the lasso he put it around the pony's neck; then he jumped off and came towards me, all the time holding on to the lasso in case he also should sink in. Whenever a horse sinks into a quicksand hind-legs first, it is of no use to try to pull him out from in front, but to save him one has to pull in such a manner as to make him fall on his side. This frees his hind-legs and gives him buoyancy, and then one can usually rescue him. Should the animal be left alone he will gradually sink in and finally drown, and the more he struggles and fights the quicker will he sink. Working like Trojans we finally rescued the guide's pony, and in case the same thing should happen to him again I waited until he had safely reached the home shore.

In riding across such rivers it is advisable to wear spurs and to have something ready to whip the horses with, for if they step into a quicksand and are hurried along, it will often prevent them from getting stuck.

Following the coast, roughly half-way between Lima and the border of Ecuador, we came to Trujillo, one of the biggest towns in Peru. As things go in other countries, this place would merely be called a large village, and a not very attractive one at that. Some of the oldest families in the country live there, and most of them keep up the customs and traditions of their Spanish ancestors.

What the town lacks in interest is fully made up by the ruins of Chan-Chan, which are situated a few miles north of the place. As I have mentioned before, the first civilisation known to have existed in these parts was the one of the Chimus, that at a later period was followed by that of the Mochicas. It is to the latter that Chan-Chan is attributed. The Mochica empire extended for some 450 miles along the coast, and Chan-Chan was its capital, estimated to have had between 80,000 and 120,000 inhabitants. Being a keen dabbler in South American archæology, I did not miss the opportunity to visit these remarkable and interesting ruins, but as they spread over a vast area I was unable to study them as thoroughly as I should have liked.

Many of the high adobe walls still remain intact, and what is left of the houses, squares and palaces gives the visitor a fair idea of what the place must have been like centuries ago. To-day all is dry and sandy, but in the olden times all this area was irrigated, the water having been conducted there by wonderful canals, some of which are believed to have been underground. Several vast, deep, stone-lined reservoirs can still be seen, and one place suggests that it might have been an artificial lake. In the neighbourhood there are several high hills which were entirely made by man, and are presumably graves of ancient rulers or nobles. Not only near Chan-Chan, but whilst on my way north from there did I see some of these cyclopean constructions.

History tells us that a fabulously rich treasure was found in one of these 'huacas,' as these adobe hills are called. This happened in the time of Toledo, the fifth viceroy of Peru. Garcia Toledo, a relative of the viceroy, heard rumours about two enormous quantities of treasure that were hidden near Chan-Chan. One of these was known as the 'pejo grande' (big pejo) and the other as the 'pejo chico' (small pejo). An Indian by the name of Chayhuah knew the place and the entrance to the 'pejo chico,' but refused to reveal his secret, for the Indians honour their dead and respect the things that are buried with them. After every method of persuasion had failed to get the secret out of Chayhuah, he finally agreed to show Garcia Toledo the place, but only after the latter had solemnly sworn that nothing would be taken out and that the secret would never be told to anybody else. However, once the greedy Spaniard had seen the mass of precious ore and stones with which the grave was filled he forgot his promise, for according to ancient documents 'five million ounces in gold and silver' were paid to the king of Spain in fifth, a proportion the Crown demanded in those days. The hill where this treasure was found has caved in at the top, which today resembles the crater of a volcano, for many have been the treasure hunters who have dug there, all hoping to find the 'pejo grande.'

Earthenware pottery and vases of the painted, sculptural type are frequently found among these ruins and in graves in this region. Most of the 'huacos,' as these pots are called, represent animals, different fruits, or human beings. They are painted in two or three different colours, and some make noises when they are being filled with water. For instance, a pot that represents a parrot will screech, a snake hisses, and an owl hoots. I saw a remarkable piece that represented the head of a woman, and when it was filled with water it made a moaning sound and tears rolled out of the eyes.

Although a special law prohibits the excavation of ancient relics many people make a side income by searching among old graves. On Good Friday I noticed an unusually large number of men digging, and I was told that the belief exists among them that this day is particularly lucky, and that many, who ordinarily never search for antiques, dedicate all Good Friday to treasure hunting. In Peru such people are known as 'huaqueros,' and it appears that many have been lucky, but unfortunately their finds are usually lost as far as scientific collections and museums are concerned, and the government would do well to make stricter laws and regulations to protect the country's unique wealth in archæology.

Not only in Peru, but also in other Latin American republics, a newcomer cannot help but be amazed at the super-abundant crop of 'doctores' and 'generales' who seem to grow wild in these fertile lands of milk and honey, whereas in other countries these relatively rare plants have to be carefully cultivated and scientifically helped during their period of growth and formation. One of the members of a foreign military mission, which was reorganising the army of a certain southern republic, told me that the greatest difficulty they had bumped up against was to get rid of some 600 generals, but even then that is not so much when it is considered that one flourishing Latin American republic that has an army of 10,000 men has no fewer than 1,145 generals, which is not at all a bad percentage when compared with some of the better known armies of the world. Yes, dear reader, at last you hear of armies where Napoleon's remark that every soldier carries the field-marshal's baton in his kit is true.

Even in the smallest village the civil (usually uncivil) 'autoridad' never fails to make his weight and importance known, and his word is the alpha and the omega of right and justice. I am told that the legal codes are perfect, and I am given to understand that all 'abogados' (lawyers), who are even more abundant than the generals, have a collection of books containing the laws of their respective countries. But even during my short sojourn in some of these republics I had ample opportunity to see that the word of a village or town mayor, or chief of police, carries more weight than all the legal codes, judges and 'abogados' combined, and furthermore I came across quite a number of men holding high political positions who could neither read nor write.

After the day's heat, I wandered to the main plaza of Trujillo one evening, and as a pleasant breeze was blowing I sat down on a bench that happened to be unoccupied. I was just lighting a cigarette when a policeman came running towards me. He was very excited, for the few hairs of his drooping Chinese moustache were fairly quivering, and even his dark half-caste complexion showed red under the dirt and grease. Rattling a curved sword which once upon a time must have been the property of an operetta company, and showing an imperfect row of yellow fangs, he ordered me to leave the bench, for this, he thundered, was permanently reserved for the 'prefecto' (mayor). Without being aware of it, I had committed a hitherto unheard-of crime in the good town of Trujillo, and so, having offered my sincerest apologies to the 'vigilante,' I began to wander round the plaza once more, whilst people eyed me like horrified children watching a sword-swallower perform his trick.

In small towns and villages it is not safe to walk anywhere but in the middle of the street in the early morning, for that is the unofficial time when all the filth that has collected during the night is thrown out of the windows. Luckily Mother Nature has provided the 'gallinazos' (buzzards), which do the work of street-cleaners and sanitary police, and it is inconceivable what would happen if these birds suddenly ceased to exist; furthermore, their usefulness is officially recognised, a law existing to protect them.

Continuing our difficult journey through hot sandy wastes, we entered the fertile Chicama valley where a German company cultivates sugar-cane, cotton, etc. This is probably the best that Peru can show in agricultural enterprise, and I appreciated sleeping in decent quarters once more, eating good food and tasting a bottle of cold imported beer. As in the regions of Lake Titicaca, I was on several occasions taken for a Chilian spy along the coast of Peru, and once or twice things looked distinctly ugly for me. What on earth a spy might be looking for in these God-forsaken places, I do not know, but when one considers the ignorance of the people there, one must be surprised at nothing.

The river Santa was the one that gave me most trouble. At the time it was in full flood, and the people thought it would be impossible to swim the horses across the wide, swift river. However, I knew the animals could perform the feat, and as I had no intention of waiting for an indefinite period for it to go down I decided to make the attempt. Natives strongly advised me not to be foolish, for they warned me that the river was very tricky and that if I missed a certain place there was no other chance to land the horses and they would be carried down to the sea.

I heard so many terrible things about the Rio Santa that I went to have a look at it. About half an hour's ride through a veritable jungle, flooded by the waters of the river, brought me to my destination.

I must admit that I did not like the look of things, for not only was the other bank far away, but the mass of water came down with a roar, boiling, seething and tumbling, carrying with it branches and trees, besides which, as some friends who accompanied me explained, there were several rocks just below the surface, and if a horse swam over any of them he would be ripped to pieces. In places where two currents met there were large whirlpools, and it did not take me long to realise that it would be very dangerous to make the attempt unless one happened to be thoroughly acquainted with every detail of the river.

In normal times cattle are swum across by 'chimbadores,' who thus earn their living, but when the waters are high nobody ever tries. When we had discussed the question my friends went to look for the best of these men, to ask his opinion. After a long wait he arrived, and having carefully studied the river said that he had his doubts about any animal reaching the other bank, as there was only one possible landing-place, and if this was not reached the horses would be lost. I had been in some bad rivers before, and on every occasion my animals behaved admirably, so I did not hesitate to assure him that they were capable of performing the feat. Finally we arranged to meet next morning and to make the attempt.

The news spread like wildfire among the natives, and next morning a large number of curious people arrived to see the show, some on horses or mules, others on foot. When we reached the proposed scene of action some were already there waiting for us, and even on the rocks on the opposite bank others had taken position.

People cross some of these rivers in a basket slung on a cable, and the one across this river is the longest I have seen, ending on a high rock on the other bank. I unsaddled, and the things were taken across by means of the cable. When I thought everything was ready one of the local authorities, who had been very friendly with me, came up and bluntly told me he would not allow me to enter the river, for such a thing amounted to rank suicide, especially as I did not know the tricks and dangers of these wild waters.

I could already see myself returning a beaten man and waiting for days, or maybe even weeks, before being able to reach that other bank, and just then I saw the 'chimbador' standing near. I offered him a good sum of money if he would swim my animals across, and to this nobody had any objection, for these men are wonderful swimmers and know every inch and trick of the river. At first he refused to consider my offer, but when I agreed that he could leave the horses if he saw that they could not reach the only landing-place and save himself he promised to try.

For a long time he studied the seething river, and sent a few men to different points upstream to signal should branches or trees come floating down. I advised him to mount on Mancha and to leave Gato to follow behind loose. The former would never let anyone but myself ride him on dry land without bucking, so we coaxed him into the water where the man mounted without trouble, and as soon as the 'all clear' signal was given they started to wade out, and in a few moments the current swept the three downstream, Gato following close behind his companion.

The people on the bank had made bets as to whether or not the horses would cross, and I must admit I passed minutes that seemed hours, until at long last there was a loud cheer from many throats and both animals waded out on the other side nearly half a mile downstream. The Rio Santa had been conquered in full flood.

I crossed by the cable and continued the journey, but my adventures for the day were not yet over, for on reaching an 'hacienda' where I intended to pass the night I found the 'peones' (workers) in an uproar. Indians and mestizos were gesticulating in groups, and I heard that one had attempted to kill another. There being no doctor within miles I was asked if I could do anything for the wounded man. I found him lying in a hut, fairly soaked in blood. He was obviously wounded deeply, and his lungs were damaged, for he was coughing up blood. I washed the wound, and as there was some laudanum in the medicine chest I gave him a solution of this to drink. The man who had attacked him was in a small hut that served as prison, and when I went to have a look at him I found him with both legs fixed in strong wooden stocks. He was an Indian, and with his long hair and savage looks was anything but attractive.

During the night my host came to call me, saying that the prisoner was attempting to escape. I hurriedly dressed, took my electric torch and a revolver, and went to see what was happening. When I approached the prison door a stone hit me in the chest, whereupon I made ready for rough work. Playing my torch into the hut I saw the Indian with a dagger in his hand, and it was easy to see that he had dug around one of the posts that held down the stocks. The man was roaring like a wild beast, and it was obvious that he was ready to make a fight for freedom. The only thing to do was to disarm him and then make him safe for the night. Accordingly I picked up a board, and holding it in front of myself rushed at the man and kicked him so as to make him lie down, but he managed to injure my right hand slightly. As soon as he was down Indian men and women rushed at him, some kicking him, whilst others tore his hair. To make him safe he was taken out of the stocks and bound with a rope. I could hear him moaning and complaining, and when I came out in the morning he was still lying in the courtyard surrounded by Indians who had kept an eye on him throughout the night. He was still in the same position as when I had last seen him, and when I requested his guard to loosen the ropes a little they told me he was no longer bound. When I examined the man I could not help feeling sorry for him, for the ropes had cut in deep and he was bleeding in several places. His eyes were bloodshot and he was more dead than alive, the only sign of life he gave being a faint moan every now and again.

I was glad when I was on my way again, and often wondered later what happened to both the assailant and the victim; I do not think I shall ever forget the Rio Santa.

Religious processions are often held and I shall always remember the one I saw in one small village. Long files of miserably-dressed people came slowly along the uneven and dusty road. Every person held a candle, the light of which cast strange shadows on the faces. In front several men carried a bed on which lay a figure representing Christ. Never have I seen anything so horrible; for the sheets had been splashed all over with red paint, or the blood of some animal, and the face of the figure was also smeared in the same way. Every now and again the procession stopped, and a band of four musicians played a mournful tune to which a man sang in a loud, wailing voice.

I know nothing more uncomfortable than arriving in one of these villages after a long journey, covered with dust and sand and dripping with perspiration. There is no chance of having a bath nor of changing clothes, and then one has the prospects of sleeping on the floor of some hut or police station with all the imaginable and unimaginable insects worrying one throughout the night.

In some of the dungeons I have seen conditions that defy the pen, and when later I was given the privilege of visiting modern American prisons I could not help remembering the unfortunate beings who positively rot away in certain South American 'calabozos.' The prison yard usually made a safe corral for my horses, and very often I slept in the place in order to be near them. Thus I had the opportunity of speaking with many prisoners to pass away the time, and many are the stories I heard from them.

Prisoners are supposed to receive ten cents per day, but as often as not the 'comisario' keeps this. For food they depend entirely on their friends or families, and every day one or two convicts leave the prison with an armed guard to go begging for food for those who have nobody to feed them. More than once I have seen the soldiers who loaf around the prison go through the bucket to see if there was anything special in it, and pick out the morsels that most appealed to them, sending the rest in to the hungry prisoners.

A law called 'ley vial' was passed, forcing every man to work for one or two weeks per year without remuneration, chiefly at road building. In spite of the necessity, I could not help considering this law exceedingly hard on the poor class, especially on Indians, and an offence to personal freedom.

In some villages there seem to be more Chinese than whites, and the majority are merchants. A Chinese newspaper has quite a large circulation, and often I saw notices stuck up in the streets written in this Eastern language. The Chinese merchant owes his success to his thrift, and the native cannot compete with him. He is his own cook, gardener, washerwoman, bootmaker, etc., and every penny he makes is saved. As far as I could see, the only pleasure he seems to indulge in is to play Chinese music on old-fashioned gramophones.

Saturdays are called 'dia del pueblo' (day of the people) and beggars are allowed to go from house to house, begging. This does not mean that one sees none on other weekdays, but merely that on Saturdays regular processions of them worry and molest one.

In many villages water is sold in American petrol tins, and when one sees huts, roofs, fences, etc., made with them one cannot help but wonder what people would do without these tin cans. Water is brought from some stream and is carried by burros or in Chinese fashion, a tin at each end of a pole balanced on the shoulder of the carrier. The donkeys are usually living skeletons, and are so used to being clubbed that they hardly take any notice of the blows they receive all day long. Quite a number have their ears cut off, and when I enquired the reason for this I was told that it is done to improve their looks and to prevent ticks from settling in them.

After many long journeys through sandy deserts and a few miserable villages we reached a little town called Lambayeque, not far from the great Sechura desert. The prison yard was full of horses which seemed about to die from thirst and starvation. They had been stolen and were waiting to be claimed by their rightful owners. The police were too lazy to take them to water, the river being about half a mile distant, and naturally never dreamt of feeding them, as this would mean expense that would be charged to the owner whether the animals had food or not. I drove the whole troop to water with my animals and, having made a fence for mine in a corner to separate them from the others, I bought all of them a good feed, although thus, probably, only prolonging their sufferings.

In many of the police stations where I slept I saw pathetic things written on the walls; such as, 'Here suffered innocently for two months Juan Rodriguez, a victim of his shameless political enemies.' Or another: 'The good and patriotic Peruvian citizen, Pedro Alvarez, starved and cried here for six months. The innocent are in jail, the guilty are in their homes living in luxury.'

In several cemeteries also I saw funny inscriptions. On the wall over one grave was written: 'Here lie eternally the mortal remains of X for having stolen a mule belonging to Y'; and in another place I found the following: 'Here lie the bones of XX, a good man but a bad fighter.'

In order to avoid the big Sechura desert I had to change my route and swing towards the Andes again. Leaving Lambayeque we followed a trail to Olmos, a small village on the outskirts of the 'despoblado.' The trail led through forests, over hills and through prairies with pretty flowers; a pleasant change after the eternal sands of the coastal regions. The horses went without a bit, so they could eat as they went along, and I was delighted to watch them pull off big mouthfuls and enjoy themselves. We passed through a gap in the mountain called 'portachuelo' (big door) and arrived in Olmos late in the evening, where I again made the police station my headquarters.

The 'comisario' and the only 'vigilante' were about to leave the village next day, so the two of them celebrated the occasion by drinking and serenading all night. Had the quality of tone been as good as their lungs it might have been all right, but as this was not the case I had but little sleep.

When I went to see the horses in the morning I found them at the gate of the paddock into which I had turned them the night before, and it was easy to see that they had eaten nothing. The paddock was full of tropical vegetation to which they were not accustomed, and judging by the tracks they had not ventured to penetrate further in. Later I often found the same thing happen, and I am convinced that fear of the unknown kept them near the spot where they had entered and where I left them. Taking my sleepless night and the horses' empty stomachs into consideration I decided to stay over for one day and to take the animals where they would find grass. Thus I spent the whole day some three miles out of the village.

In the evening I returned to get something to eat for myself, and to see if anybody could give me information about the trail ahead through the 'despoblado.' Some government official, accompanied by his wife and several 'arrieros' (mule drivers) had arrived whilst I had been out grazing the horses. This important gentleman was a mulatto, and his appearance was striking if not convincing. He wore a blood-red shirt, light yellow boots and leggings of the same colour; his thin beard had not seen a razor for many days, and his skin was greasy. His wife had a greenish-yellow complexion and was fat enough to compete with the heaviest the world has seen. Her shoes were several sizes too small for her, but this would hardly trouble her as an unfortunate mule had to do the walking for her.

In the evening I was sitting in the only hut where they had offered to cook for me when the couple squeezed their way in through the small door. The man objected to eating in the same room with me, and as he was obviously of great importance and unlimited power I was requested to go behind the hut and to eat with his servants, whom I found very much his superiors, comparing them according to Darwin's theory. These mule drivers gave me some good information about the trails ahead, and I found them very genial and pleasant fellows.

I had heard many hair-raising stories about the 'despoblado' of Olmos, stories of bandits, starvation, dying of thirst, condors swooping down to attack dying travellers. However, these tales were not new to me, and the only things that disturbed me during the night were numerous rats. One of these even went as far as to nip one of my ears. In the morning I found my saddle-bag with a big hole in it, the pests having gnawed their way through to get at the sugar and biscuits, in spite of the fact that I always took the precaution of greasing all leather things with castor oil, which rats and mice dislike, and usually hung them up to prevent hungry dogs from eating them.

I thoroughly enjoyed the whole trip through the 'despoblado.' Thanks to the almost miraculous rains of the two previous years there was an abundance of high grass, so high in places that I could not see over the top unless I stood on the horse. The trees were literally covered with beautiful creepers that formed natural tents, and parrots were flying about in flocks and wood-pigeons cooed mournfully. Where the country was open and rocky, large green lizards and 'iguanas' (large, horny, grey lizards) were basking in the sun, the former having a peculiar habit of moving one of the front paws as if beckoning one to approach. Occasionally a snake would silently glide away, frightened by the heavy steps of the horses.

There are a few solitary huts in this region, but these are only inhabited when grass grows. Sometimes years pass without a trace of green to be seen excepting the tough trees. Near these huts are big, deep, wood-lined wells, called 'norias.' Long after the grass has dried up, animals (chiefly goats) are watered there, and thousands of doves and other birds come there to quench their thirst. The climate being hot, the huts are merely made of sticks stuck into the ground, and the roofs are formed of dry, coarse grass. Beds consist of four posts driven into the ground to which two others are fixed lengthways. Across these are placed a number of sticks, which are generally loose.

Late one afternoon, as I approached one of these huts, a woman came running towards me, obviously in a great state of excitement. When she had sufficiently recovered her breath to speak she told me there was a large snake in the roof of her hut and that the reptile had tried to attack her, and she implored me to come to her rescue as her husband was out in the 'monte' (bush) and would not be back until night. When we arrived near the hut the children were there, shrieking as if the very devil were after them. I poked the roof with a large pole, but not a trace of the snake could be seen. Presently the husband appeared, and as we could not locate the reptile we set to work boiling water in tins, and when all was ready I climbed on the roof and poured the boiling water over it, the woman handing me the tins whilst the man waited with a stick to kill the snake should it come out. No sooner had I emptied the second tin than I heard shouts below, and the woman ran away with the children. I at once jumped down, and there saw the man chasing a large blackish snake around the hut until he finally succeeded in killing it. At that very moment I heard a hiss, and a similar snake passed right between my legs. I almost believe that I beat the world's record for high jump without a run whilst the reptile made good its escape.

Nothing would induce the woman and her children to sleep in the hut that night, for she was convinced that the snake that had escaped would return to avenge its mate.

About half-way through the 'despoblado' the scenery changed completely. We travelled through semi-tropical forests where I saw many aigrettes, but, although their tail feathers are highly prized, nobody shoots them here, and in consequence they are very tame and one can approach quite close before they fly away. After several journeys I came to a fence, and by following it finally arrived at an hacienda. Here I might remark that one rarely finds comforts on the average Peruvian estate, rich as the owners may be, for they live but little better than the Indians and mestizos who slave for them.

A short distance before reaching a village at the northern end of the 'despoblado' we had to cross a wide river. 'Chimbadores' have the concession for this particular river, and even if the traveller takes his animals and cargo from one side to the other without their assistance they have the right to make their usual charge. Under the circumstances I had my pack taken across in their canoe whilst the horses swam behind.

The local authorities treated me with every consideration, and as I had to go to Piura, a town near the coast, they offered to take care of my animals whilst I was away. Very much against my principles I had to accept their offer, and I did not forget to promise a good tip to the policeman who was put in charge of them, if he looked after them well.

This district is very different to the rest of the Peruvian coast. Heavy rainfalls are frequent and the houses are roofed with round tiles or with the tough bark of a certain tree. The roof considerably overlaps the side of the house facing the street, in order to give shelter during heavy downpours. Most of the houses and huts are built on ground raised between one and three feet higher than the road as this is transformed into a regular stream when it rains.

In this village I saw a pathetic sight that has its amusing side. Throughout most South and Central American countries it is common to see men and women sitting outside their huts picking certain insects out of each other's hair, acting much like our friends the monkeys at the Zoo, and it was strange to see two little girls playing with their grotesque dolls and doing the same to them. This difficult operation obviously needs early practice to acquire full efficiency in years to come.

I was fortunate enough to be able to hire a car to take me to Piura. Motoring through this sandy part has its charms as well as risks. As far as the eye can reach one sees nothing but sand, or, sometimes, stretches of tall, coarse grass. The wind blowing from the direction of the Pacific has formed thousands of half-moon-shaped sand-dunes, in shape and size much resembling bunkers of a golf links. When we had travelled about half way we met a broken-down car, the occupants of which had been stranded in this semi-desert for twenty-four hours. We crowded two women and one man into our car, leaving one fellow behind, having given him a supply of water, some bananas and bread.

I had heard wonders about Piura, but found it to be a depressing place, in fact, not much better than the rest of the villages and towns I had seen lately. Rickety houses at the doors of which loaf men, women and children, effigies of filth and misery; a few streets with pavements which look as if they had experienced heavy shell-fire, and a few brick houses that are standing thanks to a veritable miracle of equilibrium. This, and heat— terrible heat —is Piura.

From this town I made a side trip to the little port, Paita, situated on a pretty little bay on the Pacific Ocean. A railway line connects the two places, and at every station women carrying calabashes filled with cold roast chicken, oranges, sandwiches, pieces of sugar-cane, drinks, etc., sell their usually dirty goods to the travellers, some of whom have a big meal at every stop, making one wonder what is their maximum capacity.

The carriage in which I travelled rather resembled a glorified packing-case on wheels, and in it were two Peruvian officers accompanied by two women. No sooner had we started than they began to unpack baskets out of which they took chicken, bread, watermelon, cheese, oranges, cold pork, etc. I was amazed at the way they put their teeth into these, washing the food down at intervals with a drink of 'pisco,' a strong kind of Peruvian brandy. The journey lasted some five hours, and they kept on eating all the time and only started to wipe their greasy mouths and hands with the newspapers the food had been wrapped in when we were about to arrive in Paita.

On my arrival I went to quite a fair little hotel on the very edge of the bay, and when I walked into the dining-room I could hardly believe my eyes when I saw my four travelling companions of the morning sitting there, just serving out the soup, whilst the waiter was taking away the remains of cold meat and salad which is the customary first dish all over South America. The four took every course, and only after coffee and more 'pisco' had disappeared did they pull the serviettes out of their collars where they had tucked them to protect their clothes.

I was obliged to make some of these side trips in order to get money, for I carried a letter of credit and rarely more cash than was necessary to reach the next place where there was a bank.

Having finished my business I returned to Piura and visited Catacaos, a small village a few miles to the south, on the very edge of the Sechura desert, where the best quality Panama hats are made. These hats are made exclusively in the north of Peru and Southern Ecuador, and their quality entirely depends on the selection and preparation of the fibre that is grown in the low swamp-land along the coast of Ecuador.

Without wasting time I started back to the place where I had left the horses, for I was anxious to return to them and to resume the trip towards the now near border of Ecuador. When we were near the very place where we had met the broken-down car the radiator burst, leaving us hopelessly stuck. However, the driver told me a friend of his was likely to follow us with a passenger towards evening, so all we could do was to sit in the shade of the car and trust to luck. We had two bottles of cold coffee with us so we were not too badly off. After a while a fox appeared on a sand dune quite close to us and sat there observing us with intense curiosity. The chauffeur thought he would test his marksmanship and took careful aim with his automatic and fired. The bullet hit the sand a few inches to one side of the fox which gave a queer leap and then went to smell the spot where the bullet had hit; then he looked towards us as if wondering what all this was about. After a second shot had also missed, Mr. Reynard thought there must be something wrong somewhere and started off at a slow jog-trot, stopping to look back at us several times. The sun was about to set when we heard the pleasant noise of an approaching automobile, and late that night we arrived in Chulacana.

It would be impossible to follow the low and swampy coast of Ecuador, so I took to the mountains once more, and, as a matter of fact, I was glad of the prospects of a better and healthier climate in the highland. It would be almost impossible to take an overland route along the coast of Ecuador, the dense jungles and enormous swamps, not to mention the unhealthy climate, being the chief obstacles. A man on foot can always canoe across bad places; with horses such journeys are impossible.

Near the borders of some of the countries I passed through I met smugglers, and more than once they were the only people who could give me sound advice about the trails. 'Hard-boiled' as some of them were, I found them to be fine gentlemen at heart, for open-air life and hardships will always bring out the finer qualities of a 'he-man' even though he be a smuggler. On one occasion when I fell in with such a group, they invited me to feed with them and as we sat around the fire after a hearty meal, during which there was a regular bombardment of jokes, I entered into conversation with them. The boss of the 'gang' was a Turk; there were two Scandinavians, an American, a Dutchman and some natives. All the foreigners had had their troubles at home, and now they were trying to 'make good' in a new line. When I was about to leave them in the morning they were all there to help me to saddle and pack. Judging by the unusual bulk of the saddle-bags I rightly guessed that food and tobacco had been slipped into them by a rough but kindly hand during the night. After the bottle had been handed round I swung into the saddle and started off at a trot, and turning round shouted a loud 'Adios' and 'good luck'; and I meant it.

As I am writing this I can see them fighting their way up horrible trails, yard by yard, until they disappear in the cold, shifting fogs of the peaks, only to descend again into the steaming tropics. I can see their animals, in single file, winding their way along a narrow trail through dense tropical vegetation whilst the men speed them along with shouts and curses that mean nothing more than 'move on!'

In the last Peruvian village where I spent a night I slept in the office at the police station. Like all the others this room was stacked with papers and documents, some brown and yellow with age and all covered with dust. Several coffins were piled up along one wall. The chief of the 'policia' explained to me that these contained the bones of half a family. A heavy rain had washed away the cemetery, and when the relatives in Lima heard this they asked that the bones belonging to the defunct of their family be collected and sent to Lima for re-burial. I was rather puzzled how the police could distinguish these particular bones from others that were washed away at the same time, and when I enquired how this masterpiece of identification work had been performed the chief blew a puff of smoke from his black cigar and with a cunning smile told me that after all documents had for once been of use. 'Any fool,' he told me, 'can select bones of the right size when he knows the age of the person they are supposed to have belonged to.' He seemed highly amused and told me what he thought of charging for his services.

As we approached the Andes again the country became more hilly and the vegetation denser. The trees were covered with creepers bearing big pink and blue flowers. Strange 'ceiba' trees with their smooth, green trunks, thin at the bottom, thick in the middle, and again thin at the top, somewhat resembling huge Indian clubs, fascinated me with their grotesque beauty, whilst flocks of green parrots chattered as we passed. In this neighbourhood grows a certain poisonous creeper which cattle will sometimes eat, and the local name for which is 'borrachera' (drunkenness). If cattle eat much of it, I am told, they die, but usually they stop when they feel intoxicated, and then it often happens that they will fall down cliffs and thus be killed. I am told that goats especially come to grief in this line. Surely food for thought to many human beings....

It was no easy matter to follow the right trail, for roaming cattle make many paths that lead to nowhere. Necessity and experience had taught me to become quite a fair track-reader. Some mark is always left where people travel; for instance, here and there an interfering twig has been cut off with a 'machete,' the broad knife, almost as long as a sword, without which no native of the tropics will go out. Then there are places where somebody has camped or made a fire, or marks on trees where pack-animals have bumped into them. Often a burnt match will give the wanted clue, and tracks of shod animals are certain signs that one is following the trail.

The river Macara forms the boundary between Ecuador and Peru, and on the Peruvian side there is an 'hacienda,' where we spent the last night on Peruvian soil. Here, as throughout the north of Peru, I found the people very hospitable; they have not much to give, but what they have is offered with a good heart.

The climate here is delightful, for the place is situated among hills in a valley over 1,300 feet above sea level. To the north and east are high mountains, their peaks wrapped in a thick mantle of mists where the hot air, rising from the warm parts below, is condensed. Across the river, about half a mile as the crow flies, I could see Macara, the small Ecuadorian border village.

I was held up until next afternoon because the river had risen so much during the night that it was not advisable to attempt to cross it until it had gone down considerably, and in the meantime we amused ourselves breaking in a few mules belonging to the 'hacienda' where I was a guest. I witnessed some wicked bucking, kicking and biting, and some excellent riding. The waters looked safer during the afternoon, so a man came to show me the place where I could cross. Acting according to his advice I reached 'terra firma' in Ecuador without incident, and although the border is supposed to be guarded by a 'capitan' with a few 'soldados,' none of them were to be seen that day.

The Highland of Ecuador

W hen I reached the village of Macara I wished to pay my respects to the 'jefe politico,' as the local authorities are called in Ecuador, but I found that he, like the 'capitan,' was out. However, another 'autoridad' of minor calibre came to ask me what I wanted, and when I told him who I was he did all but kiss me, and informed me that they had long ago received orders to attend to me in case I should enter their country through this village.

Hearing the shouts of my new friend, who was giving loud 'vivas' for the Argentine and myself, a little crowd collected around us, wondering what all the fuss was about. By this time the horses were getting nervous, and Mancha, unaccustomed to such noise and to so many people around him, put back his ears and lifted one of his hind-legs, his usual way of showing disapproval and a fair warning to people to keep at a distance. Gato being of a more resigned temperament simply stood there with his ears down, as if bored stiff.

In the evening the 'jefe politico' arrived, and I had to spend half the night telling him and his friends all about my travels. Thanks to him and his brother officials the horses were well cared for, and even the last child went to see the 'Argentinos,' as they naïvely called them.

In spite of the invitation to stay for a few days I saddled early, and at sunrise we were winding our way up river towards the very near Andes, following a very fair trail, as things go in these parts. A steady uphill climb, partly along the river Macara and partly through dense tropical forest-land, brought us to the foot of the mountains which were towering before us, the upper regions wrapped in heavy mists. By way of contrast, where we were it was hot and 'sticky' and gnats, mosquitoes and other insects buzzed around us. Beautiful as such places are, they are malarial and unhealthy.

The 'avillo' tree is very common in Lower Ecuador. It grows to the size of an average chestnut tree, and its leaves are large and roundish and of a beautiful green. The fruit is large and round and contains seeds which are used by the natives for a strong purge. When the bark is cut an amazing quantity of milky juice flows out. People here will never cut down one of these 'avillo' trees, and if one has to be felled they build a fire around the trunk and burn it. The reason for this, I am told, is that if a person cuts one and stays near it, horrible swellings appear all over the body and face. Practically every 'avillo' is full of scars where people have had a quick slice at it with their machetes as they passed by.

I slept on my saddle, taking good care to choose a place where there were a little air and as few insects as possible. Of course, I always used my mosquito net and wherever I had my doubts about the water I put two or three drops of iodine into a glassful.

I started early, for I had been told that the 'cuesta' (steep trail) was long and one of the worst imaginable. There are many places where riding is absolutely impossible, and where one has to consider oneself lucky if the animals can pass without accident. People who have never travelled over one of those neck-breaking trails, over loose rocks, up high steps, over surfaces slippery in places, where a horse is likely to come to grief at any moment, would take a realistic description for imagination or exaggeration.

We had only a short distance to go that morning and then we started zig-zagging up a long, narrow and rocky trail. Half-way up the temperature became much lower, but the effort of climbing made us drip with perspiration. Presently we were wrapped in shifting fogs and could only see a few yards ahead. However, the higher we climbed the lighter did it get, and finally we came out of the mists. The atmosphere was clear as crystal and glorious sunshine filled me with new life; not the depressing sunshine of the low tropical regions, but the clear, invigorating and joyous sun of the mountains. After many short stops to recover breath we reached the summit, and what a panorama I beheld! It seemed as though we were on a high island, and below us an endless white ocean with mountains sticking out of it. Here and there mists, driven by swift winds, came rolling up a ravine like huge waves hungrily licking an island, or again the clouds rose slowly like the smoke of some huge fire.

My clothes were wet with perspiration and the animals were overheated, panting and dripping, but I began to feel the cold. The sudden change from the tropics to 'tierra fria' (cold land) is dangerous and it is advisable to keep moving.

For the next few days we followed trails that led over high passes and down into valleys. We passed through several small settlements where we usually spent the nights. Most of the mountains are covered with dense forests, the trees are full of moss and grey lichen, and enormous creepers twist up them like huge snakes. Below grow bushes and pretty ferns which make these forests difficult to penetrate, except by following the trail.

I had heard many stories about tigers and bad people who are supposed to make some of these valleys unsafe. One day I had taken a trail that led to nowhere and, when I found out my mistake, was obliged to return. Unfortunately, towards evening, long before the proper time, it became dark, and as we were fighting our way up a steep trail in a narrow hollow, a regular deluge began to fall. Soon the trail was transformed into a roaring stream, making it impossible to move. Before long it was pitch dark and there we were trapped in the hollow, unable to get out of it or to move. Presently lightning and thunder made things even more unpleasant, and when I found a spot where the current was not so strong the three of us took refuge there. I do not know how long I had been leaning against one of the muddy walls that trapped us in when I heard a noise like some rushing animal, and suddenly I remembered what I had heard about tigers.... The horses also were obviously frightened, for I heard them snort and move. It was so dark that I could not see an inch, but I was prepared to make a fight for it, and so I waited with my guns in trembling hands. Suddenly there was another noise, and I even thought I could smell some wet pelt. Another noise, this time right behind me, and then I was hit in the legs, not by a tiger, but merely by earth loosened by the heavy rain, and what I had taken for the smell of an animal was only the smell of wet, newly-loosened earth. Although it had long before ceased to rain we were still in the same place when the first daylight appeared. I was wet to the marrow, and I believe the only dry thing within miles was the inside of my watch. The poor horses were standing with their heads down, fast asleep, but seemingly not in the slightest concerned about the soaked saddles and pack that had been on their backs throughout the night.

Between two distant settlements part of the trail had been swept away by a landslide, and I was warned that a man and his mule had fallen down trying to cross. This meant making a detour of two or three long days, and as I had my doubts about the truth of this report, I decided to go and see for myself. After several hours we came to the spot, and a glance at the broken-off piece of rock, some eight feet, convinced me that it would be running too big a risk to try to jump the gap. There was no alternative but to return all the weary distance we had covered that day, and make the detour. Mancha was the saddle-horse that day and was going in front, and as the pack needed readjusting, I went back to Gato to do this before retracing our steps. I had been working for a while when I happened to look up. To my horror I saw Mancha moving towards the spot where the trail was missing, and before I could stop him he jumped—and landed safely on the other side. My joy at this ticklish feat soon changed into consternation when I realised our real situation. Here was I on one side with Gato, whilst Mancha was on the other, as unconcerned as if nothing had happened, as if he had only jumped across an 'arroyo' (stream) in the pampas, and not across a gap where he would have fallen down several hundred feet had he hesitated or slipped. We all know that an eight-foot jump is not much for a horse, but then the place and uneven nature of the trail have to be considered, not to mention one's nerves.

There was no time for much thinking, so I tied the pack-horse to a loose rock, and jumped across to do the same with the other, lest he continue his dangerous wanderings. Now the question was as to whether it would be safer to bring back one animal or to cross the other. After a good look at the trail I thought the latter way would be the safer. I unsaddled Gato, who jumped across like a goat, after which I brought the pack and saddle over by means of a rope, having to cross from side to side several times to accomplish this primitive and ticklish piece of engineering. Another fright, a good lesson, and many miles saved.

Buzzards, the street cleaners and sanitary police of the Pacific coast of South and Central America are also to be seen in many inland places. One evening I was sitting outside a solitary hut fixing the saddles and mending straps when I observed a little dog, of no definite breed, a kind of one-volume edition of all breeds of little dogs, staring up into the sky. Several buzzards flew over, and the dog pricked up his ears and stared after them so intently that he fairly trembled, until suddenly he rushed off and disappeared over the next hill. My host, a dark mestizo, who was sitting near me shelling corn, laughed as he noticed the way I watched the strange behaviour of his dog. He told me there must be some dead animal in the direction the buzzards flew, and the dog, fully aware of this, had followed them knowing that he would soon be able to have a good feed, a thing no canine companion ever gets from his master in these parts.

Drinking is the vice all along the Andes, and the noise made by drunkards made me lose many hours of much-needed sleep. Jogging along a lonely trail one day, I met a man who at once started a conversation with me. He said that he had sold a troop of mules in some distant village. He was riding a fine mule and had obviously been imbibing freely, the effects having loosened his tongue. At short intervals he pulled a bottle of 'aguardiente' (spirits) out of his saddle-bags and offered me a drink, a thing I always refused from strangers whom I met out in the open. In the evening we came to a hut in a valley where I was given permission to unsaddle. As alcohol was sold there, as in most huts, my new acquaintance laid in a new stock, and when it was already dark he continued his journey, saying his mule knew the way as well as he did, even during the darkest night. My host and myself made our beds on the floor and wriggled into position to sleep.

It must have been considerably after midnight when we were awakened by somebody knocking at the door. It proved to be our friend the mule dealer, who came staggering in and asked if anybody had passed with his mule. Crying like a baby and reeling about, trying hard to keep his balance, he related that he had tied his mule to a tree and he had then entered some hut to have another drink. When he returned to the place where he had left his animal it was no longer there. His mule had gone, saddle, saddle-bags, and all his money. He called upon all the saints to have pity on him, and finally dropped off to sleep, and when I last saw him in the morning he was still lying there, dreaming, perhaps, about what he had possessed only the day before.

Our trail led over mountains and hills, and again through pretty valleys. As we were slowly descending a slope the horses and myself were suddenly startled by the appearance of a huge man. He was amazingly broad and tall, and had a darkish copper-coloured skin. His features were sharp and long black hair fell over his shoulders in thick strands. He wore short trousers which did not quite reach to his knees, thus showing legs of unusual muscular development. All this and his aquiline nose and lively, very black eyes gave him the appearance of some being belonging rather to imagination rather than to reality. He slowly advanced towards us, and I noticed that he had a 'machete' in his right hand, which made me think there was going to be trouble. However, he smiled at me, showing two rows of perfect teeth, and greeted me in quite good Spanish. He enquired in what direction I was travelling and seemed altogether to be a very amiable person in spite of his looks. Whenever I was asked where I was bound for, I invariably mentioned the nearest town or village as my goal, and when I had given my usual reply the terrible looking stranger explained to me that he carried the mail from the interior and presently I saw his mule grazing behind some bushes. So for a few hours we travelled together, and then my newly made friend's trail branched off. Later I found out that he was a 'Runa' Indian. I had occasion to see many more, but never did I come across another such giant.

The 'Runas' are chiefly agriculturists and many are employed as bricklayers, street-cleaners, etc. The 'Jibaro' or 'Jivero' Indians inhabit the interior and are of a very different type. They are sometimes called 'headhunters,' but most of the stories told about their bloodthirstiness and cruelty have been invented by travellers and writers who write more with the help of imagination than knowledge of facts. True, the Jibaros are much more primitive and fiercer-looking than the quiet and industrious Runas, especially when they paint their faces or cut their flat noses and cheeks for adornment, or when they wear wooden spikes in their ears, or a spike in the lower lip, a custom especially among their women. They often cross the mountains and come to towns and villages to exchange rare parrots, monkeys, medicinal herbs, etc., for knives, gunpowder, shotguns and other articles. They arrive wearing only a cloth wrapped around the hips, or perhaps short trousers. Some bind their hair with a piece of thick string that goes from the forehead clear around the head. I have seen some wearing collars or rather necklaces made of coloured feathers, and others of dried wings of insects, of blue, green, or violet tints. They usually have long wooden lances with which to defend themselves in case they are attacked by some wild animal. They carry their loads on their backs, but the weight is supported by the forehead by means of a broad strap, the way in which all Ecuadorian Indians carry loads. It can easily be imagined how hardy these people must be if they can resist such long journeys over high mountains, wearing practically nothing to protect them against the bitter cold and snow in those high regions.

When the Jibaro kills an enemy he has a strange process of shrinking his head without spoiling its features. I have seen heads reduced to the size of a man's fist, and at one time possessed one of a girl which was the finest I have ever seen, for she looked as if she were asleep. When I grew tired of carrying so gruesome a cargo with me I gave it to an acquaintance, a thing I have regretted ever since. These heads are often offered for sale, although this traffic is illegal.

I saw a number of these Jibaro Indians arrive in a village, and all the boys followed them, teasing them and cracking jokes at their expense. At all this the Jibaros merely laughed in good humour, although I am sure they were not exactly pleased.

I was thinking about giving the horses a rest as soon as we should reach a village where I could buy them good fodder and where they could enjoy themselves in their own fashion. Adventure is often found where one least expects it, and the truth of this was proved in a village where I stopped for two days.

The horses were in a corral where they ate good grass, brought by an Indian who went to cut it some distance away, while I was living in a room that faced the one and only street of the village. A woman brought me food which was cooked in some other house, and usually curious children came to stare in through the door whilst I was eating. There being no windows the door had to be left open to admit light and air.

One poor, hungry-looking Indian boy to whom I had given some of the food that was left over was always there, and when I went to the corral he followed me like a dog. He had long hair and was dressed in rags, and only possessed an old 'poncho' (cloak) to protect him against the cold at night. He was always ready to give me a helping hand with anything and liked nothing better than to help me with the grooming of the horses, and whenever I was eating he was on the spot, squatting somewhere near the door where I could not help seeing him. When I enquired about him, the 'alcalde' (mayor) told me he was a poor orphan who lived on charity and had no home, and suggested that I take the boy with me to serve as 'mozo' as they call the mule-boys who accompany travellers. Accordingly, after some reflection, I made up my mind to take the kid with me, or at least to give him a trial. Should he prove useless, I could always leave him in the next town, where he would have a better chance to keep alive than in this miserable village.

He called himself Victor and claimed to be sixteen years of age, but I very much doubted this, giving him only about fourteen or fifteen at the outside. However, I had some kind of papers made out for him, under the name of Victor Jimenez, aged sixteen, and even thought of a suitable birth-day for him, a luxury he thought only the rich enjoyed. I sent him to have his hair clipped, and after I had disinfected him thoroughly I made him wear a new shirt and trousers I had purchased, but as he had never worn boots I did not buy him any lest he blister his feet.

I made him trot along on foot for three days, just to test his grit and to see if he would give in, but by the time we reached Loja, the first town we hit in Ecuador, the boy had proved so willing and useful that I decided to take him with me for good. Accordingly I bought him a little black mountain-pony, a saddle, a few more clothes, and—to his delight—a coat and a pair of shoes! Never shall I forget the proud way he walked down the street when he first wore those garments. It was easy to tell that he had never worn boots, for he walked along as if he were on ice, and although his feet were sore next morning he insisted on wearing his boots again to look 'It.' With the boy, travelling was much easier for whilst one looked after the horses the other minded the saddles and pack. Before this I had been robbed on several occasions, having been obliged to leave everything to look for a place for the animals, to hunt for fodder, and to take them to water.

In Loja I visited the governor, who was very courteous and who showed keen interest in my ride. The town is most primitive in every way, the only decent buildings dating back to Spanish colonial times. There are a couple of apologies for hotels where no sanitary arrangements of any kind exist. In their place one usually finds a backyard, or, of course, simply the street, where men and women can be seen relieving themselves, even in broad daylight, as unconcernedly as the dogs who act as scavengers. I observed these primitive habits in most countries along the Pacific Ocean, excepting, perhaps, in a few of the larger cities, which are fairly clean.

Even the 'whitest' people of Loja are of dusky hue, showing a strong splash of Indian blood. Religious fanaticism is one of the characteristics of all who possess this blood. Their form of worshipping amounts practically to idolatry, for they adore hideously-painted saints and dolls, and are fond of pomp and processions, in connection with which usually goes a drunken orgy.

I saw a procession in Loja in which the bishop took part. All the cracked and unmelodious bells of the many churches were being hammered by the strong arms of Indians. Two bands slowly shuffled along, each playing a different tune, whilst Indians with flutes and drums made up the front and rear of the procession. The natives of the town, and hundreds of Indians who had flocked in from far and near were kneeling, or threw themselves flat on the ground as the bishop pompously passed, blessing them. The path had literally been covered with flowers and sprinkled with scented water. By this time I was used to these processions, but never had I seen one like this. I stood there, wondering if I was dreaming or awake, when an Ecuadorian officer I knew touched me on the shoulder and whispered into my ear, 'Let us go away, this makes me positively sick.'

In this town I visited a nunnery, which was a new experience for me. Once a girl enters this one she must stay for ever, and she can never again be seen by anybody belonging to the outside world. On arrival I was taken to an entrance where my guide pulled a thick cord. Presently a small window opened which was made safe by a heavy iron grating over which was hung a heavy dark curtain. From behind this a female voice asked what we wanted. The surroundings and atmosphere suggested a voice from the dead. Later we entered the church, which is public: here the silence was broken by the mournful and monotonous voices of nuns praying up in the cloister. They have a separate entrance from the nunnery and are high up behind heavy iron bars which suggest an ancient prison. Behind this barrier there is again a heavy dark curtain that hides the nuns from view. As it happened there was a strong light behind the curtain and thus we could distinctly see the shadows of several nuns who were peeping through to see who we were.

Everything in Loja, as in all other inland towns and villages where no railroads exist, is brought in on pack-animals when possible, but large and heavy articles that cannot be loaded on beasts are transported by squads of Indians, as wagons and carts cannot be used on the steep zigzag mountain trails. I have seen pianos and heavy pieces of machinery being carried by as many as thirty Indians who construct a framework of poles, from beneath which they lift the load. Slowly, step by step, they move along, scrambling, stumbling, slipping, sweating and shouting. The food is cooked for them along the trail and they sleep out for nights until they slowly reach their goal with their heavy load, like ants pushing a large dead insect towards their nest. For this heart- and back-breaking work the carriers in this neighbourhood receive their food and 20 Ecuadorian cents, which amounts to about twopence.

The trail between Loja and Cuenca is much travelled, which makes it rather worse. The hoofs of thousands of pack-animals have worn regular steps where the rock is soft or where it is muddy, and in many places the trail is a regular trench of thick, evil-smelling mud, where animals sink in to the girth. As the mules and burros take much shorter paces than horses do, the steps worn in the trail made walking very difficult for my animals until they gradually became accustomed to taking shorter strides. These steps are called 'camellones.' The space between them is about one foot, and their depth is often as much as two feet. After a rain they are filled with water and mud, and many a bad stumble and fall have they caused us. Only sheer luck prevented my horses from suffering some severe injury or breaking a leg.

After crossing a mountain known as 'El Silban' (The Whistler), probably so called owing to the cold, strong winds that usually blow in its upper regions, we stopped in a hut in a small settlement. During the night we were awakened by somebody tapping at the door, and when we opened we found a man lying there moaning, covered with mud and blood. One of the women recognised him as the mail-carrier. He had been attacked some two miles out of the village, shot at and wounded, and his mule with the mail had been taken from him. We attended to him as best we could and fortunately the wounds were not as bad as we had first thought. According to the man, it had taken him four hours to drag himself the two miles from the place of assault to the hut. I had travelled on the very same trail earlier in the evening, so maybe I just escaped the same fate.

The country between Loja and Cuenca is exceedingly mountainous, and therefore riding is rough and tiring, but the difficult journey was worth while for Cuenca is considerably larger than Loja and superior in every respect, and, in addition, although the town has no railway communication with the outside world, almost anything can be obtained, all goods being transported to the spot on beasts of burden. The climate is exceedingly mild throughout the year, and when once the railroad reaches the town it is likely to become one of the finest in the republic. My boy, Victor, was in his glory, for never had he seen a real town before. Everything was new to him, and he was learning fast.

As alfalfa grows around there, the horses had a treat they must almost have forgotten. Indians grow it on their little farms outside and bring it into town in small bundles which they sell in the market.

The chief industry around Cuenca is the making of Panama hats. Workers can be seen sitting outside their huts, patiently twisting the long, fine fibres into the desired shape and design, and in the market-place stacks of them are bought by merchants who come to buy them up wholesale. The edges of the hats are not trimmed off, the fibres being left to stick out, so that the buyer may better be able to judge the quality, which entirely depends upon the fibre used. Consumption is very common among the makers of these hats, probably due to the squatting and stooping position they work in all day, beginning when they are mere children.

Some of the Indians who come into town wear sheepskin trousers over the ordinary ones, much resembling the 'chaps' of the cowboys, or the 'chaparreras' of the Mexican charros.

Leaving Cuenca we again followed a much-used trail where we passed numerous pack-trains on their way to and from the railroad. One evening, when we arrived at a 'posada' (inn), I found sitting there several men who had obviously been drinking freely to drown the pains and sorrows of the journey, and when we had attended to the horses, Victor and myself sat down in a corner to have something to eat. The conversation of the tipsy group kept me much amused, and when many subjects had been discussed, rather more loudly than thoroughly, probably owing to the great quantity of spirits consumed, spiritualism was brought up. Presently one of the company, a tall, dark fellow, who claimed to be a Chilian, got up and told his listeners that he could fly out of the room 'like an angel' and land outside the door, even if this were closed. His only condition was that the lights be put out and that there should be complete silence.

Everybody stared at the man of such mysterious powers with awe and respect, and when one proposed to see the miracle performed all the rest joined in. Some went to lock the door whilst Victor sat with open mouth and his eyes nearly falling out of their sockets.

The lamp was extinguished; there was a moment of deadly silence, a rush, a crash, followed by a shrill shriek of pain. Several matches were struck, and there was our magician lying on the floor, holding his badly-bruised head. The alcohol had proved too much for his imagination and the door too hard for his skull.

The mountain scenery was pretty but the trail was bad, and more than once the only fodder the horses had was bamboo, of the variety that grows up the trees in creepers and which we pulled down and piled up for the animals before we retired. In many places the trail was very muddy, and the pack-animals we passed were covered with slime from head to tail. The sufferings of these unfortunate beasts, often called 'the friends of man,' are best left undescribed. Suffice it to say, meaning no blasphemy, that my conception of hell is to be a pack-animal of the Andes.

If there happens to be a particularly deep or dangerous hole hidden under the slimy mud, the mule-drivers cut a branch and lay it over it to serve as a warning to the next passer. Once we were wading along one of these terrible trails and when we came to an open space I saw a strange shape near a solitary mule which was standing there, entirely covered with mud. As I approached, the shape began to move, and when it was in an upright position I recognised it as a man who, like the mule, was completely mud-covered. Without the formality of introduction the man addressed me in English, said that his mule had stumbled into a deep mud-hole and that he had actually been submerged under the mud for a long moment. I did not blame him for the flow of language that followed his explanation, leaving no doubt that he hailed from America. Having eased his feelings he asked me what on earth I was doing in these blessed parts, to which I answered that I was merely travelling for pleasure. 'Boy,' said he, 'you have saved my life; I was thinking about shooting myself as the biggest gosh-darned fool for ever having come here to do some surveying, but now, having met one bigger than myself, I shan't do it!'

An old story that is often told about the muddy trails of Ecuador and Colombia goes as follows:—

A gringo was riding along a narrow, muddy trail when he saw a quite good hat lying near him. He guided his mule towards it and picked it up. A gurgling voice that seemed to come from nowhere commanded, "Ey, leave this 'ere 'at alone!'

'Where are you?' asked the mystified gringo; and looking down to the spot where he had picked up the hat he noticed a round shape that looked like a human head sticking out of the mud.

'What in the name of all the saints are you doing down there?' enquired the surprised traveller. Again the gurgling, spluttering voice answered, 'Ridin' a mule. I'm in an 'urry, give me me 'at!'

A branch line of the Guayaquil–Quito railway had once been under construction, and was to extend to Cuenca and further to the south. A great part of this line had already been constructed when work was abandoned owing to politics and lack of funds; a common complaint in countries where politics are called 'politica.'

In many parts we followed the line which is cut out of the mountain sides and winds its course up and down. Here and there rains and landslides had made nasty gaps which, some day, will have to be repaired. Where the sleepers had been, put down, the horses had to walk very slowly and measure every stride, but thanks to many similar experiences they had become quite expert at picking their way, even in the most difficult places. Victor, who had never seen a railway before, became more and more excited as we approached the Guayaquil line, where I told him he would actually see an engine and a train.

Every evening when I made notes in my diary, he would always be near to watch me perform this, to him, marvellous feat. I had taught him to know the numbers up to nine and had also succeeded in teaching him part of the ABC.

When our path along the line came to a tunnel the boy thought we had reached the end of the world. It took me some time to explain to him what it was, and no little persuasion to make him follow me into its darkness. When we came out at the other side the boy's joy and surprise knew no bounds, and he begged of me to wait a little to give him time to run back to the other side once more. That night, when we were lying on the floor of a dirty 'posada' (inn), where there were more fleas than there are stars in the Milky Way, the boy suddenly broke the silence and said he knew what the 'cueva' (cave) was for.

I had no idea what cave he was referring to until he told me that the cave must be the inn where the trains and passengers slept.

About nine o'clock one morning, as I looked down across a wonderful valley with dark-green tropical vegetation, I saw the line of the Guayaquil–Quito railroad. Not long after a train came steaming slowly uphill, appearing like a miniature in the distance. Victor looked at it, then at me, but never said a word. His dream of many days and nights had come true, his one wish was fulfilled: he was actually seeing a real train!

After a few hours, always on a down grade, we arrived where the two lines meet. Here the valley forms a cul-de-sac and the Quito line zigzags up the famous 'Nariz del Diablo' (Devil's nose), indeed a fine piece of engineering. Here the trains are taken up a formidable mountain-side. There being no trail beyond this point, I had to lead my horses along the railroad track itself. An accident here almost finished our journey.

Without warning, a locomotive suddenly appeared. Quickly I hurried the terrified boy and horses along, and was lucky in finding an open space beside the track a few seconds before the engine roared past. The animals took but little notice of it, the grass that grew where they stood attracting their attention far more. Victor took good care to hide behind them; obviously he had not expected that an engine was so big and could make such a noise, but later, when the engine appeared at a zigzag below us and blew the whistle, he fairly jumped with delight.

At the foot of this mountain one steams in the hot and humid climate of the tropics, but on reaching a village at the top it is delightfully dry and cool.

Saint Peter's day was being celebrated when we arrived there and rockets were fired all day long. Two bands were playing ear-piercing and heart-rending music, and naturally alcohol was being consumed in incredible quantities. To form an arena the village plaza was barricaded off with wagons, poles, etc., the usual thing when a bullfight is to be held.

In Ecuador, owing to the lack of money, bullfights are very poor, but, on the other hand, far more amusing and humane than in the countries where the famous 'matadores' perform only when large sums are paid to them, for here the bulls are rarely killed or even injured, and no horses are used. Usually the animal is driven into the village square through an opening in the barricade, with a long rope fastened to his horns, so that he can be pulled back when he knocks over a man. Once he is within the square, he viciously eyes the crowd and begins to throw dust over his back by scratching the ground with his fore-legs, every now and again bellowing fiercely.

The Indians and mestizos then begin to take 'Dutch courage' out of their bottles, and as soon as one has worked himself up to concert pitch he jumps down from the barricade with a regular war-whoop and waves his poncho at the bull, who usually charges him at once. When one animal is tired out or refuses to charge any more he is taken out and another one is brought in. Lives are often lost and bones broken, and only if this happens do the onlookers declare the day a good one; if not, they leave in disgust and say the bulls were 'vacas' (cows).

At night there were fireworks and more rockets, things the natives always enjoy and without which no fiesta is held, and when this display was over a game of 'vaca loca' (mad cow) was started. In this a frame of wood, supposed to represent a cow, is carried by a man. Two long horns are made of twisted wire and to the end of each of these they fix a ball of rags soaked in petrol. Once these 'horns' are lit the man who carries the frame chases after the boys, who pretend to be bullfighters by waving their ponchos at him.

The following day had a great treat in store for me. The train from Guayaquil arrived, and with it some newspapers, even the appearance of which I had almost forgotten.

The National Bank of Ecuador had suspended payment, my funds were running low, and there were only two alternatives for me: go to Quito or down to Guayaquil with my letter of credit and obtain cash from some foreign bank. The latter town being nearer I decided to leave Victor in charge of the horses whilst I went down by train, a journey of about six hours. The engine-drivers and conductors of the train were all Americans, and I passed most of the journey chatting with one of the latter.

An Ecuadorian evangelist, whom I later met near the Colombian border, had hewn Bible verses in large black letters on some rocks along the line, so that travellers might read them from the train. Just before the dangerous descent of the 'Nariz del Diablo' he had written in large letters: 'Prepare to meet God'; most comforting words for nervous travellers who have heard about the many accidents that have happened there, especially before modern air-brakes were introduced; indeed, there is a 'well-populated' cemetery below, where the victims of these accidents are buried.

The further down we went the hotter did it become. We passed through several dirty villages of wooden houses, and the crowds of black and filthy people who crowded the stations made me glad to move on again. The line goes through tropical forests and wonderful valleys, while here and there cocoa plantations can be seen, until, finally, swampy parts are reached. Having arrived at the river Guayas, everybody left the train and boarded a launch that took us across to the town of Guayaquil in about half an hour.

The Ecuadorian fleet, consisting of two very old and equally rusty cruisers, the *Cotopaxi* and the *Atahuallpa*, lay anchored at a few cable-tow's lengths from the shore. One had formerly belonged to Chili and was later presented to Ecuador. The engines of both these vessels are rotten with rust, and once upon a time somebody stored sacks of cement on them, thereby not helping to improve their condition. Nevertheless, there is an admiralty up in Quito, most of its members having never seen the sea, and, of course, there are some officers and crews. The fleet is apt to sink any day, but in the meantime these 'good ships' slowly pull at the anchor chains, as the tide regularly ebbs and flows, twice in twenty-four hours.

I found Guayaquil to be a bad imitation of a modern city. Some of the streets are ridiculously wide and very bare, and the main plaza gave me the impression of a small Sahara desert with a high monument in the middle. There are some quite up-to-date stores and restaurants, but the hotels, although not bad, leave much to be desired.

Having finished my business, I lost no time, and took the first train to return to the horses.

I was glad when I was back in the highland, and it felt good to be with my travelling companions once more.

Marching on, we more or less followed the railroad towards Riobamba. Coming over a mountain we saw this town below us. It is beautifully located, just about halfway between the coast and Quito, the capital. From Riobamba one looks out upon a panorama at once majestic and inspiring. To the west stands the snow-covered Andean monarch, Chimborazo; to the east rises the Altar, so named because, draped in white and with gigantic snow candles symmetrically arranged, it resembles an altar. Blackening the horizon in his sullen wrath, the great volcano Tungurahua rises in the north.

I found a fair road leading up the valley from Riobamba to Quito. It leads along the foot of the Chimborazo and through charming little villages, mostly inhabited by industrious Indians. Fruits and vegetables grow in abundance and the climate is one of perpetual spring. Towards Quito the road passed near famous Cotopaxi, a snow-covered, cone-shaped volcano of singular beauty, towering high up in a clear blue sky.

Victor, although quite a plucky boy in other ways, was terrified of dogs, and if one happened to rush out of a hut and bark at him he nearly went into hysterics. With all the exercise and fairly regular eating he had developed an amazing appetite, and as soon as he had finished one meal he began to look forward to the next.

He had become desperately fond of the horses, especially of Mancha, for whom he always had a mouthful of something special, and he insisted on feeding him by hand. With all his fondness, he had so much respect for him that he would never venture to ride him since his first experience in that line had proved a disaster, Mancha having 'unloaded' him before he had time to think what was happening. However, the boy thought nothing of going under him, between his legs, hanging on to his tail, or cleaning out his hoofs, actions of which the horse never took the slightest notice.

For several days my feet had been feeling very hot and were constantly itching. Try what I would, the irritation became steadily worse. Victor, who had been watching me stamp on the ground several times whilst we had dismounted for a brief rest, laughed and told me I had 'niguas.' As I had never heard this name before he explained that they are small parasites that bore under the skin of one's toes. If these are left undisturbed for some time they will lay eggs, often under the nails, which must then be removed. The feet swell terribly and become very sore, and there is a great danger of contracting blood-poisoning.

When I had taken off my boots and socks the boy showed me several grey spots under the skin. With a needle he then began to peel back the skin from these places, and carefully dug in the needle at the edge of the grey spots and pulled out little jelly-like bags, about the size and shape of average pearls. This seemingly simple operation requires a great deal of skill and much practice. It is common to see Indians pick these pests out of each other's feet and, later on, on several occasions I had trouble with them, beside making the acquaintance of several other varieties of parasites, big and small.

Niguas also worry horses, attacking them just above the hoofs, but as their skin is too thick they only cause the beasts to stamp. Any grease mixed with a little powdered sulphur or camphor keeps them off, but often these simple remedies cannot be found for weeks. I have seen Indians with their feet completely deformed, resembling cauliflowers, where niguas have been left to do their work.

From the top of a hill Quito came in sight. The town is situated on a slope in a hollow and is surrounded by mountains. To the south the Cayambe glitters in his eternal mantle of white, and the abundant vegetation, typical of cool climates—eucalyptus trees and pretty flowers—makes it hard to realise that one is only within a few miles of the equator.

The boy was so excited and keen to hurry along that he did not notice that the girth of his saddle had slipped back. Suddenly I heard a snort and some wild stamping, and turning round I saw poor Victor fly over his pony's head and land on the hard road on his back. Fortunately he was only slightly bruised and shaken, and the incident furnished both of us with amusement until we rode into the city.

Quito

We had a good time in this quaint and interesting city. The horses enjoyed themselves in an alfalfa field some three miles out of town, while I stayed in an excellent hotel and made the best of every minute.

Many of Quito's houses date back to the early colonial times, and some of the churches are of great architectural merit. Wonderful gold ornaments and remarkable paintings are to be seen in some of them, but, as all churches built by the early Spaniards, their interiors are dark and gloomy. Living in Quito is the cheapest I have ever experienced, but maybe this was due to the very low exchange of Ecuadorian money at the time. Considering the ideal climate and the beautiful scenery, not to mention the historic buildings and general quaintness of the town, it is surprising how relatively few tourists make the trip up to the capital.

He who looks for the pleasures of a modern city does well to stay away from Quito, for after nine o' clock the town is fast asleep, except for a few miserable barefooted prostitutes who solicit in dark corners and in the shadows of the ancient arcades around the principal plaza. Early in the morning one is awakened by the clattering of many church bells calling the flock to mass.

I could not help noticing the number of huge padlocks which make the doors of some of the shops secure. An Ecuadorian friend of mine said there was an old joke about these padlocks. Supposing a shop is run by three partners, each one of them had his own lock. When the store is to be opened all the three have to be present to make this possible; in other words, their slogan is: Safety first!

Ecuador has an army of five thousand men, and I am told that about half of them are musicians. Nowhere have I heard so many military bands, bugles and drums as in Quito, in fact, I sometimes thought I was living in an army training-camp.

Antiques, real and imitation, are offered to visitors at very cheap prices. Even the illegal traffic in reduced human heads, previously mentioned, is carried on. Long-haired Indians, in wide white trousers, and usually wearing gaily-coloured ponchos, do the work of street-cleaners. Indian women work as road-menders and brick-carriers. They carry their loads on their backs, supporting the weight with a strap across their foreheads, and I have seen some carry loads very few white men would care to tackle. The markets are full of life, and I often wandered among the bartering, quarrelling, and chattering crowd that both interested and amused me. From Saturday noon until Monday a 'dry law' comes in force. Strange as it may seem, although I never thought about drinking in the ordinary course of events, the very idea of it being prohibited filled me with a desire to have a cocktail on these 'dry' days.

Our delightful stay had to come to an end, for I was timing my journey to reach Panama in January when the dry season, which only lasts three months, sets in, as for the remaining nine months of the year travelling through the interior is impossible, torrential rains flooding the jungles and swelling the numerous rivers.

Crossing the Line

A railroad to connect Quito with the Colombian border was started once, but was abandoned. We followed this unfinished track at times, making short cuts wherever possible. Although we walked in our own shadows at midday, the climate was delightfully cool and bracing and the nights even cold.

During the second day's journey from the capital north we crossed the line. A French scientist once marked the equator with a monument and a stone slab with an inscription; but it was destroyed and part of it was taken away by a rich man and is now lying far away as a souvenir on his estate. To-day nothing marks the equator, but thanks to my maps I was able, more or less, to realise when we stepped over into the northern hemisphere.

That evening I gave the horses the best money could buy, and included a sound patting. We had covered over 4,500 miles, and when I had a smoke that evening, sitting there watching the horses enjoy their fodder, my memory wandered back along the long and difficult trail. The cigarette had gone out long before I realised it, and when the last daylight faded away behind the Cayambe that towered up into the sky quite near us, and the moon began to give the mountain a ghostly appearance with the cold bluish light that was reflected off the virgin snows above, I wrapped myself up in my blankets, proud and well satisfied.

Our trail towards the Colombian border lay past the beautiful lagoon of San Pablo where we met many drunken Indians who were coming away from a fiesta. They were all wearing large white hats, trousers of the same colour, and red ponchos, and came along, shouting, laughing, and fighting, but none molested us.

A very steep and seemingly interminable trail took us from the cool regions deep down into the hot Chota valley. Down here we were wedged in a canyon between high mountains. The heat there was terrific, and swarms of mosquitoes attacked us. A few miserable negroes live down there, their naked children playing in the dust where a few pigs, resembling starved dogs, are basking.

Fortunately we were soon on the other side of the river, and again started a long uphill climb until we reached the 'paramo,' as the cold, damp high regions are called. Here, as in some parts of Bolivia, wild cattle exist, and woe to the traveller who is unfortunate enough to meet them.

My only experience of wild cattle was in Bolivia, where an Indian hailed me from the top of a tree. A herd of these beasts had attacked him, and he had been lucky to have been able to reach this place of safety where he had spent a whole night. I assisted him to seek his burros, which had disappeared in the meantime, and after a long search we recovered them.

Two seemingly interminable and unpleasant journeys over cold and windswept 'paramos,' the worst of which is called 'El Angel,' and we gradually descended again, and finally rode into Tulcán, the Ecuadorian border town.

As a termination to this chapter, a short description of the peculiar method by which the natives of Ecuador catch condors, or mountain vultures, may be of interest. A flat piece of tableland is selected, and here a dead horse or cow, well salted, is laid. The hunters then conceal themselves in the neighbourhood and it is not long before condors assemble to take advantage of the feast thus unexpectedly provided, and gorge themselves to the limit of their capacity. When the birds have eaten so much that they are almost torpid, the hunters rush out with lassos and clubs. The birds being unable to rise quickly owing to the flatness of the ground—they require a slope to take off properly—and their post-prandial heaviness, are easily lassoed and then killed with clubs.

Colombia

The mountains, especially the snow-covered 'Chile' and 'Cumbal,' were looking their best when we crossed into Colombia next morning. The road across the border led over a natural bridge called Rumichaca (Quichua: Stone Bridge), at the border of which customs officers, wearing dirty clothes, stopped us and demanded to see my documents, but, as in most other countries, they had been advised of my arrival and treated me with courtesy. One of the frontier patrol escorted me to the little border village where the authorities gave me a very warm welcome. From there we followed a good road; but there were many long and tiring climbs over broken country.

In this neighbourhood there are several volcanoes. In 1906 and 1924 some severe earthquakes did a great deal of damage in this region and caused the loss of numerous lives. We passed near a remarkable volcanic lagoon, the colour of which, owing to the great quantities of sulphur it contains, is of a pretty green.

As in some of the other countries we had already passed, even large villages have no running water systems. There usually is a little stream, called 'acequia,' down the main street. It is used for watering animals, washing clothes and dishes, and to carry away rubbish. At the same time it is not uncommon to see people fill their water-jugs or drink out of these 'acequias'!!

Colombia has few railroads, because it is very mountainous and the general topography is such that the construction would be very expensive and difficult. Between the Ecuadorian border and Colombia's richest and most important territory, the Cauca Valley, trails provide the only means of communication, with here and there a short stretch of road.

No rain had fallen for eight months in this district, so the horses had a very bad time of it. Everything was dry, excepting where the land was under irrigation, and when sometimes I did obtain good fodder I had to pay incredible prices for it.

We halted for a few days in a little place at the foot of the volcano, Galera, which I ascended twice. The crater is enormous and terrific eruptions have endangered the neighbourhood on several occasions. The first time I made the ascent I was accompanied by a geologist who wished to study this volcano. At the time there were no serious eruptions, only a cloud of sulphur fumes rising high into the sky. When we reached the edge of the crater we beheld a wonderful scene. In the middle there was a second and smaller crater, from the inside of which the fumes were hissing and snorting, making a noise like a gigantic steam laundry. The geologist insisted on descending the steep and dangerous walls, and attempting to reach the inner crater. After some time we located a likely place where the descent might be made, and in a little less than two hours we reached our goal.

In many places the rocks were very hot, and when I noticed that my companion was smiling at my uneasiness I foolishly told him I would go right down into the main crater. Before he had time to stop me I went stumbling down over light, loose volcanic rocks. When I was at the bottom I looked at the largest holes out of which fumes came seething.

Suddenly the rocks on which I stood began to shake and tremble, and before I knew what was happening I was wrapped in a cloud of sulphur fumes. I put my handkerchief, which was wet with the perspiration caused by the ascent, to my mouth and blindly stumbled backwards. The fumes choked and irritated me, and finally I lay down to wait for my chance. A gust of cold wind cleared a path for me and I lost no time in scrambling out of this hell. We began to fear a serious eruption and hurriedly started on our return journey. For a long time we could not find the place where we had made the ascent and with the approach of evening it became dark, and a heavy rainstorm accompanied by thunder made things still more unpleasant.

Late that night we were back in our quarters, drenched to the skin and with sore feet, and I made a vow to be more careful before entering the crater of a volcano again.

In this district the Indians wear short shirts of a dark colour, rather like Scotch kilts but without pleats. They wear no hats and go barefoot. Their hair is usually long and bobbed about level with the chin. When they walk in groups they are accustomed to go in single file, one behind the other, and when all of them, one after the other, greet one with a friendly 'buen dia,' one is apt to get tired of answering the same to each, especially if there happen to be many.

One morning when I brought the horses in from pasture I noticed that one had his mane plaited. I tried to undo it, but found it tightly knotted. I asked the boy, Victor, if he knew anything about this or if he had done it, and he immediately told me 'El Duende' had been with the horses during the night. I had never heard this name and asked for an explanation. In the meantime a half-caste Indian with whom I had spent the night had come up and assured me that the boy was right.

It appears that El Duende, according to these people, is a dwarf who lives in deep canyons and desolate valleys, where he can often be heard crying like a baby or, when he is in a boisterous mood, making noises rivalling thunder. Natives firmly believe that he is very fond of horseback riding; but, being so small, is unable to sit on the horse's back, so he sits on the animal's neck, making stirrups by plaiting the mane in such a way as to be able to put his feet in it.

The only explanation I can give for this extraordinary plaiting is the dampness in the air, which may twist the hair in such a way as to form these knots; or maybe the horse does it in rubbing against a tree.

Still advancing south we crossed the hot Patia valley where a few negroes raise sheep and goats. Wolves often do damage to their flocks which are always rounded up in corrals for the night.

Lepers are numerous and I shall never forget an elderly negro who crawled out of his hut, his face blotched with disease. This ape-like being came right up to me and held out his hand, begging for money. He even touched one of my horses, and I took the precaution of disinfecting the animal thoroughly when I came to water. Near here occurred an incident that obliged me to shoot in self-defence. An intoxicated negro insulted me, and finally attacked me with his machete.

Coming out of the Patia valley we had some tiring journeys over broken and mountainous country and had to pass some very uncomfortable nights in filthy inns or miserable huts where the dirt floor is the only bed known. Sometimes one is fortunate in being treated to the luxury of a large oxhide that takes the place of a mattress and helps to keep one's blankets clean.

Popayan is one of the quaintest little towns in all Colombia. Parks and gardens reflect the good taste of the inhabitants, and the old houses are built in Spanish colonial style. In the distance one can see the active volcano, Purace, which throws up fire and smoke. The Sotara is another volcano near there, but it is extinct. Near the town is the Rio Vinagre (Vinegar River), the water of which has a very acid flavour and no fish can live in it. The vinegar taste is attributed to the fact that the river flows past the nearby volcano which abounds in sulphur.

Continuing our march over a fair trail we passed through a district where gold, silver, copper and lead mines are worked on a small scale, and I am given to understand that the country in this neighbourhood holds great possibilities in this line.

Fodder was again very scarce so I bought sugar-cane which I chopped into small pieces. At first the animals did not like this but as time went on they took to it and derived great benefit from its nutritive properties. Off and on I had to feed them on cane, bananas, bamboo, yuca—once even green tobacco leaves—and this was by no means the end of strange menus they had on the trip. I still marvel how they never went sick with the constant changes of water and fodder, and often with the complete lack of either.

The Cauca valley is very hot, but is known as the most fertile in Colombia. A railway runs most of its length and there is a good road until, farther north, one comes once more to mountainous regions.

Palmira was the first town we struck in this valley. Quite a number of cars, and even some buses, travel between here and Cali and other towns in the district. A fairly good road makes motor traffic possible, but generally speaking, in Colombia roads are as scarce as railways. A great number of negroes live here, mixing on level terms with the whites, or those who believe themselves to be of this colour. Women can often be seen smoking cigars, some having a way of shifting them from one side of the mouth to the other with their tongues that might make many men envious.

I made a side-trip to Cali, the commercial centre of the Cauca valley. Although it is a progressive town there is nothing to be seen there; hotels are only fair but at the same time most expensive, especially high tariffs existing for people who look like 'gringos' (slang for Americans).

As we all felt the stifling heat and there was a good road, we made several marches during the night. I know nothing duller than riding by night. Nothing can be seen to distract one, distances seem enormous, and hours eternities.

'Pinto,' or piebald, horses are unknown in Colombia, thus it happened that most horses shied when they saw Mancha, and one once bolted with his rider when we suddenly appeared round a bend. To my knowledge Mancha only frightened horses in Colombia, but I observed that some in other countries seemed to look at him with great curiosity, whilst they never took any notice of Gato who is a dark buckskin, or 'dun' as this colour is sometimes called in England.

A Long and Eventful Side-Trip to Bogota

I needed information about the regions in the extreme north of Colombia and southern Panama, and the only place where I could obtain this was in the capital, Bogota. All my correspondence had been forwarded there, so it was a case of crossing the mountains and returning again in order to proceed north. There is no railroad between the Cauca and Magdalena valleys, the only means of transportation being mules, oxen and horses, and it would have been foolish of me to make the trip to Bogota and back with my animals, so I looked for a good place where I could leave them in charge of Victor whilst I made the journey alone. Near a village called Santa Rosa de Cabal I found a place with excellent pasture, and when I had made all arrangements I hired a good mule to take me over the mountains to the railroad terminus on the other side. Before I left I went to have a final look at the horses and as I walked along a stony path I nearly trod on a poisonous snake which lay there in the sun. It struck at me several times, but luckily I was wearing heavy riding boots and thick woollen stockings.

After riding my bumpy mule some thirty miles, I reached Armenia, a town at the foot of the Quindio, the mountain I had to cross next day. Most of the way the trail had been bad and muddy and traversed beautiful forests.

Next morning I started to climb up the mountain. The highest point one has to reach is called 'La Linea,' nearly 10,000 feet above sea level. From there I had a marvellous view of the Cauca valley and of the mountains around. Immediately after passing 'La Linea' the down grade begins and the trail is quite good. I spent the night in a filthy 'posada' (inn) in a small settlement called San Miguel, half-way down the mountain, and at daybreak I was on my way again, for I wished to reach Ibague by noon, in time to catch the train that was to leave at 2. The trail winds steadily down, and I passed many pack-trains of mules, and oxen with enormous horns, groaning under their heavy loads.

Pack-trains usually take four days to make the crossing. The 'arrieros' (drivers) know the places where there are grass and water, and when they unload the animals they pile up the loads to form four walls. Over these they stretch a large sheet of canvas which makes the roof of a very nice little hut. Inside they make a fire and do their cooking. With all the saddle-blankets and rugs they are able to make themselves some quite comfortable beds, luxuries which I often envied them.

As I gradually descended into the valley it became warmer. Shortly before I reached my destination the trail led through one of the prettiest coffee plantations I have ever seen. A roaring and foaming mountain stream goes through it, and the coffee bushes show a wonderful green in the shade of high trees that form a regular tent over them, protecting them against the rays of the sun. Coffee plantations require shade, except those in high places.

At noon I was in Ibague. I put the mule in a good stable, where the residents were to look after it until I should return.

The train journey towards the Magdalena river is very enjoyable. The line winds through beautiful tropical country, but the climate is hot, damp and oppressive. At the terminus one has to leave the train and take a car across the river. For pedestrians and cars there is a good bridge, but not so for the trains. A short drive and I was in Girardot, the river-port which is connected with Bogota by a railroad. A few flat-bottomed stern-wheelers lay along the banks of the river and dusky crews were loading and unloading them.

Bogota has no railroad communication with the coast, thus passengers and cargo must be transported on these primitive boats, and if the river happens to be low the run from the coast up takes as many as twenty days, or even more. Absolutely no comforts exist on these vessels, and mosquitoes and the heat help to make things worse. A German company very efficiently operates an airway between Girardot and Barranquilla, the coast town.

At 6 a.m. the train left for the capital. Gradually the line winds upwards through pretty mountainous country, the temperature and vegetation changing as one reaches higher altitudes. After some six hours we reached the 'sabana,' as the tableland of Bogota is called. Wheat is grown here and the cool climate is very suitable for cattle raising.

On the train I made the acquaintance of a Scotchman. When we started below in the hot parts he was in shirt sleeves and as we were rising to the cool regions he started to protect himself with a light sweater. Later on he put a heavier one over this, and finally, when we reached the 'sabana,' he tucked himself into an overcoat that would have made an explorer of the arctic regions envious. My friend had obviously heard many tales about terrible cold, thought we were about to reach the snow line, and was not going to run any risks.

The train sped along the flat 'sabana' for another two hours, and then we pulled into Bogota. It was a dreary day and a fine drizzle was falling. An impertinent cab-driver drove me along the bumpy streets in his rickety cab that would have been an asset to any museum. I could hardly believe that this was Bogota, the town I had heard such wonders about.

The hotel I stayed at was very good, but the prices were ridiculously high, indeed, I found the cost of living in Colombia to be the highest in my experience, and at the same time it is the country where I received least for my money.

I visited the authorities, all of whom I found to be charming and most obliging.

The town offers very little of interest. The streets are in terrible condition, uneven, and full of holes which were filled with water owing to the recent rains. I was going along on foot and as no navigation nor depth charts exist I could not tell where danger was lurking. An occasional passerby served me as pilot, but when I had put my foot into one of these holes I thought it was time to buy a lifebelt or hire a taxi. I decided on the latter, but was a sorry man when the chauffeur started to speed along. I thought I was riding as wicked a buck-jumper as ever has eaten grass.

There are many churches in the town, and the Church is said to be much more powerful than the State. To the north-east, overlooking the town, are two mountains, the Montserrat and the Guadalupe. On the former a big chapel was built, the population of the town having carried up the material. Like many churches and chapels throughout the country that of Montserrat is said to be miraculous. Here I noticed a phenomenon common throughout the countries along the Pacific coast. Practically all the better class harbour a great hatred for Americans, or anything that is American. However, I invariably found that they have a habit of aping American manners and ways, and if a man happens to have been in the States he will do his best to let one know it, and others will repeatedly use the two or three words of English they know. Mexico is the only country where I never saw this. Whilst in Bogota, a small pleasure resort was inaugurated. Imagine my surprise when I heard that it had been named 'Coney Island.' The idea struck me as being as funny as the way they pronounce it: 'Connay Eeslahnd.'

I had not come here sightseeing, and as soon as I had collected all the geographical data that existed I started the return trip to the place where

I had left the horses. Although I had met many charming people I was disappointed with Bogota, a town I found to be years behind the times, dull and gloomy.

The following extract out of *El Mundo Al Dia* (Oct. 12th, 1926) ought to prove both interesting and amusing.

The First Tragedy in El Vergel

The fiestas organised by the inspector of Las Cruzes, Dr. M., in the district of El Vergel, for the purpose of raising funds for the completion of the park which this official proposed to make in the plaza of Girardot, have taken place as fixed in the programme. Yesterday the inspector informed us that no bloody deed had occurred and that the fiesta had been very orderly. However, yesterday the first tragedy took place. During the bullfight a beast gored an individual named Marcos Aguirre who suffered serious wounds. Having been taken to the hospital he died a few moments later. This incident did not damp the gaiety of the fiesta which continued undisturbed.

I was in possession of all the information I needed about the regions north, towards Panama. Experts informed me that it is utterly impossible to make the trip across the 'Choco' and the 'Darien.' These regions are vast swamps and virgin forests, many of which have never been trodden by human foot. No land, but only fluvial means of communication exist, and to attempt to this crossing would be a foolhardy enterprise in which both horses and rider would perish. This opinion was confirmed by General Jaramillo, who had unsuccessfully attempted to take a Colombian army across these regions during the war with Panama. This gentleman had spent twenty-five years of his life exploring those parts, and is probably the outstanding expert on these regions.

My plans were made; I would forge ahead as far north as possible, and then take ship across to Colon. Accordingly, as soon as I arrived in Ibague, I saddled up the mule and started back over the Quindio. I could not afford to lose time, the rainy season being nearly due. As I had been over this trail before I thought I could travel after dark without running a risk, and this nearly caused a disaster. Before reaching San Miguel, the little settlement half-way up the mountain, a small bridge spans a deep canyon with roaring waters below. Near this bridge was a sharp curve I had forgotten all about. It was pitch dark and, when I heard the noise of the water, I knew that I was near the bridge. I guided the mule along slowly, and suddenly the animal refused to move. Try what I would, I could not make it take another step forward. After a few more futile attempts I dismounted and struck a match to see what the animal might be shying at. A cold ripple went down my back when I was aware that we had come off the trail, having missed the curve, and were at the very brink of the precipice. 'Mule sense' had saved me.

Next day I passed 'La Linea.' Near this point travellers have a habit of making little crosses with sticks and planting them alongside the trail, believing this will bring luck. Others carve crosses in the soft rocks, and in the course of time extraordinary numbers of these crosses have accumulated.

A heavy rain began to fall and the trail became rather slippery. Halfway down the other side I passed a family on their way up. Two pretty little girls with curly hair and chubby cheeks were at the head of the caravan. Just as I passed them the mule of one girl slipped and stumbled. The kiddie hung on like an expert and as soon as she had recovered balance she gave me a merry smile. There are smiles we never forget, and this was one of them. The rain was beating into her rosy face, and from her long, light-brown curls heavy drops were dripping, and when she showed me her pearl-white teeth between cherry-red lips I felt like bending over and kissing her.

Next came Pa and Ma, both looking worried and tired out, which did not surprise me. Behind them a man led a mule with two crates, one on each flank. Inside the crates were two little children who were peeping out through a small opening in the sail-cloth that protected them against the rain. At the rear came another mule, fairly groaning under a huge load of household articles, pots and pans clattering like an old-fashioned tinker's barrow. On the very top of this extraordinary load were cages with birds of various species and even a couple of cats. I have seen several such family caravans in the Andes, but I shall always remember the two cheerful and plucky little girls of the Quindio.

The rain lasted all day and throughout the night. When I was about to leave Armenia next day, I was advised to make a two days' detour over a fair road. Mule drivers warned me that the trail I had used a week before was now in a terrible condition. Thinking their report was exaggerated, and to save time, I took no notice and started back by my old route. At first I found everything as I had expected, but when I entered the forest I began to think I was lost; every now and again some peculiar landmark convinced me that I was on the right path, although it was impossible to recognise it. The recent rains had transformed it into one mass of heavy, pasty mud and water. For long distances my poor mule sank in to the girth and had difficulty in pulling his legs out of the mud.

Towards midday it became quite dark, and presently a regular deluge began to fall. To make it worse, where the trail led through a hollow, so much water accumulated that it reached half-way up the mule's flanks. In spite of my rubber cape I was soaked to the skin, and after a while I did not even trouble to raise my legs when we waded through deep water. Lightning began to flash, and ear-shattering thunder-claps shook the forest. This furious battle of the elements lasted for what seemed an eternity—and then, suddenly, there was a blank.... How long it lasted I do not know, but the next thing I remember is the sensation of sitting in a soft bed, trying in vain to see through the darkness. I remember rubbing my eyes, and seeing red and violet blotches chasing each other in circles.

Once this dance of fireworks had slowed down I gradually began to see. I had no idea where I was, much less what had happened. Looking around me I saw my mule sitting on its haunches like a dog, every now and again shaking its head. This struck me as so funny that I watched the animal for quite a while before I began to think clearly. A loud thunder-clap brought me to my senses, and it dawned on me that we had nearly been struck by lightning. When I put on my hat, which was lying near me, the roots of my hair pricked like so many pins. I had fears that the mule was hurt, but to my great relief it got up after a few pulls at the bridle.

Towards evening the rain stopped, and when I arrived at Pereira I ordered a double whack of brandy, and as I was drinking it I wished that if I have to die an unnatural death it will be to be struck by lightning.

On the next day I found the boy and the horses in excellent condition. Victor told me he had been dreaming that I was struck by lightning and that he had buried me in the mud alongside some trail. The boy had no idea I was coming back so soon. Was this coincidence or telepathy?

The Great Swamp Barrier

It certainly felt good to be with my companions again, and although the trail towards Manizales was nothing but mud and 'camellones,' I was happy to be moving once more. When we reached that town it looked like a shell-battered French village, for a fire had recently destroyed most of it, and reconstruction had begun under American engineers. I was unfortunate in finding a bed in a musty old hotel constructed of wood. With it, thousands of insects had escaped the purification of fire. To make things worse, a stranded theatrical company was crowded into the mouldy place, and throughout the night some of them practised music on different instruments whilst others danced to the tune of a gramophone, and the actresses cackled and shrieked like parrots whenever one of their admirers told a stupid joke.

Needless to say I did not make a long stay in this town, and following the mountainous trail north we stopped at a 'posada.' I was looking forward to a good and much-needed sleep, but, as bad luck would have it, I was not to enjoy this luxury.

We had fed the horses with chopped sugar-cane and had finished our supper of beans and hot cocoa, a general favourite in Colombia. Just as we were spreading our blankets on the floor preparatory to turning in, the trampling of hoofs was heard outside. Two men whom, although not in uniform, I afterwards found to be policemen, dismounted and unstrapped what seemed to be a big bundle from a third animal. This bundle proved to be a mad woman they were taking to an asylum in Bogota. The poor woman could not walk when she was lifted off, and groaned in agony when she tried to do so. I was obliged to go and construct a barricade so that my animals would not fight with the newcomers' mules, lest they get hurt, besides losing their fodder.

Many of the natives never buy fodder for their beasts when they see another traveller's animals with plenty. The construction of such barricades and the cleaning of the place, picking up broken glass, wires, etc., was a job I often had to do, and I can recommend better pastimes after a long and tiring journey than this seemingly light task which was a constant nightmare to me, but which I never neglected.

With all the noise the mad woman made throughout the night we did not get much sleep. In the morning she struggled desperately with the two men when they tried to lift her on to the mule to continue the journey, and I often wonder if she arrived in Bogota alive, for she was already in bad condition when I saw her.

The trail led over mountains and through valleys; in parts it was good, in others bad. At night we sometimes stopped at some 'posada' or in some uninteresting dirty settlement.

For some reason, inexplicable to me, most of these villages are built on the very tops of the mountains. All one is able to buy in the little shops, where such exist, is 'panela' (unrefined sugar), tobacco, unsweetened chocolate, rice, beans, sardines, and, of course, 'aguardiente' (spirits), as well as some other articles that help to make existence possible for these simple people. I often bought my horses 'panela,' of which they had become very fond. Many a time did Mancha follow me right into these little stores, well knowing what was coming his way, much to the consternation of the vendors. When I was hungry I had to eat those unattractive and dangerous sardines; but then, travellers must not be choosers there. I shall not be sorry if I never taste sardines again.

As we were nearing Medellin we had a wonderful view of the Cauca valley, with its silvery river winding north and south as far as the eye could reach. In this neighbourhood tobacco is grown. The leaves are hung to dry in huge huts with high straw roofs, the shelters being made of bamboo canes, with sides open to admit as much air as possible.

The nearer one gets to Medellin the neater are the huts and houses. Peasants passed us, going afoot with little leather bags slung over their shoulders. In these bags they carry money, cigars, etc.

I found these people to be most inquisitive. If I happened to ask any of them how far it was to the next village, a thing they never seemed to know, they would immediately bombard me with dozens of questions, such as: 'Where are you from?' 'Where are you going?' 'What is your business?' 'How much did those horses cost?' 'How much this?' 'How much that?' 'Have you any familia?' (family), which means, 'Have you a wife or wives and children?' Having been asked these questions so often before, my answers much depended on the humour I was in at the time they were put to me.

Medellin is the capital of the State of Antioquia, and has between seventy and eighty thousand inhabitants. The Antioquians are very industrious, thrifty and enterprising. The very aspect of their neatly whitewashed houses, with pretty flowers on the window-sills and neat little gardens, so very different from those in other parts of Colombia I had been through, show what the inhabitants are like. Medellin is going ahead by leaps and bounds and the progressive spirit of its people will soon make it the first town of the country. Medellin goes ahead; Bogota stands still. A railroad connects the former with Puerto Berrio on the Magdalena river, by which we were obliged to go. I was bitterly disappointed, but to make the expedition to Panama by land is impossible, as I have stated before.

Magdalena, the River of Mud
and Crocodiles

W hen we arrived at the little port new troubles began. True, there is a good hotel in the place, but I had no end of trouble to accommodate the animals. Several boats called at the port, but most of them were on their way up river, and those that were going down to the coast had no room.

Flat barges are lashed to the sides of the river boats, and in them most of the cargo and live stock is carried. Cattle are packed so tightly that it is impossible to feed and water them. I have seen a great deal of animal suffering in different countries, but I would never have believed such deliberate cruelty possible; cruelty brought about by sheer laziness and complete lack of humane instincts.

A boat arrived with two barges full of cattle. The poor animals were packed like sardines and bellowing in anguish. The steam escape of the engine faced one of these barges, and when the pressure on the boilers was too high and the valves were opened the steam hissed straight at the animals that were unfortunate enough to be rammed in near the pipe. Several lay dead whilst the others were gasping and vainly trying to stampede. Some had fallen and were being trampled on by the others, whilst groups of lousy, dark-faced men of the crew, and dusky dock-workers were looking at this hellish scene with expressionless eyes. A sheet of tin or a board hung over the pipe would have prevented all this suffering. But then this would have meant work.

Again I saw cattle being unloaded, clubbed, poked and kicked to make them drag themselves into the corral where they were given no food or water. Quite a number lay down to die whilst the 'gallinazos' (buzzards) were perched on nearby roofs and trees, patiently waiting for a certain repast.

Here the river is much wider than in Girardot, and possibly even a little more oily and muddy. Life in the village seems like a slow-motion picture, and the people move along as lazily as the very river. The atmosphere is hot and sticky; I hated the place.

I went from one dirty shipping office to another, but it was hard to get information from the uncivil and sleepy employees. Some of the offices were open and jackets were hanging on nails, but the 'empleados' were out, probably drinking 'café,' or, maybe, having a siesta. As this seemed hopeless, I went aboard several ships to speak to the 'capitanes,' but found everybody asleep, excepting the gangs of mestizos and riggers who were loading and unloading the cargo, whilst others were sitting on the bank looking on. At last, on the third day, I heard a rumour about a ship that was to arrive at noon, a ship on its way down to the coast; I had hopes that something might turn up and hastened to the shipping office, which I found open but empty.

I had waited what seemed an etermty when a dusky fellow came slouching in. He slowly seated himself but never looked at me, nor did he ask what I wanted. After a while he began to sharpen a pencil, and then opened a drawer from which he took a printed form, all the while puffing at a cigarro that matched his complexion. When he had finished with his pencil he slowly raised his eyes and looked at me, and condescended to examine my papers. I thought he would never finish filling in those forms, but somehow he managed to do it and I heaved a deep sigh of relief when he had signed them, adorning his name with a most elaborate wriggly line and endless curls that seemed to fill him with pride and satisfaction, judging by the way he admired his work of art, cocking his head from side to side while he held the 'documento' before him.

Victor was waiting with the horses, which we got on board by walking them over a plank that looked none too secure.

There were only two passenger classes on our 'good ship'. The first are permitted to sleep and walk on the upper deck, whilst the second are at liberty to make themselves comfortable among the cargo and cattle or wherever they find space. I had booked first, but when I looked for my cabin I was informed that this would cost six dollars (gold) extra. Having paid the amount I was shown what they call a 'cabina,' which reminded me of the first photographic dark-room I had entered as a schoolboy, excepting that the laboratory was relatively clean and slightly ventilated. The bed consisted of a wooden frame with nothing on it, passengers being expected to bring 'extras' with them. I set to work cleaning out the place, and with the saddles made the beds for the boy and myself.

The poor horses suffered more while travelling in the barge lashed alongside the steamer than ever they had done on the march. The broiling sun beat down on the low tin roof of the barge, while they stood in a little space between coffee sacks and got practically no air. From time to time I would throw a bucket of water on them to cool them off. I also covered the tin roof with coarse grass which I cut at night when the ship tied to the side of the bank for wood, the only fuel used on these vessels. (Magdalena boats do not travel at night but tie to the banks until daylight.)

This gave me opportunity to cut plenty of coarse swamp-grass for fodder. The mosquitoes were terrible, especially during the night when they often found an opening in the net under which the boy and myself slept. I regularly took small doses of quinine to prevent malaria, but the boy flatly refused to do this, believing this bitter substance must be poison.

The river is full of 'caimanes' (crocodiles) and some sand banks are literally covered with these ugly brutes lying there sunning themselves. The 'capitan' gave me permission to shoot, so I had some good fun picking out the largest. Whenever a particularly huge specimen came in sight the crew would excitedly call me. It is amazing how fast even the largest 'croc' can move when he is hit, and it is very difficult to kill them on the spot, their skin being so thick that the bullets ricochet off. To produce instantaneous death one has to shoot through the eyes or hit the soft place immediately behind the left foreleg where the bullet will reach the heart.

We were on the slow-moving boat for three days. The navigation is about as crude as anybody might imagine. We passed Barranca, where an American company operates an oilfield. From there a pipeline has been laid, through which the oil is pumped to Cartagena at the coast, some 300 miles away. The laying down of this pipe is in itself a masterpiece, for it leads through swamps, jungles and forests, and .the work was finished in the incredibly short time of eighteen months.

I had often warned Victor about drinking water out of any ditch or stream we came to. For his own good, I even gave him a good hiding on more than one occasion when I caught him at it. But he had a bad habit of sneaking away when he was thirsty and drinking without my permission. The result was that he contracted fever, and the mosquitoes of the Magdalena river induced a serious attack of malaria. I was happy when we were off that horrible vessel with its filthy food and unsanitary sanitary arrangements, as the Irishman would say.

From a little port called Calamar we made the overland trip to Cartagena at the coast, where we arrived without incident.

Although I looked all over the town, the only place I could hire to leave the horses was a small backyard full of pigs and mud, and it was no easy matter to find fodder, but after a long chase around I finally obtained some.

Next day, early in the afternoon, I went to pay my respects to the authorities, and only realised my mistake in arriving so early when I had already entered the government house.

At the entrance I passed several men whose shabby uniforms suggested that they were policemen. They were seated on a bench and snoring melodiously, with the regularity of waves breaking on the sea shore. I entered and looked around, but not a soul was to be seen, except a couple of skinny dogs slumbering in the shade against a wall. I ventured to peep into an office where I saw two men, obviously 'secretarios,' who were fast asleep with their feet on their desks.

I began to think I must be dreaming about the palace of the sleeping beauty. I stood there, lost in reverie, imagining myself to be exploring the palace and finding the princess slumbering on her couch and waking her up as the prince did, according to the fairy tale, when suddenly one of the 'secretarios' moved an arm to flick away a fly that had settled on his face. He opened his eyes and saw me. Without changing his comfortable position he yawned and grunted that it was half an hour before working time, and then he closed his eyes again. I returned later and was very well received by the officials, who showed me every courtesy.

Cartagena is one of the most interesting towns I visited on my ride. It was founded by the Spaniards and in those times was a formidable fortress. Many of the old buildings and fortifications stand to-day, and the dungeons are inhabited by the poor. Across the bay there is a high, steep hill that comes to an abrupt precipitous fall on the far side.

On this hill stand the ruins of what used to be a nunnery in the old times. When Morgan attacked and sacked the town his men thought they would go up there to have a look at the nuns. It is said that some of the latter, seeing the men approach, jumped down the precipice. A 'historian' put the theory before me that these nuns were in such a hurry to be the first to greet the pirates that they risked the short cut!

Whilst I waited for a ship that was to take us across to Panama, I had ample opportunity to visit some of the places of interest in and around this historical town.

Here I made the acquaintance of an American lady, Mrs. Kerr, who had lived most of her life in the jungles, shooting for the Museum of Natural History of New York. Although she was seventy years of age at the time I met her, she was like a girl of twenty in mind and body. She was running a small curiosity shop where all the 'rough necks' from the oil-fields would congregate to have a yarn with her. Even at her age she had the reputation of being a 'mean shot' and able to compete with the best. As we had a great deal in common, I spent several hours yarning about mountains, plains and jungles with her, and often since my mind has wandered back to 'Mrs. Kerr's Cabinet,' as her place was sometimes called by her friends.

The Royal Netherlands ship *Crynsson* arrived, and I was told to be ready to load the horses early next morning. We arrived at the appointed time, but were kept waiting in the broiling sun near the wharf until after 4 p.m. After standing in the sun for a few hours the poor horses began to pant with the infernal heat, and I had to cool them down by throwing sea water over them with a tin, lest they got heat stroke. Finally they were lifted on board by means of slings. Mancha showed his disapproval of such treatment by kicking in all directions when he landed on deck, but soon became quiet when he saw me arrive with an armful of the fodder I had bought for the short sea-trip.

When I had attended to everything I realised that I was not feeling well. Waiting in the fierce sun and the hurrying about all day had been too much for me. The officers and passengers were all eager to attend to me, and by evening I was feeling much better.

'Á Dios' South America!

Just before sunset, as the engines began to throb, I went up on deck to have a final look at South America. Victor was very poorly and in a terrible state of excitement, for he had never seen the sea before, and now he was on a modern liner! The horses were munching away at their fodder whilst groups of curious passengers looked on.

The sun was setting in a sea of fire, the horizon looking like a burning prairie, while the ship majestically ploughed its way through the ripples that reflected the glowing sky like fireworks. Slowly the black silhouette of the land became thinner, stars were beginning to twinkle and the ship started to sway with the swell of the open sea.

For a long time I stood enjoying the cool air on deck, thinking over the many incidents and adventures we had lived whilst travelling close on 5,500 miles from one end of the South American continent to the other. The whole thing seemed like a dream, pleasant and otherwise, but the chill of the night brought me back to reality and I went to see the horses for the last time before turning in.

Next afternoon we docked at Colon. What a difference I noticed there. The Canal Zone officials, businesslike yet courteous, some of them dressed in neat uniforms, all were attending to their respective tasks, and things went like clockwork. Mancha again objected to being hoisted off the ship, and no sooner had he been lowered on the concrete dock than he went off, bucking through the customs house. Passengers and officials ran helter skelter in all directions whilst Mancha continued his war-dance among luggage and trunks. I finally caught him, and with a few kind words and a little petting made him understand that there was no ill-feeling, and that therefore such behaviour was out of place. Although there were some difficulties about landing my horses and entering the Canal

Zone with them, the officials all joined in helping me to avoid getting entangled in 'red tape' as they so nicely called it, and by evening the animals were living in luxury in the Panama Railroad stables.

Space does not permit me to go into details about the whole-hearted assistance I was given by every official and civilian I came in contact with in the Canal Zone, and the kind welcome I was given everywhere I went. I had not been there twenty-four hours when it seemed to me as if I had been there for weeks. All the friends I had made in that short time made me feel entirely at home.

Victor was very ill, and had to be interned in the hospital, and I was fully aware that it was out of the question to take him with me, for the next lap of the ride promised to be a very arduous and difficult one. The unhealthy climate of the regions towards Costa Rica would be altogether too dangerous for the boy who would leave the hospital in a much weakened condition.

We arrived in Colon towards the end of November, and the rainy season was still in full swing. Although the dry season is supposed to commence early in December, it was still raining towards the end of that month. Heavy rains had fallen every day excepting the 14th of December, and according to the Hydrographic Office the total rainfall of the year, until December 18th, was 147.38 inches, which was only surpassed in 1915, when there were 152.77 inches. All along my route I had encountered exceptionally heavy rains and adverse weather conditions which were put down to the fact that the Humboldt current had changed its course considerably, bringing the temperature of the Pacific Ocean along the coast of South America down 5 degrees below normal on the year's average.

Now I was waiting for the dry season, which only lasts three months, to set in, and even then there was no hurry, for it would be just as well to wait a little to allow the numerous rivers to go down and to let the jungles dry up a little before attempting the crossing to Costa Rica. The horses were in good hands and were enjoying themselves, so I had an opportunity to do likewise.

When I arrived in the Canal Zone I looked more like a Robinson Crusoe than anything else, but as the sun of fellowship stands at its meridian even in Panama nobody took much notice of this.

I shall never forget the occasion on which I walked into a beautiful building in Cristobal where a dance was being held at the time. I had only just arrived and needed information. I was wearing a rain-soaked poncho and a large weather-beaten sombrero; my boots had seen better days and so had my complexion, if a man has such a thing. The well-dressed and fairskinned American ladies and girls who came to peep at me made me feel self-conscious in the extreme, for I looked so rough and dirty that I dared not do more than give a casual glance in their direction every now and again. For the first time I realised how much I had changed; I felt out of place and walked as if I were moving on ice, and as soon as I had finished my business I felt like running away and into the wilds.

After the luxury of a hot bath I lay down in a soft, clean bed, and then I began to think over matters. I put myself in the place of the people at the dance and looked at myself as I thought they must have done. I wondered if I had degenerated, what degeneration was; but after some mental debating I came to the conclusion that I had only become rough, yes, very rough.

In the morning I bought myself clean clothes, and when the barber had finished making the best of a bad job, 'dolling me up,' I felt like a new man. How light the shoes felt, how thin and clean the new suit, and how ridiculously small the newly-purchased hat! When I saw myself in a mirror I felt like an impostor, but I was happy, my vacations had begun. I did not worry about what was ahead of me, and the horses had all they could desire. When I met some of my newly-made acquaintances, who were soon to become good friends, they did not recognise me until I spoke to them.

This was the first time I had lived among Americans, for I had never been in the United States. I had previously known a few who hailed from there, but not enough to be able to form a correct opinion about so big a nation. To judge a country by its tourists abroad is ridiculous, but unfortunately is often done, and the impression some of them are apt to make is often not one that reflects credit on the nation of their origin.

The Canal Zone is supposed to be 'dry,' but even if this were the case, one has merely to cross the street to Colon, on the Atlantic side, or to Panama City on the Pacific, and there it is as 'wet' as in 'dry' New York or Chicago. In these former towns, which belong to the republic of Panama, if politically such a country exists, one finds one bar alongside the other. In addition there are some cabarets and scores of houses of ill fame. Tourists leave their money in the former, whilst soldiers mostly frequent the latter, especially on or immediately after pay-days, when they squander their dollars and very often their health.

The difference between the Panamanian and American side is as great as that between day and night. If it were not for American sanitary inspectors and influence, no white man could live in those towns, and were it not for the Canal and the amazing accomplishment of sanitation of these formerly deadly regions, Panama, to-day, would hardly figure on the average map at all.

The Silent Canal

It would be out of place if I tried to describe the Canal; technical men as well as expert pens have often done this, so I will limit my description to a few personal impressions only. Engineers kindly showed me round and explained many technical details to me, but I am afraid I might just as well have been listening to Einstein lecturing on the fourth dimension. However, bad as I was at understanding, I was a good listener.

The control house at the Gatun Locks was of particular interest to me, for, in spite of its intricate mechanism, the actual manipulation and control of the locks is simplicity in itself. When a ship approaches a special crew fixes cables to electric trolleys, called 'mules,' and these steadily pull the vessel into the lock. In the control house there is a complete miniature set of locks on a large marble table, and this set indicates every movement of the real locks without. The only difference is that the miniature sets do not fill with water, the water level being shown on indicators that resemble large thermometers. When a ship has been moved into position for the next movement of the locks, the operator in the control house is advised by telephone. By turning a small handle on the table, the engines that open or close the gates, move the safety chains, or govern the water valves, are set in motion. A most intricate and ingenious 'fool-proof' device, more complicated than any Chinese puzzle yet invented, prevents the operator from making a mistake. Should he, by carelessness, try to turn a wrong handle, an error that might have disastrous results, this safety device would make the engines refuse to work.

Every man being trained for his particular job, things at the Canal go like clockwork; there is no shouting or wild excitement. What a difference between this and some ports I had seen. Often did I wander to Gatun, where I could have sat for hours watching the ships being put through the locks, and as I sat there, admiring and fascinated, I called it 'The Silent Canal.'

I had made friends with a Canal pilot, and one day he invited me to accompany him through on a ship. On board the captain of the vessel did everything to make the day a pleasant one for me, and the pilot saw to it that I should learn something.

Unless one keeps the eye on the compass one is bound to lose direction completely. I thought I had developed a good sense in this line, but when at one point the pilot turned to me to ask me where north was I was

completely out. He told me that even expert navigators invariably lose
their bearings at this very same point, unless, of course, they consult the
needle. This is due to the fact that there are several twists and turns, owing
to the nature of the hills around.

Good Times

The army and navy officials were particularly nice to me, and I was
shown as much as time permitted. On Christmas Day I had dinner
with the 4th Field Artillery, in Gatun, and a very enjoyable evening I spent.

After having stayed for some time in Cristobal, on the Atlantic side, I
shifted over to Ancon, on the Pacific, where I stayed for some days.

At the post office something happened that always amuses me when I
recall it. I had gone to buy some stamps and when I saw the word 'gold'
written over a window and 'silver' over another, I naturally went to the
one marked 'silver.' Instead of attending to me, the clerk made a sign to
me as if indicating me to go over to the other window marked 'gold,' and
then turned away. Although I am not of Scotch origin I did not like the
idea of going to 'gold,' silver was quite enough for me, especially as I had
only paper notes, silver and nickels on me, so I returned to 'silver' once
more, and then the clerk realised that I was a stranger. He explained that
'gold' was exclusively for white people and 'silver' for the coloured.
Much relieved, I boldly stepped over to 'gold,' where I obtained what I
wanted, but as I walked away I could not help thinking that whoever
thought of this classification must have been colour-blind, or else possessed
of a very extraordinary sense of humour.

Among people in the Canal Zone the Pacific and Atlantic coasts are
often called Gold and Silver coast respectively. Very soon I became
familiar with these terms, which are used throughout the Zone, and,
needless to say, I never blundered again.

One day I was invited to visit the 'Tarpon Club,' which is situated just
below the spillway near the Gatun Locks. I was informed that tarpon is
about the gamest fish that swallows a hook. I used to think I was a bit of
a fisherman myself, although my arms are not abnormally long.

When I was invited I heard so many stories about tarpons that I hardly
slept the night before I was to make their acquaintance. I was told that
the Prince of Wales and other celebrities never missed the opportunity of
doing some tarpon fishing on their way through, and heard that the
Prince had caught none on the occasion when he went to the club during

his visit to Panama. If he did the same kind of fishing we did, I should not be in the slightest surprised if this report were true.

When the visitor enters the 'Tarpon Club' he sees a huge stuffed fish, almost the size of a small whale, hanging up, and he is informed that this is the largest that has been caught there since Cleopatra went through the Canal to meet Anthony. He is then requested to divest himself of his clothes and to put on short trousers and wickedly-spiked shoes, in order not to fall whilst wading on the slippery rocks. When I had done this, a rod with a huge brass spool, more complicated than the instruments of an astronomical observatory, was thrust into my hands. When a small fish, to serve as live bait, had gone through tortures that rivalled the most ingenious of the Spanish Inquisition, I must have looked rather pale, for presently a crafty arm was put into a locker and out came a bottle medicine. The rest of the fellows crowded around and with eager eyes watched the cork being drawn. After awhile another Sesame was opened, and a second 'Scotch tarpon' was fished out of it.

The medicine began to take effect, and as time went on the fishing stories became more befitting the place, until at last the huge stuffed specimen hanging there seemed like a mere minnow. Towards evening somebody suggested going out to see if the river was still running its usual course, or, if perhaps it had changed colour, which I thought was a sure sign that the fishing promised to be good. By this time what, some hours before, had been live bait, was now the healthy corpse of a small fish, but as I was sure that tarpon were not very particular about their food I did not change it.

For some time we cast our lines into the swift, deep waters, and then, one by one the company returned to the club house, saying the fish must have become tired of waiting for us so long. I began to think there was something in that, and started to take in my line. What was my surprise to find a small fish wriggling on my hook when I lifted it out of the water. At first I thought it was merely my bait that had come back to life, or that the medicine had affected my optic organs. Upon close observation I found that a fish slightly bigger than the bait was on the hook.

I at once returned to the clubhouse and related every detail connected with my wonderful catch. I could only bring forward two theories: one, that this fish wanted to commit suicide; the other, that it must have been an elder brother or sister of the ill-fated bait who, during heroic efforts to free his unfortunate relative in order to give it decent burial, had had the misfortune to become hooked, with lamentable results.

The shades of evening were already falling when a group of heroes came out of the clubhouse; the day's sport had been a strenuous one, for it takes

A Bridge

Where even a tight-rope walker might not always be at ease. Spanning
an awe-inspiring chasm in Peru, this wobbly structure sways so much
that nervous travellers are often blindfolded, strapped on a stretcher,
and carried across by the Indians

Ancient Indian Fountain

In a settlement in the Peruvian Andes

Amazing sunsets and cloud pictures appeared
at points 10,000 to 15,000 feet above the sea

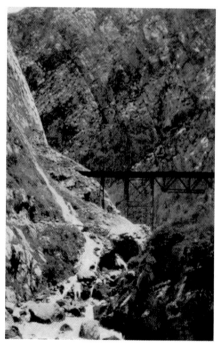

A TRAIL
Under a bridge of the Central Peruvian Railway

THE VAST DESERTS
Along the Peruvian coast are veritable infernos.
For days the horses waded in deep, burning sand

A SETTLEMENT IN NORTHERN PERU

Pre-historic Ruins
Of San Juan de Teotihuacán, near Mexico City. The origin of these
temples and two colossal pyramids which stand in the close vicinity
is likely to remain veiled in mystery

Runa Indian Women of Ecuador

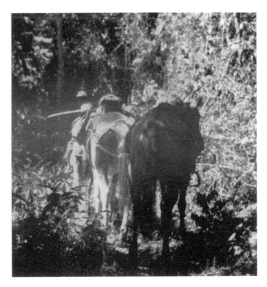

VICTOR, AN INDIAN BOY
Of Ecuador, who accompanied the author as far
as Panama, leads the way into a jungle forest

FRONTIER FORMALITIES NEAR RUMICHACA
(Stone Bridge), a natural bridge which marks the border
between Ecuador and Colombia

'MANCHA' PASSES A PACK OX
On a Colombian trail. The ox can carry a much heavier
burden than a pack mule. In mud he is also steadier

THE HORSES STAND HEAD TO TAIL
Fighting flies off each other. Despite heat, the author often wore
a thick sweater in the tropics to ward off mosquitoes and
because it tore less readily than a shirt

A dense, verdant mat of ferns, vines,
giant 'elephant ears' covers the earth in
Colombian jungle regions

THROUGH JUNGLES THE PACK WAS KEPT AT AN IRREDUCIBLE MINIMUM

CROSSING THE PANAMA CANAL
The author, assisted by an American Canal Zone policeman,
taking the horses over the Pedro Miguel lock

A GUIDE LEADS THE WAY
Towards the mountains and dense jungles between Panama and Costa Rica

THE HUT OF A PANAMANIAN JUNGLE DWELLER
To make a clearing these half-caste Indians cut and burn trees
and shrubbery and plant beans, bananas, tobacco, etc.

READY FOR THE POT
Despite popular belief to the contrary, food is not
always plentiful and easy to find in jungles

IN THE DENSE, DARK JUNGLE
Near the Panama–Costa Rica border, This frontier
has been surveyed, but has no landmarks

FERRYING 'MANCHA' ACROSS THE RIO LEMPA
In Salvador, Central America. This is the only river where a ferry
was used for the horses; when bridges failed, they swam

THE LAGOON OF COATEPEQUE, SALVADOR, AT SUNSET
This lagoon is the crater of a volcano which mysteriously filled with water

A DETACHMENT OF GUATEMALAN SOLDIERS
Here the author halted for one night

SPANISH RUINS IN ANTIGUA
From this old capital of Guatemala,
Spain's governors supplanted much
of the older civilization of the
earlier Americans

THE 'PALACIO MUNICIPAL'
Of Old Guatemala

AN INDIAN PROCESSION
Through a village near Lake Atitlan. About 60 per cent
of the people in Guatemala are pure Indians

A GUATEMALAN INDIAN GIRL

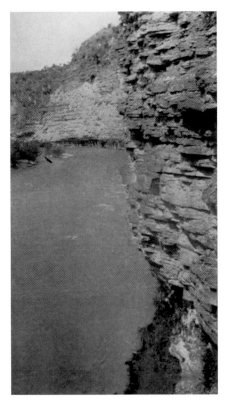

THE CANYON
Of the Rio de las Vueltas in southern Mexico

A BELLE OF TEHUANTEPEC

GIANT CACTUS PLANTS IN MEXICO

When these soldiers—who escorted the author through bandit-infested regions in Mexico—got tired of walking they commandeered donkeys from owners along the route a 'he man' to be a good tarpon fisher—and I realised it.

Victor came out of hospital, but his physical condition was not good enough to allow him to continue with me; fortunately, however, a friend gave him a job in a mechanical workshop where he was given a wonderful chance to make a good start in life.

The evening before I left him he asked me if he might spend the last night with the horses. He had become desperately fond of them, especially of Mancha, whom he would fondle all day, and I shall never forget the way the boy expressed his sorrow when we left him. Having no further use for his pony I sold it to a friend in Panama, where he found a good home.

We started our trip towards Costa Rica early in January, following an excellent concrete road to the Pedro Miguel locks where we crossed the Canal.

A Question and Its Answer

I have been asked countless times how on earth we managed to cross the Panama Canal, and this eternal question has become a regular nightmare with me. Hardly anybody ever asks me how we crossed the numerous rivers that have no bridges, or how we travelled long stretches of swampland, but every other person I meet wants to know how we crossed 'that Panama Canal.'

In order to satisfy those readers who might also be wondering how such a stupendous and amazing feat can be accomplished, I will explain how very simple it was. The Gatun and Pedro Miguel locks each have a very large water-level gate, and when these are closed one can drive over them with a car. All the other lock gates have railings to enable pedestrians to walk over them with safety, but these gates are narrow, and it is not permitted to take horses over them. However, the wide water-level gates at Gatun and Pedro Miguel are frequently used for this purpose by the army. Near the latter locks there is also a ferry that takes horses, mules and wagons across, and this also is used chiefly by the troops.

When the gate was closed I walked my horses over it. Then I took leave of some friends who had come to bid me 'bon voyage,' and started towards the U.S. army post on the other side near the famous Culebra Cut, a Canal Zone policeman accompanying me to show the shortest way there.

Mancha Suffers a Slight Accident

N ear a signal station, overlooking the bend near the Culebra Cut a
photographer wished to take some pictures of us. Just after he had
done this, I noticed that Mancha was lifting his near hind leg. Upon
examining it I found that he had a deep cut just below the pastern joint.
He must have cut himself when he stepped into a wire that was lying on
the path where we had made a short cut to save time and distance. He was
very lame by the time we arrived at Camp Gaillard, as the army post was
called, and the policeman took me to the guardhouse, where the officer
on duty immediately said that he would see that I was assisted.

I was very puzzled when I heard the soldiers speak to me in very
broken English, and also when I found that the majority did not understand this language at all. All wore American uniforms and had the
regulation equipment, and on a mast fluttered the stars and stripes. Rather
perplexed I asked for an explanation, and was told that this regiment
consisted almost entirely of Porto Ricans, with the exception of the officers and a few men.

Presently the officer on duty introduced me to the commander, who
immediately offered me the hospitality of the post until Mancha should
recover, whereupon the horses were taken to the quarantine stable where
the veterinary officer came to examine the poor cripple. His verdict was
that the injury was not serious, but that, owing to the location of the cut,
it would be some time before the animal would be in a condition to
proceed. The news was not very encouraging, for I was afraid I might not
reach Costa Rica before the rains set in again if I happened to be held up
too long; however, there was no help for it, so I was given a room and soon
settled down to army life.

My opinion of American hospitality was already a high one, and it would
be impossible for me to go into details, relating the countless favours that
were shown to me. When I reached the U.S. I found that the same
wonderful spirit exists there, and unfortunately I am only able to express
my sincere appreciation and gratitude in feeble words.

When the annual army and navy manœuvres in Panama began, Mancha
was still unfit for travel, so I was invited to accompany the troops to a
provisional camp which was pitched some twenty miles west of the
Canal. By this time I was quite at home among the troops and had many
friends among the officers and men. Sitting near the camp kitchen and

listening to the soldiers' talk was my chief delight, and many a good yarn and song did I hear there, and in return used to tell them a few out of my repertoire.

All good things have to come to an end, and so had my delightful stay with the boys. Mancha was fit again, but with the good fodder and inactivity he had become rather too fat and soft. I returned to Camp Gaillard where the horses were, and next day set out with an almost completely new outfit, excepting the saddles, with which I would not have parted for anything. Straps and buckles had been renewed during my temporary absence, and the saddler had made me a splendid set of new saddle-bags, the old ones having long ago seen better days. The horses had new shoes fitted on by an expert army blacksmith, and I was given two spare sets, nails, and new tools to work with. I had often watched the horseshoers at work and had been given some good tips by them, and their advice helped much to improve me in the art of shoeing a horse.

I returned to the provisional camp where I spent another night, and, keen as I was to continue, I was sorry when the moment of parting arrived. My delightful vacation bad come to an end, and I was about to leave a place and people that had found a warm place in my heart.

With Victor left behind, I would be all alone again with my two faithful equine companions. I was fully aware that I would encounter serious difficulties ahead, but something seemed to tell me that we would win through. To strengthen that feeling, being on Panamanian territory, I had bought a bottle of something special which I then handed round, every man taking as big a 'swig' as his waiting friends allowed him; then I swung into the saddle and went off at a slow, steady trot. A chorus of voices shouted 'good bye and good luck!' after me, and I knew I needed much of the latter.

Westward Ho!

There is a good road into the interior of Panama republic as far as Santiago; but, unfortunately, in many places it was difficult to find fodder, furthermore, the horses were at times literally covered with wood-ticks and other insects. I found that a mixture of vaseline, sulphur, and camphor lightly applied to the coats of the horses, especially on the legs, gave excellent results, and I sponged myself every night with creosote diluted with water. In spite of this, I was often full of little red ticks called 'coloradillas,' which I picked up in the grass shrubbery where I had to graze the horses. The irritation these pests produced almost drove me crazy at times. Around the waist, where the belt made pressure and rubbed, I was raw and bleeding. The perspiration running into these sores burnt so much that I had to apply distilled water with a 6 per cent solution of cocaine, which temporarily had a soothing effect.

Most people are under the impression that the republic of Panama extends from north to south, and that the Canal goes from east to west. This, however, is entirely wrong, for the Canal goes more or less from north to the south. Travelling towards Costa Rica, the sun rises behind one and sets straight in front, or, in other words, one travels from east to west.

After riding along through jungle-land for two days, we came out into open prairie. The villages we passed through were very primitive, but I found the people quite pleasant. In one of these villages I went to speak to the 'juez' (mayor and judge combined), to see if he could help me to find fodder for the animals. He was a mulatto and it was easy to guess that he did not belong to the anti-alcoholic league. When he saw me and the horses with their new equipment he took me for an American deserter, so, in order to convince this all-important personage that I was merely an ordinary civilian out for a little fresh air, I showed him my documents. I do not know whether it was ignorance or excess of alcohol, but having turned the papers upside-down and in every direction, and after painful efforts to get them in focus, he gave it up as a bad job. He called a dirty, barefooted friend who started to spell out the whole contents slowly, while he himself sat there like a Roman emperor, and nodded every now and again, grunting, 'muy bien' (very good) to show his weighty approval.

After what seemed an eternity the 'scholar' finished his spelling out of my 'documentos' and the 'juez' began to question me. He wanted to know where Buenos Aires was, and if the Argentine was the capital of Europe, if we had a king or a president, if we had a religion, if the señoritas were fair or dark, etc., etc. Being used to dealing with such people I quite enjoyed all this and answered every question to his full satisfaction.

Carnival time began, and everybody was 'de fiesta.' The national dance of Panama is the 'tamborito' (diminutive of 'tambor': drum) and in all my life I never wish to *hear* one of these dances again. In different villages I was kept awake for three consecutive nights by the infernal noise the 'band' and dancers made, not to mention the drunkards and occasional fights without which carnival would not be 'carnaval.'

The members of the 'band' sit or squat along one wall and beat primitive wooden drums with the flat of their hands, producing different rhythms and varying the noise from loud to unearthly. This thumping is kept up for an hour at a time, and often even longer. Every now and again the dancers yell out a short chorus, consisting only of a few words, such as 'quiero madrugar,' which means: 'I want to dance till sunrise.' The women stand on one side of the room, most of them barefooted, and the men on the other. When the rhythm has worked a man up to dancing pitch, he hops in front of one of the women, who then comes forward a few steps and begins to hop about, her motions much resembling a cork bobbing up and down on the ripples of a duck pond. The man never holds the woman, but hops about in front of her, and kicking his feet about as if he were standing on hot bricks, and then suddenly he will double up and spin around like a puppy trying to get a wasp off its tail. When the man has had enough he simply goes away, and the woman returns to her original place, where she has to wait until she is favoured again. Whites and blacks mix on level terms at these dances, just as they do in everyday life. I have seen white men giving the 'glad eye' to 'midnight blondes' and 'snowballs' doing this to white girls.

I was again terribly burnt by the sun, and what with the pain of this and having to try to sleep just alongside places where they were enjoying themselves dancing the tamborito, drinking and fighting, I was more tired in the morning than I had been when I arrived on the previous evening.

Panamanians are very fond of cockfights, and near most huts one can see fighting birds tied by one leg to little stakes driven into the ground. Unlike in Peru, where cocks are taught different fighting methods I have already described, the birds here are trained to fight with the beak and with their natural spurs, which are carefully scraped and sharpened with a knife so as to make them as formidable as possible. Of the two styles the Peruvian seems to be less cruel to me, for a fight only lasts a few seconds, whilst the Panamanian cocks sometimes fight for a long time until they are hacked and torn to pieces.

We passed through the little port Aguadulce, and from there on to Santiago where the governor treated me with great kindness. Here the road from the Canal Zone comes to an end, and the aspect of the country changes completely. The country is hilly and covered with shrubbery and trees, and the continental divide can be seen to the north.

Santiago is quite a fair little place, but life is very monotonous, for the only diversion men and women have is to wander around the plaza in the evenings and cast glances at each other, or for the young men to hang around the church awaiting the exit of the señoritas, who have been driven into its gloomy shadows by the little secrets of the heart.

The peasants are very dark and use short wide trousers reaching just below the knees. With these trousers they wear white shirts which are often embroidered. These shirts are not tucked into the trousers, but are worn outside. This dress is called 'chingos.' Wearing the shirt outside has its advantages for two reasons. First of all it is cooler, and secondly the 'paysanos' (peasants) can put their hands under them to scratch themselves, a thing they do all day long, and which seems to be their chief occupation between seed time and harvest.

The Panamanian is a born fighter and very clever with the 'machete,' and at one time revolutions used to be the national sport, but since American influence has put a stop to this pastime, Panamanians are supposed to have taken to hard work. I believe there must be a great deal of truth in this, for I have seen many who liked work so much that they lay down to sleep alongside it.

From Santiago on we followed a narrow trail through shady tropical forests. Enormous creepers twist up the trees in the silent but terrible struggle for light and existence. We had to cross several tricky rivers, but at the time, luckily, only a few had enough water to cause difficulties.

Once Gato suddenly stopped and refused to move further, so thinking that perhaps the pack had slipped I dismounted to have a look at it. There was a very strong smell of creosote, and upon examining the pack I found that the bottle that contained the fluid was broken and that the unfortunate animal's left flank was covered with this strong substance, which had oozed through the canvas of the saddle-bags. He must have bumped against a tree and thus broken the bottle. When we reached a stream I washed him as well as I could, but by that time there was a huge swelling, and a few days later an enormous piece of hide came off, leaving him with a nasty raw patch. It was some time before this healed up, and not until a few months after that had the hair again grown where he had been burnt.

In some places near the coast, the jungle and forests are not so dense, and there are patches of prairie land where cattle are raised. I watched a cow defend her new-born calf against many buzzards which were all around them on the ground trying to peck the little one's eyes out. The cow was bellowing in desperation and fury, and in vain tried to fight off the birds. The moment she was a few paces away from the calf other birds made a dash at it. Many young animals fall victims to these otherwise useful birds, unless they are kept near the huts until big enough to defend themselves.

According to stories I had heard and read, Panama ought to be literally carpeted with snakes, but these reports must have been exaggerations. On the whole trip I had very little trouble with these reptiles, but possibly this was due to the heavy steps of the horses that frightened snakes away before we reached them.

South American Indians, particularly the Paraguayans, wear around their ankles feathers, which are often thought to be a decoration. In reality these feathers have a very different use. The Indians wear them whenever they go out into the forest or along the narrow trails, for should a snake strike at them, the deadly fangs are not likely to reach the leg but strike at the anklet of feathers.

I know of several cures that are effective in case of snake bite, scientifically prepared serums and a few other preparations that are supposed to be good. I had some serum at one time, but unfortunately the delicate tubes broke with the many falls and knocks the pack suffered along the rough route.

I always had a supply of permanganate of potash, and for a long time I carried 'curarina,' which is a Colombian preparation, the last bottle of which I presented to a sheriff in Texas who told me he would try it on his wolf-hounds which, he said, were frequently bitten by rattlesnakes.

I have heard of many superstitions and beliefs which are supposed to save one's life in case of snake bite, and it may be of interest to readers to know some of these.

Certain South American Indians believe in a most extraordinary and original cure. If one of them has been bitten, the 'doctor' lays him on the ground in an open space and the members of the tribe start a shuffling dance, holding on to each other in single file. They chant and slowly move around describing snake figures. Every time they pass the victim they each spit at him. This strange dance is kept up for hours and—stranger still—the 'patient' usually recovers.

Snakes have a dislike for garlic, and to prevent them from entering a house people in many parts rub the doorsteps and other openings that lead into their habitations with this strong-smelling vegetable, while others affirm that no snake will crawl over a rope made of horse-hair.

In different places on my journey, I heard peasants say that snakes will suck the milk out of cows and goats, and that these become so used to this that they will return to the same spot every day and at the same hour to be 'milked.' I have also heard of snakes that are supposed to suck women's milk whilst they are asleep, doing it so gently that they never wake up. Since I returned to Buenos Aires a similar story was published in the newspapers, and this case is claimed to have happened recently in the northern section of Argentina.

Should a man be bitten and have no remedy handy, the powder out of a cartridge can save him if he acts quickly. cut a piece of flesh out where he was bitten, and immediately pour the gunpowder into the wound and thus he will burn out the affected place and prevent the poison from spreading into the blood. Again people use corrosive sublimate which they sprinkle on the ground or on their trouser-legs, believing that the smell of this keeps snakes away. In this connection I might remark that it is a well-known fact that snakes dislike any strong smell.

Among the gauchos of the northern parts of Argentina there is an old belief that no snake will ever bite deer and that the strong smell of the latter frightens them away, and for this reason some men who must sleep out in the open often carry a piece of untanned deer-hide with them, firmly believing that this will keep snakes at a distance whilst they are asleep. Old gauchos have told me that if a deer finds a snake it will move around its enemy in a cirde, all the time letting a fine thread of saliva dribble from its mouth. According to these people, the snake will not crawl over this saliva, and thus shut in a small circle will wriggle in terrible fury and very soon die. I do not know how much truth there is in this, but the very fact that intelligent people have told me identical stories makes me think it would be worth while for some man of science to make an investigation.

Some of the domestic cats in Panama are excellent snake-killers. Once I was resting in a little hut when I was called outside. I witnessed a thrilling and interesting fight between a cat and a fair-sized snake. For some time the cat looked at the reptile without moving whilst the latter was curled up in a position to strike, flashing out its forked tongue. Suddenly the cat began to jump around it, pawing with the speed of lightning. After some time the snake became stupefied and, before I knew what had happened, pussy had the wriggler by the neck, if a snake has such a thing, and made off into the bush.

On another occasion I saw a cat steal a snake's eggs. The cunning feline robber did this by teasing the snake away from the nest, and when the reptile was far enough away the cat rushed up and carried away one of the oval jelly-like eggs, repeating this performance until the nest was empty.

In Panama I heard that if a cat is bitten it will eat the snake's gall, and thus save itself. Many people there believe this to be a cure for human beings, and I have seen them keep the gall-bladders in alcohol. If anybody is bitten they rub the wound with this snake gall and then swallow it, and, according to them, with excellent results.

In these parts a jungle man told me of another cure he believes in. He said that if a snake bites a person he must walk backwards without looking where he is going. Of the first plant he touches he has to eat as many leaves as he can, and then, as this good jungle man affirmed, he will infallibly recover.

In the western section of Panama, that is to say towards Costa Rica, live the Chiriqui Indians. Most of them, including the women, file their teeth to sharp points. Like the South American Indians they are of distinct Mongolian type, and obviously are of the same origin. Many of them come among the whites where they work on plantations. I have seen quite a number of whites who have copied the Indians and had their teeth filed, being convinced that this protects against decay, and soon I became so used to seeing these pointed teeth that I took no more notice of them. The Chiriquis sometimes paint their faces with vegetable colours, especially when they have their annual dance out in the jungle. These dances are called 'balserias,' and no Indian ever washes the paint off himself but lets time and nature do this.

A 'balseria' is a mating dance which helps to mix the blood of different tribes. Once a year the Indians of the mountain sector meet. Before they assemble a large piece of jungle is cleared to leave as large and flat an open space as possible. This clearing is then divided by a fence in the middle, and when everything is ready the tribes arrive. Candles made of grease are placed on the posts which form the division. During the first night all is silence and everybody fasts. On the second night fires begin to flicker and 'chicha' (corn beer) is made and consumed in large quantities. Here, as in Bolivia, the corn is chewed, with the only appetizing difference that this is done by the girls about to be married, whereas anybody with or without teeth does this in Bolivia. On the third night everything is ready, and the dance begins.

Women do not take part in this, but sit behind in their respective camps where they watch and wait. Any prospective husband is placed in front of a man who is armed with a pole; they then shuffle along whilst everybody chants a monotonous song. When the chanting reaches a certain point, everybody goes into a sudden silence, and the men with the poles direct hard blows against the legs of the dancers in front of them, usually aiming at the part behind the knees. If the young man resists the blow, or succeeds in avoiding it with a quick motion, he is entitled to go to the opposite camp and choose a wife. According to his assets or means of support he is allowed as many wives as he is able to keep. When the 'balseria' is over, one newly-married man stays in the new clearing, where he builds his hut and settles down.

I felt much relieved when we reached David, the most important place in the interior of Panama. Travelling through the shady forests would have been pleasant had it not been for a mass of roots that made progress slow and dangerous. Both horses had several times caught their legs in them, and each of them had torn off a shoe. I had no spare sets with me and would have been in a tight fix had it not been for an American Army official who had very thoughtfully sent four sets ahead to David for me.

I had a very short but extremely pleasant stay in this little town, where I soon made many friends. Long before I had heard marvels about the place but I found it to be anything but attractive. Neglected houses and huts, a few stores, a couple of churches which threaten to tumble down at any moment, a plaza with weeds growing between the cobble-stones, a dirty 'hotel,' a great deal of filth, and much heat—this more or less describes David.

One evening I was invited to go to the theatre. I was staggered, for I never expected such a luxury to exist in this place. However, I found out that an old shed had been filled with chairs borrowed from neighbouring houses, and some sort of stage had been erected. About seventy spectators were eagerly awaiting the moment when the improvised curtain would be lifted. The girls were dressed in their best, powdered and painted, but I must confess that some were extremely pretty and attractive, and wore their dresses with grace and elegance. Of course the elder set of the same sex made great efforts not to be left behind, and I had fears that some of the chairs might not be able to support their weight. The performance was one of those heart-rending dramas, and the actors were Spaniards whose accent betrayed them as hailing from Galicia.

I knew that the next lap through the jungles and over the continental divide would be very difficult and risky, and so I looked for a guide, but it was no easy matter to find such a person, for nobody seemed to know anyone who had made this crossing. However, after a long search I heard of a man who, many years before, had made a similar journey when he tried to save himself and his mules during a revolution, and with the help of a friend I ran him to earth. He was a half-caste Indian, some fifty years of age. He said that he did not remember the way he had gone, and was not at all keen on doing another such trip.

He further told us that he had started out with two companions and twenty mules, but that he had lost eleven of them on the difficult march. This was certainly not the kind of news to help encourage me, but I was determined to try my luck once more, and at last, when I had discussed things for a long time and had offered the man very high pay and a substantial present should we reach the Costa Rican capital safely, he accepted my proposals, and within two days we were equipped and ready to start.

I had to buy a sturdy pony, the man's pack being too much for my already heavily-laden animals, and so that the guide might ride when he was tired of walking. Like most jungle men he usually much preferred to go afoot, leading his pony with one hand and holding his 'machete' in the other. No Central American goes into the woods without this very necessary tool and weapon, and in many parts they wear it in a leather sheath like a sword. I had acquired one which I fixed to the pack-saddle, and countless times I had to use it to cut fodder or to clear the way for the horses. This instrument has accounted for more deaths in revolutions than firearms, and jungle men are not afraid to face even tigers with them.

There is plenty of game in the interior of Panama; tigers, black leopards, tiger-cats, wild pigs, deer, tapirs, wild turkeys, etc., are often hunted. Game is particularly plentiful in the neighbourhood of the Chiriqui volcano, and near the coast are regular paradises for alligator hunters.

From David we made a short journey to a little place called Concepción, which is the last village before one enters the forests and jungles. When we arrived there was some kind of fiesta in progress and, of course, plenty of cockfighting and drinking. In the interior of the Panama republic most inns have a cock-ring, which consists of a circular fence, some three feet in height, made of bamboo canes. This keeps the birds in, and outside, all round it, stand the spectators, who usually bet all the money they have.

In most places the flies and mosquitoes are thick, apart from the long list of other insects to which one has to grow accustomed. A story is told of a foreign traveller who arrived at an inn long after the midday meal was finished. Much to the stranger's surprise he could not see a single fly in the house. He asked the innkeeper how on earth he managed to keep the place free of them. 'Señor,' answered the native, 'Panamanian flies, like the people, are blessed with a rare intelligence, and well do they know the meal hours. At 6 o'clock this evening the flies will again come swarming into the dining-room, just in time for our next meal, but in the meantime they have gone into the backyard where they have a dead horse and other titbits.'

Into the Green Labyrinth

From Concepción we travelled through forests, following narrow trails that lead in all directions. The huts where we spent some of the nights were extremely primitive. Food was very scarce, and unfortunately I was too liberal with my supplies, giving a great part of them away to people who enviously watched us eat good things whilst they only had small portions of yucca (a root), rice and beans. The result of my misplaced generosity and soft-heartedness was that we were soon left with nothing in our saddle-bags but clothes, instruments and ammunition.

The Rio Chiriqui was a hard nut to crack, for it happened to be rather high and extremely turbulent when we came to it. The further we progressed, the denser became the jungles and the forests. We were twisting and winding through thick vegetation; above our heads the high trees formed a roof through which the sun could not penetrate. Every now and again we came to a small open space where beautifully coloured butterflies fluttered about and humming birds darted among the flowers. Soon the country became very hilly and the trail more difficult. Looking down on the jungle forest from a hill, the thick green roof, covered with creepers and parasitic plants has the appearance of a rolling prairie.

We saw occasional herds of wild pigs and troops of chattering monkeys. The latter seemed quite annoyed at our invasion and often threw berries and dry sticks down at us. To amuse myself I sometimes fired a shot, and then they all disappeared as if by magic. Birds that whistle strange double notes could sometimes be heard answering each other; but what we liked best was the call of the wild turkeys. I shot several of them and they made excellent eating.

A few natives have settled down in jungle clearings where they grow tobacco, rice, beans, yucca, and a little sugar-cane. To make their clearings larger they fell the trees and hack down the bushes, and towards the end of the dry season they set fire to them.

The huts of these people are very original and we stopped in several of them. The roofs are high and made of dry palm leaves. Poles are laid under them to form a kind of ceiling or 'first floor,' where everybody sleeps. Below this is the kitchen and dining-room combined in one. The stove is simply a hole in the dirt floor where the fire is kindled. The walls are made of posts and cane, and the door is always barred at night to keep out dogs, or maybe some prowling beast. In the evenings it gets very cool, and after the meal we would usually sit around the fire where I heard many strange stories of mystery and superstition, as well as many wild-beast and snake yarns. Only the men spoke, whilst the women and children sat huddled in the corners listening with awe.

When everybody was ready to sleep we would all climb up to the 'bedroom' under the roof. To reach this one has to climb up a thick, notched pole that serves as ladder. Men, women and children all sleep together, and our presence did not seem to disturb them in the least. Whilst we were sleeping in one of those huts a woman gave birth to a child. This very natural happening caused practically no trouble or disturbance, and next day the woman was up and about, just as she had been the day before.

I saw many 'huacas,' as the old Indian graves are called. They are always covered with a large flat stone, and treasure has been found in some of them. For this reason many have been disturbed by treasure-hunters.

The native settlers have a strange kind of yodel call which they like to make echo through the forest.

I never tied my horses, but turned them loose near the hut in which I slept. They never went more than a few yards away, and I could hear them stamping and grazing all night, and every morning they were waiting for me at the door. Both were terribly afraid of the jungle at night, and when there was no grass near I had to cut some and bring it near the hut, for they refused to be left alone and would not eat when I staked them out in the coarse jungle grass. I tried it once or twice, but no sooner had I left them than they started to call me, and when I returned to them I found them trembling with fear. This was probably due to the fact that they had been born in the wilds and could scent wild animals and danger.

With our solitary open-air life Mancha had developed his natural instinct of observation, and by this time he was like an excellent watch-dog. Long before I could detect anything he would sometimes lift his head, prick up his ears, and sniff the air, opening his nostrils wide. Presently he would become restless and sometimes he gave a soft nicker, as if trying to speak. After a while a man might appear, although often I could discover nothing, but I was fully aware that the horse must have smelt some animal or had heard a strange noise. Once when we were nearing a little stream the horses became very nervous and troublesome. Mancha had been all nerves for some time, and when we came to the muddy edge of the stream the guide pointed to some spoors that were still filling with water and said, 'tigre' (tiger). Our arrival must have frightened the beast away, but I was amazed and puzzled how Mancha could know the smell, tigers being unknown in his 'querencia,' as the Argentine gauchos so prettily call the region where a horse is born. 'Querer' means 'to like' or 'to love,' and 'querencia' is the noun. It is a well-known fact among range people that any horse or cow will always return to its 'querencia' if it can escape and if there are no fences to prevent it from so doing. I have known animals to travel almost fabulous distances, crossing mountains, rivers and deserts to appear finally back in their 'querencia.' With the progress of civilisation they have less and less opportunity to give us proof of this and other wonderful instincts they still possess.

An Unmarked Border
in the Midst of Jungles

The border between Panama and Costa Rica has been more or less surveyed; as no landmarks exist it is impossible to tell when one crosses the line. Furthermore, in many places it is very difficult to follow the right trail, animal tracks leading one astray, and on several occasions we went the wrong way. Here and there a fallen tree obstructed our path and then we had to clear the track with our machetes. I was amazed at my guide's skill with his blade and the speed with which he could cut. Near a stream he once detected recently-made tracks of a big tapir which they call 'macho de monte' in these parts. I unstrapped the rifle and we followed the spoor. Unfortunately the big brute saw us in time and disappeared into the bushes through which we could not possibly fight our way.

Our supplies were running low, and we had come across no game for some time when we struck a solitary hut in a jungle clearing. We were hungry, and looked forward to the prospects of a good meal. The inhabitants of this hut told us that they were very short of eatables and that one of their members had gone far in search of rice and beans, but that he was likely to be away for some days yet. The news did not help to cheer us up, and we looked at each other like children who have broken mother's favourite pitcher, until somebody suggested that we go out hunting wild turkeys or wild pigs. We pushed through thick, almost impenetrable jungle for hours but saw no trace of game. The gymnastics of climbing over and worming through the creepers and bushes had begun to tire me when a troop of large black monkeys came jumping, high up, from tree to tree.

One of our party suggested to shoot, for he said we were not likely to bag anything else, and as I agreed that a monkey in the hand was worth two wild turkeys in the bush, I made ready to fire. The monkeys were flying from tree to tree and reminded me of trapeze acrobats in a circus. When I had a good chance I fired several shots in quick succession. I heard two or three heavy thuds and knew that some of my shots had taken effect. One monkey had been badly wounded and remained hanging high up on a branch. My second shot made him fall again, but once more he caught hold of another branch below. Thus in stages the poor animal fell lower and lower, until it finally hit the ground heavily near us. I rushed up to give it the *coup de grâce* with my machete, but when I saw that it was a mother monkey with a baby hanging on her back I hesitated. Both looked at me in terror, and I felt ashamed of the crime I had committed. Presently the baby monkey let go its dying mother and climbed some ten feet up a creeper where it started to howl and lament like a human being. The mother monkey looked at me and then at her young one, all the time moaning and gasping for breath. I could no longer stand this horrible sight, and to finish this pitiful scene I stepped forward and with a sharp blow put the poor animal out of misery. I shall never forget the expression of terror in her eyes and the way she held up her hands to protect herself against the deathblow.

The men picked up the dead and slit their tails to make a loop which they slipped over the monkeys' heads in order to be able to carry them by their tails as if on rifle-slings. Then we started our weary and tiring journey back towards the hut. I had no idea where we were, for with all the twisting about, and the excitement, I had completely lost my bearings. The jungle people have a wonderful sense of direction and never lose themselves, even in parts where they have never been before. Every time I looked at those large black monkeys on the men's backs I felt more and more like a common murderer. Their long arms were dangling about and their open, glassy eyes seemed to be staring at me with reproach, whilst their open jaws gave them a horrible grinning expression. I firmly made up my mind never again to shoot monkeys, unless out of direst necessity.

Arriving back at the hut a large tin of water was made to boil and into this the dead animals were dipped. Then the people proceeded to pull out all their hair, and when this was done the monkeys looked more like human beings than ever. They cut off their long fingers and the heads and cleaned them out. Once they had been cut into small pieces these were boiled with yucca roots and a handful of the few beans and rice that were left. This dish is called 'mono adobado' (stewed monkey). Hungry as I was, I could hardly make up my mind to taste it, for I felt like a cannibal. Next morning I woke up so hungry that I made a big meal of it; the beast within me had got the upper hand. The meat was extremely tough, but the soup was very tasty. The natives say that this dish is of great nutritive value, but even many of them refuse to eat it, unless driven to it by necessity as we were then, and once more on another occasion. As far as I am concerned, I would sooner try Voronoff's monkey glands than another pot of stewed monkey-meat.

We were some distance from the sea and near the continental divide. At night we could see fires along the mountain, from which we were separated by jungles that have never been trodden by human foot. These fires were made by very primitive Indians who inhabit these—to white man—unknown parts.

Having travelled in the damp heat all day, we came to a small, clear river where we undressed before crossing to the other side. Seeing a nice clear pool a little distance up stream I went there and was just about to plunge in to have a swim when, at the last moment, my guide saw me and shouted 'lagartos'! (crocodiles). Needless to say, I did not dive in, although I did not believe that crocodiles came so far up from the coast. Looking around the edges of that pool, I could see two or three dark shapes, like big logs, just under the water. I took my revolver, which was lying with my clothes, and fired at the biggest of them. In an instant what had been a beautiful still pool was transformed into a bubbling, seething flood, the wounded crocodile lashing about madly until he made a dive to the bottom.

Next morning the guide went back to the pool to see if he could find the dead 'croc,' and after some delay returned with a tin full of crocodile fat, which is used as a cure for rheumatism, sore throats, cuts—in fact, for almost every human complaint, much the same as 'grasa de potro' (horse's fat) is used in the pampas of Argentina.

Before reaching the Rio Grande de Terraba we came out of the jungles and rode over hilly prairie-land. The scenery was very pretty and the climate pleasant, and to my surprise this seemingly excellent land for cattle-raising was uninhabited. This may be due to the fact that it is difficult to reach, being wedged in between jungles, swamps and the mountain range to the north, but surely some day these regions will be transformed into a regular paradise.

The Rio Grande de Terraba was low, but even so we had considerable trouble in crossing it. The guide said that we must be very careful and he swore that many of these rivers had an 'encanto' (evil spell) which often pulled horses below the waters to drown them, especially if they happened to be fat. This seemed quite explainable to me, for it is obvious that the fatter an animal is, the sooner will it tire whilst swimming.

We again entered a dense jungle forest, but as a big piece of this was on fire we had to make a detour. In some places we rode among smoulder-ing tree-trunks, and finally were hopelessly lost. We knew our direction, but it was impossible to go that way, for the jungle could not be pene-trated anywhere except where there was an animal track or a foot trail. We were forced to cross and re-cross the Rio Grande de Terraba higher up, and to make things worse a heavy rain fell, and I began to fear we would not be able to reach civilisation before the rainy season set in again. The country was very hilly and the horses frequently slipped, stumbled and fell, and as we had to advance with utmost caution our progress was naturally very slow. My boots were falling to pieces and some of the saddle-straps had rotted and were broken. We had to fix things the best we could with a very tough and flexible kind of creeper which helped us to get along. It is not difficult to imagine how great was our joy when we reached a small settlement called Buenos Aires, some forty miles from which there is another small place called Palmares.

To reach San Jose, the capital, from there one has to cross the 'Cerro de la Muerte' (Death Mountain), which is very high and difficult to climb.

The original settlers of both Buenos Aires and Palmares were criminals who had been landed at the coast and turned loose. Even to this day the Costa Rican government deports criminals to these isolated regions, and I met two German priests who were doing their humanitarian work among these people, who live on growing tobacco and agriculture. While I stayed in Palmares I slept in a small wooden chapel and had a very pleasant time with one of these priests. He might well serve as an example to the majority of Spanish and native members who are a disgrace to the order.

One day a child died, and the relatives brought it into the chapel for the burial service. They carried the corpse in a small box and some of the men were so drunk that they could hardly stand. The good priest made the service as short as he could and then literally dragged some of the most intoxicated out of the place.

The people of this place were held in terror by two outlaws, the brothers Altamira, who were making things very unsafe at the time. They had killed several men and had assaulted various huts. Having been warned, we rode along the trail well armed and ready for any emergency, although I was well aware that we would not stand much of a chance if they happened to waylay us in the thick underbrush.

Climbing Up to the 'Middle of the World'

I knew that the horses would have some very bad days until we reached the other side of the mountain, so I gave them a good rest and all the fodder we could find. When we left the settlement the people came to give us all sorts of little gifts, consisting chiefly of the finest tobacco leaves they had picked out of their stock, but I could not accept all that was offered to us, for the pack was already full. It nearly made my guide weep when

I refused some of the offers, but it could not be helped. I often tried to roll a cigar, but never succeeded in performing this seemingly simple trick. However, the guide was very clever at it, so we were sure that we would at least have plenty to smoke for the next week or so, by which time I hoped to reach San Jose. I purchased a few provisions, and although I hated to do it, I packed three live chickens into a small basket and strapped it on top of the pack.

Many were the terrible stories I heard about the 'Cerro de la Muerte.' Some said the mountain had formerly been bewitched and that the devils had been tamed by firing guns. One man told me that there was a place where the dead were standing up like tree trunks, frozen stiff, and the devils danced among them at night.

Before we reached the foot of the mountain it began to rain and the ground became so slippery that the horses continually slipped and fell. We could only scramble a few yards and then we had to stop for breath or hack steps so that the animals could get a grip with their hoofs. This went on for some hours until we reached higher altitudes, where we entered oak forests. There the temperature was cool but the perspiration was falling off us in drops. The guide's pony had fallen so often and was so tired that it began to refuse to get up, so every time it fell again one of us had to pull in front whilst the other helped the animal to rise by lifting it by the tail. Late in the evening we came to a shelter that had been built by government men some years before. We cut small palm leaves which formed the only fodder we could find, but in spite of their toughness and bitter taste all had disappeared by morning. The night was bitterly cold but we built a fire and one of the hens was soon in our cooking-pot with some rice and yucca.

Next day we continued the difficult ascent, stumbling over a regular network of roots of the huge, lichen-covered oak trees. I feared that a horse might break a leg at any moment, but luck was with us. After some anxious hours we came out of the timber-line and from there had a wonderful view of the jungles below. Through holes in the shifting fogs we could sometimes get a glance of both the Pacific and Atlantic oceans in the distance.

Finally we found another shelter where we prepared to spend the night. It was bitterly cold and a little spring nearby was completely surrounded by ice. It was easy to see that my horses were accustomed to this, for they did not step on the icy edge but began to paw and break it to make sure that they would not fall into a deep hole. The guide's animal seemed puzzled and nervous and only drank when I offered him the water in my sombrero. Some coarse grass grew near there, so I turned the animals loose. This point—slightly over 11,500 feet above sea level—is called 'Muerte' (Death), but this fantastic name did not seem to affect our spirits as we watched the second hen broiling in the pot whilst we puffed away at our cigars. During the night the moon was so bright that I thought it was early morning, and as I could sleep no more I went out to keep the horses company. They seemed glad when they saw me and all followed me when I went where the grass was better and where they had feared to go alone, their instinct for danger having kept them near the shelter where we slept.

I sat down and wrapped a heavy poncho and a blanket about me and blew puffs of smoke into the icy night air. I observed that the horses felt the cold, for every now and again they gave some of those peculiar little snorts horses give when the cold air freezes their nostrils. Sitting out there on the mountain all alone, my thoughts began to wander, as they had often done before when I was on some lonely Andean peak. The soft, cold, silvery light of the moon gave the mists below a ghostly appearance. I felt lonely but happy and did not envy king, potentate or ruler. Here was I, as it were, between two continents and two mighty oceans, with my faithful friends of hundreds of miles both making the best of a bad meal beside me, but I knew they were satisfied, for experience had taught the three of us to be contented, even with the worst.

My thoughts wandered back to my boyhood and to the school bench for which I had an inborn dislike. Then I recalled some incidents of my boisterous age and chuckled to myself. As I tried to penetrate the infinite distance, pictures of city life appeared before me, the strife for wealth and fame, the hurry and worry of mankind, some rising, others falling, foolish pleasures, the struggle of humanity, and then I came back to reality—where was I? —Strange coincidence. La Muerte—Death.

When the first purple streaks on the horizon announced the arrival of a new day I returned to the shelter to prepare coffee. The horses followed me in hopes of something good and, although we had none to spare, each one received a good chunk of unrefined sugar which they munched until their mouths foamed and dribbled. After a welcome can of hot coffee we started out, following the bare ridges for some time, and then we began the descent. We slipped over rocks and stones and had to pick our way step by step. Dark clouds began to collect, and suddenly a terrific downpour set in. With it a strong wind blew that made it impossible to protect ourselves against the icy water that soon seemed to penetrate to the very marrow.

The guide stumbled along with his head down and his teeth chattering. I always carried a flask of 'aguardiente' (cane alcohol) in case of sickness, and knowing this the poor man could resist no longer. He asked me for a cupful which I gladly gave him and took one myself. To this day I cannot explain how we got the horses down these slopes without crippling them. Towards evening we found another shelter where we warmed and dried ourselves near a fire we had built. My boots were all in pieces now, and my feet had been cut by the sharp rocks. We were again in an oak forest, and once more the animals had to be content with a feed of leaves of small woolly palms that grew here and there among the hoary giants of the primeval forest. The rain lasted throughout the night, and I realised that we had beaten the rainy season—and defeat—by barely twenty-four hours.

Before proceeding I greased my sore feet with the fat of the last chicken and patched up my boots the best I could. The mud and the roots were terrible and we waded up to our knees in many places. After what seemed an eternity we came to the first habitations, two lonely huts, and from there the trail was much better until we hit the first outpost of civilisation, a village consisting of a few houses.

Not far from there we met a few men carrying rifles and shotguns, and when I enquired what this signified they told me a huge tiger had killed several cows and they were looking for him. The evening before one of their members had gone to the village to see if he could borrow dogs to help in stalking the beast. While we were following the trail down my guide pointed to the tracks of a horse and, with a meaning whistle, at some others that obviously had been made by a tiger. The clayey nature of the soil, which had been softened by the rain, made the tracks very clear, and we could see that the tiger had followed the man and horse and had only turned back into the forest when near the village.

Civilisation Once More

I n the first village we came to I found a telegraph office and sent word to the Argentine minister in San Jose, advising him of our safe arrival in civilisation. The local policeman put his humble hut at our disposal and whilst we cleaned and dried our drenched and muddy clothes he was busy preparing us as good a meal as circumstances permitted, and the good man saw to it that the horses should lack nothing.

The distance from this village to San Jose is about eighty miles and, as this part is all inhabited, several other villages and a fair road exist. In spite of the torrential rains that fell all the time, we covered the distance in two days, having had to pass a very bad night in an abandoned hut where we shivered in our soaking wet clothes and blankets until morning.

San Jose of Costa Rica

Towards next evening, from the top of a mountain, San Jose came in sight. The sun had broken through the clouds and we had a wonderful view of the vast valley in which the town stands. Full of cheer we began the descent towards our goal, but before we arrived there another heavy shower had started to pour down on us. Both the guide and myself had grown shaggy beards, and we must have presented a gruesome sight when we finally rode through the streets of the town. Two policemen guided us towards the Argentine Legation where a number of government officials had gathered to give us a welcome. On this, as on other similar occasions, I felt uncomfortable and embarrassed, for the people there were all dressed in their best, whilst I had, as usual, arrived dirty and in rags. My boots were literally falling to pieces and were covered with mud and my poncho and clothes were dripping like a wet sponge. However, I had to step inside, shake hands with everybody, and make superhuman efforts to raise a smile every now and again. Feeling sorry for the guide and the horses, who were outside in the rain, I finished a glass of champagne as quickly as I could and then asked to be excused. The chief of police had kindly made arrangements for the stabling of the animals and, having seen them and the guide comfortably accommodated, I went to the hotel where a room had been reserved.

At the legation I had been given mail which had been forwarded there for me and I immediately started to read some of it. My room was nice and warm and, before I realised it, I had dropped off to sleep, and when I woke up twelve hours later I was still sitting in the same position, with the only difference that the clothes I was still wearing were dry by that time. I went to see the guide and the horses and then had a thorough clean up, after which I returned to bed where I slept for another twelve hours. What a glorious feeling it was to be in a soft, clean bed again, nothing to worry about and, above all, no insects.

I had sent my city clothes ahead from Panama, so I was able to disguise myself as a 'gentleman' again and thus do the rounds, paying my respects and seeing the sights. San Jose has very little to offer in this line, for besides the small but tasty National Theatre, more or less the Paris Opera on a small scale, and, maybe, the Chapuy Asylum, there is nothing much to be seen in this city. The asylum is surrounded by beautiful parks, but as it is exclusively for lunatics I did not venture inside. Leather articles are a speciality of this town, and these are of excellent quality and workmanship.

Thanks to the considerable elevation, the climate is cool and agreeable, but during the wet season it rains practically every afternoon.

Railroad lines connect the town with ports Limon on the Atlantic side and Puntarenas on the Pacific.

The sight of San Jose that no visitor ought to miss is the evening promenade of the elite in the principal plaza. This seems to be the chief delight of both sexes, young and old. I had seen similar evening parades before, but the promenaders of San Jose obey an all-important unwritten law. The bandstand is in the middle of the plaza and around it, as though along the sides of a big square, the people walk. The ladies 'float' around to the right, or anti-clockwise, whilst the men slowly and stiffly swagger in the opposite direction, eagerly eyeing or solemnly greeting the señoritas as they pass them again and again, round after round. Only married or engaged men, when in company of their chosen are allowed to walk in the 'ladies' direction.'

One evening, when I happened to be free and alone, I went to have a look at this fashion parade and solemn occasion of self-advertisement. I had been watching for a while, and I must admit that I have rarely seen so many exceedingly pretty and well-dressed girls as were parading in this plaza. Contrary to my expectations the majority were fair and wore their dresses with the 'chic' of Parisiennes. When I saw an open gap among the people I took advantage to take a walk around with the crowd. I was smoking a cigar and admiring the shapely ankles of a girl who walked in front of me, and I must have promenaded round the plaza two or three times when some friends of mine beckoned to me.

I had noticed that the people were all staring at me and first I thought there must be something wrong with my clothes. Finally I came to the conclusion that they must have recognised me, and so took no more notice of them, but now my friends pointed out to me that I had been walking in the 'ladies' direction,' and explained this ancient and accepted custom of the town to me. Even to-day I tremble when I think how near some horrible death I must have been when I innocently broke the great, unwritten law of San Jose de Costa Rica!

Alongside the main plaza is another paved square, where the 'second class' people, as they call them, have their separate parade, which is carried out strictly under the same rule as among the 'first class.' I observed that the difference of the two classes is chiefly in the colour of the skin and the quality of the dresses. The 'second class' girls are slightly darker than those of the 'alta sociedad' who proudly float around in 'first,' although a few of them looked rather whiter than they really were, thanks to the 'poudre de riz' which they had liberally applied as a fairly effective camouflage. The main, and all-important difference between the two classes is obviously the purse, the quality of the gowns being ample testimony of this fact.

I found the people of Costa Rica to be the most pleasant in Central America, fairly industrious, thrifty and peace-loving, and, as far as I could judge, this little republic is more advanced than its Central American sisters: I shall always remember its officials and citizens as exceedingly hospitable and pleasant. From here my guide returned to Panama by ship, with many presents from different people who admired him for the way he had stuck to his job. As things go among his people, he returned home a rich man.

Side-stepping a Revolution

Prospects for crossing Nicaragua were none too rosy, for a revolution was centred in the very parts I had to ride through. Everybody advised me not to try the trip, lest I lose the horses or more. Through the Argentine Legation and other official channels I gathered whatever information was available, but when both the revolutionary and the government representatives of Nicaragua in San Jose put it to me in strong terms of recommendation not to enter their troubled territory, and I had received telegraphic advice from Buenos Aires not to run the risk, much against my will I had to give up the idea of making this ordinarily easy and short trip through Nicaragua.

Whilst waiting for news and developments, I made a short sight-seeing trip by train. At every station numerous beggars came to molest the passengers, whilst dogs and buzzards were fighting for bones and other scraps which people threw out of the windows of the carriages, for here, as in Peru, food and refreshments are sold at practically every halting-place. The dogs and birds scramble for the food thrown to them, and the buzzards seem to be no more afraid of the people than tame hens are.

I was admiring the incredible mixture of canine breeds and buzzards fighting for something to keep them alive when the train began to move towards a steep descent where there were several large curves. All the skeletons of dogs suddenly started off in a mad rush. This puzzled me, but soon I found out the solution, for when we had rounded several bends I saw all the mongrels awaiting our arrival below. They obviously knew that the shortest distance between two given points is a straight line, and had made this short cut in hopes of receiving another tit-bit below.

Having completed all my plans and preparations, we made for the port of Puntarenas, where we took ship for La Union, in the little republic of San Salvador.

Puntarenas is situated on a narrow peninsula, and the town, with its musty buildings, mostly made of wood, is as unattractive as its hot and damp climate. The streets are sandy and most of the people go barefoot. The view across the bay to the north is pretty, the exuberant vegetation and the mountains in the distance forming a picturesque background. The ships anchor outside, and are only reached by launches and lighters, a circumstance that made me feel very uneasy considering my horses had to be loaded. To put them aboard was no easy task. I had to put them in crates built for the purpose, lower them from the wharf on to a lighter, and then swing them on board; a very dangerous proceeding, with so many inexpert and excitable half-castes yelling and fussing about.

Once on board the S.S. *City of San Francisco*, the horses were soon the pets of everybody. The chief officer, Mr. Wagner, who had formerly been in the U.S. cavalry, did his utmost to make them happy and comfortable. There were several passengers on board, and among them a couple of globe-trotters who had been on the ship all the way up from Panama. They were 'walking' around the world, but obviously preferred to avoid the nasty and uninhabited parts, such as the stretch from Panama to Costa Rica. They were on their way direct to San Salvador, where I later heard that they had told people all about tigers and snakes in the Panamanian jungles which they had seen in the distance from the ship. We called at Corinto, in Nicaragua, and then at Amapala, which is a port on a small island near the Hondurenian coast. From there a two hours' run took us to La Union where the horses were unloaded again.

San Salvador

I n the Central American republics they seem to pick the darkest and most ignorant men to fill the posts of port captains and officials, which is apt to give visitors a bad first impression of the country. The only republic where difficulties were placed in my way by such people was in San Salvador. First they tried to twist money out of me, and when they failed in this attempt they tried to have their revenge by confiscating my firearms. Finally I thought the time had come to put an end to all this nonsense, so I took the offensive, which proved to be the best defence, and when the dusky officials realised that they had put their foot in it they tried to make up for it by apologising in the most flowery lingo they could think of. I did not waste much time in La Union, and with a bad first taste of the country I started the ride towards the capital. Years ago a wagon road had existed, but since a rickety railroad has been constructed this highway has been neglected and is useless to-day, except as a path for mules, burros and horses.

After a journey in stifling and oppressive heat we halted in a small village. A child had been buried that day, so I did not get much sleep, the mourners spending the night drinking, dancing, fighting and howling like wolves on a moonlight night. I was told that this is the custom among these people when a child or a spinster dies. When a joyful chord is struck on the guitar, everybody dances and sings, and when the chord is a sad one this is the signal for howling, wailing and drinking. Judging by the condition most men were in, they had freely answered the 'sad' chords.

Many yellow and black weaver-birds had made their pretty bag-like nests of horse-hair which hung down from the trees along our path. The natives say that these birds nip the tail-hairs off horses whilst they are asleep.

The republic of San Salvador is densely populated, and, as in other Latin American countries, my chief delight was to visit the invariably dirty market-places, where the essence of national life can be seen, and where I often had to buy my food from some stall. I ate as little meat as possible, and never fish, which, owing to the climate, is dangerous unless it is absolutely fresh. Regular swarms of flies cover the meat, and it is a regular habit among the sellers to wave them away with their hands whilst mechanically saying 'shoo,' and I have even heard some whistle at them whilst they temporarily buzzed around, only to settle down again with apparently new appetites.

On entering and leaving each village and town I was stopped by the police. Usually the 'vigilantes' were dark and greasy and clad in rags that were supposed to be uniforms. They demanded 'documentos,' name, and any other detail that occurred to them, and had not been for the official recommendation I was fortunate enough to possess, I really believe I should still be lingering in San Salvador. These precautions were due to the country being under martial law, and to prevent revolutionary movements.

Chinese merchants abound everywhere, and when one day a dusky vigilante stopped me for information, a group of these collected around us, together with some tough-looking loafers. The vigilante tried to look as officious as possible and took out what was supposed to be a notebook, ready to pretend that he could read and write. When I showed him my official pass this was too much for him, so he handed it to an 'educated' bystander to read out, which he did slowly and painfully. When he had finished spelling out the contents of this weighty documento, a roar of laughter broke out, and a Chinaman went so far as to push the vigilante's dirty sun-helmet over his eyes. How the mighty can sometimes fall.

San Miguel was the first little town we touched. Some eight miles away is a volcano which has the same name as the town, and which shows great activity at times. Along the road many large lizards basked in the sun, and practically naked women washed near the streams, whilst their usually numerous children were playing around them. The land is extremely fertile everywhere; coffee and a great variety of tropical fruit being grown. The heat in the daytime was oppressive and sweltering, obliging me to make the journey short and to let the horses cool down a little wherever we found a shady spot. We met a few bullock-wagons with creaking wooden wheels. Most of these vehicles are covered by wooden arches, over which skins are tied to make a roof as protection against sun and rain. The native men are dressed in loosely-fitting white trousers and a shirt or blouse of the same colour; as a rule these clothes are hanging in rags and are very dirty. They wear wide-brimmed straw hats with high crowns, and rarely go out without a machete in their hands or hanging from their waists, like swords, in leather sheaths.

We passed several groups of prisoners who were chained together in twos, mending the road under the supervision of armed guards.

In the towns and villages I usually kept the horses in the hotel (?) backyard, and paid some man to bring the fodder there. I had several reasons for doing this, one being that this kept them free from ticks and other parasites which immediately covered them when out in the open.

Traversing quite pretty and hilly country we came to the river Lempa which is the biggest in San Salvador, and there we had the luck to find a ferry-boat, the first and only one we used on the whole trip. The experience being a new one to the horses, the loading and unloading of them were none too easy, but once on the primitive craft, which was manned by two men rowing in front and one steering behind, the animals seemed quite unconcerned.

I had unloaded Mancha and took him up the bank where I put him under a shady tree and then, whilst I was busy coaxing Gato off the boat, I noticed that Mancha was snorting and nervously looking around. When I had taken the other horse up the bank, I went to investigate the cause of the trouble and soon found a big snake curled up in the grass near Mancha. When

I had killed it we proceeded to a little town called Cojutepeque.

Here I was kept awake all night by the noise of bands, rockets and drunkards. A religious fiesta was on, and in addition to this a group of 'distinguished' young caballeros were celebrating the occasion of having received their doctors' degrees, a natural event in most young men's lives here, provided they are of 'buena familia,' wear boots, collars, and maybe a necktie. The celebration was held in the courtyard of the dirty hotel where I had taken quarters. The stupendous scholars were making interminable speeches in turn, thunderous cheers and applause acknowledging the hearers' appreciation of any particularly clever twist of ultra-flowery lingo, of which even the most humble peon (worker) is very fond.

Riding through a Salvadorian village during siesta-time reminded me of visiting prehistoric ruins. Not a soul was to be seen, and only the drumming of the horses' hoofs on the rough cobble-stones disturbed the almost uncanny silence. The heat rose in waves, and sometimes I could see into a mud house through the open door, and had a glance of a man or woman sleeping in a hammock. Towards evening people began to stir again. Men appear at the doors, blinking their sleepy eyes at the glare of the sun. They stretch their stiff limbs, yawn, and scratch themselves, while the women go to fetch water, balancing big calabashes or round water-jugs on their heads.

Shortly before we arrived at San Salvador City we passed close to Lake Itopango, which looks exceedingly pretty, entirely surrounded as it is by mountains.

The outskirts of the capital are inhabited by the poor. The roads are made of very rough cobble-stones, and the filth lying about is something indescribable. Peels and skins of fruit, old sardine tins, and other refuse were scattered everywhere. The centre of the town is very different, for the streets are well-paved and clean, and the little parks are quite pretty and neat.

An officer sent his orderly to stable the horses, but, having a presentiment, I went to see to what kind of a place he was taking them, and was not surprised when I found them in a backyard that would hardly have been fit for a self-respecting pig. Luckily a Swiss gentleman came to the rescue and put his little farm in the outskirts of the town at my disposal.

The principal building in San Salvador City is the 'palacio de gobierno' (government house), where I went to pay my respects. From outside, the place is quite nice, but the interior, especially the courtyard, is very different. Rubbish was lying about, and vigilantes were sleeping on benches or lazily leaning against the walls. In one 'sala' a crowd was assembled, listening to a display of verbal acrobatics. Suddenly a black fellow, dressed in what was supposed to be a palmbeach suit, came running towards me, and to my surprise only stopped when his face was but a few inches from mine, and then he began to bark at me, spraying me like a barber, with the only difference that his spray of saliva had a strong garlic odour. Once his first excitement had somewhat cooled off, I was able to understand what he was spluttering at me with the speed of a machine-gun. I had dressed especially for the occasion and, having no other clothes, had put on a pair of clean white riding-breeches, brown top-boots, a soft white shirt with a suitable necktie, and jacket. When I had looked at myself in a mirror, before leaving the hotel, I thought that even the Prince of Wales would take his hat off if he happened to pass me, but my attire did not seem to please this black fellow, who turned out to be the 'mayor-domo' (principal porter) of the palacio. He thundered at me that only military people had the right to enter this sacred place wearing breeches and riding-boots, and that my offence constituted an insult to the president, to himself, and to the republic in general. Most people who were on business in the building wore no boots, jackets or collars, but obviously this is etiquette there.

The mayordomo's verbal barrage was so heavy that none of my occasional words directed at him reached their objective. Presently he started to push me towards the nearest door, but when I took a firm grip of his wrist he shut his mouth like a rat-trap and listened to me. When I had explained who I was, and on what errand I had come, he turned as white as his colour permitted and gave vent to the most elegant stream of apologies I have ever heard, and he was still going on with it after I had left him. The officials I met were exceedingly pleasant, and in some cases highly refined and educated.

During my ride I had opportunities to get an insight into social and educational conditions of the countries I passed through. As a rule, the upper classes in most Southern republics are exceptionally bright and quick at learning, but, on the other hand, they are usually very shallow and superficial. They pride themselves on the smattering of philosophy they possess, and their chief ambitions are in the political line; the easiest way to wealth and power.

The average young man of 'buena familia' is a born reciter of poems, and is generally very effeminate, temperamental and soft. Speech-making is a common form of disease among them, and in a fit of oratory they can touch on social reform, bits of history, philosophy, extracts of famous poems; in fact, anything from Napoleon down to second-hand teeth, but when it comes to executing any of their ideas and stupendous projects, they find that they have spent all their energy in making the last speech, and take things easy until new strength, vigour and inspiration have accumulated for another display of verbal fireworks.

Every time I looked at a half-finished monument or public building I could not help wondering how many orators had strained their lungs and vocal chords during the laying of the foundation-stones, and I tried to estimate how much of the funds had evaporated into space in the same way as the speeches had done.

Near the capital is the San Salvador Country Club, where all the native anti-Americans make desperate efforts to ape their pet aversions, and let the world know that they have mastered half a dozen English words. At the time 'Oxford' trousers were the height of masculine fashion and, not content with the already very wide 'bell bottoms,' some of the young caballeros had them tailored so wide that they looked almost like crinolines.

The way to tell the general level of culture in any country is to judge the lower or, better said, the poor classes that constitute the vast majority, and in this respect I am more afraid of being disbelieved than disputed if I were to state my straightforward opinion and facts about some of the countries I passed through.

When the chief revenue of a nation is the taxation on alcohol, which is distilled and sold by the government, it is apt to make one think.

In San Salvador the 'peones' (land workers) receive starvation wages of a few pence per day, and two meals of beans ('frijoles') and mashed-corn 'pancakes' ('tortillas'). To make the latter, corn is boiled and then mashed between two stones. When the paste is ready it is flattened between the hands and put to bake as an earthenware plate over the fire. From Panama to the U.S. border this was the chief food I had.

Naturally the Salvadorians have their evening parade around the plaza, and were it not for this daily social event the average woman would never leave her house at all. Some of the señoritas are distinctly pretty but as a rule they are of a darkish hue, and really white women are as rare as bathrooms in the native hotels.

From the capital towards the Guatemalan border the trip was easy and very pleasant. On the way I made the acquaintance of some charming people who were all very hospitable. I visited the beautiful Lagoon of Coatepeque, which in reality is the crater of a volcano filled with water. It lies in a deep hollow, and measures roughly one and a half miles across. On one side, behind the surrounding mountain ridges, one can see the smoke and fire of the famous volcano Yzalco, often called 'The Lighthouse of Central America,' since its bright eruptions may act as guiding beacons to mariners at sea.

The last little town we touched in San Salvador was Santa Ana, not far from where the best coffee in the country is grown on the slopes of the extinct volcano after which the town was named.

When a South American Indian or half-caste woman has anything to carry about, she will always bear it on her back, wrapping the load up in a poncho or cloth. In Central America things are carried by cleverly balancing flat baskets on the head, and I noticed that women who are thus carrying things have an upright, swaying, and rather dignified way of walking.

Native women are much like their sisters all over the world when they are out marketing. What ladies do in the large stores in the cities, these women do in the markets which are their paradises. There they wander from stall to stall, fumbling the goods here, asking the price there, testing, fingering, smelling and tasting, gossiping and chatting, laughing loudly, and whispering softly, and generally buying but little.

In some parts of Central America a large spider which lives in holes in the ground is a danger to horses. I heard several theories about how they are supposed to attack horses, but was never able to ascertain to what extent they are correct. Some people say that the spider, frightened by the heavy steps, comes out of its hole and squirts a liquid on the horse's legs. Others believe that, in order to make its nest, it clips the hair off the pasterns, just above and around the hoofs. I do not know how much truth there is in either theory, but the fact is that terrible sores break out just around the upper or soft part of the hoofs, and, unless they are promptly attended to, they will finally rot off. A mixture of tannic acid, iodine and glycerine, mixed in even parts, is a good cure for this dangerous form of poisoning, or again, hot water and salt, or just hot milk, are also said to give good results.

Near the Guatemalan border I stopped in a small settlement where I was given quarters in a small adobe hut. During the night I was awakened by the music of a 'marimba,' a kind of xylophone of which Salvadorians, and to a greater extent the Guatemalans, are very fond. Marimbas are of ancient Guatemalan-Indian origin. The good people were giving me a farewell serenade which they kept up till nearly sunrise. A good marimba band is well worth hearing, and clever musicians will even play classical pieces on them, although the instrument is not exactly appropriate for such music. Each man uses a separate marimba set, in appearance like a long table full of wooden notes which are struck with two hammers, one in each hand. Young men often hire such bands, and during the night marimba tables are mounted in the street, outside some señorita's house, and a serenade is given. Many a night I was kept awake by such notturnos, that become tiring in the long run.

Whenever I was about to cross the border of a new country I was quite excited and curious, wondering what the future had in store for us, and if luck would favour us as it had done all the way to the point we had reached at the time.

When my friends, the marimba players, had finished it was nearly time to rise, but much as I appreciated their attention I heartily blessed them for having done me out of several hours of much-needed sleep. I thanked them for the treat in the morning, after which I followed a good road that led towards the now near Guatemalan border.

Guatemala, the Land of the Quetzal

From the Salvadorian border to Guatemala City there is a fair road, but many steep inclines must be negotiated. During certain times of the year cars make this trip, but one wonders how!

The prospects of reaching the highlands and healthy cool climate pleased me and filled me with eagerness to go on. At the border there were two houses. In one lived the telegraph operator, in the other the border inspector. They had received orders from the capital to assist me if I needed any help, and thus I was allowed to proceed into Guatemalan territory without being molested with the usual formalities.

I had ridden some distance through delightful hilly and wooded country when a group of soldiers stopped me. All were barefooted and wore high-crowned straw hats with wide brims, and were armed with old-fashioned Mauser rifles. A fellow who was either a corporal or a general wanted to know what right I had to carry fire-arms. I might have returned to the border with them, where my friend the inspector would have vouched for me, but this would have meant a considerable loss of time and distance. I had no special licence for firearms, but when I remembered my old hotel bill (it had been paid) from San Salvador which I still had in one of my pockets, I pulled it out and showed it to the fellow. I do not know whether it is experience, instinct, or observation, but somehow I was able to tell if a person could read and write, and only very rarely did I make a mistake. In this case I had judged right, for this imposing-looking document, the hotel bill, immediately worked the miracle, and I was given a free pass.

We skirted a pretty lagoon and soon began to climb up the winding road. We crossed through the remarkable valley of Mita, and later, from above, had a fine view of it. In this valley there are many small hills of volcanic

origin. All are of similar shape, like sugar loaves, and I could not help imagining what this place must have looked like ages ago when all these
craters spat out fire and smoke. It seemed like an unreal and delightful
dream to see lovely fir trees once more. Some of the hills were covered
with regular forests of them, and I deeply inhaled the strong scent that
came from them. I was glad for the horses, for there was plenty of good
grass everywhere, not the coarse and watery type of the tropical lowland,
but the strong and aromatic varieties of cool and healthy regions.

Cold rains set in and every day we were soaked to the skin by heavy
showers. Thunderstorms in Guatemala are most imposing, and the
thunder seems to be unusually loud and deafening. In spite of the adverse
weather conditions and heavy mists I rode along happy and satisfied. The
government officials I met at times were all very obliging and ready to
make things easy for me.

I had been warned to avoid stopping in a village called Guilapa. This
place had had a very bad reputation for murder and assault for many years
and, in spite of a contingent of soldiers, expressly stationed there, conditions had not changed. However, although I tried to pass through the place
in the daytime, I arrived there so late in the evening that I had to stay
overnight. Luckily I had a recommendation to the 'coronel' and another
to the 'capitan,' and so I asked them if I might spend the night under their
wing. To this they immediately agreed, and I was invited to accommodate myself as best I could.

The soldiers' quarters consisted of an adobe house with a backyard,
where I put the horses. The village, like all others of its type in
Guatemala, was filthy and depressing. The bare plaza, with its dilapidated church that had not been open within the remembrance of
generations, and a few irregular rows of tiled shacks is about all there
is to be seen. A few ducks enjoyed themselves in pools of slimy, stagnant water and pigs were wallowing in the mud, or roamed about
scavenging. The soldiers were mostly dark half-caste Indians and wore
what had once been blue uniforms. Their headgear was any kind of hat,
straw or felt, and the lucky ones wore heavy sandals. The rifles were of
all sorts of ancient models, and the gun-straps were made of bits of rope,
hide, and even of string. Some of the officers had no uniforms, but as
a distinguishing mark they wore stripes on their sleeves and machetes
instead of swords.

Here, as in Mexico, the soldiers are not fed by the State, but have to go
to stalls or huts to purchase their food. A couple of fellows volunteered
to show me a shack where an old woman prepared and sold food, and naturally my guides expected me to give them a meal in return for the trouble

of taking me there.

I was no novice when it came to looking after myself, and long before anybody else thought about it I had cleaned the floor in the best corner, arranged my pack and saddles, and laid out my bed. As usual, the saddle served as pillow, whilst the by this time battered sheepskins and horse-blankets took the place of mattress. Whenever I could find it I bought insect powder, which I freely sprinkled into the wool of the skins.

Late in the evening an army contingent, on their way to a border village, passed through our place. They did not march in formation, but any way they liked. Some came far ahead, singly or in pairs, and half an hour must have elapsed before the last stragglers came plodding along. Some time after about twenty men had thus passed, the officer in charge appeared, mounted on a mule. He had obviously halted along the road at a few huts where 'aguardiente' (alcohol) is sold, for he was so drunk that he nearly fell off his mount.

When it was dark the soldiers burnt splinters of fir wood that served as candles in our 'barracks.' Presently some prisoners who were locked up in dark and musty 'calabozos' in the backyard were brought before the 'coronel' in twos. They were examined and cross-examined, thundered at and insulted, but only one was turned loose. All the others were once more cooped up in the darkness and stench of the jail.

I was sitting with the officers, who were drinking aguardiente, smoking and spitting, when suddenly some shots were heard. The few lights that were flickering in the village went out as if by magic, and the soldiers made a wild scramble for their rifles. Nobody was keen on going out into the darkness, where they might at any moment fall into a mud-hole or something worse, so they only moved out when they had been given orders to do so. After a while the last soldier came back, but without prisoners, and at once began to tell a story that ought to have qualified him for a generalship on the spot. Everybody listened to his vivid description of the perils and heroic minutes he had lived. It was easy to see that every listener admired the fellow's vivid imagination and colourful way of expressing himself, and I am certain that even the would-be hero did not expect anybody to believe him. At the same time he was aware that his story entertained and pleased, so he continued the narrative, expressing himself in the best fancy language he could think of.

In this village an old vendetta existed, and the 'coronel' told me that nobody had ever given a murderer away, although even children had been killed in the street in broad daylight.

It was midnight before the first thought of sleeping was entertained. Officers and men merely curled up on the dirty floor, some inside, where

I was, others outside in the corridor. The officers had blankets to cover themselves with, but the men simply slept in their uniforms.

As we approached Guatemala City the country became more populated. Presently from the top of a hill the capital came in view, and an excellent winding road took us down into the plain in which the city is situated.

It was raining in torrents when we entered the town, and some of the streets resembled rushing streams. Light bridges on wheels were placed to enable pedestrians to cross from one sidewalk to another. These bridges are always kept ready in the same places, so that if it rains they can at once and easily be placed in position. I found an excellent stable for the horses, and later went to the 'Hotel Palace,' which is very good and up to date.

Guatemala City

The capital of this republic is relatively new, having been built after the town that is now known as Guatemala Antigua (Old Guatemala) had twice been destroyed by eruptions of the nearby volcanoes. Antigua, as the old town is called for short, is some twenty-five miles to the north-west of the present-day capital. A few years ago the new town was shaken by a severe earthquake, and the amount of damage done can be seen when one visits the outskirts of the city, where rows of villas still stand in ruins.

There is very little of interest to be seen in Guatemala City, but its hilly surroundings and the delightful climate make up for this.

A few trams run to the outskirts of the town. These public conveyances are propelled by old Ford engines, and I ventured to make a journey in one of them when I went to see a cleverly-made relief map of the republic in a park outside the town. This map is made to a 1/10,000 scale horizontally and 1/2,000 vertically. It is made of concrete, and running water marks the rivers, lakes and oceans. On my way back the tram derailed, and the driver asked me to help him to lift it back on the rails. Having failed, after two or three strenuous efforts, I thought it would be less work to walk back to the hotel.

Marimba bands entertained visitors, and the 'alta sociedad' of town came in to dance to their music. Here, as in some other southern republics, I again noticed that all the American-haters try to look as American as possible at these dances, using any odd word of English they happen to know in preference to their own language.

Whilst in this city I saw a man who had been kept in a dungeon below the San Francisco church for sixteen years. This happened during Cabrera's time. The food and water were lowered through a hole to the prisoners below, and those who died were hoisted out through the same opening. Considering what this man must have gone through during those sixteen years it was a marvel to see him still alive, but the horrible experience had slightly deranged his mind; and no wonder!

I had been extremely careful all the way, and had taken every precaution against malaria, but I had become so confident that I would never get it that I had been careless in San Salvador, and the result was that I had my first attack of fever whilst I was in Guatemala Cjty. I had obviously contracted it below in the hot parts of Salvador, and had several nasty attacks later, paying the full price for my carelessness, especially when I suffered in places where I had to sleep on the ground like a dog, and travel instead of being able to lie up. However, in spite of several violent attacks, I never let it interfere with my ordinary programme, as will be seen later.

I enjoyed my stay in this capital, where I soon made many friends, and where the horses recuperated so much that Mancha bucked when I mounted him again as I was about to leave. The people who had come to see me off were amazed at this, and no wonder, for who had ever heard of a horse bucking after having travelled well over 6,000 miles, and this under the most trying conditions imaginable?

Old Guatemala

A good road, winding through wooded and hilly country took us to Antigua, where I spent two delightful days.

Before the town was destroyed, nearly two centuries ago, it had 80,000 inhabitants and no fewer than forty-four churches, the ruins of most of which are standing to this day. The only building that was not seriously damaged during that disastrous volcanic outbreak is the massively-built town hall, which is still as good as new. The ruins show how splendidly everything had been built, especially the churches. Huge arches and pillars remain standing, and many of the ruins are overgrown by vegetation. In some, Indians have built their huts and made shelters, where they live almost like cave-dwellers.

Overlooking the town are three famous volcanoes; the Acatenango (12,000 ft.), the Volcan de Fuego (Fire Volcano), and the Volcan de Agua (Water Volcano), not one of which has been active for many years. The last two are thus named on account of one having shot out fire, cinders and smoke, whereas the other spouted out exclusively water, and in such quantities that this was chiefly responsible for the destruction of the old town.

The climate is eternally spring-like and almost anything grows here. Fine big trees give shade everywhere, and beautiful glades afford pleasant walks. Except for a few tourists who visit the place there is very little movement in Antigua to-day.

Volcanic Regions of Singular Beauty

The next two journeys were delightful. In parts we followed a good road, and then again an excellent trail. Fir and eucalyptus trees grew everywhere, and fine cornfields waved in the cool breeze. Hereabouts live numerous Indian farmers. Many of them passed us along the road, carrying loads of fruit, vegetables, pottery, etc., to the distant markets. The men wear short aprons, made of wool, all of which are of the same black and white check design. Under these aprons they wear short trousers that barely reach to their knees. The costumes of the women vary in colour, but I observed that when several women came along the road together the colour of their dresses was usually identical. I saw some very fine types among these Indians. The men are usually of splendid physique, but the women seem to be rather small around the hips. The language in this part is Kachikel, but the majority of the natives speak Spanish fluently. White men among them are known as 'ladinos' (i.e. 'clever').

On reaching the summit of a high hill, after zigzagging higher and higher among the strong-smelling fir trees, I beheld one of those sights that will always live in my memory. Far below at our feet Lake Atitlan came into view. Its mirror-like surface of a deep blue reflected the surrounding mountains and the snow-white clouds that looked like huge airships. The lake is more than 4,500 feet above sea level, and rivals anything Switzerland has to offer.

After having admired this beautiful panorama for a while we followed a good but steep trail down. At times we were under shady fir-trees, then among high grass and sweet-scented flowers, or, again, we were bordering giddy precipices, the walls of which rose perpendicularly from the forest below near the lake. A German owned a small hotel beside the lake, and as there was an abundance of excellent fodder, I stayed there two days to give the horses a treat. Every day I took them to the lake, where we bathed and enjoyed ourselves like three beings of the same flesh and blood. Around the lake are several Indian villages, while American Evangelists have a missionary station on the very beach, near a village called Tzanjuyu. What on earth they want to teach these peaceful, industrious and exceedingly happy Indians is more than I can understand.

But few mortals live so easy and 'soft' a life as these missionaries do in their neat, imported bungalows. They have all kinds of luxuries, including two motor launches with which they skim over the crystal-clear lake, fishing and enjoying themselves. The Indians take next to no notice of them, excepting when a feast and free feed are promised them and, I am told, sometimes even money. On these occasions photographs are taken, to show the well-meaning supporters abroad how the 'savages' flock to their new spiritual leaders for 'food.'

What is the good of putting the Kachikel language into writing and then translating the Bible into it, when the few Indians who go to school learn to read and write in Spanish? My experience with Indians has been that they never learn to understand the Christian religion as we do, and if Kipling's famous 'East is east and west is west' is true, it is much more so with the South and Central American Indians. The Spaniards forced their way of worshipping upon the unfortunate Indians, and although many to-day adore images and wooden saints, these have merely taken the place of the old idols, and the sun, the moon, and the stars remain still the mystical background of their adorations. Some missionaries try to do away with images and outward signs and endeavour to implant Christian sentiment, forgetting that they are dealing with people of such utterly different mentality, people who will never be able to see their point of view. Sentiment, like musical and other talents, is inborn and can never be implanted, but where it exists it can be cultivated. White man has but few morals to teach the Indian, and it is superfluous for me even to go into details why I think so. Suffice it to mention war, murder, commerce, prostitution, refined vice and hypocrisy, things that are beyond the range of understanding of any pure Indian when considered on the scale we know them.

Charity begins at home; so let us start by cleaning the Augean stables of our big cities before we go abroad teaching the Indians and 'savages' our vices, which is necessary to make them understand the contents of the Bible and the teachings and principles that are to guide us.

Whilst I was in Tzanjuyu the Indians held a religious procession. An old church that was badly damaged during the big earthquake in 1825, still stands, but there is no priest attached to it, so the natives carried on on their own. Battered and discoloured old saints were brought out and slowly carried around by the men. Ahead walked two Indians beating big drums, whilst another played a small, shrill flute. The women were seated on the ground in the market square, whence they watched. Most of the men who took part in the ceremony had obviously freely partaken of 'guaro,' as their favourite strong drink is called, and some had great difficulty in walking along. Behind this strange procession followed a few more Indians, who set off one rocket after another. Finally the saints, one of which was a Spanish conquistador carved in wood, were taken back into the ruined church, where I followed to see what was going on inside.

In a niche, on one side, was an ancient altar over which an old mural painting was still to be seen. The floor had been sprinkled with fir needles and flowers, and on the altar were all kinds of strange saints to which the Indians bowed, or in front of which they threw themselves flat on the stone floor, remaining there for some time, not unlike penitent dogs. One 'saint' was a modern white doll, dressed up in Indian clothes, and in one place lay a coffin with the crude shape of a human being in it, which the drunken Indians went to kiss. In some corners and niches groups were squatting ~ the floor and drinking, whilst some lay about so badly intoxicated that they appeared to be dead. As I was accompanied by the 'alcalde' (mayor), several Indians came to kiss my hands, which is a custom among them.

To this day many Indians here believe that white men are 'hijos del sol' (sons of the sun) and that they, the Indians, are 'hijos de la luna' (sons of the moon). They say that the sun, being more powerful than the moon, the whites, being its children, must necessarily rule over the Indians.

When we came outside the church, the beating of drums called together the people, and a government proclamation was then read out, both in Spanish and Kachikel. The Indians were being reminded that taxations were due, and of what would happen to them should they fail to answer the call. I had by now so often seen both Church and State officials oppress the natives by abusing their authority that it no longer made me sick at heart as it had done before. I had become so used to it that I could look on as I learned to do at bullfights when the defenceless horses are ripped open and gored to death, sights that made me feel bilious and ill the first time I went to a bull-ring whilst in Lima.

From Lake Atitlan I took a short cut towards Quezaltenango. This trail led over mountains and was rough in parts, and we had to pass through the village Nahuala, which I had been warned to avoid. It is inhabited exclusively by Indians, who will not tolerate the presence of a white overnight. In Guatemala, as in most Central American countries, the sale of liquor is State monopoly, but the Indians of Nahuala pay the government a certain sum each year for not sending alcohol into their district. This is about the equivalent of what the government would collect as liquor tax were it not a 'dry' place!

When I arrived, I immediately went to visit the priest in order to see if he would give me hospitality and shelter for the night. He and the schoolmaster are the only whites the Indians allow to stay in their village after sundown. The priest's house stood alongside the church and was surrounded by high adobe walls. At the entrance gate stood two Indians who acted as guards, two being on duty day and night. I found the priest to be an excellent person and, strange to say, his opinion about the majority of his kind in these countries coincided with mine. When he took me outside to show me the place, two Indian guards followed us like shadows, with their arms crossed over their chests. The priest told me that these guards follow him wherever he goes within the district of the village.

The language of this district is Quiché, which sounds pleasant to the ear. More out of curiosity than necessity I learnt a few words, and used them as often as I could. 'Tabaná jum topoc,' for instance, means 'do me the favour,' and 'jagüe uimac be Xelajú'* means 'which is the way to Quezaltenango?'

After leaving Nahuala we continued over bad mountain trails at first, and later descended into a valley, where we struck a good road that took us into Quezaltenango. This town is of some importance and is a commercial centre where many Germans have settled down during recent years. I was given a very warm reception by everybody, and was obliged to stay for two days. A group of enthusiastic Mexicans came to visit me, and gave me a foretaste of Mexican hospitality and friendship.

During the course of conversation I told some acquaintances that drunkenness had caused me a great deal of worry and discomfort all along the route, for wherever I went intoxicated people molested me or made things unpleasant. I was told that in this town the police had a special two-wheeled push-cart with which 'gendarmes' went around at night to pick up drunken people. As I did not believe this, my new acquaintances took me out to prove it to me; after having seen a few 'corpses' loaded the sight became monotonous.

An excellent road, of recent construction, that wound and twisted over mountains took us safely to San Marcos, a quaint village near the top of a mountain in the extreme north-west of the Guatemalan republic.

Before I reached that place I spent a very uncomfortable night in a small settlement along the route. I had accommodated the horses in a fenced-

---

Xelaju is the Indian name for Quezaltenango.

in backyard and was sweeping the rubbish and dirt out of the room where I thought of sleeping, when two villainous-looking fellows arrived and began to watch me. After a while one of them approached and offered me some 'guaro' out of a bottle. Naturally I refused to drink any of it, and so the man returned to his companion and both began to whisper in low tones. When a second attempt to make me drink had again failed, both began to insult me, using such a vocabulary that I almost admired them for their command of the language. I took no chances that night, and, needless to say, I did not sleep inside, but under a low shed made of old petrol-cans near the horses. I had not been lying there long when Mancha began to snort and, peeping out of my shelter, I could distinctly see the shape of a man who was sneaking along in the dark. I waited until he had almost reached me, and then fired a shot into the air. My .45 Smith & Wesson was within a foot of the unsuspecting man's head when I pulled the trigger, and I should not be surprised if he was still running when daylight appeared.

San Marcos was the last village we touched in Guatemala. Thanks to its elevation above sea level the climate is very cool, in fact, after sunset it gets quite chilly, and the nights are often cold. There are several volcanoes near here, some of which show great activity at times and have been known to cause great losses of lives and property. The Tajumalco (some 12,500 feet) is the highest in the republic.

Towards the Mexican Border. A Glorious View–Descent into Steaming Tropical Lowland

W hen we left San Marcos a short climb brought us to the top of a mountain whence we started on a very steep descent over a rough and stony trail. Vegetation typical of cool climates covered the mountainside, but as we gradually came lower the plants—according to the elevation—were those of the semi-tropics or tropics.

I had been invited to stay in a coffee plantation belonging to a German settler, situated about half-way down the steep slope. The hospitality extended to me was as delightful as the glorious view from this lovely spot. Above towered the mighty Tajumalco; in the far distance below the steamy tropical lowland of Mexico could be seen, and occasionally the glimmer of the Pacific Ocean penetrated the curtain of mists. To the right, *i.e.*, to the north-west, the peaks of the mountain range extended until they faded away in the distance in the direction of the Isthmus of Tehuantepec, and in the opposite direction they continued towards San Salvador. Crystal-clear waters came bubbling and foaming down the mountain near the house, and beautiful waterfalls made a continuous roar which, together with the mild breeze, made me feel pleasantly sleepy. I could have stayed in that little paradise, with its lovely flowers and ferns, for months, but each time I looked to the northwest something seemed to tell me 'go on.' Had I not listened to this call, the chances are that I would have lost my dear old pal Gato, as will be seen soon.

After I had taken leave of my excellent host we slowly picked our way down, following a short cut that led from the plantation down towards the Mexican border. Gradually, as we descended, it became warmer and warmer, until at last the air was steamy. With the change of temperature the vegetation became more exuberant. Large-leafed tropical plants were growing everywhere and insects made the horses swish their tails and throw up their heads in vain efforts to rid themselves of the pests. The sudden change from the bracing, cool climate of the highland to the hot and sultry atmosphere of the coast made the perspiration ooze out of our pores and produced a feeling of depression and complete loss of appetite.

Back in the tropical regions once more, I vainly tried to sleep in the oppressive heat whilst swarms of insects buzzed around my net. Sleeping under a mosquito-net has its advantages, but the want of air and the heat that collects under it make one feel very uncomfortable. Many a night have I passed under my net-tent without being able to sleep for more than a few minutes at a time, rolling from side to side until I was glad to rise and light a fire and pass the rest of the night smoking and watching the horses; smoking, I mean, when I was lucky enough to have a good supply of 'comfort.'

One morning when I went to take the horses to water I noticed that Gato had gone lame in the right fore. At first I thought he had possibly twisted his leg whilst coming downhill over the rough and stony trail, or that he had perhaps been kicked during the night.

We went along very slowly, as Gato seemed to find it difficult to walk. I was quite excited when I reached Rio Suchiate and saw the small steel bridge, the middle of which marks the border between Guatemala and Mexico. A detachment of Guatemalan border officials, who were expecting me, gave us the farewell in that country, and half an hour later we stepped on the bridge and crossed over. We were on Mexican soil!

The Land of the Charros

From the first moment we wearily stepped on Mexican soil at the bridge near Tuxtia Chico until we jogged over the international bridge across the Rio Grande into Texas at Laredo, Mexican hospitality and friendship almost embarrassed me.

True, all was not a joy ride, and I had a good taste of the consequences of a revolution that lasted nearly all the time it took us to cross that wonderful but turbulent country, a distance of some 1,500 miles from the extreme south to the north by the way we went.

A detachment of well-armed guards stopped us when we had crossed the bridge into the land of the 'charros,' as the picturesque and virile Mexican cowboys are called. When I told the guards who I was they all embraced me in true Mexican style and gave long and prolonged 'vivas' for the Argentine republic. A bottle was immediately brought out and handed round, food and cigars appeared as if by magic, and I had to answer a regular shower of questions.

After I had taken a photograph of the officers, together with my horses, an escort showed me the way towards the nearest village. Gato went so lame that we had to halt several times to give him a rest. The news of our arrival soon spread all over the neighbourhood, and numerous army officers, officials and people came to give me a hearty welcome into their country, and within a few hours I received telegrams from the capital, some from the government, others from societies etc., all containing congratulations and welcomes. A veterinary surgeon of the Mexican army, who happened to be in the neighbourhood, immediately came to examine Gato, whose leg seemed to be getting worse. After a careful examination the veterinary surgeon located the trouble. A nail had been driven near the quick of the hoof, causing an abscess and, by degrees, serious trouble had developed. We cut a large hole into the hoof to give the matter inside an outlet, and after a few days the invalid showed great improvement.

Both horses were stabled under a shed in the backyard of the dirty hotel where I stayed, and the only fodder they had was a coarse swamp-grass which was daily brought into town on burros. In addition to this I gave my animals a certain amount of corn, but only a little, as it is very heating in tropical climates. The invalid had practically recovered when, on going to feed him early one morning, to my surprise I found a mule tied next to him, and my poor horse all cut and bruised where he had been kicked during the night. The spiked shoes of the mule had cut deep into his flank, and there was a nasty cut in the left knee. The pain made him put all his weight to the right side, which had given the trouble before. The owner of the mule had arrived late at night after I had gone to bed, and as no fodder was to be obtained at so late an hour he had obviously tied his animal alongside mine that it might eat some of his.

My regret was that he had not placed his mount next to Mancha, for in that case the story would have been the reverse. I never saw Gato show fight or retaliate if he was kicked or bitten but Mancha made up for that by immediately attacking any strange animal which came near him. However, he was not treacherous with men, but gave a fair warning by lifting one of his hind-legs and putting back his ears, and although he had been dangerous when he was first tamed I have never known him hurt anybody, for people always took his unmistakable warnings seriously and kept at a respectful distance when he showed signs of annoyance.

Gato's knee became so bad that he could no longer lie down, and soon a terrible abscess set in. For a whole month I worked at him, and finally he looked so bad that some who saw him thought the kindest thing would be to kill him to put him out of misery. Naturally I would never agree to this, and when I realised that his recovery in that bad climate was impossible, I communicated with the Argentine Embassy in Mexico City and arranged to send the cripple there by train. Fortunately we had reached Tapachula, where the line from Guatemala to Mexico City passes. Had this accident happened anywhere else I should have had to sacrifice the animal.

When all was arranged, sympathetic friends helped me literally to carry the invalid to the station where we bedded him down in a wagon to send him to the distant capital in charge of a reliable man. I had a big lump in my throat when the train disappeared around a curve, for I really believed I would never see my dear old Gato again. Accompanied by my friends I returned to the shed where Mancha was desperately calling his companion, as Gato had done even when the train had begun to move. Until late that night I remained with Mancha, drinking more of the strong Mexican 'tequila' than was physically good for me; but it helped mentally.

I wondered if the two of us could successfully fight our way through as far as Mexico City, after which the rest would be relatively easy. Would the swamps along the coast, or the mighty Sierra Madre rob us of victory that was practically in sight, or had our luck changed? These and similar thoughts ran through my head like whirlwinds all night.

Although the delay of one month in this place had caused us to miss the best time for travelling along the swampy coast, and the rainy season had set in, I was determined to continue. I had full confidence in Mancha and, after all, this was part of the game. We had suffered a severe set-back, but in spite of the handicap I had visions of final victory and felt that we would beat even the elements, which now seemed to have gone against us in the same way as luck had done.

The people along the coast of the Mexican State of Chiapas are much like the Guatemalans, and during my forced stay in this region I had ample opportunity to observe them. Any Mexican government official can easily be distinguished from the ordinary private person, for it seems to be his privilege to wear a .45 automatic and a belt well studded with bullets.

One day some officers took me around the town. As we passed a group of drunken soldiers some of them began to insult their superiors. Before I knew what was happening a free-for-all fight had started, knives were drawn, and shots popped in all directions. Suddenly I received a sharp blow from behind that made me see stars unknown in astronomy. People who happened to be near at the time ran helter-skelter for safety as though an earthquake were taking place. When the commotion was finished I turned out to be the only man hurt, and until wise Mother Nature had done her work I had to 'wear' a most undignified black eye.

Chinese merchants run many of the small stores, and many children show that they have a good splash of Chinese blood running in their veins.

The average man in this neighbourhood is a vicious smoker, and even little children can be seen puffing away like their elders; in fact, some seem to take to cigars as soon as they leave their mothers' breasts.

Every morning a large group used to assemble in the hotel, some to play cards, and others to roll dice whilst drinking their 'aperitivos,' and this was the time when all the news was discussed. There was plenty to talk about, for at the time the Spanish heavyweight boxer Uzcudun had lost a fight to a 'gringo,' as Americans are called in Mexico, and, not only this, but Al Capone in Chicago was in serious difficulties with the American authorities. On one occasion a little Spaniard, who had never been known to have done a day's work, was wagging his tongue as if he were in training for a talking marathon. When he came to summarise his speech, this human loud-speaker warned the listeners that all these happenings were certain proofs that the 'gringos' were endeavouring to absorb and exterminate the Latin race!

Every now and again, when he felt dry, the little Spaniard asked somebody to stand him a drink, whereupon one of the amused audience would turn to the fellow behind the bar and shout, 'Bring the "gachupin" another mouthful.' 'Gachupin,' is not a very complimentary name Mexicans have for Spaniards, for whom the majority harbour a great dislike.

Some evenings a disgustingly fat Turk mounted a roulette table in a back room, and 'lifted' the money off those who hoped to do the same to him.

The village where I spent my forced stay prides itself on a tram-line that connects the plaza with the station. As in Guatemala City, the two or three tram-cars they have are propelled by old Ford engines and come rattling along with radiators boiling over and foaming like old war-horses.

During my last few days' stay here it was obvious that political trouble was brewing, and everybody felt as if sitting on the crater of a volcano just about to break out in eruption. Minor shooting affrays had already taken place, and the whole police force was changed by disarming them late one night, throwing them out in the street and putting new men in their place. It was both interesting and amusing to watch the new 'vigilantes' when they were learning how to load rifles, things they had obviously never handled before.

The lap from the Guatemalan border to Tehuantepec, some 250 miles, leads chiefly through low swampland and jungle forests, and travelling is at any time difficult, much more so during the rainy season which had already set in. Friends advised me to take a guide along with me, but although we hunted high and low we could find nobody who had ever travelled the whole distance. True, some had walked along the railway line, crossing the swamps and rivers over the many bridges, but we could not do this and had to go another way, as these are specially built to make it impossible for animals to walk over them. Finally, however, a man who had been recommended to me agreed to accompany me, although he had never been far along that route. I bought a horse for him and another to carry the pack. I was very careful in the choice of them and picked animals that were accustomed to the swamps and coastal climate. Should they prove useless in the mountains I could always exchange them for others later, if need be.

A Difficult Stretch

In spite of the adverse weather conditions I was glad when I sat on Mancha again; and heading him in the direction of the Isthmus of Tehuantepec I was ready to tackle the next lap, which promised to be another tough proposition.

We had not ridden far when we entered forests, and shortly before midday a heavy rain began to fall, as it does during the rainy season, with almost mathematical precision at 11 a.m. every day in this part. The bad road grew narrower and narrower until it became a soft and muddy trail. Mancha was used to mud and ploughed his way through like a tractor. The guide had the bad luck to fall into a deep mud-hole, and I had not finished laughing when we came to a river where Mancha stumbled on a slippery rock and fell on his side, the strong current rushing over him. I got a good ducking, but as it was hot and the rain had already soaked through my clothes it made but little difference. Only for the first two days could I call my man a guide, for after that he did not know the country any more than I did. However, he was a splendid fellow and a great help. He was a good jungle-man, always happy and cheerful, even when things looked bad, and I shall always remember Angel Riso, as he was called, as one of nature's gentlemen, uneducated and crude, but faithful and honest and with the heart of a lion; in short, a typical Mexican gentleman of the poorer class.

The rain was so heavy that we had to stop in a little settlement called Huehuetan, which consisted of a few straw-roofed huts, and as my guide had some friends there we were given shelter in one of them. It was inhabited by an elderly woman, her son, two other women and several children. The hut had only one room which was kitchen, living-room and bedroom in one, and whilst I was watching one of the women boil an 'iguana' with rice and beans in a pot, I was trying to figure out how the little crowd of us could be accommodated for the night. Iguanas (the Mexican variety) are large, dark-grey, horny lizards, with a row of spikes along their backs. They live on big old trees or in holes under their roots. As far as appearance is concerned, a full-grown iguana, which is about a foot and a half in length, without counting the equally long tail, is about as repulsive a prospect for eating as I know. However, once cooked they are quite tasty, and in some parts of Mexico are considered a delicacy.

Obviously the man had been out iguana hunting, for against the wall lay several more. I went over to have a look at them, and found that they were still alive and, to prevent them from biting, holes had been cut through their upper and lower jaws, through which a thin but tough kind of creeper had been passed and then firmly tied around so as to keep the mouth shut. To make escape impossible the forelegs of these unfortunate reptiles had been broken and tied to their hindlegs, holes having been made through their feet that were secured together with bits of creeper. Suffering untold agonies, these iguanas have to linger until death relieves them when they are killed for cooking.

The rain seemed to increase in violence, and once it became dark everybody huddled around near the fire to eat, and afterwards to tell terrible stories of dangerous rivers, crocodiles, bandits, etc. The children snuggled up against the women, who were squatting on the mud floor, and their dark eyes showed the fear they felt. The only light there was came from the flickering fire. The horses were outside, the newly-acquired tied to trees and Mancha loose. He must have been looking for shelter from the wind behind the hut, for every now and again I could hear him stamping. Every time he did this the children, whose imagination had been worked up to terror pitch, would give a nervous twitch, and their little hands clutched tighter on the women's skirts. The man told us we would have to cross a stream next day in which there was a particularly big, fierce, and cunning crocodile, which had even attacked men on mules whilst they were crossing a certain ford we would have to use. He said that the reptile had done so much damage that the men of the neighbourhood had joined together in vain attempts to kill it. By this time my guide was also beginning to feel nervous, and presently he stood up and, raising his hands above his head, shouted in a high-pitched tremolo voice, 'Santisima Virgen Maria' (Most Holy Virgin Mary), after which he bowed and made the sign of the cross. The women did the same and, guiding the hands of the children, made them go through the same motions.

My man asked me for two candles, articles I always carried in the saddle-bags. He then took down from the wall a dirty battered image of the Virgin of Guadalupe, the patron virgin of Mexico, and, placing it between the two flickering candles on a box, began to go through all manner of strange movements, at the same time imploring the Virgin to ask San Ignacio to have mercy on us and to protect us against accidents whilst crossing rivers. A sudden gust of wind that came in under the door blew out both candles. There was a shriek of horror, and everybody commented that this meant a refusal on the part of the Virgin to act as intermediary. The guide turned to me and reproached me for not carrying an image of San Ignacio among my requisites for a long journey. Confessing my barbarous ignorance in this line, I admitted that I did not know the powers of this particular saint, although his name seemed familiar to me. All the grown-up people then began to tell me that he was the river charmer and protector of travellers on lonely and dangerous trails.

When we had debated the situation and the possible causes that had made the candles go out, my guide suggested that he might have omitted something in the preliminary ceremony, before speaking to the Virgin. He lit the candles once more and, having gone through new actions that struck me as most comical, he told the Virgin of Guadalupe that he could not speak directly to San Ignacio as he had not his image, but he humbly begged and implored her to forgive him for molesting her and to do him the favour to act as intermediary for him, and to ask San Ignacio to assist him in his troubles and to protect him against accidents. All this he said in most flowery and ornamental language, and when he had finished he again went through some strange actions, then blew out the candles and replaced the image of the Virgin on the wall. When this had been done he expressed his satisfaction and said that he was almost sure that his petition had been heard and would be attended to.

The average Mexican of the lower classes is essentially mystical and superstitious, and nearly everybody wears some religious medal on a string around the neck. I have seen many who, instead of a medal, wore a small piece of canvas on which, at one time, probably an image of the Virgin of Guadalupe had been printed, but which in time had disappeared with the perspiration, grease and dirt. These tokens of luck, or talismans, are never taken off once they have been put on.

I have read several books and different articles that dealt with the religious situation of Mexico. American magazines and newspapers have off and on published such material, but at a glance I could tell that the authors of them had either been influenced by money to write as they did, or else that they had a complete lack of understanding of the Mexican people, whose language they probably do not understand, or with whom they have never been in close contact. Neither space nor inclination permits me to go into details about this much-discussed and little-understood situation, which I have debated at all angles and among all social classes in that wonderful but troubled country, but I am convinced that there has never been an anti-religious movement in Mexico, rather, a strong drive against a certain religious institution or body. To any clear-thinking person it must be obvious that religion is purely spiritual, and an institution material, although the latter may be what we call a religious one. In Mexico religion has been used by many for ultra-material purposes, and the attack successfully directed against that highly-organised body does not imply an attack against a philosophy that has so many different interpretations and, alas, ways of exploiting and fettering ignorant people, as undoubtedly has been the case in this country.

Everybody in the little hut was making ready to sleep; skins were spread on the floor and, as it was hot and sticky in spite of the rain, all began to undress. The women did not seem to worry about our presence and did this quite unconcernedly, and when they had finished they wrapped blankets around themselves to keep off mosquitoes. I had been asleep for some time when I was awakened by water dripping down on me from the roof, and wishing to shift to a dry place I struck a match, but as there was no space anywhere I had to remain where I was, and it must have been early morning when I again closed my eyes. The smoke of the fire awoke me, and when I looked about me I found that every-body was up and busy, although it was still practically dark. The rain had stopped, and when I went outside, Mancha, who was grazing, greeted me with his usual 'good-morning' nicker. After a canful of tasty black coffee we groomed the animals and saddled up.

The almost unrecognisable trail wound through jungle forest where it was impossible to ride. Branches, twigs and leaves obstructed our path, and often the guide had to make use of his machete. For long stretches we waded through murk and slime or water, and luckily my man was familiar with this region, or else I should have been hopelessly lost. At times even he had his doubts about our being on the right track, and in several places he made me wait whilst he went ahead to investigate. Between curses we discussed the 'Ford of the Bad Crocodile,' as we had already named the one about which we had heard the evening before.

After several hours of painfully slow progress, wet and muddy up to our waists, we came to a wide, slow-flowing stream that looked more like a long pool of stagnant water. Big, wide-leafed jungle-plants were grow-ing everywhere, and mosquitoes buzzed around us in clouds. We soon found a place that looked like the ford we had been told about, and prepared to cross over to the other side.

To keep the contents of the pack dry, we lifted both wings of the saddle-bags and fixed them in an upright position, and to prevent the load from over-balancing I tied a rope over the top and secured it to the wide girth. I told the guide to do likewise on the other side, but somehow he only secured the top and forgot to tie the rope to the girth. When all was ready we started to wade across, the guide going in front whilst I followed behind driving the pack-animal before me. The water reached half-way up the horses' flanks by the time we neared the opposite bank, which was some ten feet high. We made for a steep, narrow gap, and presently the guide's horse scrambled out of the water, followed by the pack-animal. It was not easy to get out of the ford as it was fairly deep and the bank steep and slippery, and I was just about to reach safety when the load fell off the horse in front of me. As I had tied it to the girth on one side, the frightened animal bolted up the incline, dragging the saddle-bags behind. I hurried Mancha out of the water, and when we came to the top of the bank I saw the pack-horse rushing in and out among the trees, dragging the load with its precious contents behind him, kicking it every time he had a chance. As natives in this part will accept no other money but silver pesos, I was carrying a fair supply of these in the pack, which also contained different instruments, field-glasses, medicines, clothes, etc. With every kick a puff of white came out of the pack, and I suspected that either the talcum powder or bicarbonate of soda tins had been damaged.

Suddenly the frightened animal came tearing straight at me, and Mancha got such a scare that he reared up, staggered backwards, slipped, and both of us tumbled backwards into the water. Somehow I suddenly remembered the old 'croc,' and to this day I do not know how I stuck on the horse, although I was under water for some seconds, and this with him on top of me. When I reached high and dry land again, I found the pack-horse lying on the ground entangled in a mess of pack, girth, lasso and rope. I soon freed him and then, with bad presentiment, started to investigate the damage.

The saddle-bags were ripped open in several places where they had been kicked. One camera, the third broken on the trip so far, was bent into a useless wreck, whilst instruments, medicines, sugar, beans, etc., were all mixed together, and smelt something like a concoction of haggis, sauerkraut, and Limburger cheese; but, worst of all, nearly all my silver pesos were missing. I threw away what had been rendered useless, washed other things, and then laid them down to dry.

The guide stood there, scratching his head and apologising, for he knew that his forgetting to fasten the rope to the girth had caused this disaster. 'Que suerte' (what the luck), he said, 'that the crocodile was not near when you fell back into the water!'

Then began the search for the lost coins. The spilt powder and the trodden-down plants helped us considerably to see the way the horse had bolted, and soon we began to recover some of my lost treasure. Somehow I suddenly remembered the days of my childhood and the game of searching for Easter eggs, and, to the amazement of the man, I burst out laughing. When evening came we were still groping about among the plants and the grass, and when we began to feel hungry I washed the spilt medicine off some beans, and then cooked them together with some onions. When we started out in the morning I was still some sixty pesos short, but then the little melodrama of the day before was worth this price.

We slowly forged our way through dense jungle and soft swamps, passing within sight of a high ridge on which stands a big, solitary, cone-shaped rock, a singular landmark. The natives say that it is 'encantado' (bewitched), and that if anybody eats of the cocoa that grows near it, or takes away the seeds, that person is sure to die a sudden death.

For the next few days we suffered terribly. It rained in torrents and we had to guess our way through dense jungles and treacherous swamps. There were quite a number of streams and rivers which we had to cross by swimming, the swampy nature of the banks often making landings very difficult. Formerly a trail had existed which led along the foot of the near mountain range, but owing to the coming of the railway, and to the revolutions, this fell into disuse and is now impassable, being completely overgrown with vegetation. Flocks of parrots and red and blue cockatoos flew over us, and big monkeys looked down from the trees.

Some of the world's finest hardwood, rubber and chicle trees grow in abundance, but, owing to the political unrest, these must remain there like hidden treasures until, some day, conditions change. Formerly some of this wealth had been exploited, and we came across two or three 'haciendas,' the ruins of which bore testimony to what revolutions can do.

For long stretches at a time the ride changed into a struggle through mud and water, and often we were obliged to go afoot, almost dragging the animals behind us. We had to swim one pool and river after another, and the only satisfaction we had was to give vent to our feelings by swearing almost without interval. The perspiration was running down me in streams, and the rubbing of the clothes against my skin had chafed it, producing an irritation that made me feel as if I were covered with red ants. Along these coastal regions there are many tigers, crocodiles and other game, but none of them ever troubled us. Once a train surprised us as we were following the line which, in that particular place, had been built by filling in and raising the track in a stretch of swamp. We were bottled in like rats, and the only thing for us to do was to rush the horses into the water and there wait until the train had passed. One of the animals refused to follow, and as the train approached he tore away and began to race ahead of the engine. Luckily he did not stumble on the sleepers and, at the last moment, when I thought the train would hit him, he jumped off the track and fell into a soft swamp; when the fright was over we had a tough job to extricate him.

Let me just give one example of how bad travelling was in this part. From one point to another, separated by a distance of not quite twelve miles, we struggled over ten hours, and this without ever resting more than long enough to recover our breath.

On the outskirts of a village I was stopped by a detachment of soldiers. The sentry rattled an old Mauser at me, the loose screws sounding like an old-fashioned set of false teeth. He demanded to see my licence for carrying firearms, and when I produced it he said that this was a matter for the comandante and escorted me into the village where a regular little fortress had been built with sandbags near the plaza. The comandante was most polite and obliging, and apologised for having had to molest me, and explained that these precautions were necessary as a revolution had broken out, the Generals Gomez and Serrano having started an insurrection against the Calles government. Although I had had suspicions that trouble was brewing, I did not expect a general revolution, and the comandante's news filled me with apprehension.

My guide, who had been chatting with a group of soldiers, came to tell me that he had no desire to accompany me any further, and that he wished to return home to his wife. He had proved to be an excellent fellow and such a valuable help that I tried everything to make him change his mind, and he only gave in when I promised to present him with both of the horses I had bought after I had sent Gato up to Mexico City.

It was in a small village in the State of Chiapas that I had the first taste of the revolution and there I saw what crimes can be committed with impunity. A young man, about eighteen years. of age, whilst walking up and down the only street, enjoying the cool breeze of the night, passed near the house where a few soldiers had made their quarters. The officer in charge, who was intoxicated, commanded the young man to go home and to bed and, as might be expected, the youth did not obey and continued to walk up and down. Suddenly the officer snatched a rifle from one of the soldiers and fired at the inoffensive boy who fell wounded in the middle of the street, where he lay in agony for over an hour until he died. Nobody dared go to his assistance, for the officer had ordered all his men out and commanded them to shoot should anybody approach the dying man. Experience had taught me not to interfere in other peoples' affairs, least of all in foreign lands, and thus I merely watched, indignant, disgusted, but silent.

Travelling was bad until we reached a place called Tonala, where everybody turned out to greet us and to admire my Mancha, who, probably owing to his colour, was given the name of 'El Tigre de las Pampas.' I heard nasty rumours about the revolution and bandits who were making things unsafe in the neighbourhood and in parts we would have to cross before long. I had heard many similar yarns in other countries before and had taken next to no notice of them, but this time I knew that they were not imaginary or far-fetched. I feared more for Mancha than anything else, for horses are in great demand in Mexico, especially during revolutions, and my animal's fame had travelled before him, and I was afraid an attempt might be made to steal him.

When I left Tonala I shook the hands of many who had treated me like a brother; happy did we meet, happy did we part, and, maybe, happy shall we meet again.

Things began to look very ugly, and when we arrived in the next village I was told that it would be foolhardy to continue, as bandits were busy between there and Tehuantepec. Here I saw another disgusting sight. In broad daylight a man stabbed another in the plaza, and the offender was caught by some army officers who happened to be near. They hit him in the face with their .45 automatics, transforming into something resembling a half-cooked black-pudding what moments before had been a healthy head.

My two new horses showed the strain of hard work, and so I had to stay in Jalisco for four days to give them time to recuperate. I took advantage to gather whatever information was available about the regions ahead of me, but the outlook was none too rosy. A general who was in charge of the troops stationed there assured me that I could not go far without being assaulted, bandits having become very active with the outbreak of the revolution.

Whilst I was in this place an amusing thing happened to some workmen. Every day a train took them some distance out where they were mending the line, and an armed escort always accompanied the workers to protect them against possible attacks. Indeed, all the trains that passed carried troops to keep off bandits. As time passed and nothing had happened, the soldiers became so confident that they left their rifles on the train and went to amuse themselves in the forest. An engineer had hooked his field telephone to the main wire and was trying to get communication. After many futile attempts he began to lose his temper and eased his feelings by using 'wrong number language.' 'Hello, hello, —, —,' he yelled, 'anybody there?' Just as he said this he received a sharp dig in the ribs, and turning round he saw a rough-looking fellow with a rifle who once more prodded him. With a nasty grin the intruder said, 'Yes, here we are, you 'rechingado'; hand over your gun and money or I'll plug you!' All was over in a flash; rifles, ammunition and other useful articles had vanished, together with the cunning bandits who had obviously well planned this clever 'coup.'

The unfortunate engineer himself told me this story in the evening and showed me some black bruises where he had been prodded with the rifle. However, after a stiff drink he felt better and began to see the humorous side of the incident.

A dusky general called upon me late one night to impart the news that he had received orders from the War Department to supply me with an escort. I am certain that I should have lost my horses had it not been for this great service with which the government favoured me. I doubly appreciated this courtesy, for I was fully aware that every available soldier might be wanted at any moment. It was arranged that this escort should see me through to the next place where troops were stationed, and there be relieved by a new one. All commanders of the different detachments had been telegraphically advised, and thus I travelled well guarded until

I reached Oaxaca, up in the mountains, whence I preferred to travel alone again. My first escort belonged to the cavalry, but the men were all highlanders and were unaccustomed to the hot and swampy coastal regions. Their horses, which were of American origin, were practically useless, bad swimmers, nervous, and totally unfit for roughing it under prevailing conditions. Not only did my first escort's horses prove to be next to useless, but I noticed the same lack of stamina and adaptation to climatic conditions among the others that accompanied me later. I would like to see one of our well-fed, highly-strung, high-stepping snorters that waste all their energy in prancing around and tossing foam into the air, do a few days' travelling over bad trails and through swamps, and this on any food it might rustle. The difference between a range pony and a thoroughbred for hard work and roughing it is as great as that between an elegant cabaret-dancer and a sturdy, weather-beaten Indian.

I lost no time, and as soon as my escort was ready we started out, with good prospects of a few adventures. Ten soldiers and one officer were to see me through as far as the next army detachment. The uniforms of the men were of an extraordinary mixture. The officer wore a big, straw hat with a high crown, no shirt, but only a singlet and riding-breeches. The saddles were of various types, some having done service in the U.S. cavalry. I had to hire a special guide to take us through the swampy forests, for none of the men belonged to this part and were not familiar with the paths and trails. Not far out of the village the officer pointed to a tree on which he had hanged some bandits a few days before. In Mexico, people who have thus been put to death are usually left hanging to serve as a warning to others, but I will not go into details, although this was not to be the last time I witnessed such gruesome sights. Executions are such common occurrences during revolutions that people take hardly any notice of them, and even the condemned face death with no more fear than the average man would feel before having a tooth extracted. In novels and in the moving pictures we are often made to believe that one American is worth a hundred Mexicans, but people who believe this have not had the opportunity to see what these men are, be it in fighting or in dying.

I have seen Mexican soldiers lie down on the hard ground after a day's march, and go to sleep without a bite of anything to eat, and rise again in the morning, ready to go on, and this in a cheerful mood. A few 'frijoles' (beans) and a 'tortilla' (corn-cake) is all they need to keep fit, and should these fail, the soft inner leaves of the maguey plant, berries and some roots, will keep them going for an indefinite time. Frijoles and tortillas are Mexico's classical dishes, and he who objects to them should not travel in the interior of that country, for in most places there is absolutely nothing else to eat.

Our guide took us towards the coast, far away from the railroad. It rained heavily, but none of us minded this because it helped to cool us a little. In several places we had to swim, and for long stretches we waded through slimy pools filled with typical swamp vegetation. We halted in a little settlement where we all crowded into a mudhouse. Some of the escort's horses already showed signs of giving out, and lay down in the mud without touching any of the coarse grass we had cut for them. Although wet to the marrow and covered with mud, the men were quite cheerful, and when I turned up with a bottle of 'comiteco' (a strong drink) that I had bought in a hut, they were as happy as if they had been at a champagne party. One man had brought a red glass in his kit, and at night he filled this half-way up with oil and stuck a wick into it, which was held up on a float of wire and cork. When it was alight he placed the glass on a box in front of a little image of the Virgin of Guadalupe, leaving the light to burn all night.

During the conversation, that changed from one subject to another, some discussed the Virgin of Guadalupe and the Virgin Mary. One man said the Virgin of Guadalupe, being 'prieta' (dark), was 100 per cent Mexican, and that the Virgin Mary was white, and belonged to the gringos. This subject was soon dismissed with shouts of 'Viva la Virgen de Guadalupe; abajo la Virgen Maria!' (Long live the Virgin of Guadalupe; down with the Virgin Mary!)

The language of this region is Zapoteco, which is of old Indian origin. Most natives, when talking among themselves, prefer to speak in this language, although all of them master Spanish.

Next day we continued our march towards the isthmus. The first half of the journey was bad and we had to swim one or two nasty places. Mancha was by far the best horse in the water and, unlike the other animals, he would never get bogged in soft places, seeming to possess a wonderful instinct for avoiding them. He always swam across first to explore the way for the others. Towards midday we came to pretty open and hilly country. Every now and again a hare would jump up and run through the grass that grew in abundance everywhere. I had never seen such hares before, for all had white hindquarters, though the front half of the body was of the same colouring as the European hares. I shot one to examine it, and found it to be identical with the hares I had hitherto known, excepting for the strange colouring.

Our guide suddenly pointed ahead, where I could see a man on horseback in the distance. He said that this must be a bandit, for no one else would venture to ride here alone now. No sooner was the man aware of our presence than he started off at a gallop, and immediately several of our soldiers began to chase after him, but before they could reach him he had circled around towards the swamps and forest-land. After about an hour the soldiers returned with a pony tied to a rope. They said that the fugitive had managed to reach a wide stream where he had had time to unsaddle and to swim across and escape into the brush where pursuit would have been next to impossible. The guide recognised the pony as one that had been stolen some time before.

One evening we halted in a miserable village where we had to sleep on the floor without a bite to eat. During the night dogs were continuously barking, a sign that always made me feel uneasy. I had put Mancha in a small corral not thirty yards from where I lay, and had carefully tied and padlocked the gate so as to make it difficult for any person to open it. Padlocks are necessities if one travels in some Latin American countries, for, beside chaining the corral gate, one can secure one's doors which rarely have locks but merely two rings.

The soldiers had tied their horses to a row of stakes, giving Mancha the preference of the corral, where he might be alone and roll if he wished. The escort's animals knew each other, but as Mancha was a stranger they always fought with him. I got up several times to look at my horse, and always found him munching away happily, and finally I fell soundly asleep.

When I awoke again it was still dark, and as I had an uneasy feeling I immediately went to see the horse again. To my surprise the corral was empty, and striking a match I found that a place had been opened in the fence. I rushed back to advise the officer and to get my electric torch and revolver. I shook the officer and told him what had happened, and without losing time raced back to the empty corral. Thanks to the torch I could see that the heavy dew on the grass had only recently been disturbed and followed the track, which led towards a sandy stretch where it was impossible to see any hoofmarks.

I returned to see what the soldiers were doing, and found them all soundly asleep, so I again shook the officer, who jumped up with a start. He did not remember my having called him before although he had answered me, but within a few seconds everybody was rushing through the dark in search of the missing Mancha.

I went with the officer, and he, seeing an early riser sitting at the door of a hut, asked him if he had seen a horse pass. The man pleaded ignorance, but the officer was not satisfied with him and threatened to shoot him if he did not speak the truth, and to my surprise he simply commanded the man to show him the way the horse had gone and to run in front of us, and when he pointed his gun at him the frightened man almost squealed: 'No estan lejos, ya voy!' (They are not far, I'm going).

To give the alarm the officer then fired a few shots into the air, and I believe that this trick saved the situation, for about a quarter of a mile out of the settlement we found the horse coming towards us with a rope around his neck. Our foxy guide then told us that he had seen three men driving a 'pinto' horse before them, and as he had tried to escape in the direction they had come from they had roped him, and that even when he was tied he had refused to follow them. Mancha had always been frightened of a lasso, and this had obviously saved him.

In recompense for his services our guide received an unmerciful kicking, and I am sure that he believed it, and was almost grateful, when he was told to consider himself lucky that he was not going to swing on a tree for not having spoken the truth when he was first asked if he had seen anything.

We were out of the bad place now and very near the Isthmus of Tehuantepec. A large detachment of the Civil Guard had set out to meet us and to extend the first welcome, but somehow we missed each other through following different trails. In the regions near Tehuantepec the people are of a very different type, being taller than those along the coast of Chiapas. They have pleasant features and the women dress in long skirts that reach down to the ankles. They are very fond of richly embroidering their dresses and usually wear gold or silver necklaces with many coins on them.

My escort accompanied me as far as the next army post, where they were relieved by new troops. By more or less following the railroad in the direction of the Pacific we arrived in Tehuantepec without incident, although numerous bandits held the peasants of the neighbourhood in terror. On arrival we were given quarters in the City Hall, an ancient building with arcades and a big courtyard that was littered with rubbish and filth.

Old Tehuantepec

The women of Tehuantepec enjoy the reputation of being the prettiest in Mexico; their spirit, courage and beauty have made the women of this region famous for generations. Many of them are perfectly white, due to the cross breeding of French and Spanish. The costumes of the 'Tehuanas,' as the women of Tehuantepec are called, are most picturesque. I had the opportunity of seeing them at their best at a dance given in my honour.

Towards evening men and women paraded down the main street, some riding on ox-wagons decorated with flags and foliage, whilst others went afoot. Behind the wagons came the band, followed by the men, who marched in two long files. All were dressed in loose white blouses and white trousers and wore large Mexican sombreros, and then, last but not least, came the 'pièce de résistance,' the women. They were also in two-column formation, and slowly walked along, all dressed in their very best, only costumes of the region being worn. Many had large, fan-shaped head-gear of starched white cloth or lace. These head-dresses were very becoming, especially as all the women, without exception, had a very grace-ful carriage. Only a few wore shoes, and I had noticed before that women who are accustomed to go barefoot have invariably a similar, graceful and swaying walk, whereas our modern city girls merely waddle along when they go unshod. The 'Tehuanas' wear loose-fitting blouses with short sleeves, moderately open around the neck, and richly embroidered in front and behind. The long skirts are of different colours and designs, and adornments are arranged in circles around them. All the dresses were made of fine material and I noticed that each ended with a white bordering a little above the ankles.

At night a dance was held. A sandy square had been levelled and covered with a big sheet of sailcloth. Around it a fence had been erected, and arches of foliage and gaily-coloured flags made the place look most attractive. Electric bulbs of many colours had been fixed everywhere, the light of which made the ladies' dresses look doubly bright. There were some very graceful dancers among the merry throng, and nobody thought about going home until early dawn. Mexico is the Latin American coun-try where national customs have not disappeared with the modern invasion, and every citizen may justly be proud of the picturesque tradi-tions of his beautiful country.

I was almost sorry when the commander of my new escort told me to make ready to start immediately after sunset. I had spent four delightful days in old Tehuantepec, but then I had to remember that I was not on a pleasure trip.

Had it not been for the revolution I should have crossed the isthmus to Port Mexico on the Atlantic side, more or less following the railway line, but this would have been unwise because the fighting was centred on that side, and a well-organised gang of bandits had for some time past taken advantage of the favourable topography of the country around there to carry out their unpleasant activities. Accordingly there was no other way out for me than by crossing the Sierra Madre towards the highland in the direction of Oaxaca.

The other escort had already returned to their headquarters, and I heard that they had captured several bandits on their way back.

We planned to ride during the night, partly to avoid the heat of the day and partly for other obvious reasons. Every member of my new escort knew the country well, and so there would be no difficulty in finding the way. I was given a fine send-off by many friends, and soon forgot about pleasure, settling down to my job once more.

We rode in single file through sandy country, among bushes and trees. Soon it became dark, and whenever the comandante, who rode in front, had his doubts about the trail, he used a flashlight to examine the place. Stars glittered in the dark sky and thousands of insects chirruped. Here and there a glow-worm showed his greenish light in a bush, or the silence was broken by the shrill shriek peculiar to most night birds; the rest was the trampling of many hoofs or the occasional snort of a horse. When riding at night one has the sensation of sitting very high above the ground and distances seem endless. Long after midnight the moon rose over the mountain ridges and bathed the rugged country in its cold, bluish light, making the outlines of the huge cactus plants look almost ghostly against the moonlit horizon. Some stood on hills like solitary giants on guard whilst others seemed to grope upwards like fantastic beings of the deep.

The sharp crack of a rifle brought us to a halt like one man. There was a rustling of firearms being unstrapped, and then all was silence again, excepting an occasional snort of a horse that had scented danger. Some of the men slipped off their heavy sandals and silently disappeared into the darkness of the bushes, and they had not been gone long when a loud 'alto!' (halt) rang through the night, and presently several voices were heard. Soon the soldiers returned with a man who was immediately questioned, but he pleaded to be quite 'inofensivo' and said he was on his way to the nearest village. The comandante was not satisfied with the man's answers and we all went to examine the place ahead where he had been captured, and after a short search we found a rifle hidden in a bush. The man pretended to know nothing about it, but when we went through his pockets we found some ammunition that fitted the rifle, which had obviously been fired only a few minutes before. Without further ado the comandante ordered the man to be bound and taken along with us, and I never knew what happened to him after the escort had left me.

Shortly after daylight we came to a swift mountain river. The men proved to be excellent in the water, and their horses, who were of the region, swam across as if it were only a duckpond, and we soon reached a poor settlement by the name of Jalapa del Marques, where we had something to eat and then lay down to have a rest; owing to the heat and swarms of flies, however, sleeping was impossible.

Towards evening I had to go to a dance that had been organised in a hurry, but I must confess that I should have enjoyed a good sleep much more. Although there are no railroads, telegraphs nor telephones in any of these far-away places, it is amazing how fast news travels, and thus our arrival was expected in most places we touched.

The occasion must have been a good excuse, for already at that early hour some of the men showed the effects of alcohol, and, although the people belonged to the poor peasant class of Mexico, the dance was a merry and jovial affair.

In this part they have a special dance, exclusively for old women who amuse themselves as much as the younger onlookers. The band (!?) strikes up a loud and merry tune and the old women hop into the centre of the gathering with big neck-scarves in their hands which they wave in imitation of bullfighters, and presently the men come in and rush at the scarves like enraged bulls. Every time they have a chance they smack the old ladies where the back changes its name. The women try to retaliate, and this goes on until they give up, tired out. This dance, if such it can be called, is thoroughly enjoyed by everybody, and I saw nothing but clean and harmless humour displayed.

As soon as it was dark we all made ready to continue our march towards the sierras. The country was very hilly and broken, and in places the trail was rocky, or again we rode through forests or among a mass of cactus plants. Another fiesta was in store for me in the next small village we touched and where my escort was relieved by a new one.

Of course there are no hotels or even inns in any of these small, primitive settlements, where it is rare to see a stranger pass. We slept on the floor in front of the 'town hall,' and the horses were made safe in the courtyard. I was very tired, for, in addition to all the hard riding, I had not had much sleep lately. However, try as I would, I was not allowed to retire to rest until most of the men were drunk. A few had given trouble, and to make them safe until they should recover they were locked up in the 'town hall,' where they kept me awake by bellowing all night.

My new escort was not ready to start, so at last I was able to have a good and much-needed rest for one day. A heavy rain fell that afternoon, and when some of the soldiers who had to accompany me were frightened and ran to church to pray, I had a good guess that they were afraid and probably not used to these wild mountain rivers. Their long-legged and fine-boned horses did not inspire me with more confidence than the men, and I feared that they would be about as much use in swift waters as a pocket in a shirt.

The next lap, over the sierras to Oaxaca, some 140 miles, proved to be a hard nut to crack. We were now in very rugged, rough and mountainous country again, and as heavy rains had fallen the bridgeless rivers were nasty propositions. Quite a number of the soldiers were unable to swim, and Mancha's tail was in great demand where waters were deep and swift, several soldiers hanging on for dear life. He was by far the steadiest horse in the water, and where he had to wade over rocks, with a strong current reaching half-way up his flanks, he was remarkably clever at forging his way through. Sometimes two or even three of us would get on him to weigh him down more whilst others caught hold of his tail. Somehow he never objected to strangers mounting him on such occasions, when otherwise he would have bucked them off, When wading across swift-running rivers, horses often get giddy and fall, but luckily my animals never seemed to be affected that way. If the rider's head begins to feel 'swimmy' the best thing is not to look at the water but to fix his eyes on some object in the distance. Where the current was so swift as to make it hard to keep standing, Mancha had a way of turning his chest against the current and moving slowly sideways. He had learnt this trick by himself, for obviously he had found out that in this way he offered less resistance to the water than by exposing his flanks, and it was easier for him to keep his balance. Often the water and foam splashed high over his head and body, but in spite of it he kept serene and slowly continued towards the bank.

The part we were going through was practically uninhabited, but once or twice we camped in tumbledown huts that had long ago been abandoned owing to the revolutions.

For the first time I had omitted to bring a spare set of horseshoes with me and, as bad luck would have it, Mancha had to lose a shoe just then. Luckily I noticed it in time, and after a short search we found the lost treasure. I had a few nails but no hammer, so I made one out of a stone, and after no end of trouble managed to tack the iron on again.

Half-way up a mountain we had to sleep in a solitary, ruined hut. The roof had fallen down in several places, and there were some big holes in the adobe walls. Late in the evening several Indians who were on their way to Tehuantepec arrived, and so space for sleeping was scarce. I lay down in a corner but, tired as I was, I could not sleep, for so many insects of all sizes and kinds worried me, that I thought I must be lying on an anthill. I went outside to undress and shake my clothes, and then I sat down and began to smoke whilst I watched the animals graze, and, to pass away time, I went to have a look at the sleepers, whose strange positions and the expressions on their faces fascinated me. A fire was still glowing in the middle of the mud floor and the bright moon shone on some of the men through the open roof.

When the first daylight appeared we had already travelled some miles, for a long and hard march was ahead of us. We were hungry, but nobody ever mentioned it; Mexicans rarely complain—they take things as they come. When we came to a small village we had ample opportunity to make up for arrears, for the little the poor inhabitants had to offer was given to us with open hearts. We had shot a deer, of a kind that abounds in these mountain forests, and every man cut himself a piece, and soon these were sizzling on sticks over a fire, and when kindly villagers came with hot tortillas, frijoles and coffee we soon forgot our troubles.

I was well received throughout Mexico, but as the natives themselves had often very little to offer I had to put up with a certain amount of discomfort. More than once some kindly village mayor brought me a clean pillow. This made sleeping on the hard floor more comfortable, and I could not but appreciate this courtesy; to this day I wonder where and how these pillows were obtained.

Between Tehuantepec and Oaxaca there is a certain amount of traffic. Arrieros drive their burros over the rocky trails to sell corn and other agricultural products in the distant town. They use 'aparejos' (pack-saddles) with wide breast and tail straps which are often well decorated and embroidered with coloured wool. Many of these aparejos bear inscriptions in large letters, such as: 'Adios Muchachas' (Good-bye, girls), 'Fuerte Andamos' (We are going strong), 'Adios Amigos' (Good-bye, friends). The costumes of the men are entirely different here. They wear large felt hats, and jackets made of soft buckskin, with many tassels on them. These jackets are excellent wind-breakers, and, in addition to protecting against the weather, look most picturesque. In some villages the band came to serenade me at night and, much as I appreciated the honour, I must admit that I couldn't say the same about the tone of the instruments. In more than one place the well-meaning musicians kept on playing until early morning, doing me out of hours of needful sleep.

My escort was already left without horses, and when some of the soldiers got tired of walking they simply commandeered burros from the Indians along the route. One or two men were mounted on such small animals that I thought they must break their backs, but somehow the poor little brutes seemed to hold out in an amazing manner.

During a night march a soldier stepped off the trail in the dark and shot down a precipice with a shriek. We all thought that this was the last of him, but presently we heard him calling to us from not far below. I carried an acetylene lamp, which was of great value when my torch failed. Once I had it burning we found that the man had fallen on a large rock that stuck out of the mountain-side like a shelf. By means of my lasso we hauled the poor fellow back to safety. Fortunately he was only slightly bruised and shaken, and was able to continue with us when one of his companions offered him his precious burro.

It was a weary procession that arrived in a little town some eighteen miles from Oaxaca. My escort was completely played out, but not a man had given in. Even the soundest were footsore and tired, and others were as lame as their unfortunate burros, the owners of which had followed us on foot in order to reclaim them once they were no longer required. When we passed some stalls where not too clean food was sold, I invited the men to help themselves, and there was no need to ask them twice. We did not worry about cleanliness just then; all we wanted was something to fill us, and this we had. Whilst gobbling up the food I looked around, and to my delight saw small bundles of green alfalfa stacked up for sale in a market stall not far from ours. I went over and bought as many as the poor burros and Mancha could eat, and soon both men and animals were enjoying themselves.

There is a good road to Oaxaca, and as the men were not in condition to proceed I left them next morning and continued alone. It was quite a change to be by myself once more, and I had a better chance to observe things as I went along. I have been asked countless times if I did not find it dull and lonely to be on my own out in the wilds. Although very talkative when in company of friends, I never feel in the slightest dull when I am alone. The company of a horse or a dog is a wonderful thing, and with Mancha and Gato I never felt the want of any better. The work of feeding and looking after them had its recompense, for they helped to pass many hours away that would otherwise have been—excuse the expression—an empty hell. Usually there was so much to see and to do that the days passed like so many hours, and many a long conversation did I hold with the horses, who were always glad to hear my voice. They learnt to understand quite a few words; thus they would prick up their ears and look around nervously if I asked them 'que hay?' (what's up?), or they would sniff the air if I said 'puma' (South American lion). 'Chuck-chuck' meant fodder, and 'agua' water, and these they knew as well as a baby does 'daddy' and 'mummy'; if I happened to say, 'vamos, vamos,' they woke up and stepped out faster, and a slow 'bueno' never had to be repeated to make them stop.

The wide and sandy road towards Oaxaca was very busy the day I rode over it. Men and women trotted along it on foot, others were mounted on burros, mules or horses, and covered ox-wagons with solid wooden wheels slowly rolled along, creaking and squeaking. Inside sat men and women, dressed in their best and making merry, playing guitars and singing songs of the region. Alongside the road were stalls where food and drinks were sold. The reason for this unusual movement was that the annual 'fiesta del tule' was held on that day. The 'tule' is a famous old cypress tree which has stood for many generations in a village that derives its name therefrom. There are several of these gigantic old trees in Mexico, but the one I saw here is the biggest I came across, and it is claimed that this cypress is over 5,000 years old. Once every year huge crowds assemble in this village for a fiesta that lasts two or three days.

Late that evening we arrived in Oaxaca, a nice town up among the mountains. Mexican Indians, like their South American cousins, have many superstitions, some of which are very similar. Shortly before we entered the town I saw a cross alongside the road where Indians go to wish. If two stones are tied together with a string this is supposed to make the person who has done it the owner of a pair of oxen, and a maguey leaf cut off and put on the ground with a pebble in it means marriage and a baby, the leaf representing a cradle. The Indians of Oaxaca, not unlike the Bolivians, make hollows in which they place crosses, and to leave the 'sufferings' of a journey behind they place a stone or pebble in one of these hollows.

I was delighted with my stay in Oaxaca, where everybody, from the governor down, did his best to make me happy and comfortable.

Oaxaca

A trip was arranged to show me the remarkable ruins of Mitla which are some thirty miles from the town. A large party of us left in cars, and after a pleasant drive over not too good a road I was able to admire this gem of construction and art of a civilization that has long disappeared. The ruins are noteworthy for their artistic designs in different and complicated patterns, entire walls being covered with them. All are made of hewn stones, cleverly and absolutely evenly pieced together. The corners of the building that had probably once been the principal temple are perfectly perpendicular, although their complicated designs made such precision most difficult. Many of the priceless stones and decorations had been taken away from the ruins by the Spaniards to build a church near there; a testimony of ignorance. It was easy to tell that these ruins are often visited by strangers, for Indian vendors of cleverly homemade 'antiques' soon flocked around us offering articles, which came down in price every time we refused to buy them. The Mexican government has been placing a permanent guard over the ruins to prevent ignorant souvenir hunters from damaging them. In an underground passage that had recently been excavated a pillar beside which the guard, who acted as guide, insisted on telling each one of us how long we would live. This he did by making us go through performances of standing and taking spans and other measurements, and I noticed that he was very generous in his allowances of years, probably in hopes that we would be the same with the tips.

In Oaxaca there was a great deal of excitement about the revolution. Under the arcades of the town hall—a stately old building that dates back to the Spanish colonial times—bulletins were placed on the walls, and crowds of men, many of whom wore the large, classical Mexican sombreros and coloured ponchos with Aztec designs, were reading the latest news, or listening to others doing this for them, whilst little groups stood near discussing the situation.

Although I was invited and almost begged to remain in the town longer, I had to think about moving along, so after a delightful week I was again ready to see if we could accomplish what I considered would be the last problematic and really difficult lap, that is to say, the trip from this town to Puebla. Of course, I guessed that all would not be roses from there to the U.S. border, for there are large stretches of uninhabited semi-desert towards the north but, compared with what we had already been through, I thought the northern regions of Mexico would be relatively easy to cross.

The military authorities in Oaxaca had been particularly attentive and kind to me, and when I left I was accompanied by a fresh escort. The horses they had were 'green' and only half tame, and to make things livelier, some of the soldiers were no horsemen—in fact, one of them had never ridden before. As soon as we were out in the open country the horses began to act worse than ever, and at times I might have believed myself to be at a Wild West Show. Those of us who were accustomed to the saddle, or who were lucky enough to be mounted on tame animals, had plenty to laugh at, and every now and again we had to chase after a horse which had 'unloaded' his would-be rider. Possibly it was due to carelessness, or owing to the fact that the animals were too wild, that none of them had been shod, and the result was that some horses began to go lame when their hoofs had worn down on the rocky ground.

The Federal Army, to which my new escort belonged, was on the qui vive, for it was expected that General Serrano of the revolutionary force, which was bottled in near Vera Cruz, might attempt to escape by crossing the mountains and forests towards the Pacific coast.

It was evident that my escort, with horses in such condition, could not make the journey over the mountains that now lay before us. When we prepared to spend the night in the police station of the village we had reached the soldiers made sure that the horses would not disappear overnight by packing them into the fair-sized jail and then locking it! The unfortunate animals were wedged together like sardines and were given nothing to eat until morning, and the officer said it would do them good to fast and suffer a little, as this was likely to take some of the 'brios' (spirit) out of them. The escort was not sorry when I explained that I would sooner travel alone, and when I pointed out that their horses were unfit for mountain travel, especially without shoes.

In the Sierras

I had the choice between two routes: one through enormous, deep canyons, and another over mountains where a road had existed once upon a time. I decided on the latter, and in two days we were safely on the other side, after tiring journeys up and down steep and broken slopes. A fine drizzle had fallen all the time, and owing to the altitude the damp cold was very penetrating. On the other side we came to a beautiful valley where trees were laden with fruit. Golden mangos bent down the branches and birds with bright plumage were flying about. I again slept outside on the floor under the arched corridor of the municipal building in a little village named Chilar. The 'presidente municipal,' as the village mayor is called, saw to it that I should have the best of the little the good people had to offer, and when I left I was given a guide, for the trail was tricky and we had to swim a wide and swift mountain river, the Rio de las Vueltas.

The aspect of the country soon changed and we were now in vast valleys among a mass of mountains where huge cactus plants grew and where the ground was either rocky or sandy.

The Rio de las Vueltas (River of Bends), so named because of its many twists and turns, was very dangerous and wild, and, what was worse, when we had successfully crossed it, we had to do the same again the next day, some twenty miles further along. Fortunately I could take the pack and saddles over the long and giddy railway bridge, and then find a suitable place to swim and land the animals. The difficulty when crossing a swift river, or a boggy swamp, is not the getting into it nor the actual swimming, but the getting out of it, for often one finds no place where to land. In swift waters submerged rocks or tree-trunks have to be looked for, for should a horse strike one the chances are that he will be ripped open or crippled.

I was often mistaken for an officer, and people came to ask me for news about the revolution.

Mexicans are often represented as lovers of revolutions or as bandits, but I found that the vast majority are the very opposite, and all these good people want is peace and quiet, for the peasant in that country is an exceedingly industrious and hard-working man. Up to recent times lack of education was the chief obstacle to progress, but under the presidency of General Calles a wonderful start has been made to educate the masses. It is obvious that in a few years things cannot be accomplished that have taken other nations many generations to bring up to the present point and, furthermore, one has to consider the enormous percentage of pure Indians and mixed breeds that exist in Mexico, people who have a different mentality from ours, and who as a rule are adverse to education.

To cite only one example of what has been accomplished in the educational line, let me mention the State of Oaxaca where the majority of inhabitants are Indians. During the presidency of Calles no fewer than 1,100 schools were opened, and even if these are very primitive it cannot be denied that this is a wonderful start. Fanaticism, superstition and revolt, like ugly bats, will be driven back to their dark caves by the rising sun of Mexican education, and even if some of the failings attributed to President Calles be true, some day his name will be written in golden letters in the history of Mexico, as the father of education, a road builder, and an enemy of moral oppression.

The trail led through vast and imposingly wild valleys, or again along precipitous and dizzy mountain-sides until we came to Tehuacan, a pleasant little town where excellent mineral springs are exploited. I had been very unwell and feverish for the last two days, and feared another attack of malaria. The local military commander called on me and told me he had received orders to give me an escort, but informed me that as he expected trouble at any time he could only spare a few men, and that he considered it would be safer for me to travel alone, for should I, with a few men, run into a rebel force, the chances were that we would all go through the hoop. When I enquired about bandits he said that some had been active lately and that a few people had been killed by them. He left it to me to decide about the escort, and after I had debated the chances with him I thought his plan of travelling alone would be the safer, and as things turned out I was not molested at any time. Terrified villagers told me that the warning I had been given was by no means an exaggeration, for only the night before I came to a certain village bandits had raided it, looting firearms, money and food.

My fears about malaria had not been misplaced, for I was now very sick

and weakened by lack of sleep. It is bad enough to be down with this fever
in a comfortable bed with medicines at hand, but when one has to ride
all day and sleep on a hard floor in some municipal building, or in any
hut where one might be given food and shelter, malaria soon weakens the
system. I was so sick and shaken up that I felt as if my bones were breaking with every step of the horse. I had not slept for two nights, and even
the roots of my hair hurt when I touched my head; a certain sign when
one is really bad with malarial fever. However, in spite of all this, there
was no other way out but to continue, and I am certain that I would not
even have defended myself if I had been attacked. Everything I did was
mechanical; thinking had ceased, and I plodded along without observing
things around me. Luckily I soon improved a little and when I came to
the mesa I began to take a new interest in life.

These parts are very different from anything I had seen before. Rolling,
sandy stretches spread before the eye, with cactus plants and a variety of
palm bushes growing in abundance. In the distance the snow-covered
volcano Orizaba made the most beautiful background imaginable. The
sky is clear and of a deep blue, and marvellous cloud effects of rare delicacy of colour make Mexican skies unforgettable.

Our arrival had been expected in Tepeaca where I was given the first
real taste of a popular reception. Ill and tired as I was, I did not wish to
disappoint the people, and although I had the sensation of watching a flickering moving picture of the early days, I tried hard to act as if I were
enjoying myself. When it came to eating I could not face the ordeal, and
had to admit that I was not well. A glass of brandy and quinine was all I
felt like taking; alcohol to stimulate, and quinine as medicine.

Tepeaca is an important agricultural centre, close on 6,000 feet above
sea level. At night it was bitterly cold, but in the day-time the temperature was very agreeable. Every Friday the 'Tianguis' is held, as the
important weekly market is called, when enormous crowds flock into
town, and buyers from various States come to do business.

Shortly after the Spanish conquest Tepeaca was very important, Cortes
declaring it the capital of 'New Spain.' He ordered the convent of San Francisco to be built, a fortress that was impregnable in those days, and
which even now stands in perfect condition. The town has twenty-one
churches, the cathedral being the most noteworthy among them for its
rare architecture. In the main plaza stands a monument which was erected
in 1547 and on which a public clock has been installed during recent years.
Around it at the top is a platform where those condemned by the Spanish Inquisition were chained to rings in the presence of thousands of 'fieles,'
as the believers were called, who looked on in awe from below whilst the

'holy work' was performed. Near the town is a spot that to-day is known as 'Santos Sepulcros,' where valuable archæological objects have been found, together with bones of interest to medical science and anthropology. Some of the human skulls, that are estimated to date back 2,000 years, show that in those days the scourge of syphilis existed, and more notable still, human teeth have been found with incrustations of oxidium and gold, which were used as ornaments to distinguish the chieftains and great men of that epoch.

Although it was only eighteen miles from Tepeaca to Puebla, and the road good, I thought I should never get there. I was so ill and my body ached so much that I could not ride, so I made almost the entire journey on foot whilst hanging on to Mancha. We passed crowds of picturesque Indians who were on their way to the market at Tepeaca. Some drove laden burros before them, whilst others trotted along with their loads on their backs.

The news of our arrival soon spread through Puebla, and whilst I was in the town hall paying my respects to the authorities, Mancha and the pack-horse were outside in charge of a policeman. When I came out, the crowd that had collected followed us to the military quarters where my animals were to be stabled. The fact that we were only expected to reach this town on the next day was a blessing in disguise, for I was too ill and worn out to stand the strain of another popular reception. I spoke to a few newspaper men and delegates of societies who came to invite me to fiestas or to greet me, and when they realised that I was ill they took me to one of the most noted doctors in the town. He gave me an injection and recommended a good rest, but although I tried hard to sleep in the comfortable hotel, all my efforts were in vain. Next morning visitors called, and at midday and at night I had to go to dinner parties, and it is not difficult to imagine what I felt like. In the evening of my second day in the town I was given another injection, after which I went to a dance, and next morning the 'Charros' gave me a fiesta where I witnessed splendid horsemanship and skill with the 'reata' (lasso). On the following day, after a third injection of quinine, I attended another dance and was only able to leave it in the early morning when it was time to saddle up, whereafter I rode twenty-seven miles to a place named San Martin, where I had visions of putting in a good sleep at last. However, my calculations proved to be wrong, for I had just finished accommodating the horses when motor-cars arrived to take me back to Puebla, and in spite of my trying every excuse to avoid going, my arguments were of no avail. A policeman was put in charge of the horses, and I was packed into a car and driven back to Puebla, where I pretended to be enjoying myself all night, and at eight o'clock in the morning I was back with the horses and made ready to start.

We followed an excellent road which winds over the mountains, connecting Puebla with Mexico City, and when I had energy enough I admired the wonderful panorama around me. Beautiful forests cover the mountains, and high above and quite near tower the two snow-capped volcanoes, the Ixtaccihuatl and the Popocatepetl. (Both these names are of ancient Aztec origin, the former meaning 'Sleeping Woman' and the latter 'Smoky Mountain'). Many cars passed during the day, and I had to dismount every now and again to speak to people who had come to greet me, and I am certain that I should have fallen asleep had it not been for these distractions. In the evening I heard the droning of many motors, and after a while a long line of motor-cycle police from the capital came speeding along. To my surprise they stopped when they reached me, and one of them introduced himself as the chief of the Mexico City Traffic Department. He embraced me in typical Mexican fashion, and from that moment he has been one of the countless friends I made during my long and unforgettable stay in that beautiful city.

My new friend told me that a reception had been arranged in my honour and asked me to push ahead until I came to a place where stood the remains of what had at one time been a wealthy 'hacienda' (estate).

I had covered some thirty-five miles when I unsaddled, and as there was no fodder for the horses nor good food for myself, the city police arrived in cars some two hours later, bringing me all and more than I required. I was so tired that I could hardly sleep, and I was glad when my small alarm-clock advised me that daylight was not far off.

A woman in a hut prepared me a cup of coffee, and whilst I was sipping it I heard voices outside. A cinema operator and some photographers had run me to earth, and soon I was being 'shot' at all angles. One of the newspaper men who had also arrived let me into a secret that made me forget everything else. He told me that among the many surprises waiting for me, my old companion Gato was on his way out to greet me, together with a crowd of charros and other riders. He added that the horse had entirely recovered and was full of life. This piece of news filled me with such joy that I started off at a fast trot, paying scant attention to an aeroplane that circled overhead, giving me a welcome, and I hardly noticed the cars that passed me, the occupants shouting loud 'vivas' in our direction. I kept on trotting fast, and although Mancha was perspiring freely I made him go at this pace, for I was in a hurry to see Gato, and I wondered if he would recognise Mancha and myself and how he would act.

Far ahead I could see a crowd moving towards me, and judging by the cloud of dust they raised I rightly guessed that this was the vanguard of the charros who had left the city before sunrise to come to meet me. Soon I could distinguish their large hats, the gold and silver embroidering glittering in the brilliant sun.

When they had dashed up to within fifty yards of me all gave loud cheers, whilst occupants of cars clapped their hands. After this all was a whirl-wind; some embraced me, others slapped me on the back, there was a trampling of many hoofs, the shouting of many voices—I was bewildered and felt as if all this were a strange dream. Presently the circle around me opened and I saw the head of my old pal Gato. I forgot everything around me and went to pat his neck, to tickle his nose, and to rub his forehead, as I had often done before when we were all alone out in the open. When he saw Mancha he gave a low nicker, opening wide his nostrils and slightly quivering his upper lip. The two horses then sniffed each other whilst I examined Gato, whom I found to be in wonderful shape, not a sign of his accident being visible.

An open-air luncheon had been prepared in an hacienda near there, so the whole crowd went to eat and make merry. The charros were dressed in their best festive costumes, and the saddles and trappings of their horses were equally splendid and costly. Some of the ladies wore the national costumes of 'chinas poblanas,' and a fairer sight could not be imagined. The Argentine Minister and other members of the foreign diplomatic corps were present, some of them on horseback, while others had come in cars. The chief of the Mexico City Police headed the charros, most of whom were society people or high government officials. However, formality was put to one side, and everybody ate, drank and made merry, whilst photogra-phers and cinema operators were busy taking some happy groups, and later a few short speeches were made, during which a special delegate gave me the official welcome to the City of Mexico. Of course the humorous 'birds' were not missing, and several kept the crowd in roars of laughter with the witty remarks for which Mexicans are noted. Then there were one or two of the clown type, a Mexican poet, and a well-known Argentine business man of the city being the outstanding characters among that class, and soon all eyes were focused on them, especially when the cognac and champagne began to take effect on them. I was in my dirty travelling clothes and felt rather out of place with a two days' growth of beard, and I was still feeling the effects of malaria and sleepless nights, but I success-fully acted as though I were feeling fresh and well. After a while we started out in the direction of the distant city, and many people who had in the meantime arrived in cars were waiting outside. All joined the procession, whilst two rows of police in motorcycles and side-cars accom-panied us. In each side-car were two men with rifles, and I was told this

was a precaution owing to the state of affairs at the time, and the many
government officials who were among us. It was a splendid sight to see the
crowd of charros and ladies ride through the centre of the city, their
picturesque costumes showing off to full advantage on the lively steeds with
flowing manes. It had been arranged that my horses should be stabled in
a riding academy, where more refreshments were waiting for us.

As soon as I could do so I made a bee-line for the hotel where rooms
had been reserved for me. Although many hunted high and low for me
to ask me out on a 'parranda,' as Mexicans call a spree, I left word with
the servants I was 'not in,' and was able to put in a sleep that lasted close
on twenty hours, after which began a continuous round of banquets, fiestas, and excursions which continued for three solid weeks.

Mexico City

M exicans are born horsemen and lovers of adventure and the open
air, and therefore our journey appealed to them and, without
meaning to boast, I must add that, as a nation, they were the ones who
best understood the significance and valued the merit of my undertaking,
and showed their appreciation accordingly.

Of all the banquets I have ever attended, the most brilliant and
picturesque was given to me by the 'Asociacion Nacional de Charros.'
It was very appropriately given in the Don Quijote hall in one of Mexico's
finest hotels. The diplomatic corps was well represented, and all the
participants who were charros wore the typical costumes of the different regions to which they belonged. The value of the sombreros alone must
have represented a fortune, for all were embroidered in gold and silver,
and some were even studded with precious stones. The famous Mexico
City police band delighted everybody with music, and when the banquet
and the speeches had come to an end, artistes sang some of Mexico's classical songs, and the traditional dance, the 'Jarabe Tapatio,' was executed
by various couples. To describe all the receptions I was honoured with
would take up too much space, so I must limit my remarks to the most
outstanding.

I visited most of the leading government officials and some of the
foreign diplomatic corps, and had the honour of meeting Ex-President
Calles in the old castle of Chapultepec, being greatly impressed by his frank
manners, virile appearance and keen sense of humour. Although it is
obvious that he has a strong and inflexible character, there is a kindly look

in his dark and penetrating eyes.

Probably the most popular act was the bullfight, the taurine art being almost frantically admired by the masses. I was requested to 'partir plaza,' or, in other words, to ride into the arena, halt in front of the president, and ask him for the key, after which I had to return, open the gates and lead in the 'cuadrilla,' riding in front of the colourful procession. The 'cuadrilla' consists of the bullfighters and helpers. People who do not know the Spanish language usually call a bullfighter 'toreador,' a word that does not exist in that language. Bullfighter in Spanish is 'torero,' and the man who does the principal work; the playing of the bull at close range, and the killing, is called 'matador' (killer) or 'espada.'

An amusing thing happened whilst I was performing the opening ceremony, the request to do which being the greatest honour that can be bestowed on a person in a Mexican bullring, and which must be done on horseback. Knowing nothing about bullfighting, I was told exactly what I would have to do, and on the fatal day, when the huge concrete bowl was filled to full capacity with a mass of excited humanity, I was ready below the stands in the semi-darkness.

Although punctuality does not bother the average Mexican, a bullfight begins with unerring precision on the tick of 4 p.m. To delay by one minute would mean the wrecking of the place, and might even bring about bloodshed, so when the hands of the large clock in the arena near the sixteenth hour of the day, the crowd is worked up to such a nervous pitch that people give vent to their feelings by shouting and yelling. To make sure of being punctual, I had taken good care to be on the spot an hour before time, and when I heard the frantic yells from without I suggested that the show should be started when it was still ten minutes early. To my surprise the Spanish matadores with whom I was conversing gave me looks as if they had suddenly discovered me to be a leper, and although they had been groomed with the utmost care and their faces were well powdered, they showed the paleness that had come over them; when they recovered speech, they told me that even such an idea had never before even been conceived, and implored me to wait until the big hand of the clock was covering the black mark that indicates the exact astronomical hour of four.

At last the critical second had arrived, a bugle blew, and the gate swung open. Mancha, who had shown signs of nervousness before, propped and snorted, and I had to use the spurs. Being unaccustomed to such treatment, he shot forward into the bullring like a rocket whilst thousands of voices cheered wildly. The sudden change from dusk to bright sunshine, and the strange surroundings made the poor horse a bundle of nerves, and presently he lost his temper and began to goat jump, his usual preliminaries before starting his old Patagonian war-dance. I had my work cut out, and to make things worse, the crowd began to wave handkerchiefs and yell more than ever, and in the midst of all this, I suddenly remembered that I had not particularly tightened the girth. With the type of saddle I used this is very serious, so all I could do was to sit tight and ride by balance as much as possible. After a considerable amount of trouble, and to the delight of the crowd, I arrived in front of the president, and then rode back across the arena to lead in the cuadrilla. By this time Mancha had cooled off sufficiently to limit his acrobatics to nasty prancing only, but I was glad when I had finished my job and completed a circle around the big ring, part of my duty before making my exit. Just when I was about to ride out I became careless, and the old boy seized the opportunity to buck his way out in great style. I don't mind admitting that I was glad when I was seated in the balcony that had been constructed to accommodate the guests of honour, and during the excitement of the bullfights I could not help wondering what I would have done down there if my saddle had turned!

The 'Asociacion Nacional de Charros' gave me a show, inaugurating their new grounds, where I saw some clever roping, excellent riding, and steer-throwing. The Mexican way of steer-throwing differs from the American cowboy 'bulldogging,' for the charro races after the steer, catches hold of his tail, and once he has put his right leg over it he makes his horse cut away to the left, thus throwing the steer. Although this feat might appear simple to the casual observer, it requires good horsemanship, strength, and great judgment to accomplish it.

This fiesta ended with national dances and a bullfight, the chief of the traffic department, General Gomez Velazco, being the matador. No horses were used, and although the bulls were on the small side I was glad to be up in the gallery, and not in the ring.

The Mexican Press also gave me a banquet out in the floating gardens of Xochimilco, the Venice of Mexico City, and later the motor-cycle police amazed me with their daring acrobatics and dangerous stunts.

Invitations to theatres and an outing to the famous pyramids of San Juan de Teotihuacan and many other acts of sympathy delighted me, and kept me on the move every day.

Together with the members of the small Argentine colony I had the pleasure, in a small measure, of repaying our Mexican friends for their numerous acts of friendship by giving them an 'asado criollo,' as the way of roasting steers and sheep over a fire out in the open is called in the Argentine.

One of the most beautiful sights I have ever beheld was when I was driven far out of town during the night to see the sunrise from the top of a mountain named 'Cerro de la Estrella.' The vast valley of Mexico spread below us, wrapped in inky blackness, and the bright lights of the town glimmered in the distance like fairy lights and bright glow-worms. The mountains stood out against the moonless sky like rugged, black silhouettes, while thousands of stars gave a faint light. By degrees the horizon to the east began to assume a dark violet and greenish-blue colour, and as the light became stronger these colours changed into every possible tint, whilst the peaks began to glow. When the first sunrays flashed over a ridge, nobody in our small party could resist any longer, and as in a concert, when a master has amazed the audience with a faultless execution of a particularly fine passage all of us cheered and applauded. The Great Architect of the Universe had shown us one of His masterpieces.

I believe I should have been royally entertained for an indefinite time longer but, besides feeling the strain, I had to prepare to continue our march, which promised to be much easier from here on. I was sorry to have to leave so many good and kind friends behind, but it had to be done sooner or later.

I spent a few days taking leave of everybody, and giving the horses some preliminary jogs after so long a rest in excellent stables with the best and richest fodder. Every day the horses had visitors, and a little bird told me that two prominent ladies of the American colony never failed to make a pilgrimage to the stables to offer some special tit-bits to Mancha and Gato, who had won their admiration and affection and, although I never met these ladies, I have had a soft spot in my heart for them ever since, and I am sure that the horses would be on the look-out for them, as they were then, should they ever be back in those same stalls.

All final preparations completed, I decided to leave the city next day. To my surprise crowds of mounted charros were assembled near the stables, ready to accompany me out of town for some ten miles, where, after many embraces and fervent handshakes, I sadly watched them disappear behind a cloud of dust. These charros, who were mostly high government officials, had left their work to do me this last honour, as they had done the day I arrived. Au revoir, charros; he-men, gentlemen, friends!

The Mexican Mesa

Although the rebels had been defeated by the Federals, trouble was by no means over, and minor skirmishes took place here and there, and I could not help feeling the unpleasant undercurrent that existed.

We followed an old highway which had been destroyed at the time when Carranza's revolutionary army marched towards Mexico City from the north. This old road has been practically abandoned since, and the ruins of formerly prosperous estates could be seen all along our route, which led over rocky hills in some parts.

I was glad to have warm clothes, for in the mornings there was a nasty nip in the air. Some of the sandy plains we came to later very much reminded me of the Bolivian altiplano. Near some of the settlements large water reservoirs have been walled-in in hollows, with walls made of large rocks holding the water back at the bottom end. Maguey plants grow everywhere, and from the juice of these 'pulque,' sometimes called 'Mexican wine,' is made. The maguey plant and pulque are the curse of the country, for owing to the abundance of this plant, which will grow where nothing else can be cultivated, the drink made from its juice is very cheap and within the reach of everybody.

The making of pulque is very interesting. When a maguey plant has grown to a certain size the centre leaves are cut out with a knife, and a hollow is made in the direction of the roots. After a few hours this basin-like hollow is filled with a clear and very sweet juice which is later collected by putting the end of a long, flute-shaped calabash into it. At each end of this implement small holes are bored, and by dipping one into the juice and sucking at the other, this primitive, but effective instrument is filled with the liquid, which is then emptied into goat or cowhide skins. It is left standing thus for a night and then the pulque is ready to be consumed and is taken into the village or town in skins, loaded on burros, one on each side. The beverage has a peculiar 'medicine' taste, but often it is flavoured with fruit juice and other ingredients.

To make 'mescal' and 'tequila' the big roots of the maguey plant are dug out, and after being steamed for some hours, which is done in huge ovens, they are crushed under a big stone roller, which is turned by an ox or a mule pulling on a pole. The juice, thus squeezed out, runs into tanks where it is left to ferment, being distilled later. Alcoholic drinks, together with 'marihuana,' have caused a great deal of degeneration in Mexico. Marihuana is a weed that is smoked mixed with tobacco, having a similar effect to opium on a person, except that it is not quite so strong a drug, but, on the other hand, more of an irritant.

Marihuana intoxication affects people strangely, the majority becoming violent, whilst others, instead of speaking normally, whisper as if communicating some important secret. The drug is a great favourite among soldiers, and, although the growing of the weed is strictly illegal, it can be obtained almost everywhere if one 'knows the ropes.' I understand that during latter years, especially since the prohibition law has been in force in the U.S., large quantities of marihuana have been smuggled across the border, and, of course, tequila and mescal fetch good prices and have found ready acceptance among Americans, especially in the Southern States. I had ample reason to believe that there must be truth in this rumour, for when I was riding along the highways in the Southern States, I used to amuse myself counting the empty flasks and bottles that had been thrown into the ditch by passing motorists, and the daily average I reached was astounding, although I was only able to count, more or less, on one side of the road!

Riding over the high mesas I got lost several times, the old road being completely overgrown with grass. Indians who live in low stone huts with straw roofs inhabit these parts, and the many cross-trails that exist are apt to mislead even the most expert traveller who does not know them well.

I had to sleep in strange places, and I was glad that nobody there knew who I was; it was a pleasant change not to have to answer the same old questions everybody in towns put to me.

The people of San Juan del Rio were on the look-out for me, and when I was within a few miles of the little town a crowd of charros came out to meet me. I had not bargained for more receptions after Mexico City, but soon I found out that I had made a great mistake. When we rode into the town people came rushing out of their houses and cheered, and I noticed that posters were stuck on some walls, advising the public of our expected arrival and calling upon them to help to make the reception as brilliant as possible. When I left the capital I intended to cover the distance between Mexico City and New York in as short a time as the horses could without suffering, and had it not been for all the receptions, I am convinced that my animals would have given a good account of themselves and that it would have taken many attempts to lower their record.

San Juan del Rio entertained me for three days; there were dances, luncheons, fiestas and speeches, and when I heard that the next town was already preparing to welcome us, I gave up the idea of making good time, and began to wonder if we would ever get out of Mexico at all. I envied aviators, for after all, they can travel undisturbed and in relative comfort once they are in the air, but I had to stop every time I was asked to do so, and there was no way of dodging.

The governor of the State happened to be in San Juan at the time, and so he gave a luncheon in an hacienda outside the town where a merry crowd gathered. The most classical of all Mexican dishes, a 'mole de guajolote' (stewed and spiced turkey) was served, and plates were filled with 'chile' (Mexican pepper). Some of the chile eaten in Mexico is so 'hot' that I could not possibly eat it, but the natives swallow it with glee, although it brings tears into their eyes. After a mouthful, they immediately drink pulque. When the witty governor saw that I shied at the chile, he jokingly told me that it was rather like a fierce dog, for once it knows a person it no longer bites. The band of an orphan asylum supplied the music, and when the majority were full in every respect, the speeches began, even the prisoners who acted as waiters being allowed to show their skill in oratory which they used unsuccessfully, trying to take advantage of the governor's presence to ask for freedom.

In this little town I met Sydney Franklin, a boy of some 25 years of age, and the only American bullfighter. He was born in New York and had taken up this strange profession in Mexico, where he had lived for some years. He showed a certain amount of skill at the time, and people who understood the taurine art told me that he promised to become a star some day.

Throughout this State a member of the Charro Association accompanied me with a servant of his, and I was delighted with the company of this gentleman who had travelled many countries in former times. He was dressed in the costume of the region and wore large 'chaparreras' (chaps) made of tiger skin. I was sorry when we came to the border of the next State, where my companion turned his horse's nose towards home again.

In the historical town of Queretaro another reception had been prepared for me, the townsfolk turning out in a body to welcome us.

Among other things a 'jaripeo' (rodeo) was given in the local bullring, where I again witnessed some daring and skill. The most remarkable feat performed was when a charro tied his rope, ending in a running noose, around his neck, and, when thus tied, roped and threw a wild horse. The slightest mistake in judgment would probably have been fatal, but even after having done the trick once, he twice successfully repeated it. To make things more difficult, he did all manner of fancy twirling and skipping through the rope before lassoing the animal, which he did without stopping to take aim, bringing the horse down in a flash.

I shall never forget how a man of the crowd suddenly appeared in the bullring and came staggering towards the place where I sat. It was obvious that he had been celebrating freely, and that in consequence his balance was not what it ought to have been. When he was directly in front of me he saluted in real bullfighter's style and proclaimed to the universe that he would ride any bull in my honour. The crowd greeted this promise with wild applause, for it was obvious that we were in for a bit of very dangerous fun.

A lively and very nasty-looking bull was then let in and lassoed, and when a rope had been tied around his body to afford the would-be rider a grip, the man was helped on and the animal released. The bull started off like a rocket, bucking and at the same time trying to dig his long, sharp horns into the rider on his back. It was not long before the man lost his balance and fell off, but his left hand remained stuck under the rope by which he had been hanging on, and the infuriated bull dragged him along, all the while throwing his head back and ripping open the unfortunate fellow's shirt. The crowd was wild with delight, although it looked as if the man would be killed any moment. Finally, his hand became freed and he fell to the ground. The bull turned to charge, but, drunk as the man was, he jumped to his feet and began to run towards the inner barrier of the ring. The bull's horns almost touched him during this race for life, whilst the crowd, more pleased than ever, stood on its feet and cheered. The poor man was far too busy to listen, and when I thought the beast must inevitably get him, he threw himself over the barrier, landing like a sand-bag on the other side. The bull crashed into the barrier and the man, who was not even hurt, got up and ran even farther away, to a place of entire safety. Even if this fellow had not proved to be a champion rider, he has probably made a world's record for quick sobering-up, and never have I seen or heard of more appreciative spectators than those in that bullring.

Only very few charros are professionals, most of them being modest ranchers, excepting those in the capital, who belong to the 'alta sociedad.'

Whilst in Queretaro I visited the spot where Emperor Maximilian of Austria was executed by a firing squad. A small chapel has been built there, and the rough pine coffin in which he was carried back to the town is in a small museum in the municipal hall.

A few days before I visited the place a shooting had taken place there, and the walls and windows was riddled with bullet-holes. One projectile had smashed the glass case and ripped open the sides of the coffin in which the stains of the emperor's blood can still be seen, the most remarkable being where his blood-covered hand had rested. During the recent shooting a man had been killed just alongside the coffin, and a bullet which had glanced off the top of his head had lifted off tufts of his hair which remained stuck to the wall and ceiling in a most singular manner. A pool of dried blood showed the place where the man had fallen, and when one of our party looked around he found the revolver of the victim under some wooden steps, where it must have been flung as the man was falling.

Had I been a souvenir-hunter, I could have taken away some of these gruesome and historical relics, for I was even offered a splint of the emperor's coffin, but somehow such things only appeal to me in museums—after all, their proper place.

A large party of us motored out to a famous hacienda that had originally been a nunnery. The main building, with its solid stone arches and spacious courtyard was imposing, but when wild horses were brought into the corral outside, none of us had time for admiring the old building; what we then wanted was action and fun, and plenty of it we had before long!

This hacienda made pulque on a large scale, so after we had finished our rough play in the corral, we proceeded to the 'pulqueria' (pulque factory), where I was made to sample every variety. Indians were doing the work in the place, and shortly after sunset I saw them going through a strange ceremony.

All lined up in two rows inside the pulqueria near the door, and then the foreman stepped between them and started to yell out a long-drawn 'Ave Maria' in a high-pitched voice, the two words being answered by the others in a similar fashion and in one long breath. When their lungs were empty, they made a quick turn towards the door, and stepping out like soldiers, they said 'Buenas noches' (good night) like one man, and then passed out into the open through the arched door which had once upon a time been the entrance to the main chapel of the nunnery.

I was assured that the pulque we were sampling was new and harmless, but unless it were my Panamanian monkey diet beginning to affect me, it must have been otherwise; the main thing was that my hosts were delighted, for I had partaken of their salt; I had tasted their pulque.

In every village and town we were greeted by crowds, any rancher or charro who had a horse available riding out to welcome us. When we left one place the horsemen accompanied us half-way to the next village, where a new delegation awaited us, but the riding with a crowd had one great drawback, for we were wrapped in a cloud of dust for hours at a time. In several places even the church bells were rung, and there were more fiestas than were good for me. In fact, I began to envy my horses for the rest they had during the nights. My good Mexican friends did not realise that they were only making merry for two days in each place, whereas I was taking on a regular relay, day after day.

From Queretaro on, I rode through a vast, sandy plain that extends towards the north-west between two mountain ranges that can be seen in the distance. The haciendas which used to exist at one time have practically disappeared, having been abandoned or destroyed during the revolutions, and the land around is a semi-desert, shrubbery and cactus plants being the only things that seem to thrive there, besides a few weeping willows at long intervals where there is water. Even in the few old estates that existed, very little was to be found, only a few pieces of the most necessary furniture being kept, in order not to attract ransackers during troubled times. I saw some of the wilful damage and wholesale destruction that had been done to such places, especially where Carranza and his army had passed. They had carried everything before them like a cyclone; cattle, poultry, wagons and household articles that might be useful to them, and what they could not take was burnt or otherwise destroyed.

As but few settlements exist, and these are separated by long distances, I was left to travel alone again, and although water was difficult to find, and the land was practically barren, I was glad of the change. The natives in these parts usually dress in what is supposed to be white. They wear large, high-crowned straw hats, trousers, and a white apron, of which one corner is lifted by tucking it under the belt. Instead of boots they use 'huarachos,' as their sandals are called. The majority of these people are Indians or mestizos, and although they are somewhat shy and slow in answering a question when one first meets them, I found them to be quite pleasant once the ice is broken and one has their confidence. They are very hardy people, and if given a chance, are good workers. The wages they receive are insignificant, for c.50 per day (about one shilling) is all they can expect; with this they must keep themselves, and as they almost entirely exist on tortillas and frijoles, this is possible.

Throughout Mexico I noticed that every hacienda had its church and chapel in former times, and several owners told me that this was an unwritten law, the breaking of which meant persecution by the Church, but schools and hospitals were not necessary and hardly existed. I had ample opportunity to hear people discuss the religious situation, and although many miss their daily services, I have met none who wish the Church to exist again as it did in former times, with its heavy taxation and other forms of exploiting the Mexican people and giving them nothing in return but blind fanaticism, and keeping them back from modern progress and education. I have no doubt that these evils were the foot of all the trouble in that country, and should the pendulum during the sudden clean-out have swung somewhat the other way, this is bound to adjust itself again, once the ousted party realises that a return to former conditions is out of the question.

In the important town of San Luis Potosi we were given another rousing reception, entertainments lasting for a whole week. The local charros gave a splendid exhibition of their skill in the bullring, and one of them performed a trick that I had never before seen or heard of. Riding his horse this charro chased a wild mare and, when he had the chance, he jumped on to her back. When she had unsuccessfully tried every vicious trick in her repertoire to shake him off, the charro spurred her into a gallop, and then called his tame and splendidly-trained saddle-horse, which immediately came alongside the racing mare, whereupon the man jumped gracefully back into the saddle. This trick is named 'Paso de la muerte' (death pass), and is one of the finest pieces of horsemanship I have ever seen performed, for not only does it require a great rider, but a perfect training of the saddle-horse, a thing about which the average cowboy, charro, or gaucho horse-breaker knows very little. It is one thing to be a 'bronco-buster' and another a horseman, and the mixture of the two is rare to find.

The long stretch between San Luis Potosi and Saltillo in the north is practically all one vast desert lying between two sierras which appear like two shaggy, dark blue lines in the distance. Cactus plants and shrubbery break the monotony of the journey through this sandy plain where we passed an occasional Indian goat-herd sitting in the shade of the large cactus plants which resemble huge pipe organs, whilst his animals fed on the shrubbery around him. Goats are the only animals that seem to exist in these arid regions, excepting rabbits and hares, which sometimes jumped up in front of us, frightened by the trampling of the horses' hoofs. This part of Mexico very much resembles Santiago del Estero, in the Argentine, which is situated about the same latitude south as this is north of the equator.

At long intervals we passed miserable stone huts with straw roofs where the goat-herds live, and sometimes I called there to see if they could spare a little of the usually salty and dirty water they stored in some hollow near the habitation. I considered myself lucky when I could buy myself sufficient tortillas and frijoles to make me forget my raving appetite, and more than once I had to go without even these. I had only one meal a day, besides a can of coffee in the morning, and the poor horses did not fare much better, having to exist on any dry cornstalks I could buy, or on leaves and twigs they could pick up; and very clever they were at finding them. Lack of nutritive fodder never seemed to weaken them, but when money could buy it, I gave them as much of the best as I could obtain, and incidentally this expense was considerable.

Whirlwinds were continuously lifting sand in high columns which danced about in the distance and around us like strange mythological giants.

I had been especially requested to pass through a small mining town, and as things turned out, I was lucky to have written to the mayor, accepting his invitation, for when we arrived in a small settlement, some twenty miles before our goal, it was already dark. The place seemed to be deserted, for not a soul was to be seen. After riding up and down the one and only street, a door opened and a man appeared. I asked him for the 'presidente municipal,' whereupon he slowly moved to another house, where he knocked. Several people came out, but the mayor was not among them, and then this reinforcement joined in looking for the wanted man, until finally we ran him to earth. Soon he brought a large key, a thing I had long ago learned to recognise as the key of the 'town hall,' which invariably is an adobe hut like any other building, except that it has a door with a big lock, and a dark gaol where all kinds of insects wait for their next meal when a prisoner is brought in, prior to being brought before the 'juez' (judge) in the capital of the district. I was given quarters in the office (?), where I prepared my bed by pushing two long wooden benches together, and placing my saddle blankets on them. The horses were in the filthy back yard, which is usually the favourite latrine in such settlements; as is the custom in some Latin American countries where lavatories have never been heard of among most of the country people. The back yards of the 'town halls' are the preferred places for discussing politics and hard times, weather conditions and social events, whilst squatting where the walls afford shade.

Before leaving this subject, I must mention an amusing thing a man told me in Panama. The Rockefeller Institute has installed a sanitary-pit near every house. Inspectors see that these are kept clean for the sake of public health, and the neglect of these expensive installations is sometimes punished with a fine. 'Señor,' this Panamanian told me, 'since the gringos have invaded our happy shores, liberty has ceased to exist, for even the doing of our necessity has been put under control!' This man, like many others, does not seem to appreciate what the Anglo-Saxon race has done towards the sanitation of the world.

When I asked the mayor of the little Mexican settlement where I could purchase food and fodder, he told me that it was so scarce in the place that they could not spare any, and I was just getting ready to spend another night on water and tobacco only when a policeman arrived on horseback. He had been sent by his chief in the mining town to look out for me, and to order the presidente municipal of this settlement to attend to me. As if by magic, everything that an hour before was not to be had, coffee, frijoles and hot tortillas, turned up, and soon the horses were tearing dry corn-stalks to pieces, and the formerly disobliging mayor could not do enough for me until I left.

Next day I was met by many riders who had come to escort us into their town, where I had to remain four days.

When we reached the outskirts, the municipal band, consisting of some twelve men, struck up a march and took the lead in the procession. The tone of the instruments was not exactly up to the mark of the Mexico City Police band's, but the intentions and enthusiasm were certainly not inferior.

Without meaning to be sarcastic, I cannot refrain from describing our march into this little town, for even at the time I could not suppress a smile, and when a gentleman who was riding beside me asked me what I was amused about, I told him outright, making him and others who heard me roar with appreciation. The band did not walk in step, every man choosing his own pace and length of stride. In front walked a blind kettle-drummer, and when he went in the wrong direction somebody headed him straight again. Next came the brass instruments, every man blowing until he was red and blue in the face, and behind them, immediately in front of me, hobbled a piccolo-player with a wooden leg, and whenever the distance between him and the rest of the band became too big, or my horse threatened to step on him, he hopped along full speed to catch up with the others, never interrupting the playing of his high, shrill notes.

When we were already near the plaza a horse-cab came tearing along, the skeleton of an old nag, which by some miracle had escaped being used in a bullfight for years, fairly bouncing into the air. A bearded man, the player of the big drum, was coming along late. Behind the cab ran what must have been his boy, carrying the drum-stick the father had probably forgotten in his hurry. As soon as the man was out of the dilapidated vehicle, and had strapped on his important instrument, he began to hit it with all his might, although he was still some distance from the procession. I always appreciated these village bands, for their unpretentious efforts were well meant and many of the musicians showed talent, although their instruments were old and battered and the quality of their tone distinctly poor. We halted in the main plaza, where the speech of welcome was read from a balcony, where-after the band entertained the crowd by giving a special concert.

I enjoyed myself thoroughly at the different fiestas that followed, and among other things witnessed another bullfight, where one animal was 'dedicated' to me, which means to say, killed in my honour. When this is done, the matador comes in front of the person to whom he intends to dedicate the bull. Having saluted, he turns round to face the beast, and in doing so, cleverly throws his two-cornered hat towards the honoured person, a gesture that is elegant, somewhat arrogant and not easy to perform with grace.

Now, every time the hat is thrown to anybody, that person is expected to put a gift, in the shape of a banknote or a cheque, into it; and bullfighters are accustomed to good presents. As fate would have it, I had not taken more than a few pesos (Mexican currency) with me, neither had I a cheque-book handy so there I sat, holding this blessed hat on my lap, as an old maid might hold the dead body of her favourite cat. However, Mexicans are sharp and quick-witted, so only a few painful seconds passed until a friend rightly guessed my plight and came to the rescue by lending me the necessary. Quite unintentionally, this bullfighter had made me feel such an ass that I felt more like putting a charge of high explosive into his scented hat, but as the show went on, and my sudden fright wore off, I began to have more kindly feelings towards the fellow who was coolly facing death down in the arena, but I made up my mind to be more careful next time; *experientia docet!*

Next day we ate a 'barbacoa' (barbecue), made with the killed bulls' heads. The Mexican way of preparing a barbacoa is most original. A hole is dug in the ground. and lined with stones, and in it a fire is made, charcoal or wood being used as fuel. When the hole and the earth around it have been made very hot, the fire and ashes are taken out; the bottom of the pit is covered and the sides lined with maguey leaves. The meat is then placed into the hot hole, covered with more maguey leaves, and finally everything is completely covered up with hot ashes and earth. When this has been done in the evening, the barbacoa is ready to be dug out and eaten next day at noon. The bulls' heads were still very hot when they were dug out, and were so tender that the juicy meat literally fell off the bones.

When we left we followed the Laredo–Mexico City railroad line wherever possible. The country here is very arid and water scarce, and the few people who live in poor settlements, separated by long distances, make their living by combing out 'ixtle,' the fibre of small, shaggy palm trees, and 'lechuguilla,' the leaves of the maguey plant. With these fibres, ropes, brushes, etc., are manufactured, the maguey variety being particularly good for 'reatas' (lasso for roping animals).

The weather was ideal for staying indoors and huddling near a cosy fire, for a strong icy-cold wind swept the mesa, and the sky was of an ugly dark grey. As I had been in the tropics for so long, and possibly owing to malaria, I felt the cold doubly, and whenever I shuddered I thought my bones must fall to pieces. Often I used to dismount and get between the two horses, and making them go at a fast trot, I did all manner of gymnastics by catching hold of the pack-saddle in one hand, and the riding-saddle in the other. The horses did not seem to mind this in the least, for they would keep up their fast trot or slow gallop until I let go and dropped behind. These tricks warmed me up considerably, and at the same time we made good headway towards the next place where we hoped to find something to eat.

Hereabouts the huts are built of palm wood, and the roofs are covered with dry maguey leaves which much resemble round tiles, when cut for the purpose of roofing. Although the people are very poor, and the cold winds were howling, the warmth of their simple but generous hearts made up for what nature did not provide, and I found excellent hospitality everywhere, and whatever food these poor people had was at my disposal. I always insisted on giving them a present in the shape of money before I left, but usually it was quite a struggle to make them accept it. Hills came in sight ahead, and I was glad to know that we were nearing the end of the long, wide valley of San Luis, in which we had travelled for many days.

When we came to an hacienda, I rode to the entrance, where several men stood observing my movements. Having said 'buenas tardes' (good evening) I asked for permission to unsaddle, which was immediately granted. After a while the men asked me where I came from, and when I told them they were delighted and slapped me on the back and went to fondle the horses. I observed that all were in fits of laughter, which rather puzzled me, but soon I was to know what the joke was about. They confessed that they had taken me for some defeated revolutionary leader escaping towards the U.S. border, and when I heard this I joined the laughter.

A similar incident had happened to me in a village in one of the Central American republics where a dusky policeman in a ragged uniform hung around me for quite a while, looking at me from every angle. After some time he slouched away, only to return with my friend the 'comisario' (sheriff), who immediately roared with laughter when he saw me. He then told the vigilante to show me the 'thing,' a remark that made me wonder what was coming. The poor man with a blush, if such a thing was possible under his dark, greasy skin, slowly took a printed picture out of one of his torn pockets and handed it to me. It was the photograph of a Swedish bank cashier who had disappeared together with a considerable sum of money, and, according to the text below the picture of that gentleman, it was suspected that he had escaped either to Central or South America, where the bank had distributed these photographs, hoping somebody would identify the man. The reward offered was enough to make a rich man out of the lucky captor, and obviously the policeman had already had visions of castles in Spain. The only resemblance I could see between myself and the man on that photograph was the colour of the skin, but probably white men were all alike to this poor vigilante, much the same as negroes are to me.

A cold trip, over high hills at first, and then along a steady down grade brought us to Saltillo, an important town which stands below in a hollow or pan. Here the famous 'sarapes' are made, coloured cloaks without which no charro's or 'china poblana's' equipment is complete.

From this town I headed the horses towards Monterrey, covering the distance in two days. A fair road exists, but in several places it was difficult to distinguish the right one from others that went in different directions among the mountains one has to cross to reach the plain in which Monterrey stands.

For a long distance the pass in the mountains leads through a narrow and deep gulley, mountains towering high on both sides. The rock formation of these sierras is very shaggy and broken, producing some strange effects. Two peculiarly-shaped peaks are especially worthy of note, 'El Agujero' (The Needle Eye), so called because near the pointed peak a circular hole goes clear through, showing the sky on the other side. The other is named 'La Silla' (The Saddle), having the appearance of a Mexican saddle with the pommel in front.

When we reached the outskirts of Monterrey I could hardly believe my eyes when I saw neat bungalows with pretty lawns in front of them. For the moment I had forgotten that we were nearing the U.S. border and that these practical houses were due to American influence, which can already be felt there. This town is utterly different from any other I had seen in Mexico, for even from far away I was astonished to see more factory chimneys than church towers. It is the most industrial town in the republic, the outstanding factory being the big modern brewery, where excellent light beer is made, much of which finds its way into the U.S.

Although I was invited to stay a few days in this town, I immediately continued towards the border, where my correspondence had been addressed, and where I planned to take a good rest.

Over Barren Plains Towards the Rio Grande

A modern road that is to connect Monterrey with Laredo was under construction at the time we passed, but as only a short piece was finished it was more of a hindrance than a help to us. The distance to the border along this road is a little over 140 miles, and as the country is practically a desert, we came to only one small village that deserves the name of such. When I rode up to the municipal building a few men were seated on a bench. One of the group, a tall dark fellow, who made a striking picture with his large charro hat, smiled when he saw me, and told me that although he never had the pleasure of meeting me, we were old acquaintances in a sense, for he said he had been on the look-out for me for a long time in Central America. This naturally surprised me, and when I asked the smiling fellow to be more explicit, he explained that he had fought as right-hand man under General Moncada in Nicaragua, and that he had been watching for me there to advise me to keep out of that country, should I foolishly have attempted to cross it during those turbulent times. He added that I ought to consider myself lucky to have been so well advised about giving Nicaragua a miss, for he was convinced that the least I would have lost would have been the horses. To my amazement he handed me over a map I had lost in Central America, telling me that for a long time he had hoped to have the pleasure of handing it back to me personally.

The weather was again bitterly cold, glacial winds whistling through the horses' manes and blowing sand into our eyes, making them run with tears.

A few goats and scraggy small cattle keep alive with difficulty on the coarse shrubbery, which is the only thing that grows on these dull and sandy plains. One day an enraged cow attacked us, but she turned tail when I fired two shots into the air. For two nights I had to sleep in very poor huts, where there were more fleas than frijoles, and I was thankful when I saw the skyline of Laredo, the border town.

In the northern part of Mexico I had to make the acquaintance of a new kind of insect, although I thought every possible species had sampled my blood. I had been itching badly for some days and was sure that I was only being worried by some particularly hungry or vicious fleas, but in spite of using every cunning trick for stalking them, surprise attacks, flares, and in short all the 'fleacraft' I had acquired with long and painful experience, my attempts at even getting a glimpse of them proved futile. I began to wonder if such things as flea ghosts exist, but, just as I was giving up my thorough investigations as hopeless I saw something move along the seam of my shirt, inside which I had my head like a photographer focusing a camera. On further inspection I found a small, transparent, torpedo-shaped insect, and putting it between my nails I crushed its hard shell, which gave way with the classical crack. Revising all the seams and possible hiding places, I discovered quite a number of these little crawlers, and soon found a way of exterminating them.

I saw a crowd of horsemen coming from Laredo in our direction and rightly guessed that they had come out to meet us. Soon members of the border police, a few charros, and others came dashing towards us, headed by the chief of the customs house. Not only had the thoughtful and considerate gentleman brought the official welcome with him, but being well acquainted with the poor and practically uninhabited region we had just passed, he had with him a basket full of excellent food, and a bale of alfalfa for the hungry horses. When we had eagerly stuffed down as much as we could hold, we started towards the near town, accompanied by two long lines of horse-men. The military band played us into the place and later, after a few speeches had been made, we sat down to a banquet and everybody made merry. The best place that could be found for the horses was the bullring, where they were all by themselves and had ample room for rolling and moving about, but had my two pals realised what kind of a place they were in, they would surely have felt like a person sitting down to a champagne dinner in a place of execution. I was lodged in a neat little cottage where I was left to rest undisturbed, an act of consideration on the part of the authorities which I much appreciated.

Sitting in a comfortable armchair, whilst smoking a cigar, my thoughts wandered back to many strange places; I laughed at some of my old misfortunes, and a regular review of panoramas and faces passed before me. Before retiring to my comfortable bed I could not help going for a walk down to the river, where the international bridge leads across to U.S. territory. I could hardly believe it to be true that we had won our way through. I went down to the muddy bank and sat down to look at the lights of the high buildings on the other side of the river. Again I watched people and cars crossing the bridge to and fro; merry American revellers who came across into Mexico to go to the cabarets and dance halls where it is 'wet,' and others returning back to 'The Land of the Free,' hoping the flask they were hiding 'for luck' would not be discovered by the border officials who are there to search for them. When my eyelids became heavy I got up and returned to the bullring, where Mancha and Gato were having a good time among the fodder they had scattered all over the place, and when they came to rub their noses against me I patted them, saying, 'Well done, old boys;' and they seemed to understand that I was happy and very pleased with them.

Texas at Last–Victory in Sight

My ride through Mexico had been most interesting, but in spite of all the hospitality and splendid receptions, I must admit that I crossed over the international bridge at Laredo with mixed feelings. I was sorry to think that I might never again see the many friends I made in that beautiful country, but, to admit the truth, I was partly glad to leave it, for the fact is that I never felt safe, especially in some parts, and I considered myself lucky not to have lost the animals through assault or robbery. On more than one occasion things had looked distinctly 'hot' for me, but somehow I always managed to pull through.

Everything had been arranged with the American border officials so that there should be no difficulty, and I owe great thanks to the American consul in Nuevo Laredo for the kindly interest he took in me.

When dealing with little officials, there is always one among them who wants to give the impression that he is the centre of gravity of the whole department, and that without him the nation would go to rack and ruin. I had the misfortune to run into one of these at Laredo. He was a Polish Jew, a fat, stumpy little fellow who wore huge horn-rimmed spectacles on his shiny red nose, a most unfortunate defect for a border official of a 'bone dry' country, but which, for argument's sake, and giving him the benefit of the doubt, I will put down to the tight fit of his uniform. This 'hundred percenter' was so officious and rude that I was sorry he was not talking to me on the other side of the bridge, but the chances are that he would have known better, and after all, every dog is entitled to bark in his own kennel.

I had a wonderful time as the guest of the army at Fort Mackintosh, and in this connection I must mention that this was the case in every army post I struck on my journey through the States, where all doors were open to me, and where I made many friends among officers and men.

The change from one side to the other of the Rio Grande, as the Americans call it, or Rio Bravo, which is the Mexican name for the same river, is like that from night to day. In Nuevo Laredo there are no paved streets, and pools of stagnant water oblige one to pick one's way. Most of the houses are made of wood, and cleanliness is only known as a word that figures in the dictionary. The only thing Nuevo Laredo has better than Laredo Texas is the water supply, which is excellent. Laredo on the Texas side is like a paradise when compared to the other, for the streets are all made of concrete, the houses and neat stores are of ultra-modern type, and even skyscrapers tower into the sky. The hotels, although much smaller, compare favourably with New York's average giants, but —the most striking change of all—big hats, red neck scarves, and guns in holsters on belts studded with bullets are unknown!

The land on the Texan side of the river is all under cultivation, onions, oranges, grape fruit, and different vegetables being the chief products. In fact, to-day Texas is the biggest onion supplier of the U.S. It is obvious that something must be wrong in Mexico, for although the land on the southern side of the river is exactly the same as on the Texas side, it is a semi-desert and scarcely inhabited.

A great surprise was in store for me when I rode into Fort Mackintosh, for a sergeant, who had been so good to my horses in Panama, came running up to greet us. Whilst we were on our way up from the Panama

Canal zone he had been transferred to this post, where he once more took charge of my pals, and he certainly knew how to look after them! One half of the 4th Field Artillery was stationed in Panama, and the other in Fort Mackintosh, so I met several officers and men whom I had known whilst we were in the Canal Zone. My horses certainly took full advantage of 'Uncle Sam's' oats and the variety of excellent fodder that was systematically given to them, and Mancha seemed to be feeling as proud and honoured as I did when the troops passed in review before us.

At last I was able to buy myself a complete outfit of clothes, which I needed to attend the many parties, dances and luncheons to which I was invited, and later I always sent my trunk ahead from one town to another.

During my delightful stay in Laredo I had another slight attack of malaria, and I shall always remember the kind way in which both the commanding officer of the fort and his wife looked after me. When I left the border to follow the highway towards San Antonio, a mounted detachment accompanied me for some distance and the band played us out of the post. The civilian authorities had extended every courtesy to me, and the public and the Press had given us an enthusiastic welcome, so after the mounted detachment had left us to return to Fort Mackintosh I watched them disappear in the distance, and when the skyline of Laredo began to fade away, I could not help saying, 'I hope it's only 'au revoir,' Laredo!'

To describe my ride through the States in full would be somewhat dull, owing to the similarity of conditions in most places, but it may be of interest to mention some of my impressions and observations, also some of the difficulties I met with—difficulties I never expected to find. Concrete roads are excellent for cars, but they are very tiring and hard on horses; and heavy motor traffic makes horseback riding anything but pleasant. Today, also, the problem of stabling horses in American towns is not as simple as it was once. Stables have given way to garages in most villages and towns, and sometimes even on farms. Taking all in all, I believe I enjoyed my trip through Texas and Oklahoma more than through the Eastern States, but this may have been because everything in America was then new to me.

Between Laredo and San Antonio there is very little to see, for once I had ridden out a day, I came to the end of the cultivated land, and the country much resembled the part between Monterrey and Laredo in Mexico. Coarse shrubbery is about all that grows there and only at long intervals did we pass some wooden farmhouses that are none too tidy or clean in appearance. An irrigation system has been planned on a gigantic scale by which water of the Rio Grande will some day make a fertile plain out of this region. Land speculators and real estate agents have already been busy down there, and once a week a special train of 'home seekers,' as the Texans call the prospective land buyers, are brought down from the North to have a look at the place, which is boosted sky high. I saw two or three of these trains come down, and somehow I could not help comparing them with the cattle trains we are accustomed to see in the Argentine, on their way to the freezing plants. Out of every window hung two or more heads, looking at 'The Promised Land.' Undoubtedly these regions will give big returns some day, but I am afraid the buyers will not live to enjoy them.

As we neared San Antonio the flat country became more fertile, and we passed through several nice little villages, where the trio of us enjoyed wonderful hospitality. The Texans were the people in the U.S. who took the greatest interest in my horses, and many came long distances in their cars to have a look at them. Quite a number of the men wore the traditional high-heeled cowboy boots and sombreros, a combination that is very becoming. Every house was open to me, and my only difficulty was to refuse the many invitations I received every day, without hurting people's feelings. The horses were the centre of admiration of large groups that used to collect around them, and even if there happened to be no stable handy when we arrived in some places, willing and practical hands soon fixed up a suitable place, and fodder was brought along in a car. More than once some enthusiastic lady brought a packet of Quaker Oats as a special tit-bit for the horses, and I even had to keep an eye on them to see that they did not overdo the feeding.

The majority of the landworkers are Mexicans, or of Mexican descent, and the comments I heard about them were all very complimentary. They are very hardworking and thrifty, and even a very insignificant salary satisfies them. Cheap Mexican labour makes it difficult for American hands to find work in the fields, and some day this will give rise to a knotty economical problem; in fact, Mexican labour in Texas and other border States has already provoked serious trouble and is the basis of several bills in Congress to place all Latin-American immigration on a quota basis—aimed entirely at Mexicans.

Although I did not expect to find Texas as it is often represented in cowboy films or by novelists, I must admit that I was somewhat disappointed with the few farms of any size I saw, and as for cowboys—I might just as well look for sabre-toothed tigers prowling about in Hyde Park. I did see some who acted the part of cowboys pretty well, but I am afraid if they came down to the pampas they would feel like the babes in the wood among the gauchos. I saw several whizz past us in cars, with a fully-saddled pony in a trailer behind on their way to a small field, maybe ten or twenty miles away, where they work among the few cattle they possess. When the day's work is done they load the pony again to return home. I am told that real cowboys still exist in other parts. I do not know, for I have only ridden some 2,000 miles through the States, not counting side trips by car and by aeroplane, but the fact is that I have never seen a 'wild' cowboy.

I have been at several 'rodeos,' where I witnessed some marvellous riding and roping, the same company touring from State to State with the regularity of astronomical seasons, and incidentally, the 'cowboy' who won the roping in one of these 'world's championships' was from New York, where he learnt his tricky, but, in a practical way, useless art. Yes, times have changed, and will go on changing; even in the Argentine the influx of foreigners is gradually changing the gaucho into a modern freak who fits neither into a town nor into a saddle. However, as the Argentine is essentially a cattle-raising country on a large scale, 'camp life' as it is called there, will always continue so long as man eats meat, and no mechanical device will ever take the place of the horse for working the vast herds of stock.

'Dude ranches' are other commercial innovations of modern times in the U.S. A few ponies are kept, together with some 'drug-store cowboys' whose job it is to act the 'tough hombres.' Rich people from the industrial towns come to stay at these family hotels, where they equip themselves with huge sombreros, high-heeled boots, fantastically designed 'chaps,' etc., and then go out to do the 'shooting' with cinema and other cameras, in order to show their friends at home what a rough life they led out in the Far West or down in wild and woolly Texas.

Nowhere did I enjoy myself more than in San Antonio, where I spent quite a number of days as the guest of the army at Fort Sam Houston, which is the largest army post in the U.S. Kelly and Brooks Field are two important army flying centres situated a few miles out of town. Not only was I entertained at dances, polo games, etc., but I was given the opportunity to get an insight into the splendid organisation and *esprit de corps* that exist in the U.S. Army, and, in fact, I was shown so many things of interest that I was unable to take them all in.

Before being taken up in a 'plane I was dressed up in overalls, helmet and goggles, until I looked 'airworthier' than participants in the Schneider Cup races, and when the method of releasing the parachute had been explained to me, we circled up until the hangars and the city of San Antonio looked like miniature toys below.

Whilst wondering what I would do if I had to jump and release the parachute, it struck me that the present-day system of releasing them in America has one great defect, for this is done by pulling a ring that is over the region of the heart. I am not criticising the system from a mechanical point of view, but as this usually effective life-saving device depends on a man's almost subconscious movements in a psychological moment, I think that there is room for improvement, and that a way should be found to attach the releasing ring to the hip-flask.

With all the entertainments it looked as if I should never reach my goal, but the day came when I had to take leave of my excellent hosts. Among the officers I had made so many friends that I felt like leaving home when a mounted detachment accompanied me for some miles out. Had it not been for the heavy traffic and the many people who continually stopped me to shake hands, I should have enjoyed the ride through the pretty country to Austin, the capital of Texas, where I started another round of entertainments. In practically every town and village where I stopped the same thing happened, and with all the speeches I had to make at Rotary, Lions, Kiwanis, and other clubs, societies and schools, I nearly ran dry of material and jokes.

The climate in Texas is very changeable and tricky, and strong winds sometimes rise when the day has promised to be warm and pleasant. A yarn that is often told in these parts well illustrates such sudden changes, and goes as follows: —

A farmer worked with a team of mules, and the day was so hot that one of his animals suddenly died from heat stroke. The farmer ran back home for help, and by the time he returned the other mule had frozen to death!

Mancha and Gato were sick with distemper for a few days, but luckily the attacks left them with no bad after-effects. They must have picked up the germs in some stable or drinking trough, and this is the only time I have known them to have been sick.

Whenever I stayed in hotels I admired their cleanliness and excellent service, also the cleverly disguised way in which the 'bell-hops' and porters let you know that if you want a drink, you need only ask them for it. More than once bootleggers had the impudence to phone me up and to ask me point-blank if I wanted any 'corn' or genuine (?) Scotch delivered at my door, 'just something reliable to entertain callers,' as they put it.

The prohibition law has probably been more discussed than any other; its pros and cons having been thrashed out in open debate and put on paper by the pens of many writers highly qualified and otherwise, and I was heartily sick of the subject which was brought up countless times during my stay in the country.

Although—or because—I am a bachelor, American women have been of unusual interest to me, not so much on account of their, generally speaking, attractive looks and fine physique, but owing to the place they take in society, in business, and in other activities, and on account of the extraordinary freedom they enjoy. In America, I venture to say, woman enjoys more freedom than in any other country, and the written, as well as unwritten, laws give her more protection than it does to man. In China, tradition is said to rule the home, in other countries I have known it is man, but in the U.S. woman is supreme. American girls particularly fascinated me by their free and easy, yet graceful and essentially feminine manners, Victorian bashfulness and false modesty being entirely strange to them. Immediately after speaking to a girl for the first time, I had the feeling that I had known her for years, and spoke to her as if she were an old college pal of mine. In Europe and in South America, co-education is practically unknown after the age of twelve, but in the States boys and girls grow up together, and probably the free and easy ways that struck me about the girls are due to a better understanding and absence of shyness between the two sexes. In spite of being opposed to the co-educational system, I must admit that this is one of its important and far-reaching advantages. In business and industry, the American woman is rapidly catching up with man, and, in spite of that, I observed, that home life flourishes, and that the children enjoy all its benefits.

In America no classes of pedigree humanity exist, the American's society pass is his pocket-book, which, when all is said and done, has the same power where man is man, for what would be the use of a title anywhere without money?

Americans' independent and democratic spirit can best be detected when one observes factory hands going to their work. In Europe the average workman and small employee looks humble and often even depressed, whilst the American swaggers along at an easy, self-possessed gait, with his shirt-sleeves rolled up and his lunch-can slung over his shoulder; he feels as 'good' as his employers—and he is. I had the pleasure of visiting many industrial plants, and whenever the 'bosses' who showed me round stopped to talk to a workman, he answered them as man to man, and not as serf to feudal lord. This is one of the external manifestations of social equality.

From the day I crossed the border, until I rode across the toll bridge over the Red River into the State of Oklahoma near Denison, the Texas Rangers were excellent friends to me.

The Texas Rangers are a small body of special State police, consisting of a very reduced number of men who are picked for their upright character and bravery, and the spotless record and the tradition of this small but highly-efficient force has been kept up to this day.

In former days the Texas Rangers were a mounted force, as the 'Red Police' or the Canadian Mounted is still to-day, but with the fencing in of fields and the coming of concrete highways, automobiles are now used to 'range' about. I had the pleasure of covering many miles in their company, all the rangers being dressed like any other citizens. They are frequently represented as men wearing the traditional cowboy costume, and who are supposed to be mounted on circus-trained bucking horses, but he who expects to find them so would be rather disappointed, for I doubt as to whether all of them are at home in the saddle to-day.

San Antonio, Fort Worth and Dallas are the largest cities I visited in Texas, and there for the first time I really felt the dynamic and assimilating spirit of America. Architectural masses rise high into the sky where only yesterday Indians camped, and beautiful country homes stand among carefully and scientifically cultivated fields that a few generations back were the grazing grounds of herds of scraggy long-horned cattle.

I had a glaring example of how the prohibition law is not enforced in some cases, when a certain wealthy landowner, and well-known figure in athletic-promoting circles turned up at a public show very drunk, and sitting where the enormous crowd could see him, pulled a bottle of whisky out of his overcoat, and drank until he fell off his seat. The authorities who saw him did not move until he had whipped out a revolver and fired two shots that might have hit anybody. Even when he was disarmed he continued the public scandal and threatened the police, and after he had ignored two summonses to appear at court, he was finally fined to the colossal tune of $1! I wonder what would have happened if any other man had been discovered taking a quick drink out of his hip flask?

Some of the country stores in Texas bear strange and humorous advertising inscriptions, among the best I have seen being:

BROWN'S STORE—'Anything from a rat-skin to a ranch'; and,
JONES' STORE—'Anything from a cradle to a tomb stone,'

and I believe they were not exaggerating. These country stores much resemble the Argentine 'almacenes,' where almost anything from white elephants to guitar strings can be obtained.

The Southern accent is as different from the northern as a Scotch 'hielander's' is to a London cockney's, and I noticed that no love is lost between the North and the South. In a mule barn where I had stabled the horses I heard an argument between some old Texans and a New Yorker who was touring the South.

Although it was cold at the time the latter wore a kind of Harold Lloyd straw hat, horn-rimmed spectacles, and bell-bottomed trousers. He was criticising the Texans' way of dressing, their bad English, etc., and when the argument became so heated that I thought they were coming to blows, an old fellow with a battered old sombrero got up and having spat some of the tobacco juice out, said: 'Anyway, you—cayn't speak no good English yerselves, you—Northeners think you know all about everything, but you just don't know nothing; you—is just one heap of bull,' and pushing him by the shoulder he added with a threatening look, 'and now you'd better quit,' and the fellow did!

In the South I occasionally found old mule barns which had survived out of the many that existed and which have been turned into garages and filling stations. These barns seem to be favourite meeting places for loafers and gossipers, who sit in groups discussing the bad times, to say nothing of every man, woman and mule in the neighbourhood, now and again emphasising a particularly weighty statement by spitting out tobacco juice. In some corner, well hidden from public view one may also see some rolling the dice on a little mat, playing the classical game of 'craps'; dimes and quarters changing hands with astonishing rapidity. To be a good 'craps' player a man has to master a special vocabulary and must be a bit of a contortionist, for some magic words and movements are said to attract luck. Negroes are particularly picturesque and amusing to watch, and I should not be surprised if the Charleston originated during a 'craps' game in some southern mule barn.

Whenever a fellow rises after having given somebody a meaning wink, and the pair 'fades away' around a corner, one could have a safe bet that they are going to have a swig of 'corn' or some other 'moonshine'; —yes, the old mule barns that remain are real havens for local characters, where troubles are invented and forgotten, and where the most important schemes of national importance are discussed in heated debate, which is held in language not so much parliamentary as expressive, whilst the well-fed mules stand there, seeming to listen with the boredom of an old judge who is hearing his thousandth case of intoxication or public disturbance.

In Texas there are strange contrasts of yesterday and to-day, for I have seen farmers ploughing fields with teams of big, heavy mules, preparing to sow the year's cotton, whilst a regular stream of automobiles sped along the concrete highway, along which the Waco-Fort Worth electric trains raced, big steel towers holding the high voltage cables in a seemingly endless line that stretches from horizon to horizon over the plains; the continuous purring and humming of many motors is sometimes drowned

by the droning of an aeroplane overhead, but the farmer slowly continues along his furrow with an occasional 'giddap!' to urge on the mules.

The main topics among the farmers seemed to be the weather, politics
and prohibition and it struck me that the average American is either a
republican or a democrat the main point, as far as this average individual is concerned, being that if he belongs to one party he is simply
opposed to the other.

After the State of the horned toad and the blue bonnet, as Texas is often
called, we crossed into Oklahoma, following the same highway north.

A visit to the MacAlester State Prison was of unusual interest to me,
especially as I was told that this particular institution ranks among the most
modern and up-to-date in the U.S. I know many high-class public schools
where pupils do not enjoy half the comforts prisoners do in that
particular penitentiary, and I have an idea that it would take me quite a
long time before I would become penitent if I were made an inmate of
the place.

During meals, which are served in a hall that looks like a huge auditorium, the prison band, consisting of forty-five men, supplies music that
is as excellent as the food, and in the courtyard there is a commissary where
'soft' drinks, cigarettes, etc., are sold at cheap prices. The men have to work
in the prison factories, but their hours are reasonable, and even bonuses
are given for extra work done, some convicts earning enough to keep their
families supplied with the necessary money to live.

The prisoners are locked up in their cells only during the regulation
sleeping hours, and I was amazed at the excellent and spotlessly clean beds
they had, luxuries which I am sure the majority never knew before
entering the place. No keys are used for locking and opening doors, all
this being done by electricity from a central place. I was shown the room
where the 'juice shooting' is done, as they humorously call electrocuting,
and I found that the place, and the death-cells alongside, had something
about them that makes one feel 'goosey.'

Undoubtedly Americans are the greatest advertisers and boosters in the
world, even the badges so many wear in their buttonholes and the insignia
on their cars are all there to 'hit the eye.' Many people in other countries
are apt to feel annoyed when they see photographs of this and that in
America, advertised as the 'biggest' or 'smallest' in the world, but the
educated American merely smiles when he comes across most of such
pictures and propaganda. I must have passed half a dozen swimming-pools
along my route which are advertised as 'The World's Largest,' to mention
only one variety of pseudo world-beaters, and some forty miles before
we arrived in Washington D.C. we passed near a farm on which was

written in large letters: 'HOME OF WORLD RECORD BULL "ROLLO PONTIAC FAYNE"'—and I believe that farmer was right!

I had read so much tourist propaganda about the Indians of Oklahoma that I almost expected to find them living in wigwams, and hunting buffaloes, and in my dreams I could see myself madly galloping over endless prairies with hordes of yelling and blood-thirsty Indians, with painted faces and flowing head-gear, hoopeeing behind me, whilst I cursed myself for not having made the detour via California and Alaska to New York.

Well, I met many of these Indians, but if I had not been told they were such, I would have taken them for Mexican labourers, and instead of being able to cast glances at the Hiawatha beauties of my dreams, I found the Indian women dressed like whites, and the majority of them were fat and ugly.

I visited a school for Indian girls, where they enjoy every comfort and good education. To-day many of the Oklahoma Indians are very wealthy, rich oil deposits having been discovered on the barren land the government had by mistake so generously given them as a reservation. They dress as whites do, excepting a few who still cling to the poncho or blanket that takes the place of an overcoat. The pure Indian here looks much like his South American cousin, the colour of skin, coarse black hair, high cheekbones and dark slit eyes being identical. Many whites are proud of claiming a splash of Indian in their blood, but when one puts aside fiction, and considers historical facts, there is very little to be proud of, for the North American Indian was much inferior to his Mexican and South American kin of days gone by. For some of these, like the Mayas, the Aztecs, and the Incas were highly civilised and advanced in various sciences and arts; whereas the North American Indian was merely a nomad hunter and a savage, as the Indians of the pampas and further south of the South American continent used to be, and they, like the North American Redskin, have left nothing to show that they ever existed but a few flint-stone arrow-heads and other primitive stone implements and weapons.

Alongside the rushing traffic I felt like a snail moving along, but at the same time I had ample time to observe things I should otherwise have missed.

The majority of motorists in the States seem to have no consideration for anybody along the road, and this to my mind shows a sad lack of education and want of gentlemanly instincts.

I had a great deal of trouble with 'road hogs' who seemed to outnumber the relatively few whose character qualifies them to drive a car, and many a time did they deliberately drive across the road to 'shave' my horses, obviously not even realising that they were endangering their own lives as much as ours. Off and on different objects were thrown at us, and once even an empty bottle, whilst shouting: 'Ride'm, cowboy!'

Taking all in all, I was as disappointed with the farms as I was with the general level of culture in the States. True, I met the most charming and refined people, but on the other hand, I found the lower classes to be very ignorant and common, especially north of the Mississippi.

As to the farms, I expected to find them to be models in every way, but the wooden barns and pools of stagnant and muddy water, and the general appearance of the places left much to be desired. On the whole, I found the farmers to be ignorant, lacking even the most elementary knowledge, and not knowing the world beyond the small radius in which they live.

The average Argentine 'estancia' is far superior to the best I have seen in America, the quality of stock, installations, and even the machinery used being better. If I described some of the leading 'estancias' with their modern homes that are veritable palaces in some cases, the surrounding parks, flower-gardens, swimming-pools, polo pony stables, etc., I am afraid I might be disbelieved. I visited some fat stock shows in the States, and when I was told one of them was the 'finest in the world,' even though I am no expert, I could not help smiling to myself.

Near most farm-houses in Oklahoma, cyclone cellars are built, in which people take refuge in case of danger, rather as people did in Europe during the World War when enemy aircraft made raids. Whilst I was on my way through those parts a cyclone swept a strip of the country, and I could see the incredible devastation it caused, everything having been swept away where it had passed. I tried to avoid staying in towns whenever this was possible, for outside, along the highway some of the farms make a side income by taking in tourists, posters outside the gates of such establishments advertising the fact. If there was no stable available, there was always some small paddock where my horses could graze, and they enjoyed this much more than being under a roof.

A great part of the wealth of the U.S. is concentrated in the industrial north, where the Southerner's money goes to buy automobiles, agricultural machinery, etc., and where the brokers enrich themselves, thanks to the farmers' products of the south. This is one of the sore points between north and south and, at the same time, a problem of vital importance, but difficult of solution. True, Oklahoman and Texan oil-fields give fabulous returns, but only a relatively small number of people benefit by them; the livelihood of the vast majority being earned on the land.

I rode through the beautiful, wooded Ozarks when they were at their best. It was the strawberry season, and enormous quantities of 'berries' were being shipped north. It is calculated that an army of 65,000 pickers is wanted for the harvest each year. Here and there we passed big fields where peony flowers are cultivated, and at the time these were in full blossom, and streams of cars with tourists came along the roads to see this beautiful sight. To avoid being molested by curious people, I had disguised myself as a farmer, but even then some recognised me, which was probably due to the colour of Mancha, who was so 'pinto' that one could not help knowing him after once seeing his photograph. More than once when I was walking about the villages in the evenings, farmers who were short of strawberry-pickers came to offer me a job, and they must have taken me for one of the loafers one so often sees hanging about when I refused.

Several times I was mistaken for a horse trader, and farmers came to offer me their 'old grey mares,' and others came to ask me the price of my animals. I always took advantage of such opportunities to have a good joke, and when I told the would-be buyers my price they walked away as if in a hurry to 'phone up the nearest lunatic asylum.

The horses must have enjoyed the trip through the hilly woodland of the Ozarks as much as I did, for all along the sides of the highway juicy clover grew in abundance, and many a drink did they have out of the clear and rippling streams we found at short intervals.

Unfortunately, many of the tourists positively spoil the pretty country, and soon they were my pet aversion. The very sight of a car filled with a vulgar and noisy crowd made my blood boil, and when I saw them litter the most picturesque spots with paper, empty bottles and cans, my inward rage knew no bounds. I am not tarring all tourists with the same brush, but the fact is that many of them are veritable pests.

The accent of the Southerners is as pleasant as their expressions are original and to the point, and the short 'howdy' on meeting pleased me as much as their 'I hope you good luck' amused me on parting.

The nearer we came to St. Louis, the heavier became the traffic, and with a lead horse the danger of being run into was considerably increased. I was seriously considering leaving one horse behind and finishing the ride on the other, but the question was to find a suitable place to leave him, where he would be well looked after. When we arrived in St. Louis I had the good fortune to meet a wealthy manufacturer who happened to be a great horse lover, and he immediately offered to take charge of one of my horses. As Gato had been the unlucky one in Mexico, I decided to leave him on my new friend's beautiful farm, just outside the city bounds, where he received the best of treatment, whilst I continued towards Washington on my faithful Mancha.

I made my stay in St. Louis as short as possible, and although I missed Gato's company, I was much relieved when I crossed the Mississippi by one of the long bridges. With one animal I could travel much easier and faster where traffic was bad, and I had less work in finding fodder and accommodation.

St. Louis is not an attractive town, the industrial quarters being gloomy and dirty; even the main streets have something depressing about them. Some of the parks and surroundings make up for what the town lacks, but above all, I noticed one thing about it, and that is the extraordinary number of good-looking girls I came across everywhere. Now I am not going to claim that St. Louis has the prettiest women in the world, but although I have extensively travelled many countries, and this not only in the American Continent, I must say that I have never seen so many attractive and neatly-dressed girls as I did there. When I remarked this in one of the clubs where I was entertained, somebody got up and said that New Orleans had St. Louis 'beat' in this respect. As I did not know the former place, I was unable to give my opinion, but I have an idea that that enthusiast was a native of New Orleans, and, of course, there is no place like home!

If I were a painter I would find it impossible to put a woman or man as a typical American on canvas, and I do not think that such a type exists, physically speaking; there is too great a mixture of blood of all nationalities, and in many cases even of races, not sufficiently boiled down or crystallised to allow the production of a type that can be said to be representative. Many Americans are of the Teutonic and Scandinavian types, others distinctly Anglo-Saxon or Latin, and all are slowly being mixed in this melting-pot of nations, much as in the Argentine which is beginning to be a veritable Babylonia.

The further east we advanced, the closer together did we find the towns, and the less pleasant did riding become.

In most hotels in the U.S., a society called The Gideons places a Bible in each room, and on the other hand, the management of the establishment thoughtfully hangs corkscrews on chains, and fixes bottle-openers on the walls, and whilst the clauses of the prohibition law are in a frame under glass inside the door, a crystal jug and tumblers are placed on a tray on the table alongside the Bible, the iced water and other incidentals being as easy to obtain as they are likely to be poisonous.

Notoriety and publicity seekers abound in the States, and at the same time that I rode through the country a coast-to-coast foot-race was in progress, which was merely a novel advertising stunt, and an effort to pick up a few dollars. I came across all sorts of people who were on transcontinental publicity stunts, and the way they advertised, and the thrilling accounts they gave the newspapers of their adventures, made me feel as if I had only been on a Sunday school outing. I saw an Italian 'cowboy' from the 'Wild West' who was on his way from San Francisco to New York on a mule and, as he had no money and as I felt sorry for his starving animal, I gave it a feed of hay and oats. Another fellow was pushing a golf-ball from New York to Los Angeles, and soon afterwards an elderly man passed us, marching from coast to coast, playing a violin as an advertisement for some make of boots. Later I saw one on roller-skates, then one on stilts, and others who were merely tramping and 'sponging' their way through.

We stopped in beautiful Indianapolis for a few days and then proceeded to Columbus (Ohio). Unfortunately, the governor of the State was absent, but I shall always keep his warm letter of welcome to the city as one of the most treasured souvenirs of the whole trip. I was splendidly entertained by the different riding clubs that flourish there, and was glad to see that riding is again on the increase in the U.S. In most towns of any size and importance riding clubs exist, and the numbers of members are fast increasing; obviously people realise that a daily ride is not only a wonderful recreation, but also a great health-preserver.

Some farmers have formed a society that affords mutual protection in case of theft, and the notice of membership which those who belong to the society have fixed on their gates rather amused me, for it read: 'Member of Horse-thief Association.' I have an idea that all horse-thieves in America are on the list of unemployed, unless they have taken to easier and more profitable occupations, such as boot-legging or kidnapping.

After Columbus we made for West Virginia, where we arrived immediately after crossing the Ohio River, and where we again made excellent friends who could not do enough to make our stay as pleasant as possible. The hilly country around these parts is charming, and I was taken out for long drives through the Eastern panhandle of West Virginia, which is very mountainous and beautiful. The 'mountaineers,' as the inhabitants of these very wooded hills are called, are surprisingly conservative, and in many cases even bordering on the primitive, which fact is all the more surprising when one considers that they are within a stone's throw of the large cities of the East.

We crossed over the wooded Cumberland mountains, which are sometimes called the 'Blue Ridge,' a ride I enjoyed thoroughly. Mancha often lost his footing on the slippery concrete, especially where down grades were steep, but after I had him shod with rubber padding he had no more difficulty in keeping on his feet.

In many places the road was fenced in on both sides, and in one of these (to horsemen) dangerous traps we nearly had an accident that might have ended my ride when we were so near the goal. Notices are placed for the benefit of the few who walk along the highways, advising them to keep to the left side of the road, or, in other words, to face the traffic. However, I found that my horse shied at cars that came speeding towards him, and often passing close to him, so I kept to the right where the traffic overtook us from behind. Even if a car or bus almost 'shaved' us, Mancha took not the slightest notice of it, and continued calmly jogging along. On this occasion I followed the right-hand side of the road as usual when a car came towards us on the other side, a man (?) at the wheel and a lady sitting behind. The driver deliberately crossed the road towards us, and as there was a fence, the horse could not jump in the ditch, a thing I often had to make him do to avoid serious accidents when ungentlemanly drivers tried their jokes on us. Before I could do anything the car hit my horse violently, knocking him down, and opening a gash in his flank and left hind leg. The driver did not stop, and before he disappeared around the curve he honked the horn and waved his hand at me.

If I had been armed, which was never the case after I had crossed the U.S. border, there is no telling what I would have done to that man. There lay my dear companion who had taken me over mountains, through deserts and jungles, over a distance of some 10,000 miles. Had all our efforts been made to reach this spot, and be robbed of victory through the guilt of a low-down 'road-hog,' and this when we had almost reached the goal? Surely fate could not be so cruel and luck adverse after having been kind to us in places where I had sometimes expected we could not pull through. After the first shock Mancha rose, and although he bled profusely, I found that no bones were broken. I washed him down at a stream, and at a farm-house I obtained iodine, with which I disinfected the wounds. Although I informed the police by 'phone, giving the number of the car and other details, I never heard from them, although they promised to communicate with me; I shall always remember that. If I had been travelling in an aeroplane instead of on a horse, and somebody had wilfully damaged a part of my machine, this would have been broadcast and printed as an unparalleled outrage and scandal, but as things were there was a difference; yes, I must say, a vast difference!

During my ride through the States I had two incidents with boot leggers; one when I left the highway to follow a path into a wood where I intended to rest for an hour or so. I was looking for a spot where there might be good grass, and had gone quite a distance without finding a suitable spot when a rough-looking fellow stopped me to ask what I was doing there. As it was obvious that he was not sober, I simply continued, but I had not gone very far when another ruffian held me up, and this by pointing a shot-gun at me. He asked me what I was after, and when I told him, he merely told me to 'get' and not to dare to come 'interferin' around there again, or else there would be trouble. Naturally I thought I was trespassing on private property, and having apologised returned to the highway. When I again passed the drunken fellow on my way back, he was even more unfriendly than he had been before, and threatened to 'shoot me full of holes' and made other unpleasant but obviously sincere promises and threats, such as I had never heard even in Central America or Mexico, places that are reputed to be very 'tough.'

That evening, when I told some acquaintances about this strange happening, I heard from good authority that 'moonshiners' were working some stills in that wooded neighbourhood; and as the sheriff is elected by public vote, many of the voters see to it that the man of their choice is a non-interferer — and I was given to understand that it pays in every sense of the word.

The second incident happened to me in a town when I was looking for the stable where I had left the horse. Just before going to bed, I usually went to have a last look at the animals, and on this occasion I had gone down a wrong street and was vainly looking for the stable in the semi-darkness. Suddenly a tough customer confronted me and looked me all over, finally asking me what I was 'hangin' around there for. I told him I was endeavouring to locate a certain stable, and to my surprise the man offered to accompany me there, and although I did not trust him much, I accepted his offer. We soon arrived, and whilst I was inside I noticed that my guide was talking with the owner of the stable in low tones. Before I left I went to thank the fellow for his assistance, whereupon he asked me if I wanted a drink, and when I refused the offer he wanted to know if I was a 'friend,' and before I left him he said: 'You'd better be a friend, or else you'll have a job to get out of this town!'

We passed through the Cumberland Narrows, and after two or three days left the last rolling hills of the mountains behind us, and on the five hundred and fourth actual day's travelling after leaving Buenos Aires, from the top of an incline, the dome of Washington's mighty Capitol appeared ahead.

The night before I had advised friends that I would arrive, and a newspaper man who had motored out to interview me had carefully explained to me which road to follow so that I should not miss those who were coming to meet me.

However, in spite of his detailed description, I went the wrong way, and only realised it when I found myself lost somewhere in the lower part of the city. I had come at a fast trot so that nobody would stop me to ask questions, but when I realised that I had missed those who had driven out to meet me, I began to try to find my bearings again. I looked for a policeman, but, as usual when one wants one, I could find none. Finally, I came to a drug store, where I decided to telephone to the Argentine Embassy to tell them that I was hopelessly lost somewhere in the 'wilds' of Washington, and to ask them to send a rescue-party to search for me. Accordingly I tied Mancha to a lamp-post, and just as I was about to enter the drug store I heard a gruff voice shout, 'Hey, mister, what the hell do you mean by tying that horse to the lamp-post. Do you think you are out in the "gawdam" country?' I turned round to see who was thus addressing me, and to my amazement a 'cop' stood there; he had appeared as if by magic. When I had made myself known to him and had explained the sad plight I was in, he laughed very heartily and held the horse for me whilst I went to 'phone, and when I returned he was still chuckling to himself and patting Mancha's sturdy neck.

At the Embassy I was informed that everybody had gone to meet me, and so I left word that I would wait where I was until they should return. The policeman showed me a shady spot where I could wait undisturbed, and when an Italian fruit and vegetable vendor passed with his cart, I bought a few bunches of carrots, of which Mancha was desperately fond, and sitting down near him, I watched them disappear, one by one. In due time the 'rescue-party' arrived, and escorted me to the Wardman Park Hotel, where Mancha was put in a comfortable stall in the luxurious stables belonging to the establishment. Photographs were taken until I was sick of it, and then I was free to speak to those who had come to give me the first welcome. Until late that night I was kept busy answering the telephone, reading cables, and interviewing reporters who asked me the same questions I had answered countless times before, including how I had crossed 'that Panama Canal.'

I had been in Washington several days before I was free to have a look at the city, a thing I always liked to do absolutely on my own. Social calls and visits to different clubs kept me busy all day, and I had by no means a pleasant time.

The capital of the U.S. is certainly one of the finest towns I have ever seen, and is quite different from any other I had ridden through. Most of the wide streets are lined on both sides by splendidly-kept and shady trees, and some of the parks, squares and monuments show rare taste in beauty and design. The Lincoln Memorial and the Arlington Cemetery impressed me most, but although the George Washington Monument or obelisk is a fine construction, to my mind it fails in many respects. I could detect nothing artistic, appropriate or original about it, in spite of it being a wonderful piece of work in its way. It seems to be exclusively used by tourists and sightseers who stand and scramble at its foot in a queue, waiting their turn to be shot up to the top in the lift to have a look at the city and its surroundings from above.

The Arlington cemetery, which is situated on a hill on the south side of the Potomac River, was once upon a time the home of General Robert E. Lee, and to-day thousands of America's military and naval men lie buried there in the shade of stately trees among the green undulations of the lawn-covered ground, where modest crosses stand in perfect rows, marking the resting-places of Uncle Sam's dead warriors, while more elaborate and impressive monuments are dedicated to soldiers and sailors of fame.

A beautiful Grecian amphitheatre, built of solid marble, is a rare gem, and looks at its best against a background of dark green cedar trees. In front of it, facing the Potomac River below, and the town on the other side, is the tomb of the unknown soldier, which, shame to say, has to be guarded since souvenir-hunters damaged it.

In no other city in the U.S. had I seen so many negroes as I did in Washington, and many of them seem to be wealthy, at least, judging by the way they overdress and by the luxurious cars in which they drive about. I heard rumours that their prosperity is due to many of them being 'booze-runners,' as Americans call a new class of law-violators who are prospering thanks to the prohibition law.

In the South, negroes are kept strictly separate from the whites. In trains and in trams special sections are reserved for them, and they are not admitted to shows, restaurants or hotels where whites go, but have their own separate haunts, yet somehow they seem to be as contented and happy as their dusky brothers and sisters in the north of the country, who enjoy much more freedom, which, I am told, is due to political reasons.

The aspect of some of Washington's finest streets is spoilt by small shacks in the middle of a row of magnificent houses, and here and there a little Chinese shop positively ruins an otherwise striking 'tout ensemble' of buildings.

I had originally intended to finish my ride in New York City; but, after two fairly serious accidents with motorcars, I decided it would be better to finish in Washington, having ridden from capital to capital. I did not wish to expose Mancha to further danger, for, after all, both horses had more than proved their worth. Considering that the short ride from Washington to New York would only amount to a stunt that might give the impression that I was seeking vulgar publicity, I shipped Mancha to New York, where, as usual, the army was again to the fore. Without being asked, the commander of Fort Jay, on Governor's Island, offered to look after my pal. From that island, which is only a short distance out in the middle of New York Harbour—and which we reached by taking a ferry-boat—one has the best view of the business district of the town, with its colossal skyscrapers, which at the time had a golden tint from the setting sun. I was held spellbound for quite a while; I looked at Mancha and then at these towering masses of concrete and steel, one the product of the wild, arid and wind-swept plains of Patagonia, the other the result of the working of human brains, initiative, science and skill. Before I realised it I was again talking to my horse as I had become accustomed to do—'Yes, old boy, this is New York, but I know the rolling pampas are calling you— be patient, I'll take you back—you deserve it!'

Busy Days

When the horse had been housed in a comfortable stable I was shown round the army post which occupies the whole of Governor's Island, and later the ferry-boat took me back to the mainland. Soon I was lost in the hustle and turmoil of New York's busy life and gazing up at the towering walls of the skyscrapers. The breath-taking traffic much reminded me of swift-flowing mountain rivers in deep canyons, the countless cars being jammed together like masses of driftwood and logs that have been washed away by the irresistible force of the waters after a storm and yet these moving masses obeyed the signals of red and green—organisation and discipline.

I was invited to make my headquarters at the Army and Navy Club, where I thoroughly enjoyed myself all the time I was in New York.

Mancha seemed to be doing the same on Governor's Island, for when I went to visit him one day, a sergeant who had wanted to ride him to give him a little exercise greeted me with the following words: 'Good morning, sir, would you mind telling me what kind of hell-pet your horse is supposed to be?' He informed me that Mancha had 'acted as gentle as a lamb' until he mounted him, and then he had 'gone off like a stick of dynamite.' After three unsuccessful attempts to ride him the sergeant had given it up as a very bad job, and was quite pleased when I told him that he was by no means the first one to have had such an experience—in other words, that this was Mancha all over.

Mr. James Walker, popularly known as Jimmy Walker, received me at the City Hall and did me the great honour of presenting me with the New York City Medal, the Argentine Ambassador, Dr. Malbran, and other personages being present during the simple ceremony. Although opposed to anything in the show line, I dressed up in the traditional costume of a gaucho for the occasion, and Mancha wore the most gorgeous ancient trappings that have probably ever been seen in New York. These things had been especially sent to me by a collector of antiques in Buenos Aires.

After a short chat with the lively and extremely witty mayor, and when I had presented him with a set of 'bolas,' some mounted policemen and a few friends in cars escorted me all the way down Broadway and Fifth Avenue until we reached Central Park, where Mancha was stabled. Whilst this seemingly interminable ride lasted I must have been the most embarrassed and unhappy man, for there is nothing I dislike more than being stared at. I wished that the skyscrapers would fall down and bury me, or that the ground would open and swallow us. Mancha behaved splendidly all the way, and even seemed to take an interest in the strange surroundings.

If any city in the world knows how to entertain it is certainly New York, and I had my full share of it, and even Mancha was shifted from one place to another, according to where his presence was required. After I had been back by rail to St. Louis to fetch Gato, both horses spent ten days at Madison Square Gardens, where they were on exhibition during the International Horse Show.

Later I returned to Washington, where President Coolidge did me the honour of receiving me in his office at the 'White House.' The audience was fixed for 10.30 a.m., and on the tick of the clock those who were to present me and myself were ushered into the President's office. In spite of the solemnity of the moment I could not help comparing this punctuality with the kind we are accustomed to in Latin America! The President was sitting at his desk and rose as we entered. He struck me by his simplicity of manner and free and easy way of carrying on the conversation which chiefly centred around the proposed Pan-American Railway and the topography of the countries I had ridden through. Before we retired the President congratulated me on our success, and, after having presented him with a small gift in the name of the Retired Army and Navy Officers' Club of Argentina, I departed highly impressed and inwardly proud.

The National Geographic Society did me the great honour of giving me the privilege of delivering the opening lecture to the society in Washington in the city auditorium, and although I fully appreciated so great a recognition, I felt like a mere atom when I stood before the microphones, making great efforts to describe our whole voyage in less than one hour, which is the regulation time given for a lecture. Judging by the applause at the end of my talk, I came to the conclusion that I had succeeded in interesting the large audience, or else that the American public is very lenient when it sees a man making a desperate effort.

Possibly this lecture was instrumental in saving mine and the horses' lives, for I had contemplated booking a passage on the ill-fated *Vestris*, and thanks to the delay I had to put off our departure. Two friends of mine sailed on her, and both had the good fortune to be saved, whilst over a hundred other passengers came to a sad end in this maritime disaster.

It was with mixed feelings that I left Washington to return to New York, where I had to make final arrangements before sailing. Everybody had been so kind to me that I felt like staying longer, but then Buenos Aires was calling me, and I was longing to be back with my people and friends once more. On December 1st the horses were in comfortable boxes on the lower deck of the Munson liner *Pan-America*, and ready to travel as the company's guests. The rules do not allow stock to be transported on these passenger liners, but once more I was given proof of American friendship and appreciation when orders were given by the head of the company that my horses be accepted, and that no fees be charged for their transportation. Not only did I enjoy American hospitality throughout the U.S. territory, but even until we landed in the docks of Buenos Aires did we enjoy the benefits of this wonderful spirit for which I shall ever feel deeply grateful and indebted.

Farewell U.S.–Back to the Pampas

Quite a number of friends had come to give us a final farewell on the ship, and I could see them waving their handkerchiefs on the wharf as we slowly glided away. Presently the engines began to throb, and by degrees the marvellous skyline of New York faded away behind a mantle of grey mist. Outside the harbour we dropped the pilot, an act which always seems to interest the passengers, and gives them the opportunity to break the ice and get into conversation, which is almost stereotyped in its sameness.

We had a wonderful trip all the way, and the sailors thoroughly enjoyed the presence of the horses. Every night a large group would sit around them and smoke their pipes whilst the horses munched away at their hay, seemingly enjoying the cool night breeze as much as their admirers did

We called at beautiful Rio de Janeiro, Santos and Montevideo, and after twenty days Buenos Aires came in sight in the far distance. In spite of the midday heat of an unusually hot summer's day, a large crowd was patiently waiting at the docks, and gave us a rousing reception as the ship tied to the side.

Soon after I was caught in a regular whirlwind of shaking hands, being slapped on the back and answering questions, and when I came down the gangway I was swept off my feet and slightly hurt by being trampled on. However, I was soon rescued, and when it was all over I began to see the funny side of it.

The horses were unloaded at once, and an enthusiastic crowd accompanied them to the grounds of the Argentine Rural Society, the very place from where we had started out nearly three years before.

As soon as the official and other receptions were over I took the horses out to the pampas again, where they will enjoy the kind of life that is natural to them. Some had planned to put them in a public park where people might go to see them, but when the idea was put before me I consulted with my friend Dr. Solanet, who had originally given them to me, and we decided that it would be kinder to allow them to spend the remaining years of their lives on a beautiful 'estancia' in the south of the province of Buenos Aires, and as I am writing these last lines I can see them galloping over the rolling plains until they disappear. out of sight in the vastness of the pampas. Still gazing in the direction where they have disappeared I have visions of many strange places we saw together, joys and sorrows, hardships and pleasures, and then the faces of many friends in far-away countries appear before me, friends in all stations of life— friends without whose moral and other assistance we could never have succeeded. Good luck to them, and good luck to you, old pals, Mancha and Gato!

POSTSCRIPT

An eventful quarter of a century has passed since I unsaddled Mancha and Gato for the last time. In most of the countries through which they carried me and my pack, many things have changed. When we started out from Buenos Aires, only two cobbled roads connected the capital with nearby towns. To-day a number of modern highways cut through the pampas, and in some of the other South and Central-American Republics roads have been built also. Taking such and other improvements into consideration, I wish to make it quite clear that the foregoing pages were written shortly after the conclusion of our journey.

Knowing only too well how 'touchy' some of my South-American friends are if anyone says—or especially writes—anything about their countries which is not flattering. I sincerely hope that nothing I have written in this book has hurt the feelings of any reader. Time, conditions and even people have changed greatly, and surely will go on changing.

Should the reader wonder what I have done since the completion of our long expedition, here is a brief summary of my activities since then. In life many strange things happen to us, and sometimes they come about quite unintentionally as far as our plans and aims for the future are concerned. Thus, after the publication of this book, I wrote a number of others dealing with various subjects, including some of my subsequent travels through different parts of the world. In my *Bohemia Junction*, as well as in *The Tale of Two Horses* and *Ming and Ping* (the last two are for children) are related a number of adventures and stories lack of space did not allow me to include in this already bulky volume. Every now and again, after having led a sedentary life for months, struggling with manuscripts, when the open spaces call me I set out to see more of this world which, despite its creaky and groaning state, continues to smile at those who smile with it. And so I carry on, not as a rider of horses now, but as a struggling author who tries to keep his balance—mental and physical—on an office chair, whilst leaning over blank sheets of accusing paper.

After their return to the pampas, Mancha and Gato enjoyed life on the beautiful 'Cardal' ranch where they roamed about at will. During the warm months, the two inseparable companions spent their time out on the grassy plain, but in winter, towards evening they trotted up to a gate there to wait until it was opened for them, when they headed for a roomy loose-box where oats, bran and alfalfa hay were in readiness for them. Early in the morning, if by any chance there was some delay in letting them out, they neighed, stamped and generally protested in order to attract the attention of the man who was in charge of them.

Some years ago when I made a trip to the Argentine, upon arriving there I hurried out to the ranch to say 'how d'you do' to the horses. After they had been driven into the corral, followed by a number of gaucho friends I approached the place where, in former years, I had had some exciting fun, and, incidentally, more than one rough tumble.

Within the circle of stout posts I was overjoyed to see my old pals. Although still some fifty yards away, I shouted, 'Mancha, Gato!' Immediately both turned round and stared at me, their heads held high, ears pricked up, and nostrils dilated. I slowly approached the corral, and entered through the gate, the men watching with intense interest. I spoke to the animals, and they slowly came towards me. When I touched Mancha's broad forehead, both sniffed me all over. To find out if they still remembered one or two simple tricks I had taught them, I stood in front of one and snapped a finger. Immediately a fore-leg was lifted, and I was allowed to inspect the hoof, and when I repeated the noise, this time snapping my finger under the horse, he at once lifted a hind leg. These tricks the animals had learnt in the wilds, ten years before, when I tried to make quite sure that no stone or other hard object was lodged in a hoof to lame them.

There could be no doubt they remembered me; but to make quite sure, I returned to the corral later. On this occasion I did not show myself until one of the men had called the animals several times. They made no response, but when I shouted their names, both at once looked up and came towards me. I made several other simple tests, which left me in no doubt that both remembered me clearly.

On a cold wet morning in January 1936, I went to see my friend, Cunninghame Graham (who wrote the preface to this book) depart from London in order to re-visit the Argentine after many years. Although 84 years of age at the time, he was determined to go and make the personal acquaintance of Mancha and Gato, so before he boarded the train at Paddington Station, I handed him a tiny bag of oats, to be given to my horses. This little bag he put into a hand bag as if it were a priceless gem. When the train steamed out of the station, somehow I sensed that this would be the last time I would see my wonderful friend's flowing shock of silvery-white hair, and that I would never again shake his strong hand; the hand which was equally dexterous with the reins, the lasso and the pen. Unfortunately, shortly after having arrived in Buenos Aires, he contracted pneumonia, and when a specialist stated that the case was a serious one and that a journey out to the pampas was quite out of the question, Mancha and Gato were transported to the city, so that he could see them from the window of his hotel. The little bag of oats I had given him in London was not forgotten, for on Cunninghame Graham's request, a lady took it to the horses, and shortly after my friend died. When his body was taken to the port to be shipped for interment in Scotland, as the huge procession slowly wended its way through the streets of Buenos Aires, Mancha and Gato, led by two gauchos, followed immediately behind the hearse. And so, like prairie riders of old, when they set out on a long journey, my friend was followed by two spare horses.

On the 17th of February, 1944, I received a telegram informing me that Gato had died that day. The telegram was followed by a letter written by my friend, Dr. Solanet, on whose ranch the horses had been every since their return from New York. Among other things I read, 'Gato died at 4 p.m., without suffering. As usual, together with Mancha he was standing at the gate, waiting for his feed of oats. When the man who looks after them approached the gate, he was puzzled to find Mancha gone, and Gato lying down, apparently asleep. Upon investigating, he discovered that dear old Gato had died, evidently from heart failure, and that he had set out on his voyage to Trapalanda where Don Roberto waits for him ... ' (Dr. Solanet refers to Mr. R. B. Cunninghame Graham, and who in his preface refers to 'Trapalanda,' the gauchos' heaven for homes.)

In a subsequent letter, Dr. Solanet says: '... I feel sorry for Mancha who will have nothing to do with any other horse. I am sure that horses sense what it means when a companion dies. They know that he can't be found anywhere. Mancha never calls Gato. He is not restive, and does not fuss as formerly he did when temporarily separated from his friend. Now intelligent Mancha is sad and lonely. He keeps on his own although I have put twenty other horses into his favourite field. It is useless; already a week has passed since Gato died, but he takes no notice of any of them, and roams about alone, far away from the others. Now I shall bring him to the stables where I am keeping a show mare for which he always had a soft spot in his heart.'

Although this was done, the mare had no further attraction for Mancha, but eventually he made friends with an old draught horse, in whose company he could always be seen, far away from the mass of other horses who grazed on the pampa.

I was in London when, early in the afternoon on Boxing Day, 1947, my telephone bell rang. Upon answering it, I was glad to hear the voice of my friend, Mr. Ralph Deakin, the Imperial and Foreign Editor of *The Times*. After having expressed the hope that I had spent a happy Christmas, he informed me that he had just received a cable from Buenos Aires, and proceeded to give me the sad information that Mancha had died on Christmas Day. Mr. Deakin explained that as the news would appear in the next issue of *The Times*, he thought it would be better to forewarn me about what I would read. I shall never forget this act of consideration. As it happened, a cable sent to me from the pampas by Dr. Solanet, arrived only on the following day.

Here I must make a correction of two statements which appeared in all the preceeding editions of this book.

In 1925, when my two horses and I set out from Buenos Aires, Mancha was eighteen years of age, and Gato sixteen; not sixteen and fourteen, as I set down their respective ages. Argentine Griollo horses are noted for longevity, especially in cases when animals are broken in when they are of mature age, say after having reached six or more years. Between ten and twenty, Griollos are at their best, and if—as in the case of Mancha and Gato—they have endured many hard Patagonian winters, they are bound to be tough, for ruthless Nature eliminates all but the hardiest, as is explained in the introduction to this book.

The many people from different parts of the world who went to the 'Cardal' ranch to see the two horses, will agree with me that neither of them showed the slightest trace or sign of having been affected in any way by the difficult journey. The very fact that Gato reached the age of thirty-five, and Mancha that of forty, substantiates this statement. Thanks to my two horses' demonstration of resistance and hardiness, the Griollo breed—which a quarter of a century ago threatened to disappear—flourishes once more, not only in the Argentine, Uruguay and Chili, but throughout South America, where breeders take a great interest in the type of animal of which my two companions were such typical specimens.

On the 'Cardal' ranch, among stately cypress trees stands a simple though beautiful stone monument, made by a distinguished Argentine sculptor of animals, and near it the two inseparable companions rest, still side by side.

In my heart there is room for many animals I have loved, but Mancha and Gato will always have a special corner of their own. The Red Gods have given me some great days and many a grand horse, but among them my two companions of the long trail will always rank as the greatest. Farewell, faithful and stout-hearted old friends!

Chelsea, London,
A. F. TSCHIFFELY
March, 1951.

PALLAS EDITIONS

The Linen Goddess
Travels from the Red Sea to Prizren
Sheila Paine

The task had seemed simple enough at the beginning:
where had the idea first come from that
that little triangle of silk embroidery,
hung with three tassels,
had the strength to fend off evil?
And where did people still believe in it?

The third volume of Sheila Paine's odyssey takes her through war-torn Eritrea and Somalia, past the ancient rock churches of Ethiopia and the tiny pyramids of Sudan, through Egypt and across the Mediterranean to Greece, ending in the bandit land of Albania.

It is an adventure across the fault lines of history, and religion too, as the Linen Goddess fades and reappears from view. 'Even amid Madonnas, petitions to Ab-Besma ab-Besma Wold, rusty bits of iron, broken white glass elephants and a myriad blue beads, it had always been there.' And after a journey through some of the least visited and most dangerous parts of the world Sheila finally catches up with the goddess surprisingly close to home.

Sheila Paine has spent the last twenty years travelling, researching tribal and peasant embroidery, and has written four books on the subject. Her extraordinary picareque quest for this undying embroidery goddess began with *The Afghan Amulet: Travels from the Hindu Kush to Razgrad*, and she picked up the thread of her journey in *The Golden Horde: Travels from the Himalaya to Karpathos*. Both of these will be reprinted by Pallas Athene. Her magnum opus on amulets will be published by Thames and Hudson in 2004.

234 pp plus 32 pp colour plates   ISBN 1 873429 87 8   £12.99

PALLAS EDITIONS

The Light Garden of the Angel King
Travels in Afghanistan
with Bruce Chatwin
Peter Levi

This is a beautiful book, a poetic evocation and worthy of a place on the
shelf beside Kinglake's *Eothen* and Robert Byron's *Road to Oxiana*
John Morris in the *Sunday Times*

Rich in anecdote and general speculation
Simon Raven in the *Observer*

It has all the glamour of a revelation. I still turn to it for inspiration.
Stanley Stewart in the *Daily Telegraph*

From time immemorial Afghanistan has been a mountainous crossroads.
Through it have come merchants with indigo and Chinese silk, Alexander the
Great, nomads from the steppes, colonies of Buddhist monks, great Moghul
conquerors and the ill-fated armies of the British Raj.

In 1970 Peter Levi, classical scholar, archaeologist and later Professor of
Poetry at Oxford, set off with Bruce Chatwin to seek the clue which each
migration left. It is this quest that gives his fascinating book its theme. How
far east did Alexander really establish himself? Who built the great upland castle
that exists on no map? Could the sculptors of Athens really have influenced
the early Buddhist artists? In drawing back the curtain on Afghanistan, Levi
reveals not a rocky wilderness ranged over by plunderers, but, in the words
above Babur's tomb, 'a highway for archangels'.

First published in 1973, this account of Afghanistan is an acknowledged
classic of travel writing. It is now reissued with fresh photographs from the
Chatwin archives and a new introduction in which Peter Levi looks back on
a lost Afghanistan, 'an island in time, a ruined paradise', and on his friendship with the young Chatwin.

234 pp plus 16 pp colour plates   ISBN 1 873429 35 5   £12.99

PALLAS EDITIONS

The Stones of Venice
John Ruskin
abridged by J. G. Links

It is a book for the lover of architecture, the lover of Venice, the lover of
lost causes... but, perhaps, above all, for the lover of fine writing.
J. G. Links, in his introduction

For fifty years, *The Stones of Venice* was read by all who went there and
thousands who could not; the sightseers whom the city captivates today
seldom have Venice's greatest guidebook with them.

The overwhelming clarity of Ruskin's vision, which would eventually lead
to his mental breakdown, makes him the most stimulating, entertaining,
aggravating and enlightening companion. At its best, his prose has a precision
and nobility that rank it with the greatest masters of the language.

His most influential book, *The Stones of Venice,* was written as part of an
impassioned polemic in favour of Gothic architecture. 'It is in Venice, and in
Venice only, that effectual blows can be struck at this pestilent art of the Renais-
sance.' This was Ruskin's war cry as he entered the now almost forgotten Battle
of the Styles on the side against 'the school which has conducted men's
inventive and constructional faculties from the Grand Canal to Gower Street.'

But first the reader must know the difference between right and wrong; he
must find out for himself the best way of doing everything. 'I shall give him
stones, and bricks, and straw, chisels and trowels and the ground, and then
ask him to build, only helping him if I find him puzzled.'

Unhappily, these exciting objectives were attained only after the expenditure
of nearly half a million words; glorious words, but too many. It is the aim of
this edition to remedy this and to put a fascinating book within reach of those
with limited resources of time. Much that was superfluous has been omitted;
what is left is the essence of a now most readable book.

272 pp plus many illustrations from the original editions
ISBN 1 873429 35 5   £9.95

PALLAS EDITIONS

Effie in Venice
Mrs. John Ruskin's letters home, 1849-52
Edited by Mary Lutyens

Even if these letters had not the special interest of being from John
Ruskin's wife, they would be absorbing in their picture of the social life
that dominated Venice at this particular period
Marghanita Laski in the *Observer*

A lively picture of the *ancien régime* re-establishing itself for its last fling.
Mary Lutyens has put so much into the narrative linking these hitherto
unpublished letters and is so at home with the vast cast of characters,
that the book is as much hers as Effie's. It is perhaps the most
radiant episode in Ruskin's life
The Times

Superbly edited by Mary Lutyens from the original letters discovered by her
untouched in the archives, Effie Ruskin's letters home from Venice give an
unparalleled view of Victorian travel and society through the eyes of a highly
intelligent and lively young woman. John Ruskin took his wife to Venice for
the first time in 1849, and while he worked on books that would define the
Victorian aesthetic ideal, Effie explored Venice with growing freedom and
independence of thought.

Rightly considered a classic both of travel literature and of writing about
Victorian art and the milieu where much of it was made and appreciated,
Effie in Venice makes a welcome return to print.

368 pp plus 16 pp b/w plates   ISBN 1 873429 33 9   £12.99

PALLAS EDITIONS

The Generous Earth
An account of life in the Dordogne Valley of France,
'the land of all Good Things'
Philip Oyler

with a new introduction by Joy Law

This glimpse of a lost time will be loved by anyone who has longed
for a vision of the Dordogne before it was transformed
by the 20th century and the British
The Sunday Times

In *The Generous Earth*, Philip Oyler 'describes a civilization which possesses
a vitality and an integrity of which the excellence of its products is but an
outward manifestation, and he describes from within, rather than as a mere
detached observer.' So wrote Lord Northbourne in his foreword to this
classic account of life in rural France, now reissued for the first time since 1961.

Philip Oyler, farmer and traveller, moved to the Dordogne after the First
World War. There, in the district between the small market towns of St Céré
and Sarlat, in the Dordogne valley about 100 miles east of Bordeaux, was a
region completely unexploited by commerce or tourism.

He found a way of life that had hardly changed for centuries and is now
no more. It was a world of true rural husbandry rooted in tradition and a beautiful countryside where the balance of nature had not been disturbed by
man. The region was rich in real wealth – crops, vineyards, stock, timber, fruit
and fish.

Anyone interested in travel, in France, in farming, good food, good wine,
and sheer good living will enjoy this book.

192 pp plus 16 pp b/w plates   ISBN 1 873429 66 5   £12.99

PALLAS EDITIONS

The Surprise of Cremona

One Woman's Adventures in Cremona, Parma, Mantua,
Ravenna, Urbino and Arezzo

Edith Templeton

with a new introduction by Anita Brookner

A strip-tease Baedeker
Cyril Connolly

Mrs Edith Templeton...sojourned in old towns of North Italy
— Cremona, Parma, Mantua, Urbino and Arezzo.
None before her has been so frank, so robust, so comprehensive.
Tremendous fun... companionable, evocative and informing
Edith Shackleton in *The Lady*

A ruthless, ironic, exasperating,
immensely amusing companion
Sunday Times

Highly original, bald, assured...a virtuoso display of personality.
She makes the reader see through her eyes
— and sharp, ironic ones they are...
Pamela Hansford Johnson in *Bookman*

Edith Templeton, Bohemian aristocrat, accomplished novelist and widow of
the physician to the King of Nepal wrote this highly individual account of
her visit to six North Italian towns in the early fifties. Wonderfully evocative of the time and the places, her vintage narrative is a gem of travel literature
but has been unavailable for many years. An introduction by Anita Brookner
to this new edition gives a beautiful analysis of the astringent wit and classic
poise of Templeton's writing.

256 pp plus 16 pp b/w plates   ISBN 1 873429 65 7   £12.99

PALLAS EDITIONS

In the Glow of the Phantom Palace
From Granada to Timbuktu
Michael Jacobs

Jacobs is an engaging, wonderfully informative
and ever-surprising companion
Jan Morris

Funny, learned and beautifully written
New Statesman

He is the ideal companion we all dream of but rarely find: patient, lively
and endlessly generous with his encyclopaedic, cultivated mind
Irish Independent

The George Borrow of the High-Speed Train Era
ABC Madrid

In this new book, Michael Jacobs follows the trail of the Moors of Spain, exiled
from their last kingdom of Granada in 1492. This extraordinary journey takes
in ruins and discos in Andalucía, masseurs and literary lions in Morocco, before
finishing in the mud mosques of Timbuktu, where, some claim, families still
keep the key to the house in Granada that they fled five hundred years ago.

On the way Jacobs conjures up a cast of irrepressibly alluring adulterers,
louche fixers, kings, professors, poets, cobblers and voyagers, in a kaleido-
scope of fiction, history, journey and imagination. How, Jacobs asks as he
journeys southwards, can we be sure who, where, or when we are?

Michael Jacobs is widely regarded as the leading Hispanist of his genera-
tion, and his books have been acclaimed both here and in Spain. *Andalucía,
The Road to Santiago* and *Madrid for Pleasure* have been published by Pallas
Athene. He is currently Fellow in Hispanic Studies at the University of
Glasgow.

224 pp, illustrated   ISBN 1 873429 36 3   £12.99

PALLAS EDITIONS

Gatherings from Spain
Richard Ford
in a new edition by
Ian Robertson

The splendid result of the toil, travel, genius and learning of one man,
and that man an Englishman
George Borrow

You may live fifty years without turning out any more delightful
thing than the *Gatherings*
J. G. Lockhart, writing to Ford

As soon as it appeared, Richard Ford's *Handbook to Spain* was hailed as a major work of literature. How far Ford had burst out of the guidebook genre was amply proved the next year when Murray's produced a compendium of the material they had forced Ford to discard from the *Handbook*. Characteristically, Ford also added much that was new, all of it treated with energy, diamond wit and irresistible charm. Much of what he describes of the Spanish character remains valid today; much of romantic Spain was already fast disappearing: 'Many a trait of nationality in manners and costume is already effaced; monks are gone, and mantillas are going, alas! going.'

For many readers, Ford remains the greatest travel writer of all. 'Time has not dimmed the scintillating perspicacity of Ford's observation, nor weakened the verve of his engaging style,' writes Ian Robertson in this new edition – the first for a generation – of *Gatherings from Spain*, which is illustrated with drawings by Ford himself, and enriched by a fully annotated index, the fruit of many years's research by Robertson, the leading scholar in the field.

400 pp plus 16 pp colour plates   ISBN 1 873429 34 7   £12.99

PALLAS EDITIONS

Edinburgh:
Picturesque Notes
Robert Louis Stevenson

Beautiful as she is, she is not so much beautiful as interesting.
She is pre-eminently Gothic,and all the more so since
she has set herself off with some Greek airs,
and erected classic temples on her crags.
In a word and above all, she is a curiosity.
Robert Louis Stevenson

'I am only a Scotchman after all, you see,' wrote Stevenson with more pride
than diffidence. *Edinburgh: Picturesque Notes* is amongst the most vivid of
Stevenson's writings, and one of the least known, since it was curiously
overlooked when his works were posthumously collected, and has only
rarely been in print.

Far from being a flattering guidebook, or even a purely picturesque travel-
ogue, this eulogy of Stevenson's beloved birthplace is as full of the louche as
of the romantic. Smells and shady characters, gloomy graveyards and spec-
tacular Pentland views rub shoulders with the suave glories of the New
Town and its smart society. Stevenson's passion for Auld Reekie never
clouded his wry wit, and his enthusiasm for the picturesque detail and the
savoury anecdote will delight readers today as much as they scandalised
contemporaries.

114 pp plus many illustrations from the original edition
ISBN 1 873429 76 2 £7.95

PALLAS GUIDES

Pallas Guides to Britain

The Pallas Guides to Britain are written by Peter Sager, who lives and works in Hamburg. A highly distinguished journalist (the winner of the prestigious Egon-Erwin-Kisch prize, the German equivalent of the Pulitzer), he has the sharp yet generous eye of the outsider, and his guidebooks are lyrical, witty, offbeat and wise. They have been rapturously received:

WALES
Certainly the best book on the country
New York Times
A passionate and fabulously detailed book
The Rough Guide
A wonderful thing *Jan Morris*
A brilliant book ... I love it. Peter Sager has opened my
eyes to my own country
Mavis Nicholson, South Wales Echo
511 pp   ISBN 1 873429 58 4   £16.95

EAST ANGLIA
His knowledge and enthusiasm are awe-inspiring
East Anglian Daily Times
A breadth of knowledge few natives could rival
The Times
A stunningly good guide – literate, amusing, colourful,
informative and lavishly illustrated
Mail on Sunday
Thorough and thoroughly readable
Griff Rhys-Jones, BBC1 Bookworm
579 pp   ISBN 1 873429 57 6   £16.95

WEST COUNTRY
His sensitive and informative writing of such locations makes me
want to seek them out and soak them up, even for a second time
Colin Brent, The Tavistock Times Gazette
Altogether a find *Salisbury Journal*
276 pp   ISBN 1 873429 08 8   £14.95

PALLAS GUIDES

Pallas Guides to Europe

From our launch title *Czechoslovakia*, which was the first detailed guidebook published to the country since the war, Pallas Guides have earned the reputation of being the best on the market. Detailed, scholarly, intelligent and approachable, they are equally attractive for the traveller on the road and in the armchair.

ANDALUCÍA
by Michael Jacobs
The best one volume guide to Andalucía *Rough Guide*
No other book can compare *Cosmopolitan*
464 pp   ISBN 1 873429 43 6   £15.95

DORDOGNE
by Joy Law
Required reading *TLS*
The best sort of travel book *The Spectator*
318 pp   ISBN 1 873429 28 2   £14.95

CZECH AND SLOVAK REPUBLICS
by Erhard Gorys
Highly informative and quite admirable *The Art Newspaper*
Rich and rewarding *Traveller Magazine*
462 pp   ISBN 1 873429 51 7   £15.95

POLAND
edited by Sebastian Wormell
No one interested in Polish culture, landscape, its people and life in Poland should be without this book *Polamerica*
This hefty book is a cultural treasure *Polish American Journal*
691 pp   ISBN 1 873429 22 3   £19.95

FORTHCOMING
THE MIDI   PROVENCE   ROMANIA   ROME

PALLAS GUIDES

Pallas for Pleasure

Based on the legendary *Venice for Pleasure*, Pallas for Pleasure are walking guides to some of the most beautiful and historic cities in Europe. Personal, idiosyncratic and always enlightening, illustrated with carefully chosen old paintings, photographs and engravings, they show the traveller how the city became what it is rather than just what can be seen today.

VENICE FOR PLEASURE
by J. G. Links

Not only the best guide-book to that city ever written, but the best guide-book to *any* city ever written
Bernard Levin, The Times

One of the most delightful and original guides ever
Jan Morris

The world's best guide book *William Boyd, The Spectator*

J. G. Links' little charmer*The Lady*

If there is a cult guide book, this is it *The Good Book Guide*
275 pp inc. 32 colour plates   ISBN 1 873429 40 1   £12.95

MADRID FOR PLEASURE
by Michael Jacobs
286 pp plus 32 colour plates   ISBN 1 873429 24 X   £12.95

BRUSSELS FOR PLEASURE
by Derek Blyth
320 pp inc. 32 colour plates   ISBN 1 873429 14 2   £12.95

AMSTERDAM FOR PLEASURE
by Derek Blyth
316 pp inc. 32 colour plates   ISBN 1 873429 47 9   £12.95

FLEMISH CITIES FOR PLEASURE
by Derek Blyth
320 pp inc. 50 plates   ISBN 1 873429 30 4   £12.95

PALLAS GUIDES

Pallas Passions

Pallas Athene publishes a number of non-series travel books chosen for their expertise, wit and yes, passion.

A272 – AN ODE TO A ROAD
by Pieter Boogaart
The most eccentric and fascinating guidebook we have ever seen
John Sandoe Bookshop
A bound folly *Art Quarterly*
Astonishing *Jeremy Paxman, Newsnight*
216 pp inc. 200 colour illustrations ISBN 1 873429 48 7 £15.95

ART GALLERIES OF THE WORLD
by Helen Langdon
528 pp inc. 212 colour plates ISBN 1 873429 46 0 £16.99

THE ROAD TO SANTIAGO
by Michael Jacobs
280 pp inc. 90 colour & b/w plates ISBN 1 873429 42 8 £12.95

AN HOUR FROM PARIS
by Annabel Simms
240 pp inc. 70 colour & b/w plates ISBN 1 873429 69 X £12.95

BUDAPEST: A CRITICAL GUIDE
by András Török
246 pp inc. 62 maps and diagrams ISBN 1 873429 31 2 £9.95

GREAT BORDEAUX WINES
by James Seely
416 pp inc. 200 colour illustrations ISBN 1 873429 21 5 £39.95

THE FOOD LOVER'S COMPANION TO TUSCANY
by Carla Capalbo
384 pp inc. 27 maps and elaborate indexes ISBN 1 873429 32 0 £12.95

If you would like further information
about titles published in the
Pallas Editions series,
please write to:
Pallas Athene
59 Linden Gardens
London W2 4HJ
or visit our website at
WWW.PALLASATHENE.CO.UK

Series editor: Alexander Fyjis-Walker
Series assistant: Ava Li
Editorial assistant: Della Tsiftsopoulou
Series designer: James Sutton

This edition published by Pallas Editions
in conjunction with Ostara Publishing 2002
Reprinted 2003
First published by William Heinemann Ltd 1933

ISBN 1 873429 70 3

Printed in Finland